The publisher gratefully acknowledges the generous support

of the Anne G. Lipow Endowment Fund

for Social Justice and Human Rights

of the University of California Press Foundation,

which was established by Stephen M. Silberstein.

Racial Propositions

AMERICAN CROSSROADS

Edited by Earl Lewis, George Lipsitz, Peggy Pascoe, George Sánchez, and Dana Takagi

Racial Propositions

Ballot Initiatives
and the Making of Postwar California

DANIEL MARTINEZ HOSANG

University of California Press

BERKELEY   LOS ANGELES   LONDON

University of California Press, one of the most distinguished university presses in the United States, enriches lives around the world by advancing scholarship in the humanities, social sciences, and natural sciences. Its activities are supported by the UC Press Foundation and by philanthropic contributions from individuals and institutions. For more information, visit www.ucpress.edu.

University of California Press
Berkeley and Los Angeles, California

University of California Press, Ltd.
London, England

© 2010 by The Regents of the University of California

Library of Congress Cataloging-in-Publication Data

HoSang, Daniel.
    Racial propositions : ballot initiatives and the making of postwar California / Daniel Martinez HoSang.
        p.   cm. — (American crossroads ; 30)
    Includes bibliographical references and index.
    ISBN 978-0-520-26664-3 (cloth : alk. paper)
    ISBN 978-0-520-26666-7 (pbk. : alk. paper)
    1. California—Race relations—History—20th century.
2. Referendum—California—History—20th century.
3. California—Politics and government—1945–   I. Title.
    F870.A1H67   2010
    979.4'053—dc22   2010008921

Manufactured in the United States of America

19 18 17 16 15 14 13 12 11 10
10 9 8 7 6 5 4 3 2 1

This book is printed on Cascades Enviro 100, a 100% post consumer waste, recycled, de-inked fiber. FSC recycled certified and processed chlorine free. It is acid free, Ecologo certified, and manufactured by BioGas energy.

To Umai, Isaac, and Norma

Contents

Illustrations

TABLES

Introduction

"Genteel Apartheid"

> One difference between the West and the South I came to
> realize . . . was this: in the South they remained convinced that
> they had bloodied their land with history. In California we did
> not believe history could bloody the land, or even touch it.
>
> —JOAN DIDION

In the 1990s, a series of controversial California ballot initiatives renewed a debate over the meaning and significance of race and racism in public life. Within a span of seven years, as the nation looked on, California voters passed propositions banning public education and public services for many immigrants (1994), repealing public affirmative action programs (1996), outlawing bilingual education (1998), and toughening criminal sentencing for adults and juveniles (1994, 2000).

At first blush, California seemed an unlikely site to stage such contentious struggles. During most of the 1990s, California Democrats, traditional supporters of civil rights since the New Deal, held a ten-point lead in voter registration rates, capturing all of the statewide offices by the end of the decade. Moreover, California voters appeared to take quite "liberal" positions on many other issues, approving ballot initiatives to increase the minimum wage and to legalize medical marijuana while rejecting measures backed by conservatives to establish a system of public school vouchers and to weaken the political power of unions.[1] The sudden upsurge of "racial antipathy" on the part of the overwhelmingly white electorate seemed an exception in need of explanation. Why, observers asked, did a wave of "racial conservatism" grip California's seemingly liberal electorate?[2]

Scholars and pundits have offered several explanations: demographic transformations fueled by a growing number of immigrants arriving from Asia and Latin America; upheavals in the state's economy, including the steepest economic downturn since the Great Depression; and a series of opportunistic political actors who used the ballot process for their own partisan gain. All of these lines of inquiry are worthy of attention and, indeed, each tells part of the story. But in continuing to search for the *exceptional* forces that drove the racialized ballot initiatives of the

1

1990s, these explanations each rest on an important historical—and thus political—assumption that deserves scrutiny. By tracing these conflicts to a unique set of contemporaneous economic, political, and social forces, we are left to understand them as a departure from broader historical patterns or continuities; as an effort to turn back the clock on the state's history of racial progress. Indeed, in these narratives, white supremacy—the ideological complex that explains hierarchy, destiny, and even fatality as an expression of innate human difference—is figured as an anachronistic and static force; progress itself is racism's greatest enemy.

Could it be possible instead that white supremacy as an ideological formation has been nourished, rather than attenuated, by notions of progress and political development? What if we imagine racism as a dynamic and evolving force, progressive rather than anachronistic, generative and fluid rather than conservative or static? What if we understand racial hierarchies to be sustained by a broad array of political actors, liberal as well as conservative, and even, at times, by those placed outside the fictive bounds of whiteness? And finally, what if the central narratives of postwar liberalism—celebrations of rights, freedom, opportunity, and equality—have ultimately sustained, rather than displaced, patterns of racial domination?

This book plows the soils of postwar California history in search of the conflicts, alignments, and political currents that preceded and produced the initiative politics of the 1990s, and it explores how the ballot propositions of that decade have shaped the state's contemporary political culture. As table 1 suggests, across the post–World War II era, California's system of direct democracy has proven to be a reliable bulwark against many leading civil rights and antidiscrimination issues: California voters rejected fair employment protections in 1946, repealed antidiscrimination legislation in housing in 1964, overturned school desegregation mandates in 1972 and 1979, and adopted "English Only" policies in 1984 and 1986.

Taken together, this longer history of racialized ballot initiatives might suggest an opposite conclusion: that postwar California political history is characterized by an unchanging and undifferentiated racial domination, with rhetorical shifts simply masking an enduring racial animus. Yet this argument rests on equally ahistorical grounds, and reinforces the conception that progress and racism are natural adversaries: racism remains because we have made no progress.

Indeed, in the postwar era, rights and opportunity have been the lingua franca of California politics—the state has imagined itself at the forefront of not only national but global progress and development, fettered only by the limits to its own imagination. During this period, we can also locate

TABLE 1 Select Ballot Initiatives Examined, 1946–2003

Issue	Date	(Proposition No.) Subject	Result
Employment discrimination	Nov. 1946	(Prop. 11) Creates a state Fair Employment Practices Commission and prohibits racial and other forms of discrimination by unions and employers	Defeated
Housing discrimination	Nov. 1964	(Prop. 14) Exempts most real estate transactions from antidiscrimination laws; nullifies most of 1963 Rumford Fair Housing Act and similar legislation	Approved
School busing and desegregation	Nov. 1972	(Prop. 21) Prohibits mandatory desegregation of schools; repeals statute that sought racial and ethnic balance in public schools	Approved
School busing and desegregation	Nov. 1979	(Prop. 1) Prevents state courts from issuing school desegregation orders in excess of federal requirements	Approved
English Only ballots	Nov. 1984	(Prop. 38) Places California on record against multilingual ballot requirements	Approved
Official English	Nov. 1986	(Prop. 63) Establishes English as official state language	Approved
Three Strikes criminal sentencing	Nov. 1994	(Prop. 184) Increases sentences for repeat criminal offenders	Approved
Immigrant public services	Nov. 1994	(Prop. 187) Declares undocumented immigrants ineligible for public social and health services, public education	Approved
Public affirmative action	Nov. 1996	(Prop. 209) Ends affirmative action in public hiring, contracting, and public education	Approved
Bilingual education	June 1998	(Prop. 227) Ends most bilingual education in public schools	Approved
Juvenile crime	June 2000	(Prop. 21) Increases penalties and sentencing for juvenile offenders	Approved
Racial data collection	Oct. 2003	(Prop. 54) Bans race data collection and analysis by state and local governments	Defeated

many of the forces and dynamics posited to be the engines of "racial progress": a generally liberal political culture, a relatively robust economy, an increasingly diverse populace, and well-organized civil rights leadership. Yet as table 1 reveals, nearly every major civil rights and racial justice issue put before a vote of the people in California during this period has failed.

This book attempts to come to terms with this apparent contradiction. The title, *Racial Propositions*, is meant to operate on two levels. It refers first to the history of racialized ballot initiatives in the postwar era, which are brought together here in a single narrative. To tell this story, I examine the conflicts and relations of power that gave rise to these ballot measures, profile the significant political actors involved, examine the discourse generated by the initiative debates, and explore the impact the measures had on the broader political culture of the state.

"Racial propositions" also references a central argument of this book: that each of these ballot measures represented a set of *propositions* about the meaning of race and racism. During the postwar period, debates on the significance of race have been marked more by contradiction and transformation than by unity and coherence. As the formal mechanisms of state-sponsored segregation withered after World War II, diverse political actors contended to interpret the meaning of race and the role of the government, private organizations, and individual citizens in addressing the legacies of racial domination. In California, a state that took pride in its identity as a forward-thinking and pragmatic experiment in social possibility, no single account could claim automatic authority. This book examines the role ballot initiatives played in this process of *proposing* and generating racial meaning and forging racialized political communities. Such propositions invoke and help constitute a broader political framework about human possibility, which marks some claims, experiences, and harms as legitimate and recognizable while stigmatizing others as specious and irrelevant.[3] The fervent discussions over these measures as they unfolded on newspaper editorial pages, at public debates and neighborhood meetings, and through campaign advertisements has made them a central site for Californians to deliberate the meaning of race, rights, and authority.[4]

APARTHEID IN THE LAND OF SUNSHINE?

In 1961, Alexander Saxton wrote a story for *Frontier Magazine* and its left-leaning readership about a state-sponsored skilled trades apprenticeship program that maintained a "curious and almost unapproachable island of segregation." While the nation's attention was fixed upon the struggles in the South, the freelance journalist—it would be two more years before Saxton entered graduate school and a decade before the publication of his influential *Indispensable Enemy*—cast his gaze west. Saxton explained that it was in "the free and sovereign State of California" where a taxpayer-supported program training tens of thousands of carpenters, plumbers, electricians, metal workers, masons, machinists, and other skilled workers for relatively high-wage positions remained almost exclusively white; a Jim Crow regime in the land of sunshine.

Saxton did not account for this exclusion in terms of individual prejudice, bigotry, and intolerance, though most observers understood the "massive resistance" unfolding in the South at the time to be a function of precisely such forces. Nor did he seek to unearth a set of extremist forces lurking in the shadows that was intent on imposing its white supremacist worldview. Instead, Saxton explored the routine procedures and preferences for admitting new applicants and hiring trained workers. It was in this quotidian sphere that notions of rights, qualifications, standards, and fairness helped authorize extraordinary racial disparities. These barriers, and the ideas that shaped them, endured even though the state legislature had formally prohibited racial discrimination in the program for more than ten years, and even as most unions took forceful official stands in support of fair employment legislation.

Saxton pointed out that "California's integrated taxpayers" were essentially underwriting the discriminatory practices of unaccountable employers and unions, which used informal, largely unspoken selection criteria to maintain their authority over these programs and jobs. Moreover, state administrators, unions, and employers either denied any discrimination existed or shifted responsibility to others in the system, stymieing efforts of the newly created state Fair Employment Practices Commission to address the problem. Saxton employed an evocative juxtaposition to describe this vexing system: "genteel apartheid."[5]

"Apartheid" is a term few Californians would use during this period to describe the racial life of their state. While formal racial segregation remained the rule rather than the exception in most neighborhoods, schools, and workplaces through World War II, unmistakable changes unfolded in the war's aftermath. The Black press frequently looked to California to imagine the early realization of the "Double Victory" over fascism abroad and racism at home. In 1948, in the wake of recent court decisions that struck down interracial marriage bans, racially restrictive housing covenants, and segregated public schools, the *Los Angeles Sentinel* declared that "Jim Crow is just about dead in California."[6] A two-page centerfold in the *Pittsburgh Courier* in 1949 on life in San Diego showed photos of a multiracial cast of citizens and workers enjoying an easy camaraderie: "Here in this thriving city which can rightfully boast about its 'heaven on earth climate,' steady progress has been made in interracial relations and increased job opportunities. . . . The model set by San Diego could be used as a fine model for future improvement in race relations in many sections of the United States."[7]

These and many similar accounts anticipated the demise in California of a powerful narrative within American political discourse. Historian Gary Gerstle uses the term "racial nationalism" to describe a political culture in which domination and hierarchy are explicitly justified and defended by assertions of racial kinship and shared origin, cast in either "biological" or "cultural" terms: "race" as an adequate explanation for inequality.[8] In the nearly one hundred years between California's admission to the union and the end of World War II, examples of unapologetic racial nationalism were prominent: organized lynchings, vigilante violence and mass killings, forms of indentured servitude, restrictions on immigration and property ownership, minstrel shows, segregated classrooms, hotels and restaurants, eugenics research, and mass-based white supremacist movements.[9] While important examples of interracial solidarity and antiracist resistance could also be found during this period, these efforts contended with a dominant political culture that defended and justified racial inequality and domination openly.   legitimacy

At the end of World War II, however, a moment sociologist Howard Winant describes as a "fundamental and historical shift, a global rupture or 'break'" in the worldwide regime of white supremacy, public defenses of racial nationalism grew increasingly rare in California.[10] Diverse political actors defined the character of the state as fundamentally forward-thinking and open-minded; a station of perpetual opportunity that had vanquished and disavowed all trappings of discrimination and prejudice. Indeed, since the end of the war, political organizations and movements from anti-tax groups and chambers of commerce to labor unions and civil rights activists have framed their claims in the rhetoric of "equal opportunity" and "equal rights." Rights and opportunity became leading narratives within California political culture during this period, expressing the basic commitments of what Gerstle describes as "civic nationalism"—a liberal creed conferring rights and privileges without regard to religion, gender, race, or national origin.[11] By transforming racial subjects into citizen subjects empowered to fully participate in the state's economic and political marketplace, this creedal vision has provided the framework and boundaries of effective and intelligible political redress in postwar California.

Los Angeles Times columnist Patt Morrison exalted this vision in a 2006 essay celebrating the paper's 125th anniversary when she argued that California's gift to the world is "the gift of reinvention, the push to the next frontier, the break through the next boundary . . . even the boundary of self. Here, we are all Eves and Adams, with no past, no class, no patterns to follow, the only limits the ones of our own making."[12]

Morrison's California seems to be the antithesis of a society steeped in apartheid. But taking a cue from Saxton, I take apartheid to mean more than open declarations of white supremacy and the policies and violence that sustained explicit segregation. South Africa's post-1948 National Party era, the paradigmatic example of an apartheid regime, was built upon a broad system of meaning making that constructed historically specific ideas about race, national identity, and social hierarchy as both natural and inevitable. By describing postwar California political culture as shaped by a commitment to apartheid, I am not suggesting that the state paralleled the development of postwar South Africa; such a comparison is easily dismissed.[13] Indeed, as California passed legislation banning racial discrimination in the state militia, employment, public accommodations, and in housing sales and rentals, and overturned laws banning interracial marriage and restricting landownership among Japanese Americans, the South African government adopted laws enforcing deeper and wider regimes of segregation. Yet even in California, as the legal architecture of racial segregation went into decline, the logics that naturalized racial distinctions and hierarchies lingered, endorsing policies that reinforced potent racial inequities. Here, I am not describing the transition from de jure to de facto segregation, but rather the endurance and transformation of modes of political reasoning and discourse that naturalized and reified specific ideas about race, subordination, and power.[14] The ideological alchemy of apartheid—a belief in the inexorability of racial segregation and hierarchy—shaped the state's political culture, fixed the meanings of racial identities and group conflicts in particular ways, and constituted an everyday political common sense for diverse Californians, including those who resisted its demands and assignments.[15]

In addition, the ballot measures examined here relate directly to the endurance of formidable patterns of racial segregation. The fair employment, fair housing, and school desegregation measures detailed in chapters 2 through 4 explicitly addressed the state's authority to challenge relations of apartheid in these areas. Ballot measures to undermine multilingual public services, eliminate public benefits to noncitizens, lengthen prison sentences, repeal public affirmative action and bilingual education programs, and abolish state collection of racial data, examined in chapters 5 through 8, also reinforced prevailing patterns of segregation and inequity.

To speak of apartheid, then, in postwar California is to inquire into a system of meaning making and policy formation that constructed compelling ideas about the inevitability of racial hierarchy and segregation even as the formal structures of racial exclusion waned rapidly and ideas about rights and opportunity were publicly valorized. During this period, California witnessed many of the forces that influential voices of the mid-twentieth century argued would spell the demise of racial subordination: a rapidly expanding nonwhite population that exercised growing economic and political power, the adoption of extensive civil rights legislation (though such legislation often became the subsequent target of ballot initiatives), the putative "liberalization" of social attitudes among broad sectors of society, a political culture that celebrated unfettered opportunity, a growing infrastructure of public resources and programs, and an expanding economy that created jobs and wealth at a higher rate than any other region in the nation.

Race-based hierarchies, however, not only endured throughout this period, they increasingly came to be understood as both acceptable and inevitable within the same political discourse that so earnestly celebrated tolerance and condemned racial prejudice. The historical legacy of these developments is evident across the political landscape of contemporary California, expressed in the racial disparities within areas such as criminal justice, housing, education, health care, employment, and reproductive rights, and the undeniable correlation between race and life opportunities they produce.[16] Race remains an indispensable ideology and social prism through which to comprehend and appraise the sources of and solutions to many of California's crises: the legacy of a prison system that leeches more than $7 billion annually in state funding while corralling more than a quarter of a million Californians into industrial cages; the shuttered libraries, parks, and hospitals across the state; the dozens of high schools that witness the disappearance of two-thirds of their student body between ninth and twelfth grades; the extraordinary inequalities in incomes and wealth evident within a seven-mile radius of downtown Los Angeles; and the chronic crises in financing and budgeting that have wrecked many functions of the public sector.[17]

To be sure, these patterns and relationships are driven by multiple and interdependent forces; race never operates as an abstract or isolated political determination.[18] As feminist theorists have long argued, race and gender are co-constitutive, often demanding attention to "the race of gender and the gender of race."[19] Race often similarly functions, in Stuart Hall's words, as the "modality through which class is lived."[20] Indeed the false dichotomy presented between race- *or* class-based explanations of political inequality is itself an artifact of racial domination, for it presumes that racial subordination only functions through isolated expressions of animus rather than broader structures of power.[21] Racial meaning can also be expressed and experienced through frameworks of nation, family, sexuality, religion, and other cultural forces.

The racial diversity of California's population certainly extends into many realms of social, political, and economic leadership, and claiming or asserting a white identity does not automatically guarantee security or mobility. But race remains critical to securing "a society structured in dominance."[22] Attending to the political labor that race performs helps resolve a central contradiction of California: how a state that so publicly reveres and symbolizes ideas of human development, possibility, and achievement treats the incapacitation and immiseration of so many of its inhabitants as both natural and inevitable.[23] It speaks to the yawning gap Joan Didion describes between what Californians "believed to be their unlimited possibilities and the limitations implicit in their own character and history."[24] Understanding how this resolution had been secured in California, the paradigmatic "blue state" on the nation's political map, offers important insight into the broader story of story of race and nation in the postwar United States.

THE ROLE OF BALLOT INITIATIVES

Qualifying a ballot initiative—statutory or constitutional legislation subject to the approval of the electorate—is no small feat. The initiative's language must be drafted and submitted to the state attorney general for approval. Petitions must be printed and hundreds of thousands of signatures gathered. A public campaign, often costing millions of dollars, must be waged in a state where the two major population centers are four hundred miles apart. And if passed, the measure must withstand the scrutiny of the courts as well as elected officials and bureaucrats who may be reticent to enforce its provisions. Since the instruments for direct democracy were first adopted in California in 1911, the vast majority of efforts to enact policy through the ballot have failed. In the first ninety-seven years of the initiative's use, nine out of ten of petitions filed with the secretary of state did not subsequently qualify for the ballot. Of those that did qualify, two out of three were rejected by voters.[25]

Political scientist E. E. Schattschneider explains that in all political conflicts "the audience determines the outcome of the fight." Once a conflict is brought into a new arena, the balance of power is likely to shift, as "every change in the scope of a conflict has a bias."[26] In all of the initiatives examined in this book, proponents took their case to the ballot only after other avenues—specifically the courts and the legislature—proved unfavorable. Following Schattschneider's maxim, after their conflict became placed before a new audience—the California electorate—the balance of power shifted. But only in the initiative discussed in chapter 2—the 1946 effort to pass a fair employment measure—were the proponents from traditional civil rights groups. In all other cases, the forces that wanted to invalidate or reverse particular civil rights protections—such as fair housing legislation, school integration mandates, bilingual education, and affirmative action—were the ones that sought to enjoin the electorate. Why?

The most obvious answer seems to lie in the composition of the California electorate. Though registered Democrats have outnumbered Republicans since the New Deal, the electorate remained overwhelmingly white throughout this period; even in 2000, as California became the first large "majority minority" state in the nation, white voters still constituted 72 percent of the electorate.[27] Exit polls have revealed that a majority of these white voters have consistently endorsed these efforts to roll back civil rights gains by large margins. The move to the ballot by civil rights opponents thus seems purely instrumental.

From this perspective, the outcomes of racialized ballot initiatives are a relatively transparent expression of the ideological commitments voters bring to bear on particular issues or policies. Indeed, when ballot initiatives appear in the accounts of historians and political scientists, they are often cited as an expression or evidence of a larger and more organic political development, an outcome rather than a cause. Thus a vote against fair employment practices or in favor of repealing bilingual education is regarded as indexing a consistent and relatively unambiguous policy position of the electorate.[28] Such an analysis led legal scholar Derrick Bell to conclude that ballot measures enable "the voters' racial beliefs and fears to be recorded and tabulated in their pure form," serving as "a most effective facilitator of that bias, discrimination and prejudice which has marred American democracy from its earliest day."[29] Other studies have demonstrated that ballot measures with recognizable racial currents or connotations pass at much higher rates than do other types of measures placed before voters.[30]

A central premise of this book, however, is that ballot measures are more than transparent plebiscites on fully decipherable policy issues. Once an issue moves from the legislature or courts to the ballot, the *outcome* of the conflict is not the only factor altered. As public spectacles, ballot measure campaigns can shape the very definition of the public good and establish the boundaries of legitimate political discourse for the future. Political scientists V. O. Key and Winston Crouch observed as early as 1939 that in California, while "most legislative issues are perceived as frictions between 'partial' interests which are seeking accommodation in a highly differentiated society," when a conflict finds its way onto the ballot "competing interests . . . will vie energetically for the privilege of bearing the burden of the public interest."[31] Some high-profile legislative and court battles or executive decisions may certainly command public attention, but most of the political and ideological labor expended in these arenas occurs behind closed doors, far from public view. In addition, within these branches of government, deliberation will typically involve negotiation, compromise, and the consideration of multiple political perspectives.[32]

Ballot measures, by contrast, especially those that receive widespread public attention, create public spectacles where competing political interests necessarily seek to shape public consciousness and meaning. Because the instruments of direct democracy by definition are intended to advance the will of "the people," these organized groups and interests must always make their claims in populist rather than partisan terms, thereby defining the very meaning of the common good. The theorist Ernesto Laclau argues that this function is essential to the process of hegemony—a political project achieves authority when its particular interests become regarded as coextensive with those of the people.[33] While this process is inherent to every political struggle, it is brought into particularly stark relief within ballot initiative campaigns, in which each side claims to represent the interests of the people while unmasking the opposition as narrow and partisan.[34] And because, at their most elemental level, ballot initiatives ask voters to cast an up or down vote on particular policy questions, their outcomes seem to express or reveal hardened public policy preferences and ideological commitments, homogenizing and unifying what are typically much more heterogeneous and contradictory currents. In this sense, ballot measures transform conditional propositions into unconditional political and ideological truths.[35]

The audience that encounters and witnesses these conflicts on the ballot can also find itself transformed. The theorist Stuart Hall cautions against treating political struggles as "an arena which simply represents and reflects unified collective political identities," thus understanding "politics as a dependent sphere."[36] Rather than starting with the premise of the self-authored political subject, whose "interests" and affinities exist independent of context and interpretation, Hall reminds us that political language and symbols help constitute political subjectivity and make meaning from experience. A political "spectacle" or conflict, as Murray Edelman argues, does not reveal the objective "facts" of a particular situation. It acts instead as a "meaning-machine: a generator of points of view and therefore of perceptions, anxieties, aspirations and strategies."[37] Political conflicts are ambiguous rather than self-evident phenomena constructed in part through "the roles and self-conceptions" fashioned by the observers themselves.[38]

The political language, symbols, and modes of address that fueled these initiative debates reveal the roles that competing campaigns played in organizing and defining, rather than merely expressing, public understanding of complex political controversies. Ballot initiatives shape and condition the very terms with which people analyze and assess issues in public life and the identity positions they claim for themselves and ascribe to others.[39] Amending the familiar formula in which racial identity is explained to be generative of political conflict, I stress that political conflict is also itself generative of racial identity, that "politics makes race" as much as "race makes politics." The debates and campaigns that arose from these ballot initiatives are important institutional locations that shape the ways that certain ideas have come to grip the social imagination. By situating the discourse fueling ballot initiatives within the broader narratives marking life in postwar California—including nationalism, masculinity, consumption, property, security, prosperity, and privatization—we can better understand their role in constructing, rather than just expressing, the ideological lineaments of this period. While there were diverse sites of racial production in public life during this period, these initiatives played a prominent role in condensing meaning and organizing and naturalizing particular configurations of power.

A fine-grained analysis of particular racialized ballot measures helps to answer a larger question of this book: how did political investments in white racial identity become sustained and further naturalized though a liberal discourse of rights, opportunity, tolerance, and fairness? To situate this question historically, and to elaborate the theoretical concerns it raises, I open the next chapter at the birth of the postwar era, as California readied itself for a future unencumbered by its bloody past.

1. "We Have No Master Race"

Racial Liberalism and Political Whiteness

In January 1944, Los Angeles mayor Fletcher Bowron announced the formation of the Los Angeles Committee for Home Front Unity to bring together leading political, civic, business, religious, and labor leaders. The committee would ensure that divisions pitting "creed against creed, race against race, color against color" did not undermine the wartime effort. "Unlike our enemy," Bowron explained, "we have no master race."[1]

Bowron's pronouncement echoed the calls of dozens of other civic unity, "human relations," and "fair play" organizations across the state and around the country during this period; Los Angeles alone was home to twelve such organizations or coalitions by 1944.[2] These groups drew from the broad antifascist, prodemocratic discourse ascendant during the war to advance what the Swedish economist Gunnar Myrdal referred to as "the American Creed," a nationally bound civic culture that conferred individual rights and privileges without regard to religion, race, ethnicity, or national origin. Myrdal's landmark 1944 study on race relations, *An American Dilemma*, emphasized that racial discrimination was a problem "residing in the heart," one that contradicted fundamental American principles of equality, fairness, and social mobility. Myrdal, like many of his contemporaries, advocated a widespread "educational offensive against racial intolerance" to address this lag or contradiction, arguing that "a great majority of white people in America would be prepared to give the Negro a substantially better deal if they knew the facts."[3]

These groups elaborated the basic ideas, commitments, and political strategies of a discursive framework we recognize today as postwar "racial liberalism." Like all political discourses, racial liberalism is best understood as variegated and contested rather than coherent and unified.[4] Across U.S. history, liberalism has often connoted a set of shared political principles and commitments—individual rights, a reliance on private property and free markets, equal treatment before the law, and a representative and limited government—that shape a particular gaze on politics, an "attitude of mind rather than a political creed."[5]

Liberalism has furnished a political vocabulary for a range of projects and purposes, with disparate political actors utilizing its key signifiers (rights, freedom, opportunity, progress, etc.) for distinct and sometimes conflicting goals.[6] But organizations and individuals that embraced racial liberalism in the immediate postwar era generally shared the belief that racism and racial subjugation were fundamentally incompatible with the emancipatory tenets of the American Creed, and they supported various types of government intervention to ensure that "private" prejudices did not encumber the public good.[7] For these groups, racial liberalism both described an idealized state of social and political relations—equal treatment under the law without regard to race—as well as a strategy for achieving that change. Progress toward racial equality would be realized when atavistic ethnocentric impulses steadily gave way to a more tolerant and inclusionary Americanism—a neutral and indeed universal form of political judgment that was inherently indifferent to social location, position, or perspective. As the organizational motto of one group based in Los Angeles had it, "If you have racial or religious hatred in your mind you cannot have true Americanism in your heart."[8]

In California, as the war was in its last throes, the rising influence of this discourse was unmistakable. For example, a Fourth of July celebration in 1945 at the Hollywood Bowl, Los Angeles's famed outdoor amphitheater, attracted fifteen thousand people to observe "Interdependence Day . . . a CELEBRATION to Promote Racial Friendliness in America." Mayor Bowron introduced the keynote speaker, Supreme Court Justice Frank Murphy, who told the crowd to be vigilant against "all manifestations of the Nazi disease we may find among our own people." His speech, titled "All Men Are Brothers," urged a "spiritual battle" against "those in our midst who have been nurtured on the myths of the superior and inferior races and who practice discrimination against other Americans because of the color of their skin or some other arbitrary racial sign." Murphy warned of the "exaltation of any race, or nationality as superior to all others." Joining Murphy on the stage were a group of leading civic figures from the region, including Los Angeles archbishop John Cantwell, Rabbi Edgar Magnin, Supervisor John Anson Ford, and James Thimmes of the Congress of Industrial Organizations.[9]

Had Myrdal located his study in California rather than the South, he would have found widespread violations of the American Creed at the time of the Interdependence Day celebration. Just a few dozen miles from the Hollywood Bowl, for example, school districts in Orange County still formally segregated Mexican American and Anglo students. Jim Crow regimes of segregation in public spaces could be observed in public swimming pools, railroad coaches, restaurants, and hotels. Large sections of residential housing in Los Angeles and many other cities in California were covered by racially restrictive housing covenants and occupancy clauses, which typically restricted ownership and residence of a property to "members of the Caucasian race," with the exception of live-in domestic servants. At the war's end, the state still had laws in place prohibiting interracial marriage and banning landownership by many Japanese Americans.[10] Some local chapters of the American Legion, Elks Club, and Cub Scouts—and even public schools—continued to sponsor minstrel shows as fundraisers.[11] And until 1941, the *Los Angeles Times* featured a weekly column titled "Social Eugenics," written by a prominent member of the American Eugenics Society who advocated for the widespread use of sterilization for "racial betterment." As historian Alexandra Stern explains, "California stood at the vanguard of the national Eugenics movement" led by an "influential sector of elite Californians that embraced Eugenics as the best solution to the state's perceived problems."[12]

After the war, these policies and conditions became the object of public advocacy campaigns, litigation, and citizen organizing by groups determined to see California set the national standard for ensuring that its fair-minded residents embraced and accepted the ideals of the American Creed. For the California Federation for Civic Unity (CFCU), a coalition of some 150 state and local organizations united for this purpose, a progressive and patriotic national identity was the enemy of racial injustice. The organization's 1949 "blueprint for action" reasoned that when business owners and managers who enforced "racial exclusions in public places" were confronted by the inconsistency of their actions, they would "invariably realize how mistaken they were before. Their business grows better, not worse. Their patrons do not object. Everyone is happier and feels a lot more American."[13] A similar group explained that its program was premised on the idea that "given full and accurate information, even on the most controversial subjects, the average American, if he has been reared in the democratic tradition, will remain fair-minded in the face of prejudice."[14]

While similar organizations and campaigns could be found across the country, California offers an exemplary location to study the contours and trajectory of racial liberalism, and the ways it both purged and produced

variegated forms of racial domination in the postwar era. That is, the sentiments expressed in Mayor Bowron's 1944 declaration, "we have no master race" and "our freedoms are for all people," rapidly become axiomatic
within public discourse in the state. Postwar California political culture
affirms the general observation that liberal ideas have "provided the essential frame within which political arguments, including those about race
and other exclusions, have had to be cast . . . they provide the boundaries
outside which arguments cannot travel."[15] And many of the policies, practices and norms endorsing and enforcing racial domination in the 1940s
were soon vanquished. Assemblyman Augustus Hawkins of Los Angeles
proclaimed with considerable pride in 1960 that "virtually every law, clause,
or word facilitating discrimination or segregation has been wiped from
our statute books"; nearly all these reforms were passed after 1935, when
Hawkins became only the second African American state lawmaker elected
in California history.[16]

Surely if groups like the CFCU had a soothsayer in the their ranks
during their heyday in the late 1940s, they would rejoice in the knowledge
that few Californians at the start of the twenty-first century have ever had
to stare down a vigilante mob fighting the desegregation of their neighborhood, encounter employment ads insisting on "white gentile" applicants,
or face punishment for speaking Spanish on a school playground—experiences not uncommon at the war's end.

At the same time, would these groups recognize in contemporary California a civic order guaranteeing "freedoms for all people," which they so
confidently anticipated would accompany the expansion of the American
Creed? How would they account for the deeply segregated neighborhoods
and school systems and the racial disparities in income, health, and lon-
gevity witnessed across the state? How would they explain why race has
endured as a potent axis of power in an age when the vast majority of
Californians seem to reject, as Justice Murphy put it, the "exaltation of any
race, or nationality as superior to all others"?

THE BACKLASH THESIS AND THE REJECTION
OF RACIAL LIBERALISM

In the last three decades, similar questions have animated an important
scholarly and popular debate. What is the relationship between the American liberal tradition and the enduring forms of domination that shape the
U.S. political order? The most influential answer to this question emerged
in the shadows of Ronald Reagan's ascension and what appeared to be an

unrelenting conservative turn in American political culture. The "backlash theory" argues that racial liberalism failed to achieve broader structural transformations because large sectors of American society, especially the white working class, rejected liberal ideals.[17] In these accounts, the beleaguered white voter/citizen/worker—weary, angry, or fearful of the looming "threat" of racial justice—reflexively struck back to limit the influence of racial liberalism and embraced a competing framework of racial conservatism. As Thomas and Mary Edsall explain in the definitive account of this process, "As the civil rights movement became national, as it became clearly associated with the Democratic party, and as it began to impinge on local neighborhoods and schools, it served to crack the Democratic loyalties of key white voters."[18]

Studies of California politics have also relied heavily on explanations of white racial backlash. The electorate's embrace of a 1964 ballot initiative enshrining in the state constitution a right to discriminate by race, color, religion, or national origin in housing, explored in chapter 3, has been described by several commentators as a populist backlash against fair housing laws. Grassroots movements against busing to integrate public schools in the 1970s and against property taxes in the late 1970s and early 1980s have been described in similar terms. Today, backlash remains the framework of choice to describe public support for measures banning services to immigrants, opposing affirmative action programs, and demanding harsher sentences for criminal offenders.[19]

The backlash narrative has proved useful and appealing to commentators on both the political right and left. For the former, it offers proof of the enduring conservatism of the populace—it was the radicalism and violence of the "rights revolution" and its coterie of feminists, student radicals, and Black nationalists that drove the Silent Majority into the GOP. It demonstrates, this position holds, the inexorable hostility most in the United States feel toward such "radical" claims.[20] To commentators more identified with the left, the backlash justifies the conviction that the New Left failed when it abandoned the "universality" of class concerns and addressed itself instead to the "particularities" of race, gender, sexuality, and other narrow "interests." White voters abandoned the Democratic Party because the Democratic Party abandoned them.[21]

BEYOND THE BACKLASH THESIS

If the backlash thesis proves appealing as a political claim, it remains inadequate as a historical explanation. As Jeanne Theoharis argues, its advocates "elide white ethnic working-class alienation and political powerlessness with opposition to desegregation, naturalizing racism as a response for politically alienated working-class whites."[22] Political scientist Joseph Lowndes points out that backlash theorists fail to confront a central question: "Why should white workers necessarily have seen increasing claims for black equality as detrimental to their own interests?"[23] By always insisting on the particularity and distinctiveness of "nonwhite" consciousness, interests, and demands, these scholars treat the white backlash that ensued as a fait accompli rather than the contingent outcome of historically specific events, claims, and struggles.

This error rests on what Alexander Saxton describes as a circular logic in explaining the causes and endurance of racism: "a system of ideas and attitudes that allegedly causes differential treatment of non-whites is said to originate as a result of such differential treatment."[24] As historian Barbara Jeanne Fields has influentially argued, "since race is not genetically programmed, racial prejudice cannot be genetically programmed either but, like race itself, must arise historically." To posit, then, that "race" or "racial prejudice" functions as a motive force of history does nothing "more than repeat the question by way of answer."[25]

At stake here are not simply scholarly debates but commitments to particular courses of political action. In 1967, Stokely Carmichael and Charles Hamilton contested the claim that overreaching demands for racial justice and civil rights incited the currents of white backlash. In *Black Power: The Politics of Liberation in America*, they explained, "The so-called white backlash against black peoples is something else: the embedded traditions of institutional racism being brought into the open and calling forth overt manifestations of individual racism."[26] Here, a subtle but important distinction must be made between taking the violence and power of these "traditions" of racism seriously without regarding them as primordial and thus inevitable. Carmichael and Hamilton argued that these conflicts required political responses and solutions. They criticized the reluctance of "almost all white supporters . . . to go into their own communities—which is where the racism exists—and work to get rid of it" and insisted that the "white middle class suburbs need 'freedom schools' as badly as the black communities."[27]

An alternative scholarly trajectory, extending from W. E. B. DuBois to James Baldwin and Toni Morrison, has sought specifically to interrogate the origins and development of these traditions of racism, insisting that a greater possibility of democracy and human freedom required their abolition.[28] This work provides an important set of analytic and theoretical tools to understand the political struggles explored in this book.

RACIALIZED LIBERALISM

In 1943, Loren Miller, a young civil rights attorney who would go on to lead a successful challenge to racially restrictive covenants in the U.S. Supreme Court and serve as one of the first African American judges on the Los Angeles County Municipal Court, wrote to a colleague about recent comments made by Los Angeles mayor Fletcher Bowron. The reform-minded mayor certainly regarded himself as a racial liberal. By the end of the war, he would support the creation of a Fair Employment Practices Commission and desegregated public housing.[29] But Bowron remained strongly opposed to the resettlement of Japanese Americans who had been forced into internment camps a year earlier, and he hoped that "some legal method may be worked out to deprive the native-born Japanese of citizenship" after the war. Bowron described Japanese Americans as "a race apart," explaining in a public address that the "accident of birth should not make being born on American soil, of parents who are alien in legal effect and at heart, citizens of the United States, just the same as the descendants of the pioneer stock that has made America great and fixed a standard for Americanism."[30]

In response, Miller wrote to his colleague: "I am very much disturbed by the rise of [Bowron's] kind of racism, and I believe it to be significant that it comes from people like him; persons who are not essentially demagogues but are rather the ordinary, slow and stodgy middle class Americans. . . . It is a smug, unreasoned feeling that 'we' Americans of the Old Stock are the elect of the Lord and can be stretched to mean that whoever and whatever challenges the Supremacy of the White Race has in some manner sinned against eternal verities." Miller admitted, "It is hard to tell how deep this feeling runs," but noted that local labor leaders had recently echoed similar sentiments, and that even the national newspaper of the Communist Party had not offered a response to Bowron's stinging remarks.[31]

Implicit in Miller's comments is an alternative conceptualization of the relationship between long-standing currents of white supremacy and the ascendant racial liberalism Bowron embraced. Miller did not suggest that Bowron was merely expressing an irrational prejudice born of wartime hysteria, or conveying an attitude that was somehow contradictory to American values. Nor did he trace Bowron's comments to a brand of extremism or conservatism. His concern focused instead on the endurance of a political subjectivity and collective identity (evident in his reference to "'we' Americans of the Old Stock") that was constituted through and determined by a particular understanding of what race meant, and the kinds of hierarchy and power it authorized. Liberal commitments to tolerance, rights, equality, and opportunity did not nullify or negate this political subjectivity, which was "ordinary" and extended to even some progressive groups. Instead, this subjectivity could constitute the terms and boundaries within which such liberal commitments could be expressed—a liberalism that was always already racial.

DEFINING POLITICAL WHITENESS

The political "feeling" that Miller described so deftly in 1944 anchors the conceptual category I define as "political whiteness." Political whiteness describes a political subjectivity rooted in white racial identity, a gaze on politics constituted by whiteness. This concept draws from and extends both George Lipsitz's observations about the "possessive investment in whiteness" and Cheryl Harris's critical account of "whiteness as property." Whiteness, Lipsitz argues is "possessed" both literally in the form of material rewards and resources afforded to those recognized as white as well as figuratively through the "psychological wages" of status and social recognition detailed by W. E. B. DuBois.[32] Harris similarly describes a "valorization of whiteness as treasured property," recognized by the law and enforced by the state, which produces a "settled expectation" that its beneficiaries will face no "undue" obstacles in claiming its rewards. Whiteness, she explains, "is simultaneously an aspect of identity and a property interest, it is something that can be both experienced and deployed as a resource."[33]

The concept of political whiteness describes how these norms, "settled expectations," and "investments" shape the interpretation of political interests, the boundaries of political communities, and the sources of power for many political actors who understand themselves as white. It does not simply describe the interests or politics of "white people," which after all are necessarily varied. It instead concerns the process by which some political claims and interests come to be defined as white. James Baldwin described an "American delusion" fostered by whiteness that leads people to believe "not only that their brothers all are white but that the whites are all their brothers."[34]

Like whiteness in general, political whiteness is a subjectivity that constantly disavows its own presence and insists on its own innocence. It operates instead as a kind of absent referent, hailing and interpolating particular subjects through various affective appeals witnessed in claims to protect "our rights," "our jobs," "our homes," "our kids," "our streets," and even "our state" that never mention race but are addressed to racialized subjects.

Political whiteness is, in one sense, a widely studied phenomenon. Scholars and observers have long sought to explain the relationship between white racial identity and political behavior and action. In most accounts, however, white racial identity is viewed as fully realized and defined, constructed outside of the field of politics. Conflicts like ballot measures merely express its preordained interests. This account, by contrast, does not view political whiteness as a fixed, a priori identity that simply becomes expressed through political conflicts. Carmichael and Hamilton's argument certainly holds true: there are deep "traditions" of racism embedded in diverse institutions and structures that shape the contours and trajectory of white political identity at any given moment. But white political identity is hardly static; it also becomes transformed and renewed through struggles such as ballot initiative campaigns.

THE HEGEMONIC CHARACTER OF POLITICAL WHITENESS

Political whiteness bears two characteristics that are central to all hegemonic formations. First, as cultural studies scholar Raymond Williams explains, "the hegemonic has to be seen as more than the simple transmission of an (unchanging) dominance. On the contrary, any hegemonic process must be especially alert and responsive to the alternatives and opposition which question and threaten its dominance" because a "lived hegemony is always a process." It must be "renewed, recreated, defended, and modified" as it is "continually resisted, limited, altered, [and] challenged by pressures not all its own."[35]

California's racialized ballot measures reveal precisely such a process at work. Taken together, they demonstrate the contested formation of political whiteness, a gaze on politics that is characterized by both continuity and change. Rather than viewing these ballot measures as primarily concerning the rights of various racialized minorities, we can understand them instead as contests over the political authority and "settled expectations" of whiteness itself.

A central assertion of this book is that the political forces that opposed civil rights and racial justice policies are the ones that have best understood the malleable nature of political whiteness, and have constantly tested the ways they could adapt and incorporate new ideas, values, and experiences. Their opponents, by contrast, rarely attempted to challenge political whiteness as a fundamental identification, treating it instead as an inexorable force of political life.

Williams's second point about hegemonic formations concerns the question of opposition. By definition, ballot initiatives are viewed as contests between opposing political projects, which presumably do not share similar ideas, commitments, or values. But Williams argues that the very power of hegemonic formations derives from their capacity to shape the terms on which they are opposed: "nearly all initiatives and contributions, even when they take on manifestly alternative or oppositional forms, are in practice tied to the hegemonic: that the dominant culture, so to say, at once produces and limits its own forms of counter-culture."[36]

Within California's racialized ballot measures, political whiteness has been sustained by forces on both sides of the initiative debates, as putative opponents often echoed and refined ideas that valorized and naturalized this subjectivity. Unwilling or unable to challenge political whiteness as a universal standard of political judgment, self-identified liberal groups played an active role in reproducing its normative assumptions, constraining the boundaries of acceptable claims for racial justice in the future. Such limitations became profoundly evident during the racialized ballot measures of the 1990s.

This conceptualization of hegemony challenges a dominant rhetorical arc long embraced by many civil rights supporters that draws a bright line between a racially egalitarian and liberal political order on one side and an ascriptive and conservative order on the other. From this perspective, the endurance of racial domination in political life is attributed solely to those who stubbornly refuse to renounce their racist commitments to the latter camp. Such representations mask important convergences in the ways diverse political actors and movements collaborated to racialize many critical policy debates in the postwar era. While the categories of racial conservatism and liberalism have some heuristic utility, particularly in describing differing policy prescriptions, such rubrics can often obscure as much as they reveal.[37]

The trajectories of racial liberalism and political whiteness in postwar California may have certainly been intertwined, but their destinations were not preordained. White political identity did not teleologically absorb the lofty tenets of racial liberalism as it progressed from ethnocentrism to enlightenment. Nor did it abruptly and intuitively reject those tenets once civil rights protesters filled the streets. Their fates were determined through political struggles, waged across time, and argued within the same normative framework. The ballot initiatives examined in the pages that follow tell one story about how the high aspirations of racial liberalism ultimately ran aground on the shoal of political whiteness.

2. "Racial and Religious Tolerance Are Highly Desirable Objectives"

Fair Employment and the Vicissitudes of Tolerance, 1945-1960

In October 1946, voters across Southern California received letters from a recently formed group called the Committee for Tolerance alerting them to a threat that would "arouse intolerance, disunity and hatred" across the state.[1] In the immediate aftermath of the war, calls for "tolerance" often summoned nationalist allegiances to defend a shared commitment to acceptance in the face of despotism and fanaticism, a civic creed forged in the crucible of national crisis. The letter's recipients might have presumed any number of issues had propelled an organization dedicated to tolerance to issue such an alert: Perhaps it was another proclamation from Governor Earl Warren calling for the protection of returning Japanese American internees? Perhaps it offered a reaction to the ongoing revelations over the expanse of Nazi concentration camps? Maybe the letter was sent by opponents of white nationalist Gerald L. K. Smith, warning that the "Minister of Hate" might be returning to Southern California? California, as much as any state in the nation, had been completely transformed by the war—its explosive population growth, rapidly industrializing economy, and its singular contributions to the nation's technological development. In this context, warnings about the specters of "disunity" and "hatred" held a particularly strong resonance.[2]

The Committee for Tolerance, however, made no mention of these issues. Its alarm focused instead on a ballot measure voters would face in the upcoming November election. Frank Doherty, the committee's chairman, declared to his readers that Proposition 11, which would create a state Fair Employment Practices Commission (FEPC) and formally ban discrimination by race, religion, color, or national origin by unions and employers, merely "pretends to promote tolerance and good will." In fact, the former president of the powerful Los Angeles County Chamber of

24

Commerce warned that "the unfair law" would "arouse intolerance, disunity, and hatred." Tolerance, Doherty insisted, was by its nature a matter of personal conscience and could not be legislated by the state.[3]

Proposition 11 has received little attention in most accounts of civil rights and antidiscrimination struggles in twentieth-century California history.[4] The measure met an overwhelming defeat on Election Day—it received just under 30 percent of the vote—leading one historian of California ballot initiatives to the straightforward conclusion that "the public was definitely not ready for fair employment."[5] From this perspective, the measure lost primarily because the forces of "racial liberalism" had yet to match the power of the prevailing "racial conservatism." In addition, in the aftermath of Proposition 11's defeat, the battle to win a state FEPC focused almost entirely on the state legislature, which finally adopted the legislation in 1959. Thus, the 1946 ballot initiative seems like a minor footnote to this broader story.

Proposition 11, however, remains a critical site for examining the ways that competing actors attempted to define the meaning and significance of racism in a time of dramatic political transformation. The measure represented the *first and last* time that a diverse grouping of civil rights, labor, religious, and "civic unity" organizations attempted to place an antidiscrimination measure before the California electorate. The Proposition 11 conflict occurred at a time when the very definition of terms such as "tolerance," "discrimination," and "unity" were deeply contested and at a moment when the authority of white political identity would become steadily transformed.

The overwhelming defeat of Proposition 11 shaped the strategies of civil rights advocates for many years to come, conditioning their understanding of how antiracist public policies could be most effectively secured and which constituencies were necessary to mobilize for such efforts to succeed. The backers of the FEPC were not an undifferentiated grouping of "racial liberals" but a heterogeneous set of activists and organizations espousing distinct political commitments, analyses, and strategies. At the same time, opponents of fair employment policies refined their own political vocabulary, fusing anticommunist and antiregulatory narratives with an emerging discourse that incorporated and even celebrated some tenets of racial tolerance and liberalism. That is, fifty years before the formal ascendance of "colorblind" race politics in California political discourse, opponents of civil rights proved remarkably sophisticated in commanding the terms and ideas of racial liberalism to serve their own political purposes.

THE EMERGENCE OF FAIR EMPLOYMENT
PRACTICES LEGISLATION

For African American and Mexican American workers in California in the 1940s, fair employment laws held particular political significance. In June 1941, the threat of a March on Washington by labor leader A. Philip Randolph compelled President Roosevelt to issue Executive Order 8802, prohibiting government contractors from employment discrimination based on race, color, or national origin. At the time, California's burgeoning defense industry, from the sprawling Kaiser shipyards along the San Francisco Bay to the massive Lockheed airplane factories in Los Angeles County, routinely consigned Black and Mexican American workers to the lowest-paid jobs, if they hired them at all. Women faced both racial and gender discrimination, which fair employment practices (FEP) laws did not address. Unions, especially those affiliated with the American Federation of Labor (AFL), continued to maintain segregated locals. The U.S. Employment Service, for its part, often tacitly supported such practices by honoring employers' requests to recruit and assign workers for jobs on a segregated basis.

Such policies did not go unchallenged. For example, the Los Angeles Negro Victory Committee, formed to end discrimination in the region's defense industry, led a 1942 campaign to ensure that Black women would not be excluded from the shipbuilding industry. As Charlotta Bass, publisher of the *California Eagle* and an instrumental force in many civil rights struggles during the time explained, "Negro women . . . decided they were going to fight untidily [sic] for food, clothing, and the comforts of life which were due to them." The women organized a mass action at the Employment Service's Los Angeles office, demanding and winning an end to the discriminatory referral practices.[6]

While the five-member Fair Employment Practices Commission created by Roosevelt's executive order had minimal formal enforcement power, it did hold a series of fact-finding hearings in Los Angeles and other cities home to major defense industries. These hearings provided civil rights groups and their labor allies, primarily unions affiliated with the Congress of Industrial Organizations (CIO), a public platform to challenge these patterns of segregation. Over the next few years, as a result of both the growing labor demand and through the political pressure applied by the FEPC, hundreds of thousands of defense jobs opened up for nonwhite workers. Though these advances were often tenuous and uneven, especially for Mexican American workers and women, the FEPC represented the first time the federal or state government had taken deliberate action to address widespread discrimination in the workplace.[7]

Civil rights groups, including the National Association for the Advancement of Colored People (NAACP) and the Urban League, had begun asking for a state-level FEPC to parallel the federal body as early as 1941.[8] In 1944, as wartime employment seemed to be peaking, these groups renewed their call for state-level legislation, protections deemed particularly important in the face of an immense peacetime reconversion process that would leave many workers idle. While Randolph and other national leaders battled southern representatives to enact a permanent FEPC on the federal level, leaders in California and elsewhere made state and local-level legislation their top priority. As the newspaper of the Randolph's Brotherhood of Sleeping Car Porters asserted at the time, "Without the FEPC, Negroes and all other minorities will face terrible days in the postwar period."[9] Historian Robert Self explains that, to these leaders, a state FEPC could serve as "the front wedge of an assault on hiring discrimination and Jim Crow unionism in California."[10]

California's leading crusader for a state FEPC law was Assemblyman Augustus Hawkins of Los Angeles.[11] An unfailing New Deal Democrat, Hawkins sponsored unsuccessful FEPC bills in the 1944 and 1945 legislative sessions. And while popular Governor Earl Warren voiced his support for state FEPC legislation in early 1946 (consistent with the GOP's 1944 national platform), he could not find the necessary backing among lawmakers in his own party; the powerful agriculture and business lobby in particular was determined to keep the legislation locked in committee. In the 1946 special session of the legislature, both a bipartisan bill supported by Hawkins and a more modest bill supported by Warren failed to get out of the Republican-controlled Governmental Efficiency Committee. The *Los Angeles Sentinel*, the state's largest Black newspaper and an unswerving champion of the FEPC, acknowledged Warren's support in principle but questioned after the failed vote why he did "little or nothing to secure passage of the measure through the legislature controlled by his own party."[12]

Hawkins, who in a later interview suggested that he had to fight Warren "every inch of the way in Sacramento on fair employment practices," had altogether lost patience with his fellow lawmakers. He told supporters in February 1946 that "any hope of passing an FEPC bill through this legislature is like believing in Santa Claus."[13] But Hawkins and his allies in the CIO, NAACP, and other faith, labor, and civic unity groups had an alternative plan. From their perspective, opposition to the FEPC arose from a small number of antilabor employers, newspapers (especially the *Los Angeles*

Times), and conservative elected officials who stubbornly refused to recognize the citizenship rights of all Californians. As the *Sentinel* asserted, "most of the fair minded people of this state—and most Californians are fair minded when they are well informed—approve a state FEPC and the real job is to enlist these Californians."[14] FEPC supporters decided to take their cause directly to the voters. Hawkins declared optimistically, "There is no doubt in my mind that the people of California want a Fair Employment Practices Act and are determined to get one."[15]

The very decision to bring the FEPC legislation to the ballot deserves consideration. While there had been examples of civil rights and racial justice activism in the prewar period—strikes among Mexican and Japanese American farmworkers, Don't Buy Where You Can't Work campaigns, the NAACP's legal advocacy against racially restrictive housing covenants in the 1920s—the statewide project for FEPC legislation was unprecedented.[16] The state legislature continued to be dominated by business-oriented Republicans and was almost entirely white: Hawkins was the only African American in the state assembly.

Why, then, at this juncture did Hawkins and other FEPC supporters feel the electorate, which in spite of wartime migrations of hundreds of thousands of Mexicans and African Americans still remained overwhelmingly white and Protestant, would approve a fair employment ballot measure? Certainly, FEPC backers were emboldened by the growing numbers of Democratic voters in the state. Given FDR's support of the wartime FEPC, such voters might be more supportive of the state legislation. From 1930 to 1940, Democratic Party registration grew from 456,096 to more than 2.4 million, while Republican registration remained at roughly 1.6 million.[17] In addition, while the emerging political bloc of progressive civil rights and labor organizations in the state was not as powerful as comparable formations in the Northeast and Midwest, in cities such as Oakland, Richmond, San Francisco, and Los Angeles the capacity of this alliance was clearly on the rise.[18] Finally, in New York, a successful bipartisan coalition emerged to pass a similar state FEPC policy over the objections of well-organized groups of employers, and similar legislation had been adopted in New Jersey, Indiana, Wisconsin, and Massachusetts.[19]

 California's FEPC supporters imagined that the ideological transformations wrought by a war against fascism and predicated on a unified notion of national citizenship would disable the prevailing discourse of racial nationalism in favor of a pluralist discourse in which economic, social, and political privileges derived from hard work and loyal citizenship rather than racial, ethnic, or religious kinship. By transforming racial subjects into citizen subjects empowered to fully participate in the state's economic and political marketplace, this liberal vision would provide framework and boundaries of effective and intelligible political redress.

As the Proposition 11 campaign revealed, however, the abstract tenets of this liberal creed were polyvalent; their political character was not guaranteed.[20] Indeed, the contours and trajectory of California race politics after the war must be understood in relation to the political struggle over the meaning of this emerging civic creed.

"THERE IS NO RATIONALITY IN PREJUDICE": RACE RELATIONS GROUPS AND THE RISE OF RACIAL INNOCENCE

Much of the support for the FEPC struggle in California came from organizations affiliated with an emerging number of "race relations" and "civic unity" groups. These groups traced their roots back to the late 1920s and early 1930s, when a range of political organizations and cultural figures sought to articulate a more inclusive conception of American identity free of racial and religious chauvinism, especially in response to the resurgence of white Protestant nativism unleashed in the aftermath of World War I. The "cultural gifts" movement, as historian Diane Selig explains, flourished in cities across the country during the interwar period and emphasized notions of cultural pluralism and distinct group-based identities to celebrate and consolidate the nation's heterogeneous character.[21] In the early 1940s, the eruption of the so-called Zoot Suit Riots and the internment of tens of thousands of Japanese Americans in California spurned the formation of dozens of civic unity and "fair play" organizations.

To take one leading example, in September 1944 the first meeting of the San Francisco Civic Unity Council brought together some 340 representatives of groups, including the YMCA, the American Friends Service Committee, the CIO Minorities Committee, the San Francisco Council of Churches, the National Conference of Christians and Jews, the B'nai B'rith Community Committee, and others. According to records about the council, "racially, the group included two Chinese, five Negroes, one Filipino, and thirty-three whites." The meeting resulted in a series of recommendations that were typical to such civic unity groups: developing training courses in "interracial leadership" and "interracial education"; eliminating segregation in housing through both policy advocacy and educational campaigns designed to "'Nail the Falsehood' that minority races reduce the value of property"; and advocating for a permanent FEPC.[22]

At roughly the same time, the Chicago-based American Council on Race

Relations (ACRR) opened a Pacific Coast office in San Francisco to address "the population dislocations during the war period, the housing situation and the worsening condition of the colored minorities." In July 1945, ACRR helped bring together a Sacramento conference of similar civic unity and fair play organizations from across the state. Within a year, the founding gathering of the umbrella California Council for Civic Unity brought together nearly fifty newly formed race relations organizations from across the state.[23] Described by one participant as "an actual movement," the new group declared its purpose to bring together "all those forces which favor harmonious living—labor organizations, real estate associations, employers, religious interests, professional groups, service groups, such agencies as the American Legion, Veterans of Foreign Wars, Chambers of Commerce, newspaper publishers, and various social agencies," insisting "there is no rationality in prejudice." Soon changing its name to the California Federation for Civic Unity (CFCU), the group held biannual statewide retreats in Asilomar on the central coast for the next ten years. Nearly every leading civil rights activist of the period had some involvement with the CFCU directly or with one of its affiliated organizations.[24]

THE CONTOURS OF LIBERAL ANTIRACISM

The various race relations organizations, labor unions, and civil rights groups brought together by the CFCU forged an analysis of racism influenced by a number of sources. The milieu of global politics loomed large—references to the Good Neighbor Policy, American brotherhood, and Roosevelt's Four Freedoms saturated their language.[25] More particularly, the work of figures such as Ruth Benedict, Ashley Montagu, and above all Gunnar Myrdal deeply influenced their understanding of the factors that nourished racism and the interventions necessary to bring about its end. These writers emphasized the scientific fallacy of racial superiority and inferiority (though rarely challenging the existence of "race") and asserted that public education and positive intergroup interactions would dispel prejudices held by a fundamentally rational public. The greatest resource in reversing this cycle was the American Creed itself, "a belief in equality and in the rights to liberty" that grew from the Enlightenment and the American Revolution. Appeals to the creed and its universality could overcome the local particularities, customs, and chauvinisms that sustained bigotry and segregation.[26]

For all of these groups, racism was, to borrow a term from Paul Gilroy, "bad ideology."[27] It rested primarily in the thoughts and the actions of the individual who, because of personal experiences or a parochial upbringing, continued to subscribe to illogical and erroneous ideas about race. Yet with the proper information and experiences, any individual could be cured of this condition, embrace tolerance, and no longer be "guilty" of racism. When this occurred on a widespread basis, resulting in changes in both beliefs and actions, segregation in areas such as housing, employment, and education would also whither. These remedies did not preclude legislative action to correct the legal underpinnings of discrimination; most race relations groups remained vigilant in their efforts to end racially restrictive covenants, discriminatory housing practices, and even biased immigration laws. But those legislative changes were necessary so that people, no longer "artificially" segregated by force of law, could shed their own prejudices and accept those from "other groups."

This notion of "racial innocence"—the self-possessed individual who decided to free himself or herself from the narrow trappings of prejudice and bigotry and fully accept American notions of equality and fair treatment—would dominate debates over the meaning of race and racism for the rest of the twentieth century.

OTHER ELEMENTS OF THE FEPC COALITION

While most members of the civic unity groups embraced a Myrdalian framework that actively promoted the civic creed as the surest bulwark against the forces of racial exclusion and bigotry, the FEPC coalition included political actors and organizations with other analyses. For example, in 1944 the ACRR hired a young Fred Ross to join the staff of its Pacific Coast Community Services office. Ross, who would become legendary in community organizing circles as a contemporary of influential organizer Saul Alinsky and a mentor to Cesar Chavez, was particularly enthusiastic about the prospects of "working directly with the people themselves in the establishment of minority or inter-minority organizations for civic action on a neighborhood or community basis."[28] Ross thus championed another important approach toward antiracism. Rather than explaining racial inequality as a function of "incorrect" or irrational ideas, this perspective emphasized disparities in relations of power. While elite allies may be necessary to support efforts against racist policies, they were not the most important constituency. To win FEPC-type legislation required the development of powerful organizations that could make claims and demands on the political system. Organization, rather than the dissemination of information, was the primary imperative.

Similar ideas drove unions that included large numbers of African American and Mexican American workers struggling against racial discrimination during the war. C. L. Dellums of the Brotherhood of Sleeping Car Porters became the standard-bearer of a growing African American labor movement in Oakland, Richmond, and San Francisco in the aftermath of the war. As Dellums would later explain, "Negroes will have to pay for their own organization, their own fights, by their own funds as well as their own energy." Dellums's Brotherhood and other Black railroad workers unions were built with "Negro leadership and Negro money" using the solidarity forged within sites of segregation to wage direct confrontations against racial discrimination.[29] Dellums played a leading role in launching the Oakland Voters League (OVL) in the mid-1940s. This labor–civil rights coalition temporarily wrestled control of the Oakland City Council from the conservative Republican bloc that had dominated city politics for many years.[30] The OVL, like the activist labor unions, drew its strength from building organization and a new notion of political community among the city's multiracial working class.

Similarly, Mexican and Mexican American workers in the citrus groves and packinghouses of Southern California engaged in spontaneous walkouts to demand better wages or working conditions. For the large-scale employers that dominated California's vast agricultural sector, race, ethnicity, and national origin had formed the de rigueur basis of hiring and the organization of labor crews since the late nineteenth century.[31] Employers believed such a racialized division of labor discouraged strikes and unionization while making it easier to recruit, deploy, and dismiss large groups of workers. Early civil rights groups and progressive unions in California, including the United Cannery, Agriculture, Packing and Allied Workers of America (UCAPAWA) and the Congress of Spanish Speaking Peoples, similarly fused a robust commitment to organizing Mexican American workers and residents with a broader platform of social and economic justice.[32]

While the actions of farmworkers and packinghouse workers rarely resulted in collective bargaining agreements or lasting unions, they did suggest a different analysis of the causes and solutions to racial discrimination in employment. These workers certainly appealed to notions of fairness and inclusion, but they understood the problem as being rooted in unequal relations of power.[33] Like the labor unionists led by Dellums, they attempted to bring the contradictions of a racially segmented workforce directly to the fore.

A final component of the pro-FEPC coalition included an array of Communist Party members, several CIO unions, and other left activists, which viewed the struggle for the FEPC as an opportunity to unite a broader working-class formation. Like Ross, these activists held that employment discrimination was not a function of individual irrationality but was a deliberate effort by business interests to divide and fracture solidarity among workers. While they also described workplace segregation and discrimination as un-American, they linked the issue to a broader project of economic democracy and union power. During the war, the CIO consistently urged the U.S. Employment Service to reject discriminatory job specifications, arguing that such discrimination hindered the effort to achieve full production.[34]

In Los Angeles, left-leaning CIO locals consolidated rapidly in the 1930s under the leadership of the CIO Council. In the wake of a short-lived sit-down strike at the Douglas Aircraft Factory in Santa Monica in 1937, more than one hundred CIO locals formed in the Los Angeles area, and many counted large numbers of Black and Mexican American workers as members. Three of the major CIO locals in Los Angeles—the International Ladies Garment Workers Union (ILGWU), International Longshore and Warehouse Union (ILWU), and United Auto Workers (UAW)—had significant communist or socialist leadership. In some cases the CIO sought to include antidiscrimination clauses in some union contracts or to desegregate all-white employment sectors.[35] While it is important to remember that such positions were much more widely embraced by union leadership rather than rank and file members, even these official positions represented an important source of antiracist politics. Other FEPC supporters, including the Civil Rights Congress and the Communist Party, offered a similar analysis, often expressed in even more strident anticapitalist tones.

Thus, the effort to win FEPC legislation was not the product of a singular racial liberalism. Instead, FEPC represented an issue in which a fairly heterogeneous group of political forces found temporary common ground. For left labor activists, communists, and socialists, fair employment represented one among several issues (such as full employment, public housing, and wage and price controls) where confrontations with probusiness forces over the terms of the postwar economic consensus could be waged. More centrist members of civic unity groups believed that discriminatory employment policies validated and helped perpetuate the intolerant individual mind-set they believed to be at the core of racial inequality. These were not mutually exclusive or conflicting positions. But the campaign for Proposition 11 remains important to examine precisely because it represented an early site in the postwar era for such groups to assert and legitimate particular propositions about the sources of and solutions to racial subordination.

BRINGING FEPC TO THE BALLOT

In California, the Committee for a State FEPC had been established in early 1945 to mobilize support for Assembly Bill No. 3, a bill drafted by Hawkins patterned after legislation that had recently been adopted in New York.[36] After the war, national efforts to make the federal wartime FEPC permanent continued to be stymied by southern Democrats, and several states in the Northeast, Midwest, and West pursued state-level FEPC policies to perform the same function.

To build public support for Hawkins's bill, the Committee for a State FEPC established steering committees in Northern and Southern California, raising funds to purchase a few advertisements in Los Angeles and Bay Area newspapers. Their campaign to win public support for the measure rested almost entirely on applying the prodemocratic aspirations of the war to the home front. Anticipating that the celebrations of freedom and democracy sounded on VE day and VJ day remained fresh on the minds of California voters, FEPC supporters in Los Angeles published a newspaper ad featuring a solemn-faced GI staring sternly from beneath his helmet: "DON'T MESS IT UP NOW, BUDDY! Be Sure That Home-Front Jobs Are Open to ALL Americans!" The long list of endorsing community leaders included Judge Isaac Pacht, who chaired the Southern California committee, future Los Angeles County supervisor John Anson Ford, writer Carey McWilliams, and civil rights attorney Loren Miller.[37]

The arguments mobilized during the legislative hearings rehearsed the attacks that would await FEPC legislation in the subsequent initiative debate. Powerful agricultural interests, represented by the Associated Farmers of California, lobbied relentlessly against the measure, as did groups of retailers and other business associations. The Associated Farmers reported to its members at the end of the legislative session that while "many sincere representatives of racial groups who appeared at the hearings on the bill" made it "unpleasant" to oppose Assembly Bill No. 3, doing so was absolutely necessary because the legislation was "vicious almost beyond description. We have no hesitancy in predicting that had this bill become law it would have not only contributed to but would have created racial strife rather than alleviate it. It was radical legislation, pure and simple." Reciting a key argument it would use in the debates to come, the article pointed to a recent walkout of ILWU members in Stockton who had refused "to work with Nisei Japs" as evidence of the folly of regulating the racial attitudes of workers.[38]

The Council for Civic Unity of San Francisco would later report that the effort at trying to get the FEPC passed by the state legislature was "futile except for incidental educational values, since it was a foregone conclusion that the State Senate, dominated by big agriculture (which likes its racial labor gang kept intact and apart), would never enact FEPC."[39] The state senate was overwhelmingly dominated by representatives from rural areas, the result of a Progressive-era apportionment plan that created legislative districts based on county boundaries, rather than on population, and rural senators remained the staunchest opponents of fair employment legislation over the next twelve years.

Convinced that Governor Warren's professed support for a fair employment bill would not transfer into meaningful legislative action, FEPC advocates concluded that they stood little chance of getting the measure adopted through the legislature.[40] Representatives from across the state gathered in Fresno to plan a strategy to bring the FEPC issue directly to voters.[41] Leaders from African American, Mexican American, and Jewish civil rights organizations, together with representatives from the statewide CIO Council, formed the core of the group. They drafted a ballot initiative that closely mirrored Assembly Bill No. 3, declaring that the "opportunity to obtain and hold employment without discrimination because of race, religion, color, national origin or ancestry is hereby recognized and declared to be such a civil and constitutional right." The measure called for the creation of a five-member commission appointed by the governor that would be empowered to "receive, investigate, act in and render decisions on alleged instances of discrimination in employment because of race, religion, color, national origin or ancestry." The commission could issue formal subpoenas, conduct hearings, and issue findings with authority of a court order. By vesting strong enforcement authority with its administrative agency and limiting the scope and manner of judicial review, the proposed legislation went much further than the public education and fact-finding body preferred by Warren. It not only outlawed discrimination by employers and labor organizations, it prevented inquiries into the race, religion, color, national origin, or ancestry of a job or union applicant.[42] One study in 1946 found that 95 percent of job openings advertised in the State Employment Service were subject to particular "qualifications" of race, creed, gender, or national origin; stipulations that the service always attempted to honor.[43]

The group quickly turned its attention toward raising the funds necessary to print the petition and support an all-volunteer effort to gather signatures. Acknowledging that it would be a "long hard fight" to win FEPC through direct legislation, Attorney General Robert Kenny, the statewide committee's honorary chair, urged donors to contribute to the campaign so that the growing problem of reconversion and unemployment would not be further exacerbated by "the poison of discriminatory hiring and firing."[44] By the early spring of 1946, the effort was in full swing, led by the neighborhood organizations, faith groups, and the emerging network of civil rights and race relations organizations. Weekly petition drives at places like the Soto-Michigan Community Center in Boyle Heights, just east of downtown Los Angeles, brought together hundreds of NAACP members, trade unionists, Communist Party members, volunteers of newly established civic unity groups, and Jewish, Catholic and Protestant activists, along with members of emerging Mexican American and Japanese American community organizations into the momentous effort, furnishing many of the 275,000 signatures gathered statewide.[45] Organizers convened large meetings in San Francisco and San Diego to explain to supporters how to gather signatures and to identify the best places to do so. At the height of the petition drive in April 1946, Hawkins told the *Los Angeles Sentinel* that in "every busy intersection in the city" and "wherever a nylon or a butter line forms . . . petition collectors are sure to be there too."[46]

Hawkins announced later in April that the campaign had collected the necessary number of signatures to qualify for the November election. "There can be no doubt whatever," Hawkins proclaimed, "that the people of this state will have a chance to vote on the FEPC at the November elections, and there determine whether or not they will countenance continued discrimination on jobs because of race, creed or color." When the secretary of state confirmed in June that the measure would appear on the November ballot as Proposition 11, the *Sentinel* editorialized, "Let's Gird for Battle." While the paper predicted there would be "plenty of opposition and well financed opposition at that," it still concluded that "it is hard to believe that any but special interest cliques, which make money out of setting group against group, will vote against the bill once they understand what it means." Though the campaign would have to educate and mobilize hundreds of thousands of voters in the months to come, the *Sentinel*, like nearly all FEPC supporters, remained convinced that California voters would not turn their backs on such a fundamental issue of freedom and democracy.[47]

THE CAMPAIGN FOR PROPOSITION 11

State campaign-finance filings suggest that the pro-FEPC effort raised approximately $44,000 in Northern California—primarily from donors and businesses based in San Francisco—and $31,000 in Southern California, including funds spent on qualifying the initiative for the ballot. Among unions, only the left-leaning California CIO and ILWU made direct donations to the campaign. With limited funds, the Hawkins-led campaign in favor of Proposition 11 consisted primarily of distributing pamphlets and leaflets to voters through volunteers and supportive organizations and through appearances at a series of public debates and forums about the measure. The campaign was able to retain a consultant, Dan Foutz, whose firm had worked in the past for the CIO as well as the conservative Merchant and Manufacturers Association.[48]

The campaign to win public support for Proposition 11 reflected the composition of the broader liberal-left coalition that backed fair employment legislation. The effort continued to press the American Creed and the obligations of applying the antifascist commitments abroad to domestic concerns as well. The pro-11 ballot argument concluded with a statement by four prominent religious leaders calling on voters to "put upon our statute books the legal guarantee that this war shall not have been fought in vain, and that the American concept of human equality, to which men look for guidance in the principles and practices of liberty, shall become at last more than a hope and a desired end."[49]

Proponents also attempted to draw upon concerns over the economic dangers brought about by reconversion and the need to maintain the purchasing power and production capacity developed during the war to save the economy from depression. A typical flyer argued that "PROPOSITION 11 leads the way toward more jobs—by creating a rising purchasing power which will result in a more prosperous state. . . . [The FEPC] helped us get national unity and full production to lick the Axis, by encouraging the hiring of ALL qualified workers."[50]

Thus, the main Proposition 11 campaign continually framed the initiative as a reasonable, measured response that would prevent discrimination from stalling California's advance in the postwar era. It stressed the FEPC's emphasis on education and conciliation and that no workers would be displaced if the measure were adopted. The enforcement provisions were necessary because "education is ineffectual unless legislation can compel a few recalcitrants to conform to democratic practices." While the campaign did not altogether conceal the ways in which African Americans and other racial minorities were particularly invested in the FEPC issue—the ballot arguments, for example, were also signed by Hawkins, *Los Angeles Sentinel* editor Leon Washington, *Pittsburgh Courier* Pacific Coast editor Herman Hill, and attorney Loren Miller—the campaign rarely suggested that discrimination was a broad problem in California, underscoring that all workers and the economy at large would benefit from prohibitions on discrimination.[51] In their attempts to win the support of white voters for the measure, they framed the issue as a conflict between a few extremists and bigots, on the one hand, and the fair-minded, democratic populace on the other.

By contrast, the California CIO's stand for Proposition 11 differed in several important ways. While the CIO participated enthusiastically in the pro–Proposition 11 campaign, they also produced voter-education materials for the November election of their own. One flyer tied the continuing racial violence in the South and the failure to pass federal antilynching legislation or to repeal the poll tax with the California effort to pass an FEPC law. "30,000 cases of job discrimination were laid before the FEPC in the 4 years of its life. Thousands of inequalities were corrected. IN 1946 CONGRESS KILLED THE FEPC."[52] Also calling for full employment, it suggested that California's entanglements with racial discrimination were connected to rather than distinct from a national crisis of racial inequality. The left-leaning Civil Rights Congress, which pressed the initiative vigorously in Los Angeles, similarly stressed the connection between the FEPC issue and broad social justice concerns. Here, white workers were urged to back Proposition 11, not only because they embraced democratic principles, but because segregation and discrimination harmed the interests and unity of all workers.

The endorsement of the AFL-affiliated State Federation of Labor in the summer did not result in broad-based activism for the initiative among its affiliated locals, many of which continued to segregate nonwhite workers into "auxiliary" locals. In Los Angeles, at the urging of the Garment Workers Union, the AFL Central Labor Council formed a Labor Committee to Combat Intolerance that worked with the independent Jewish Labor Committee (JLC) to educate union voters. The committee announced it would sponsor "a number of community-wide activities dramatically illustrating Labor's stake in the drive against intolerance." These activities included a luncheon for two hundred labor leaders featuring the Democratic candidate for U.S. Senate, Will Rogers Jr., who gave a major civil rights speech.[53] At the same time, Louis Levy, chair of the Los Angeles JLC, announced his group would initiate a "vigorous campaign to eliminate racial discrimination and bigotry among workers." Zane Meckler, a former organizer with the Worker's Defense League in New York who was put in charge of the initiative, explained that the JLC's approach would be "to fit the tolerance question into the problems of economic and political democracy." Capturing the tenor of many labor groups that supported fair employment laws, Levy suggested that it would be a mistake to isolate the "poison of race hatred and combat it alone"; better to instead focus on the "conditions which tempt ordinary people to grasp that it is the Jews, or the Negroes, or the foreigners who are taking away their economic bread and butter or cultural opportunities."[54]

Not all labor officials who favored fair employment laws supported putting the FEPC question on the ballot. C. L. Dellums opposed the very idea of placing the question before voters. As he would later recount:

> We should never set a precedent that we recognize that the people have a right to vote on anything they want to vote on. The rights I have been fighting for all my life, they are now called civil rights, I call human rights, God-given rights. White people have been using their majority and their control of the law enforcing agencies and firearms to prevent us from exercising our God-given rights. . . . We were never really asking white people to grant or give us any rights. Only to stop using their majority and power in preventing us from exercising our God-given rights.[55]

Dellums felt that putting the FEPC question to voters, even if it passed, would imply that the electorate possessed the authority to affirm or negate rights which were "God-given"—a position distinct from the civic unity leaders in San Francisco and the multiracial coalition of activists from Los Angeles that comprised the leadership of the Proposition 11 campaign. Dellums would play a leading role in the subsequent fourteen-year effort to win approval of the FEPC measure within the state legislature, and he was eventually appointed by Governor Pat Brown to serve on the state's first FEP commission in 1960.

THE CAMPAIGN TO DEFEAT PROPOSITION 11

As the November election approached, opposition to the measure began to take shape only a few miles away from the bustling Boyle Heights street corners where the Proposition 11 petition effort in Los Angeles was centered. Frank Doherty, the former president of the Los Angeles Chamber of Commerce and an outspoken anticommunist, quickly began raising money to fund a public campaign against Proposition 11. Doherty hired thirty-two-year-old Herbert Baus, a former public relations director for the chamber, to manage the campaign. Doherty, a onetime associate of Governor Hiram Johnson, knew the mechanics of the initiative system well and saw in Baus a major talent for conducting conservative-oriented public relations. The pair focused on raising money and securing endorsements, waiting until three weeks before the election to launch their public campaign.

Had Proposition 11 been launched in the 1920s or 1930s, when the Ku Klux Klan enjoyed widespread public backing and theories of eugenics merited serious attention among many California elites, Doherty and Baus could have explicitly campaigned against Proposition 11 as a basic affront to the privileges of white supremacy. Indeed, the last time an initiative with strong racial overtones appeared on the ballot—the successful 1920 Alien Land Law measure, targeting landownership rights of Japanese American farmers—proponent V. S. McClatchy stated openly in the ballot argument that "whites" must defend their interest against "Orientals, largely Japanese" who would soon gain "political control through force of numbers induced by the heavy birth rate."[56] The potent grip that racial nationalist ideology had on much of California's white populace was evident in the minimal public outcry that met the forced repatriation of tens of thousands of Mexicans and Mexican Americans in the 1930s and the wartime relocation of nearly 100,000 Japanese Americans.[57]

Indeed, even at the end of the war, several political actors attempted to build support for their projects on similar grounds. In May 1945, for example, Gerald L. K. Smith, a onetime associate of Huey Long in Louisiana, came to Los Angeles to establish a local chapter of his America First Party. Smith championed a doctrine of "Christian Nationalism" to stem "mongrelization and all attempts being made to force the intermixture of the black and white races."[58] While Smith's rallies drew several thousand supporters, they were met by a much larger grassroots movement that denounced Smith as an anti-American extremist who represented the antithesis of California's postwar promise. Los Angeles mayor Fletcher Bowron and many other elected officials roundly condemned Smith for "industriously blackening" the city's name "to serve his own special ends."[59] Anti-Smith rallies led by a broad coalition of Jewish organizations, civil rights groups, labor unions, and others drew twelve thousand protesters to Smith's appearance at the Shrine Auditorium in July 1945; seventeen thousand appeared the following month.[60] In early 1946, in the face of a number of cross-burning incidents, Attorney General Robert Kenny carried out several raids against the Ku Klux Klan. Governor Earl Warren announced, "I can think no worse calamity could befall our state or nation than to have a revival of the Ku Klux Klan either in fact or in spirit. . . . I am calling upon every public employee as well as our citizenry at large to give careful thought and attention to the eradication of the last vestige of bigotry in our state." The California Superior Court soon revoked the Klan's charter to operate.[61] In the wake of a global war fought in the name of freedom against fascism, there was a dwindling audience for brands of patriotism espoused by Smith or the KKK.

Doherty and Baus recognized the resonance of antifascist rhetoric within the dominant political discourse; Proposition 11 could not be defeated through overt appeals to white supremacy. At the same time, in opposing the FEPC they were essentially defending the right of white employers and unions to openly discriminate on the basis of race, religion, and national origin. They created the Committee for Tolerance to resolve this contradiction—harnessing an ascendant, pluralist discourse of civic nationalism to longstanding narratives of white supremacy.

The public campaign against Proposition 11, like opposition to Assembly Bill No. 3 the year before, was driven almost entirely by employers, though a handful of stridently conservative organizations and a few labor leaders also launched independent efforts to lobby voters against the measure. Doherty and Baus raised approximately $60,000 for their committee in only a few months, including $10,000 in the two weeks before the election. These figures do not include independent expenditures by many county-based associations of agricultural employers, as well as the Los Angeles Chamber of Commerce itself, which printed and mailed anti–Proposition 11 materials to sixty thousand voters before the election.[62] The committee also took out billboards across the state.[63]

Doherty used the relationships he established as former chamber president to disseminate materials against the initiative. The campaign distributed literature through business organizations and conservative groups and regularly fed press releases to papers like the *Los Angeles Times*, which printed the materials verbatim. Baus later confessed that the arguments used to defeat the measure were primarily designed to confuse and distract voters: "Like an octopus, we threw as much ink as we could in the water."[64] Yet the Committee for Tolerance did in fact emphasize a core set of arguments, hewing to two main propositions.

First, as the campaign's moniker suggested, Doherty and Baus asserted that Proposition 11 would increase division and strife. The chamber of commerce declared, "Racial and religious tolerance are highly desirable objectives. Tolerance, however, by its very definition is something which cannot be forced by law. It is a matter of individual conscience and private judgment."[65] Doherty endlessly repeated the refrain that Proposition 11 "would *emphasize* racial and religious cleavage and differences. *It does not allay them. For that reason it would inflame hatreds and work to the disadvantage of every minority.*"[66] Similarly, California Farm Bureau vice president C. O. Hoober asserted that "California's farmers, as a group, never have discriminated against workers because of race, color, or creed. In fact, agriculture hires more workers from minority groups than does any other California industry." Hoober suggested that while the "Farm Bureau would support any genuine, honest, effort to prevent discrimination . . . our investigations show that Proposition 11 is neither honest nor genuine, and that such an act would prove unworkable and impractical."[67] The *San Francisco Chronicle* concurred with Hoober, explaining that "no one can quarrel with the spirit of Fair Employment Practices without refuting the principles underlying American democracy." The paper held that the initiative simply was not the instrument to advance such principles. The *Los Angeles Times* similarly editorialized, "Admirable as it might be if race and religious prejudice ceased to exist, The Times does not believe that the disappearance of either can be helped by compulsion. . . . Prejudices by their very nature are matters of emotion rather than logic or reason."[68]

Such claims were certainly not particular to the Proposition 11 debate. The notion that government could not and should not legislate "private" morality was a popular defense against proposed civil rights legislation in the nineteenth century. Political forces deeply invested in white supremacy, such as southern opponents of Reconstruction, similarly justified racial subordination by attacking the alleged overreaching authority of the state.[69] In addition, business and Republican opponents of fair employment legislation in Congress and other states at the time also regularly invoked the "tolerance" defense.[70]

What is striking about the appeals to tolerance made by California FEPC opponents is the way they resonated so strongly within the framework of civic nationalism espoused by their opponents, revealing the contradictory character of tolerance as a political signifier. On the one hand, in this context, tolerance might signify the acceptance and affirmation of some sort of difference and the recognition of a shared and interdependent human condition. On the other hand, as the political theorist Wendy Brown argues, tolerance does other work: it can also be a deeply depoliticizing discourse, in the sense that it "involves construing inequality, subordination, marginalization, and social conflict, which all require political analysis and political solutions, as personal and individual on the one hand, or as natural, religious, or cultural on the other." This move of personalizing and naturalizing involves "removing a political phenomenon from comprehension of its *historical* emergence and from a recognition of the *powers* that produce and contour it." Inequality becomes naturalized, Brown argues, because the subjects of tolerance are marked as "inferior, deviant, or marginal vis-à-vis those practicing tolerance." That is, invocations of tolerance, even within the discourse of racial liberalism, still reproduce a political subjectivity that remains highly racialized; the plea to tolerate is addressed to an audience—a political community—that must already identify as white. Thus, by casting the question of employment discrimination in the language of tolerance, certain members of the populace continued to be marked as insiders (those who will do the tolerating), while others (those who will be tolerated) are marked as outsiders.[71] Here, even in the putatively antiracist language of civic nationalism, political whiteness—the notion that one's status within the polity is derived from an exclusionary racial identity and community—becomes affirmed and sustained rather than displaced or transformed.

Doherty and his allies could thus draw upon ideas about tolerance and even antidiscrimination while still appealing to political whiteness. Within this discourse, the assumption endured that particular immutable racial, ethnic, or cultural differences among the populace—the differences that required toleration—might still be relevant to employment decisions. The ballot argument against Proposition 11 stated that "certain minority racial groups are the most efficient agricultural labor" and that if "compelled by law to put minorities with conflicting customs, creeds and prejudices into the close proximity required for agricultural labor, inevitably friction, and in many cases, violence will result."[72] An anti-11 pamphlet expressed outrage that Proposition 11 would make it *"against the law* to specify a Japanese gardener or a colored porter or a Filipino fruit-picker or an English waiter or a Chinese cook or a French hairdresser or Swedish actress or an Italian singer or a Mexican dancer."[73] The Los Angeles County Chamber of Commerce warned its members that the measure would "deny employers the right to obtain full information about a prospective employee—race, religion, color, national origin or ancestry—for the purpose of intelligently appraising an applicant's qualifications for a particular job."[74] Here again we have a particular *proposition* about the meaning of race—a fixed, embodied notion of difference that was associated with one's "natural" role in the labor force—as well as the meaning of racism—a refusal to tolerate such differences. The proposition offered by the anti-FEPC groups articulated and incorporated many of the ideas asserted by the civic unity organizations in defense of prevailing relations of power.

Appeals to political whiteness were also conspicuous in claims made about the risk FEPC legislation posed to white working men. Doherty explained to voters, "You might lose your job or be demoted at the whim of appointed commissioners forcing another person into your place. . . . This political commission could discriminate against you."[75] The FEPC, Doherty insisted, would act as "investigator, prosecutor, judge, jury and executioner" to rob workers of due process rights and leave them subject to the whims of a heavy-handed bureaucracy that would be captive to the blackmailing schemes of those intent on taking their jobs.[76] Proposition 11 would deny "the right of free speech between one man and another freely negotiating about the right to work or the right to join a union." These threats were often gendered as well, raising the long-standing specter of racialized affronts to white women. Doherty asserted that the FEPC could insist that "you, your wife, your daughter or your sister must work with anyone the commission directs, regardless of color or race." The campaign against Proposition 11 also relentlessly red-baited its opponents on similar grounds. Doherty referred to the measure as a "Communist-inspired scheme" of the CIO's Political Action Committee (CIO-PAC) that would threaten the freedom of workers and employers.[77]

Such charges resonated strongly with a tradition among California labor unions that viewed efforts to exclude nonwhite workers from particular labor markets as fundamental to the survival of the white working class.[78] From this perspective, both antiunion employers *and* workers of color threatened to undermine the autonomy and power of organized white labor. Thus, while the California CIO Council and several other unions endorsed Proposition 11, other local union leaders organized a Labor Committee against Proposition 11. Headed by representatives of the United Railroad Workers (CIO), the State Building and Trades Council (AFL), and the International Association of Machinists (AFL), the group declared that the initiative "threatens more harm to organized labor and its members than to any other group of citizens." It reasoned that the FEPC legislation "empowers a political commission to subpoena union members, records, and private papers" and "authorizes the political commission to jail and fine union members."[79]

The Proposition 11 debate thus indexed two important transformations. On the one hand, political actors that had openly defended and profited from discourses of racial nationalism, such as the Los Angeles County Chamber of Commerce and the Farm Bureau, began quickly—though obviously not completely—to disavow such claims in favor of arguments that recognized and legitimated the civic creed. On the other hand, these same forces demonstrated how this rapidly ascendant discourse emphasizing pluralism and tolerance could be used to defend prevailing inequalities. The Proposition 11 debate reveals early in the postwar era the ways that racial liberalism, with its references to abstract ideals of equality over embodied relations of power, had limits that opponents of civil rights were quick to exploit. And while the anti-FEPC appeals weaved together long-standing narratives of racialized threats to white political authority, it is important to remember the context in which the appeals were made: a rapidly transforming political environment in which all political identities were in flux, and in which at least some white workers and political organizations did not view curbs on racial subordination as inimical to their interests.

Proposition 11 was crushed on Election Day, capturing less than 30 percent of the vote. The measure lost in fourteen of fifteen Los Angeles City Council districts; only in the multiracial Ninth District covering Boyle Heights, Little Tokyo, and the Central Avenue corridor did it prevail.[80] The initiative had a voter-participation rate of 85 percent, one of the highest in the election, suggesting the public debate over the initiative did not go unnoticed. The question here is not whether an alternative set of political arguments or strategies on the part of FEPC supporters could have secured a different outcome. Lacking polling data, voter surveys, or a clear sense of how widely the campaign materials circulated, it is difficult to make conclusive assertions about the influences that the competing campaigns had on the decisions of voters.[81] Instead, the campaign reveals ways that various political actors competed to define the very meaning of civic nationalism, tolerance, and racial liberalism.

Indeed, the outcome of another proposition on the same ballot demonstrates the challenge of making clear pronouncements about the electorate's judgments about race and racism based on Proposition 11 alone. This measure, Proposition 15, sought to enshrine the state's Alien Land Laws into the state constitution for the purpose of "closing loopholes" that allowed "Japanese aliens . . . to conceal true ownership of property." Sponsored by Republican state senator Jack Tenney of Los Angeles and Democratic senator Hugh Burns of Fresno, who were both also outspoken opponents of Proposition 11, the measure anticipated that the anti-Japanese sentiments that fueled support for internment during the war endured unabated. A recent wave of escheat lawsuits attempting to wrest ownership of farm properties from Japanese Americans had relied upon the Alien Land Laws, and such suits would have been undoubtedly strengthened with the passage of Proposition 15.[82]

Groups, including the Japanese American Citizens League, local fair play organizations, religious organizations, civic unity groups, and their allies, led the campaign against Proposition 15. Like the campaign in favor of Proposition 11 (which included many of the same groups), the effort against Proposition 15 declared "RACE HATE AND DISCRIMINATION Hurt You" and urged voters to tell their friends to "Vote American!" and reject the initiative. Opponents of the measure cited the decorated and heroic effort of the twenty-five thousand Japanese American GI's who served in the war and their right to "fair play and decent treatment for themselves and their families."[83]

Well into the war, legislation such as Proposition 15 would have found strong support among the electorate and a broad range of political leaders, invoking the principle, as Los Angeles mayor Fletcher Bowron argued, that the Japanese were "a race apart."[84] But the measure lost by nearly twenty percentage points, revealing the unstable terrain on which debates over race and racism would unfold. The same antidiscrimination and fair play arguments that failed to persuade voters to pass the FEPC helped to defeat the discriminatory landownership laws.

The opposing fates of Proposition 11 and Proposition 15 reveal an important dynamic that characterized antiracist political efforts across the postwar era. On the one hand, raising charges of extremism, attacking the spurious logic of biologically determined racial hierarchies, and appealing to national traditions of fair play and tolerance certainly had significant political resonance. Not only did such appeals secure the defeat of Proposition 15, they also shaped and made possible the repeal of a host of formally discriminatory policies. In 1946 (eight years before the *Brown v. Board of Education* ruling), a federal district court struck down the segregation of Mexican American students in the *Mendez v. Westminster* case. Within a year, the legislature removed all remaining school segregation statutes from the California Education Code. The California Supreme Court struck down antimiscegenation legislation in 1948, citing the work of anthropologists such as Ruth Benedict in arguing that "the categorical statement that non-Caucasians are inherently physically inferior is without scientific proof." The court held that the marriage prohibitions "violated the very premise on which this country and its constitution were built, the very ideas embodied in the Declaration of Independence, the very issues over which the revolutionary war, the civil war, and the Second World War were fought."[85] In 1952, the state supreme court struck down California's Alien Land Law as a violation of the Fourteenth Amendment, prompting Attorney General Pat Brown to note that all Californians should be proud that the state "will legally no longer persist in an adherence to a philosophy of a 'super race,' nor insist upon being a vindictive outpost of racial discrimination—that every one of our residents here has an equal opportunity to share in the building of a greater destiny for our State."[86]

Between 1945 and 1958, under Republican governors and within a Republican-controlled legislature, the state prohibited segregation and discrimination in the state militia, auto insurance sales, employment in public works, within the state civil service code, in employer or labor-run apprenticeship programs, in the provision of welfare benefits, and in teacher hiring and assignment. State agencies like the Department of Motor Vehicles were banned from requiring driver's license applicants to identify themselves by race, and the State Employment Service was prohibited from accepting discriminatory job listings.[87] A proposed 1952 Freedom of Choice ballot measure sponsored by state senator Jack Tenney, which would have essentially legalized the right to discriminate in broad areas of public life as a right of free association, failed to get any meaningful public support or legislative backing.[88] In all of these debates, few Californians seemed willing to openly reject the principles of nondiscrimination, equal opportunity, and tolerance. To be sure, these outcomes did not spell the ultimate demise of commitments to racial nationalism, but these developments were historically unprecedented.

On the other hand, invocations of tolerance, when expressed through appeals to political whiteness, proved quite accommodating to defenses of prevailing relations of apartheid. The campaign against Proposition 11 was not premised on a rejection of tolerance per se but on a proposition about what types of authority remained permissible within a society that had committed itself to tolerance. Some types of authority—the claims championed by Gerald Smith, the KKK, or those represented by Proposition 15—that had been legitimated for many years became stigmatized as "un-American" and indefensible. Yet other types of authority, such as the power of an employer or union to discriminate by race, gender, religion, or natural origin, became marked as not only permissible but absolutely necessary to the proper functioning of the economy and civil society. These privileges were represented, in this sense, as progressive and forward-thinking.

Many factors shaped this particular historical outcome: the exigencies of war and peace, the rising tide of anticommunism and cold war politics, the decline of left-oriented unionism, and the actions of a diverse set of political forces contending to make their particular vision of a "tolerant" society—their racial proposition—stand in for the whole. Proposition 11

thus represents more than an instrumental policy battle between competing blocs of liberals and conservatives; it also provides a window into the
ways that claims for white political authority adapted and transformed in
response to the rising influence of civic nationalist discourse. It reveals the
ways that the prevailing emphasis on individual forbearance and open-
mindedness championed by the civic unity groups intersected with the
claims of figures like Doherty, who also employed the rhetoric of tolerance
to defeat Proposition 11. If racism was indeed a question of individual
affect, "compulsory" legislation was unnecessary. It was an early lesson
in the mutability of the creedal vision and its claims of racial innocence.

THE AFTERMATH OF THE 1946 ELECTION

While Proposition 11 did not dominate the headlines the way subsequent
statewide ballot initiatives concerning race and racism would, the initiative
had an enormous impact on the strategies civil rights advocates pursued to
advance FEPC and other legislation over the next two decades. Two trends
are particularly important. First, the defeat of Proposition 11 convinced
FEPC and civil rights advocates of the enormous disadvantages they faced
in the arena of direct democracy. Even after a 1952 poll suggested a majority of California voters now approved of state FEPC legislation, supporters
feared the impact that another initiative debate would have on broader
public sentiment.[89] In 1957, the Jewish Labor Committee's Max Mont
explained to Councilman Ed Roybal (who contemplated sponsoring an
FEPC referendum in Los Angeles) that support for a referendum would be
"*worse* than outright opposition to the FEPC bill." Mont warned that "as
the referendum campaign developed, the public debate would become more
and more heated, bitter, and acrimonious [and] inter-group tensions would
develop that could set race relations back for a decade."[90] The NAACP
passed a formal statement the same year similarly condemning a proposed
statewide referendum on FEPC: "The serious question of extending equal
job opportunities to all Californians would become submerged, distorted,
and perverted in the slogans and propaganda directed at the general public
in a referendum campaign."[91] FEPC proponents understood that an initiative campaign could be generative of public ideas about race and racism
that would undermine their objectives. Not only did they focus subsequent
efforts to win the FEPC entirely on the state legislature (and in some cases,
local city councils), they similarly eschewed ballot initiatives as a means to
secure any other civil rights legislation.

The second major impact of the Proposition 11 campaign was to convince the more centrist leaders of the FEPC coalition that communists and left unionists had to be purged from the effort if it was to have any future success in the state legislature. Left CIO unions were among the most enthusiastic and activist supporters of the FEPC. But civil rights groups in general faced enormous pressures during this time to demonstrate their anticommunist commitments. The California Legislature's rabid Committee on Un-American Activities named even the moderate Chicago Conference on Race Relations among several "front organizations devoted to racial agitation" and declared that half of the sixty-three sponsors of the FEPC in Southern California, including Assemblyman Hawkins and writer Carey McWilliams, were "prominent left-wingers" and "well known Party-liners"—"submission to Moscow is chronic with these individuals."[92]

Though the mainline backers of the FEPC did not paint communist support of fair employment legislation with such a crude brush, they did not want to give their opponents the opportunity to rehearse the red-baiting attacks they unleashed against Proposition 11. The California Committee for Fair Practices (CCFP), which was formed to press the FEP law through the state legislature in the 1950s, explained that the 1946 initiative had failed in part because "the Communists intervened and tried to identify themselves with the issue, thereby sowing public confusion and accomplishing their real aim—defeat of the measure and continuance of discrimination."[93] In 1947, FEP supporters in Los Angeles refused an invitation from the leftist California Legislative Conference to work on a unified campaign for local fair employment legislation.[94] When the NAACP organized a Sacramento lobby day in 1953 in support of an FEPC bill before the state legislature, it specifically invited "all non-Communist, non-Fascist organizations" to join the mobilization.[95] Frank Williams, an attorney who served as West Coast regional director of the NAACP from 1950 to 1959, explained that "the left wing was completely excluded from the [FEPC] Mobilization" and recounted with satisfaction that even unsympathetic lawmakers commended the group for this action.[96] In response, the *People's World* reported on the "often ludicrous efforts of virulent anti-Communists among the leaders of the [FEPC] mobilization to keep it 'pure' by 'screening' from direct participation delegates from any groups considered to be 'left wing.'"[97]

To be sure, civil rights groups were quite pragmatic in following the prevailing anticommunist currents of the day.[98] Such moves generally strengthened their ability to make claims on American ideals of equal opportunity and undermined their opponents' efforts at dismissing their proposals as subversive. But the purges also came at a price. While these left organizations did not command an extraordinary membership base or grouping of votes, they were deeply committed to directly involving grass-roots members in civil rights struggles. In addition, they were often the only voices that linked specific policy proposals like the FEPC to broader calls for working-class empowerment within an antiracist framework, specifically calling on white workers to fight racial discrimination. Absent these efforts, the more tepid calls to resolve bigotry at an individual level increasingly became the singular rhetoric used to define fair employment politics.[99]

THE EMERGING LABOR–CIVIL RIGHTS COALITION AND THE FEPC VICTORY

It was not until 1959 that the California Fair Employment Practices Act, sponsored by Augustus Hawkins, was approved by the state legislature and signed by newly elected Democratic governor Pat Brown. A relatively robust FEPC law, the measure's passage reflected several significant developments in California politics since the defeat of Proposition 11 in 1946.

In the mid-1940s, California labor leaders were decidedly split on fair employment legislation, and some AFL leaders actively opposed Proposition 11. During the 1950s, the influential AFL-affiliated State Federation of Labor began to view groups like the NAACP and the Community Service Organization (CSO) as potent allies in their effort to wrestle control of state government from business-dominated Republicans. In 1953, the State Federation of Labor joined the newly formed California Committee for Fair Practices. The committee's work represented one of the high points in an emerging Democratic–labor–civil rights bloc that gained influence during the late 1950s and early 1960s. Groups like the NAACP, the CSO, the AFL, and the CIO collaborated on voter-registration drives and shared legislative interests, including the defeat of a 1958 Right to Work ballot measure sponsored by a coalition of employers and business interests.

As civil rights groups became more closely aligned with organized labor, they also began challenging the state's civic unity groups' emphasis on individual education and awareness raising among the white populace. The NAACP's Frank Williams explained to a 1952 gathering of the Los Angeles County Conference on Human Relations that in a state with "one and one-half million members of the most disadvantaged minority peoples . . . any struggle for the improvement of human relations is doomed to failure" without "roots deeply embedded in these people." He asked the group, "If

Figure 1. Fair employment supporters, Los Angeles, 1956. Los Angeles County supervisor John Anson Ford, civil rights attorney Loren Miller, the Congress of Industrial Organization's Gilbert Anaya, and Nathaniel Colley of the state NAACP at a conference at Hotel S on fair employment practice measures. Courtesy of Los Angeles Times Photo Archives, Department of Special Collections, Charles E. Young Research Library, University of California, Los Angeles.

our goal is the early realization of equality of opportunity for all people, is it proper to expend time, energy and money in the first instance to work *for* disadvantaged people? Isn't the correct approach to organize and work *with* minorities themselves?[100] Williams's critique foreshadowed a growing skepticism among some civil rights leaders about the political strategies and ideological frameworks championed by self-described racial liberals.[101]

The CCFP also concluded that the shibboleths of "tolerance" and "unity" alone would not be enough to legitimate demands for FEP legislation in the face of intransigent employers who continued to champion their own tolerance. The group produced a number of detailed reports documenting widespread discrimination within state and private employment agencies (where it found that 67 percent of job requests received in 1951 were discriminatory), the building trades, the hospitality industry, and other occupations, drawing growing attention from the media and elected officials.[102] Criticizing the public education campaign for Proposition 11 in 1946 as "poorly planned, haphazardly and almost indifferently executed," the rejuvenated FEPC effort sought to focus public attention on specific examples and patterns of discrimination while building powerful local and statewide alliances.[103]

The combination of coalition building and grassroots organizing, combined with a rejuvenated base of Democratic electoral activism, realized enormous dividends in the 1958 election, where Democrats swept nearly every statewide office, gained majorities in both the state assembly and senate, and elected a Democrat to the governor's office for only the second time in the twentieth century. During the election, Brown and his allies successfully portrayed their Republican opponents as extremist forces out of step with the state's forward-looking populace. Emboldened by these recent electoral victories, CCFP members remained resolute in the face of threats to qualify a referendum to repeal the newly passed FEP legislation. As the *California Eagle* would proclaim, "1959 isn't 1946." The paper called for a "showdown" with FEPC opponents; the repeal referendum never qualified for the ballot.[104]

As chapter 3 explores however, this emergent Democratic coalition had critical vulnerabilities. With the purge of communists and leftists from the FEPC coalition, civil rights and human relations groups silenced those voices most likely to articulate a forceful vision of racial justice connected to workers' empowerment; only the limited language of racial innocence and equal opportunity remained. While prominent labor officials declared support for a broad range of civil rights issues, much less action was taken to organize rank and file union members to these ends. In 1964, Loren Miller would assert in an address to a United Autoworkers Conference in Lake Arrowhead, California, that while some progress in desegregating unions had been made, "it is easier for a camel to pass through the eye of a needle than for a Negro to gain admittance to the portals of some unions." When such bars were lifted, leadership roles were denied. "The Negro is a second class citizen in too many unions; he is the governed, never the participant in government."[105]

At the same time, civil rights opponents were developing a wide-reaching critique of the state's role in combating racial discrimination and inequality within their growing grassroots base. Together with the political resources held by conservative business groups and the professional campaign consultants they employed, they were well positioned in the battles that loomed over race and housing.

3. "Get Back Your Rights!"

Fair Housing and the Right to Discriminate,
1960-1972

Six weeks before the 1964 presidential election, *Time* magazine reported on a California ballot initiative that was proving to be "the most bitterly fought issue in the nation's most populous state," interest in which over-shadowed "that of such relatively piddling contests as the one between Johnson and Goldwater."[1] Indeed, as an onslaught of billboards, television and radio debates, media coverage, handbills, and neighborhood meetings and rallies ensured, few California voters that fall could escape the spell of Proposition 14. Crafted by the California Real Estate Association (CREA), the six-sentence constitutional amendment sought to exempt the real estate industry, apartment owners, and individual homeowners from nearly all antidiscrimination legislation, enshrining an unprecedented "right to discriminate" in housing sales and rentals within the state's highest law. The initiative took particular aim at the Rumford Fair Housing Act, adopted by the state legislature a year earlier to address patterns of racial discrimination and segregation in housing as entrenched as any region in the nation. Avoiding any explicit justification of racial inequality or difference, or even a defense of segregated neighborhoods per se, the Realtors' public campaign asserted that "property rights" could not be sacrificed to the onslaught of "forced housing."

On November 3, 1964, as California voters elected the pro–civil rights Lyndon Johnson in a landslide, they also approved Proposition 14 by a two-to-one margin. While the U.S. Supreme Court ruled that that the measure violated the Fourteenth Amendment's equal protection guarantees in May 1967, and restored the Rumford Act and the other antidiscrimination laws the measure nullified, Proposition 14's impact was profound. Opponents identified the initiative as one of the deepest setbacks to civil rights in California during the 1960s—"a smashing blow to the teeth for racial minorities in California—and many linked the results directly to the Watts Uprising the following summer.[2] No debate over civil rights mobilized more intense attention and deliberation in California during this period than Proposition 14.

Most scholars have explained the triumph of Proposition 14 as an exemplary expression of "white backlash" against the progress of civil rights in the postwar era.[3] Proposition 14 seems to demonstrate a particularly powerful example of this political phenomenon because it suggested that even in the sunny and tolerant climes of California, thousands of miles away from the "massive resistance" of Selma and Birmingham, collective white tolerance to the advance of "racial liberalism" had limits that would prove inexorable. As historian Mark Brilliant argues, housing proved to be the shoal where racial liberalism would run aground. Brilliant captures this sentiment well in citing a letter written to Governor Pat Brown in the aftermath of the election, which declared, "Your Rights End Where My Property Begins."[4]

To be sure, the Proposition 14 election provides important insights into the sustained power and appeal of white racial identity in the early 1960s, and the way such identifications shaped the choices of voters. But interpreting Proposition 14 as the expression of individual attitudes alone—a kind of litmus test about the limits of "racial tolerance"—obscures a much more complex and dynamic story about the deep material and ideological investments in political whiteness, or the way that political identifications and communities become determined by narratives of racial difference. The Proposition 14 campaign demonstrates the ways in which competing political forces—self-identified conservatives and liberals—collaborated to sustain this powerful political identity to the detriment of broader claims for racial justice.

THE EMERGENCE OF RESIDENTIAL APARTHEID IN CALIFORNIA

For the migrants and settlers who arrived in California during the real estate booms of the late nineteenth and early twentieth centuries, the quality and status of their new lives became understood in explicitly racial terms almost from the outset. Early white migrants to Southern California, largely American born and middle class, viewed the single-family detached houses, with their large lots and landscaped yards, as ideal because of their symbolic and physical distance from the congested streets and tenements associated with the ills of turn-of-the-century urbanization.[5] Richmond homebuyers, for example, were enticed by a 1909 developer's appeal to "white men, civilized men, twentieth century Americans" who could appreciate the "beauty of owning property—real property—a HOME."[6] Thus, "homeowner" became a social and political identity animated by particular normative race, class, and gendered assumptions: a white nuclear family headed by a breadwinning father, a homemaking mother, and their immediate children—the home serving as both the foundation and index of this condition.

The extraordinary influence of Realtors and boosters and the cultural meanings associated with homeownership and racial exclusivity formed the groundwork for the extensive modes of racial segregation that shaped the geography of twentieth-century California. The struggle to sustain these exclusions, however, was always a contingent process rather than a finally determined outcome. Especially in the early twentieth century, before the proliferation of restrictive covenants and limitations that restricted homeownership or occupancy on the basis of race, Black migrants found white homeowners willing to sell or rent properties to them;[7] California's Black homeownership rate in 1910 was 38 percent, compared to 17 percent in New England and 22 percent in the South.[8]

As diverse groups either ignored prevailing race restrictions or pursued legal challenges to overturn them, the boosters, developers, Realtors, and property owners who remained invested in racial exclusion as a source of value, status, and identity were forced to take new action. Racial covenants, for example, did enter into widespread usage until the 1920s. Developers, Realtors, and owners propagated the use of covenants, occupancy clauses, and similar agreements (often going door-to-door to persuade homeowners to sign them) precisely because there were white homeowners willing and interested in selling and renting their homes to nonwhites. Indeed, if an unchanging and all-encompassing white racial animus had existed independent of such concerted action, racial covenants would have been unnecessary; the agreements would have been self-enforced.

The California Real Estate Association emerged as the most steadfast and influential leader in the effort to sustain the articulation between property ownership, political community, and racial identity. Formed in 1903 in order to professionalize the public image of real estate salesmen and allay public concern over the risk of land speculation and fraud, the CREA developed a strict "Code of Ethics" to be followed by its member "Realtors" (a copyrighted name that only members of affiliated local realty boards were authorized to use). Until 1951, this code included the principle that a "realtor should never be instrumental in introducing into a neighborhood a character of property or occupancy, members of any race or nationality, or any individual whose presence will clearly be detrimental to property values in the neighborhood."[9]

Local realty boards assumed the role of disciplining any members who violated this principle and determined which neighborhoods and tracts would be designated for "whites only," refusing to share listings with agents who openly served nonwhite clients.[10] Bodies like the Southwest Realty Board in Los Angeles formed "race restrictions committees" to organize homeowners to maintain racial restrictions, publicizing their success in the CREA magazine.[11] As late as 1949, Glendale Realtors proudly declared their city a "100% Caucasian Race Community" in the CREA's annual directory.[12]

In the 1930s, the new federal Home Owners Loan Corporation (HOLC) made racial distinctions a central determinant in appraising a neighborhood's suitability for federally backed loans. Multiracial neighborhoods in Los Angeles such as Boyle Heights and the Central Avenue district received the lowest grades on these "Security Maps," directing the vast majority of investment in housing stock toward exclusively white neighborhoods.[13] Building on patterns established by settlement, strengthened by covenants, and valorized by federal mortgage assistance initiatives, California's exploding working- and middle-class suburbs remained almost exclusively white. The 1930 and 1940 censuses of South Gate found only two Black residents in the city out of a population of nearly twenty-seven thousand.[14] As the South Gate Property Owners' Protective Association proudly declared in its handbook, its planners had recognized "the danger of allowing race restrictions to lapse too soon" so that nearly "all of the city's residential tracts have perpetual restrictions against occupancy by non-Caucasians."[15]

The Federal Housing Authority (FHA), which succeeded the HOLC in 1934, used the HOLC's rating system in its provision of mortgage guarantees to lenders and developers and even provided model covenant agreements to builders. FHA assistance poured into segregated white communities like the Los Angeles suburb of South Gate as it shunned integrated neighborhoods in South and East Los Angeles.[16] According to one estimate, of the 350,000 new homes constructed in northern California between 1946 and 1960 with FHA support, less than 100 went to Black homebuyers.[17] Moreover, as historian David Freund argues, the FHA's programs included a widespread marketing campaign that insisted that the massive new federal housing programs were in fact initiatives to unleash private capital into the free market, rather than direct state subsidies. Freund explains that these campaigns helped reinforce the idea among white suburbanites that their burgeoning communities were an achievement of the free market and their own volition, free of any government support or assistance.[18]

Realtors remained defiant even in the face of the 1948 *Shelley v. Kraemer* decision, which ruled that court enforcement of restrictive covenants was akin to state action and was in violation of the Fourteenth Amendment. In response, the Los Angeles Realty Board urged "a nationwide campaign to amend the United States Constitution to guarantee enforcement of property restrictions." The Realtors argued that such restrictions provided "a traditional element of value in home ownership throughout this nation." Because "recent decisions of the Supreme Court . . . have destroyed the values thus secured," a constitutional amendment was necessary.[19] The Los Angeles Realty Board drew up a proposed amendment and advocated for its adoption before the National Association for Real Estate Boards (NAREB) for more than a decade.

After the courts signaled their refusal to enforce restrictive covenants, Realtors proliferated the use of "corporate contract agreements" and "neighborhood protective associations" through which homeowners could regulate the sale of properties in their neighborhoods.[20] An article in the CREA's monthly magazine advised that such associations would not technically be issued with "reference to race or color, but [would be] based entirely upon personal qualifications as a good neighbor, or in other words, cultural status." It continued, "The advantage of [a home association] is that it will permit exclusion of undesirable whites."[21]

After the *Shelley* decision, local realty boards continued to expel members who violated agreed racial boundaries. Because these local boards controlled the Multiple Listing Services (MLSs), which provided access to homes available for sale, Realtors who choose to breach these mandates faced dire consequences. Few broke ranks. A fair housing group in the San Francisco peninsula reported that only three of the six hundred Realtors serving the region agreed to provide "equal and undiscriminating treatment in the purchase of homes" as late as 1960. In the same year, the Los Angeles Realty Board did not have a single Black Realtor among its more than two thousand members.[22]

After 1950, developers of large residential tracts, which supplied the vast majority of new housing in California, arguably became even more influential than the Realtors in maintaining and even expanding patterns of segregation. While the FHA after 1949 no longer allowed restrictive covenants to be directly attached to the loans it guaranteed to builders, and individual homeowners could not seek judicial enforcement of restrictive covenants on their own or neighboring properties, neither federal nor state law barred tract developers from discriminating in the sale of individual homes. With few exceptions, developers from the late 1940s to mid-1960s planned housing tracts on a racially segregated basis, including some tracts that were reserved for Black and/or Mexican American residents. The civil rights attorney Loren Miller, for example, noted in 1955 how the new suburb of Lakewood, ten miles south of Los Angeles and often regarded as the region's "finest flower," was "a bean field ten years ago, a thriving metropolis today—lily white, made white, kept white by builders with the active consent of the FHA."[23]

In the San Fernando Valley north of Los Angeles, where the population more than doubled from 311,016 in 1950 to 739,570 in 1960, patterns of racial segregation actually increased after restrictive covenants were outlawed. Fifteen of the sixteen cities in the Valley reported a Black population under 1 percent in 1960. Nearly every Black newcomer to the Valley in the 1950s, even those that arrived to work in technical jobs for the region's defense contractors, was directed to the racially segregated northern area of the city of Pacoima, where the Black population quadrupled during this time. The chair of the San Fernando Valley Fair Housing Council told a state commission in 1960 that he knew of only one single Black family able to purchase a home in a new housing tract during the previous ten years.[24] A 1963 estimate put the Black population in the Valley outside of Pacoima at 0.0015 percent. The first Black resident to buy a house in the Sun Valley district remarked, "I didn't know California had become Mississippi."[25]

Why were Realtors and developers so invested in maintaining rigid lines of segregation during this time? At a hearing that year before the U.S. Commission on Civil Rights in Los Angeles in 1960, a representative of the Los Angeles Realty Board declared racial discrimination in housing to be entirely nonexistent: "The inability of one to fulfill a desire is not discrimination: it is frustration which only the individual can overcome by personal improvement in his financial and social position." Quoting the social Darwinist Herbert Spencer, the representative insisted that a natural "heterogeneity" in society was a product of the "march of progress and of civilization."[26]

Thinly veiled references to white supremacy, however, do not explain the Realtors' actions in their entirety. Several generations of investments in racially segmented housing markets had left an enduring legacy. As historian Robert Self argues, under the HOLC, FHA, and Veterans Administration (VA) guidelines, "the most profitable real estate strategy was to treat black and white housing markets as entirely distinct entities."[27]

Open housing policies and practices risked triggering wide fluctuations in property values instead of the steady increases that the industry most prized. Covenants and corporate contract and neighborhood association agreements were built upon and helped fuel white racial identity and discrimination to this end. Self concludes that "the real estate industry came to see the promotion, preservation and manipulation of racial segregation as central—rather than incidental or residual—components of their profit-generating strategies."[28]

For their part, most white homeowners took full advantage of the privileges afforded to them by the federal government and the real estate industry, understanding the value and sanctity of their property and neighborhoods to be dependent on racial distinctions and exclusion. Hundreds of thousands of white residents abandoned previously integrated communities in Los Angeles, San Francisco, Oakland, and Berkeley for the promise of racially exclusive suburbs and then conspired to keep their new neighborhoods segregated.[29] After the war, as more people of color acquired the personal savings and income to purchase homes in these communities, they often faced well-organized and sometimes violent resistance. In 1947, the *San Leandro News-Observer* reported that the "sudden increase in the East Bay Negro population" meant "local neighborhoods are spontaneously moving to protect their property values and calling upon [a local Realtor] to assist them."[30] It was, as Self explains, "segregation's consequence," racism rationalized as economic calculation."[31]

Collectively, these investments in whiteness forged a racial geography in California as segregated and asymmetrical as almost any region in the country. In 1960, 82 percent of the nearly 35,000 Black residents of San Diego lived in only 10 of the city's 123 census tracts. The San Francisco East Bay suburb of Orinda Village reported only 4 nonwhite households out of a total of 1,600. According to a report by the Los Angeles Commission on Human Relations, between 1950 and 1960, of the 637,399 units constructed in the county, "at best only 2.2 percent were available to minority groups." The report continued, "It is indeed a startling fact that in the ten-year period ending in April 1960, only 1,437 additional Negro citizens or .87 percent have found residences outside of the Central District of Los Angeles, and in San Pedro, Venice and Pacoima."[32]

MIDCENTURY CHALLENGES TO RACE RESTRICTIONS

Though racial segregation in California remained stark through the 1960s, defending and preserving these patterns proved increasingly difficult. The national office of the NAACP challenged the FHA's use of "public tax money to restrict, instead of extend opportunities [or] to enforce patterns of racial segregation," eventually ending the federal government's subsidies for segregated housing.[33] In 1946, the Los Angeles chapter of the Civil Rights Congress formed an anticovenant coalition asking property owners to sign "antirestrictive covenants" that would invalidate any standing race restrictions. West Coast NAACP attorneys, including Frank Williams and Loren Miller, played central roles in several cases that led to the U.S. Supreme Court rulings finally outlawing covenants.[34]

By the early 1960s this activism grew more forceful. NAACP member E. J. Franklin told a gathering of more than eleven hundred civil rights supporters assembled in the Beverly Hills High School auditorium in 1963, "Everybody is upset about conditions in Mississippi and Birmingham; but they should be upset about conditions in Los Angeles." Another NAACP leader explained, "There is more racial residential segregation in Los Angeles than in any major Southern city in the United States."[35] Congress of Racial Equality (CORE) chapters in San Francisco, Berkeley, Oakland, and Los Angeles increasingly used direct-action tactics such as sit-ins at segregated subdivisions and "window-shopping days" to test whether Realtors showed properties for sale on a nondiscriminatory basis. In 1962 and 1963, an interracial group of several hundred protesters regularly picketed segregated housing tracts in the city of Torrance outside of Los Angeles; many hundreds were regularly arrested, including actors Marlon Brando and Rita Moreno.[36]

In addition, while sporadic violence continued to visit Black, Asian American, and Mexican American homeowners who bought property in all-white neighborhoods, such vigilantism was increasingly met with a visible counterresponse, and by the late 1950s, sheriff's deputies dispatched to these conflicts were more likely to disperse protesters then abet their efforts.[37] Several accounts suggest that these new homeowners almost always found white allies willing to ease their transition, and that the initial opposition they met often faded. The sustained protests and vigilantism that met desegregation efforts in northern cities such as Detroit and Chicago during this period occurred far less frequently in California after the war.[38] A 1955 report about racial attitudes in areas "in-filtrated by non-whites," based on interviews with 549 white residents in thirty-five Bay Area neighborhoods, concluded "that for the large majority of white residents, the presence of Negro or Oriental neighbors was not prominent in their respective thinking about the advantages and disadvantages of their respective neighborhoods."[39] The stark segregation that still existed in

1960 suggests that these efforts were piecemeal at best, but they challenge the claim that these neighborhoods unvaryingly resisted desegregation.

Perhaps the most important force for desegregation was the growing numbers of Mexican Americans, Asian Americans, and African Americans who had adequate income and savings to purchase more-valuable homes in white communities, some with the assistance of VA loans. From this perspective, housing desegregation was a practical imperative, not just a moral one: the housing stock to which most nonwhite Californians were confined, much of it old and dilapidated, could not meet the enormous demand. A 1963 study in Los Angeles County suggested that 26 percent of African Americans and Asian Americans, and 32 percent of the Spanish-surname population, lived in dilapidated housing, compared to only 7 percent of the white population.[40]

THE EMERGENCE OF FAIR HOUSING LEGISLATION

It was against this backdrop in 1958 that a coalition anchored by civil rights organizations, labor unions, and the recently formed California Democratic Council (CDC) brought a Democratic majority to the state legislature and helped Edmund "Pat" Brown upset conservative Republican senator Joseph Knowland in the race for governor. Within three years, with the support of Brown, Inglewood assemblyman Jesse Unruh, and under the leadership of African American legislators Augustus Hawkins and William Byron Rumford, the state passed a series of important civil rights bills. In addition to the 1959 legislation creating the Fair Employment Practices Commission, lawmakers passed the Hawkins Act to prohibit discrimination in public housing (including housing financed or insured by a government loan) and urban renewal projects, and the Unruh Civil Rights Act, which banned discrimination in all business establishments and established the legal principle that "all persons within the jurisdiction of this state are free and equal."[41] Court rulings subsequently held that real estate agents, tract developers, and most apartment owners were also included under the Unruh Act.[42]

While this legislation brought a large proportion of the housing market under the coverage of antidiscrimination law, the laws did not provide an enforcement mechanism. An aggrieved buyer or renter was still required to file a legal claim (either a civil suit or a complaint to the district attorney) in order to obtain relief—a lengthy and costly process. The standard "open housing" legislation adopted in other states called for an administrative process to resolve complaints of discrimination. In 1963, Assemblyman

Rumford introduced Assembly Bill No. 1240, the Fair Housing Bill. This legislation covered private housing financed by public sources (such as VA and FHA loans) and non–publicly assisted housing comprised of five or more units. The legislation empowered the four-year-old FEPC to receive, investigate, and adjudicate complaints of discrimination.

Rumford's bill faced an uncertain fate as the legislature prepared to adjourn in June 1963. Rumford, Governor Brown, and Assembly Speaker Unruh lobbied undecided legislators vigorously, while CORE began a sit-in in the capitol rotunda. Minutes before the legislature was to adjourn for the summer, and over the vociferous objections of several apartment owners and the CREA (which argued that no housing discrimination existed in California), lawmakers adopted the bill and Governor Brown signed the Rumford Act into law. No swell of individual homeowners traveled to Sacramento to lobby against the bill, and newspaper coverage of the debate suggested little "public outcry" toward the legislation at the time.

With the passage of the Rumford Act, California joined Massachusetts, Washington, Colorado, and New Jersey among the fourteen states in the postwar period to pass some version of open housing legislation enforced by an administrative body.[43] Like other states, California's open housing protections offered modest remedies to the crisis facing the hundreds of thousands of people excluded from the vast majority of the state's housing market. Most of the housing included in the act was already covered by the Hawkins and Unruh legislation or by a November 1962 executive order issued by President Kennedy.[44] The primary change brought about by the Rumford Act was to vest adjudication and enforcement powers with the FEPC. Complainants seeking redress under Rumford had to file their grievance with the FEPC, wait for an investigation to occur, and then participate in a voluntary conciliation process. If the case was still unresolved, the FEPC could convene a formal hearing and, if it sustained the complaint, order the homeowner or manager to rent or sell the property in question or a comparable accommodation to the complainant. If such a remedy was not available, a $500 fine could be imposed, but no criminal charges could be filed.

It is also important to note that the Rumford Act exempted properties consisting of four or fewer units and only covered single-family houses that were owner occupied and financed by a government loan. In other words, a vacant or rented single-family home (e.g., an investment property) was exempted from Rumford Act coverage even if it was publicly financed; duplexes, triplexes, and fourplexes were exempted entirely. One estimate suggested that the Rumford Act covered only about 25 percent of the nearly 3.8 million single-family homes in the state and less than 5 percent of the 857,000 duplexes, triplexes, and fourplexes. Other than vesting authority with the FEPC, its primary impact was to extend coverage to 99 percent of the 738,000 apartment buildings of five units or more. In other words, most individual homeowners remained entirely unaffected by the provisions of the Rumford Act; none of their "rights" were abridged by its provisions. These limitations are important to keep in mind in evaluating the Realtors' (and some scholars') subsequent claims that support for Proposition 14 represented a grassroots response by a beleaguered electorate frustrated with the steady erosion of their rights.[45] At least as a policy measure (rather than as a political symbol), there is scant evidence to regard the Rumford Act as "an overreaching law" that demonstrated that "liberalism had lost its sense of moderation."[46]

In addition, the Rumford Act dealt with discrimination in renting and sales only; it did not provide any assistance or relief for the many Californians who could not afford housing outside of segregated neighborhoods. Thus, the law would primarily benefit middle-income renters and buyers who could afford such housing. To be sure, open housing legislation was critical because it further signaled the state would no longer sanction or enforce racial discrimination in housing and because it increased housing options for many middle-income earners.[47] But the Rumford Act was not intended to bring about widespread integration or solve the endemic housing crisis that was facing so many Californians.

BRINGING THE "FORCED HOUSING" QUESTION TO THE BALLOT

Because of the success of open housing legislation at the state level, the CREA and the National Association of Real Estate Boards had largely abandoned their efforts to defend the legality of racially restrictive covenants, focusing attention instead on reversing the tide of these laws. Since the 1948 *Shelley* decision overturning restrictive covenants, every other strategy pursued by realty groups—including the proposed amendment to the U.S. Constitution, the formation of neighborhood protective associations, corporate contract agreements, and disciplining Realtors who broke informal restrictions—failed to win significant public support or pass legal muster. The NAREB concluded that defeating fair housing laws in California—the nation's most populous state, and one that often regarded itself as the antithesis of the Jim Crow South—could reverse the national proliferation of open housing laws.[48]

While the NAREB, the CREA, and the California Apartment Owners' Association were resolutely committed to taking the Rumford Act off the books, they faced a vexing tactical dilemma. In the Democratic takeover of 1958, Brown and other Democrats effectively portrayed their Republican opponents as atavistic extremists who were out of touch with the state's liberal and forward-looking electorate. When Brown won reelection in 1962 against Richard Nixon, he candidly expressed his support for additional civil rights legislation, including open housing measures, with little apparent backlash from voters. Indeed, the California Poll—the polling organization that would later become the Field Poll—found in a 1964 survey that voters identified "civil rights and the race problem" to be the most important issue in that year's presidential election.[49]

To roll back the Rumford Act would require the Realtors to steer clear of any language, symbols, or inferences that associated their opposition to open housing with the prosegregationist images of the John Birch Society and figures like George Wallace. At the same time, it was a policy and practice of racial segregation that they specifically sought to protect; the CREA's campaign would be built on complex and unstable political terrain.

The CREA decided to withhold its support from a smaller group that had begun collecting signatures for a referendum initiative that would repeal the Rumford Act. The referendum effort, led by a group based in Berkeley, fell sixty thousand signatures short of qualifying for the ballot, suggesting grassroots opposition to the open housing legislation was not immediately guaranteed.[50] As the CREA would later explain, it did not support this effort because a referendum would not prevent the legislature from enacting similar laws in the future, nor would it preclude county and local governments from adopting their own open housing measures.[51] Instead, as the referendum effort floundered, the CREA and the California Apartment Owners' Association, with the support of the NAREB, met to draft a more sweeping and permanent initiative to amend the state constitution.[52] As early as March 1963, three months before the Rumford Act was adopted, CREA president L. H. Wilson had proposed that a ballot initiative be placed before voters that incorporated the association's newly adapted "Property Owners Bill of Rights." Soon after, at least twenty realty boards took out full-page ads proclaiming this bill of rights in their local newspapers.[53] Calling itself the Committee for Home Protection, the CREA ultimately drafted an initiative that adopted much of the language in this document. Concise and cleverly crafted, it made no mention of race. Its operative first paragraph instead focused on the seemingly transparent and fundamental notion of property rights: "Neither the State nor any subdivision or agency thereof shall deny, limit or abridge, directly or indirectly, the right of any person, who is willing or desires to sell, lease or rent any part or all of his real property, to decline to sell, lease or rent such property to such person or persons as he, in his absolute discretion, chooses."[54]

While the initiative would come to be identified as a straightforward repeal of the Rumford Act, the constitutional amendment actually eviscerated most (but not all) of Rumford's provisions and also invalidated components of the Unruh and Hawkins acts that banned discrimination in public housing, apartment rentals, and housing construction. An analysis authored by the law-school deans at the University of Southern California, the University of California, Los Angeles (UCLA), and the University of California, Berkeley, concluded that the measure "would establish constitutional immunity for those who discriminate in the sale or rental of their property and would exempt them from present and future fair housing laws."[55]

THE REALTORS' CAMPAIGN

The CREA quickly retained a campaign management and public relations consultant (funded in part by a ten-dollar assessment paid by member Realtors), but the association decided to forgo the customary practice of retaining paid signature gatherers. The group instead mobilized its nearly forty-five thousand members, organized into 171 local realty boards, to take on the immense task of gathering at least a half-million signatures within 150 days.[56] A February 20, 1964, advertisement in the *Oakland Tribune* seeking volunteers to circulate petitions, revealed the careful construction of the issue the Realtors intended to bring before voters:

"RUMFORD ACT FORCED HOUSING"
COMMITTEE FOR HOME PROTECTION

In September 1963, the Rumford Act became state Law. Heretofore, a man's home was his castle. The Rumford Act makes a man's home subject to the whims of a politically appointed State Board. . . . The politically appointed Commission can FORCE you to sell or rent your home to an individual NOT OF YOUR CHOICE. Most people believe that a man has the right to sell, rent or lease his property to whomever he wishes; consequently they OPPOSE the Rumford Act. . . . VOLUNTEERS NEEDED TO CIRCULATE PETITIONS.[57]

Neighborhood Realtors, joined by committed political and religious conservative activists, mobilized an enormous grassroots operation, delivering and collecting petitions from thousands of volunteers through designated "area captains."[58] Local realty boards assumed responsibility for coordinating petition gathering in their areas and pressed individual Realtors to collect signatures and make additional contributions to the CREA to defray campaign expenses.[59] Apartment owners also played a significant role in this effort. The Apartment Association of Los Angeles urged its members to "regain and keep control of your property" and to protect the "American right of freedom of choice" by distributing petitions widely.[60] By late March, the Committee for Home Protection (CHP), now headed by former CREA president L. H. Wilson, submitted 633,206 valid signatures to Secretary of State Frank Jordan, reportedly the largest number ever certified for an initiative measure.[61]

The narratives in clear sight in the *Oakland Tribune* advertisement would be rehearsed throughout an intensely fought campaign during the next ten months. The Committee for Home Protection identity (first developed by political consultants in a 1948 initiative campaign against public housing) continued to draw upon a powerful cold war narrative of home and civilian defense against a menacing outsider—"the home as a man's castle"—evoking threats to a collective domestic security. The campaign materials, news accounts, and other public discourse developed by the CHP assiduously avoided most direct mentions of race, civil rights, or segregation. In its published communications, few claims were ever made that the Rumford Act would drive down property values, lead to racial strife, or would sacrifice any natural orders of segregation—arguments that circulated widely in open housing conflicts in other parts of the country at the same time.[62] Most supporters of Proposition 14 would not defend the tenets of racial nationalism explicitly.

Instead, in their campaign materials, public talking points, organized letters to newspaper editors, and fund-raising appeals, Proposition 14 supporters steeped their arguments in the rhetoric of egalitarianism and even antiracism. Incorporating dimensions of emergent liberal civil rights discourse, they portrayed racial discrimination as a regretful but individually rooted problem of morality and tolerance, one the state could or should do little to address. These arguments clearly related to the claims used by employers to discredit Proposition 11 in 1946, but they went further by incorporating some of the developing rights-based language popularized by the burgeoning civil rights movement.

The CREA had begun to deploy the language of tolerance and antidiscrimination in early 1963. As it was lobbying vigorously to defeat the Rumford Act and other civil rights legislation, the CREA Board of Directors formed an Equal Rights Committee to "inform and assist members of the Association in their understanding and responsibility in giving equal service to all clients." In June 1963, the CREA and NAREB adopted a new policy declaring that Realtors "have no right or responsibility to determine the racial, creedal or ethnic composition of any area or neighborhood" and that the Realtor should "exert his best efforts to conclude the [real estate] transaction irrespective of the race, creed, or nationality of the offeror."[63] The CREA further amended its constitution to include language prohibiting member boards from imposing "any limitation upon membership because of race, color, creed or national origin" and adopted new guidelines prohibiting Realtors from promoting panic selling or "blockbusting."[64] Thus, a year before the public battle over Proposition 14 had begun, the Realtors had already incorporated some of these rights-based claims. While the Realtors actively publicized the creation of their new Equal Rights Committee in various public forums, there is little evidence to suggest that the committee affected the actual practices of any local realty board. These reforms, however, allowed the Realtors to claim the high ground of racial innocence in their own campaign rhetoric. CHP chair and former CREA president L. H. Wilson declared in a February campaign debate that the statewide Realtors' group was "open to all races and all religions. Our constitution requires that no member board shall impose any limitation upon membership because of race, color, creed or national origin."[65] The CREA's Charles Shattuck insisted in a 1964 address to colleagues in Sacramento that Realtors have always "been devoted to keeping the state progressive and free." He continued, "In the state of California, we have no 'Jim Crow' laws. The Negro and other minority group citizens have and enjoy every single legal right you and I enjoy. There is no justification whatsoever for legislation to discriminate against the majority merely to please the minority."[66]

THE CAMPAIGN FOR PROPOSITION 14

In debates over housing desegregation in urban areas of the Midwest and Northeast, opposition to fair housing laws from white residents and real estate agents often focused on the threat posed to property values, typically cast in terms of neighborhood defense. California Realtors and homeowners made similar arguments in the 1940s and 1950s in the wake of challenges to racially restrictive covenants. By the time the Proposition 14 debate unfolded in 1964, however, the Realtors referenced the property-value claim much less frequently.

A pro–Proposition 14 editorial in the *Los Angeles Times*, which had supported earlier desegregation measures in employment and education, articulated the propositions espoused by the CREA clearly. The editorial decried "artificial laws designed to hasten the process of social, as distinct from civil, justice," insisting that "discrimination will disappear only when human prejudice succumbs to human decency." The editorial criticized the Rumford Act for "seeking to correct such a social evil while simultaneously destroying what we deem a basic right in a free society." Proposition 14, the editorial declared, "should relieve tensions between ethnic groups, leaving human decency and good will as powerful allies in overcoming prejudice."[67]

Situating Proposition 14 in the spirit of an inclusionary Americanism built upon freedom and opportunity over exclusion and hierarchy, the CREA's Property Owners Bill of Rights asserted that Proposition 14 was indeed the rightful heir to the nation's history of pluralist inclusion. It referenced the "forty million immigrants [who] gave up much to come to this land . . . for the precious right to live as free men with equal opportunity for all" and celebrated the passage of the Fourteenth Amendment as "a new guarantee of freedom . . . to guard against human slavery. Its guarantees were for equal protection of all."[68]

Proposition 14, its proponents insisted, would restore a divine, eternal, preternatural "property right"—held to be the bedrock of American freedom—that the Rumford Act had abridged. The headline of a typical CHP pamphlet announced, "OWNERS! TENANTS! NEIGHBORS! GET BACK YOUR RIGHTS! VOTE 'YES' ON PROPOSITION 14."[69] Mobilizing cold war anxieties over a "creeping socialism," another Yes on 14 pamphlet titled, "That Long, Long Arm of the Law," warned that "the Rumford Forced Housing Act's police arm is long and strong. It can reach almost any Californian—almost anyone who owns or rents a place to live.[70] The pro-14 ballot argument stated bluntly that "the Rumford Act establishes a new principle in our law—that State appointed bureaucrats may force you, over your objections, to deal concerning your own property with the person they choose." Such a policy "amounts to seizure of private property."[71]

The CHP never described its opposition as agitating civil rights organizations and almost never as people of color per se, but as a government controlled by an unaccountable cadre of elite white liberals determined to dispossess a silent majority. A broadside by a CHP affiliate based in San Gabriel explained that "the use of the term 'fair housing' and the claim that it is a 'civil rights' issue, is an attempt to sugar-coat a bitter pill by angle-playing, vote seeking politicians. Remove the sweetness and slogans

WHY 'YES' ON PROPOSITION #14?

YES Vote Will **restore** to California property owners the right to choose the person or persons to whom they wish to sell or rent their residential property.

YES Vote Will **abolish** those provisions of the Rumford Forced Housing Act of 1963 which took from Californians their freedom of choice in selling or renting their residential property.

YES Vote Will **amend** our California Constitution so that the only way future legislation could take away the freedom of choice in selling or renting of residential property would be by vote of the people.

YES Vote Will **halt** the State Fair Employment Practices Commission's harassing and intimidating the public and property owners in the exercising of their freedom of choice.

YES Vote Will **end** State police power over the selling or renting of privately owned residential property.

YES Vote Will **restore** rights basic to our freedom—rights that permit all persons to decide for themselves what to do with their own property.

That Long, Long, Arm of the Law—

The Rumford Forced Housing Act's police arm is long and strong.

It can reach almost any Californian—almost anyone who owns or rents a place to live. Owner. Tenant. Yes, and neighbor, too!

First, it reaches the owner. It takes away his right to choose his tenants or buyers.

Then it takes away a tenant's or buyer's right—the right to choose his neighbors.

If the owner insists on his freedom to choose, the long arm can reach out and make him pay a complainant up to $500; and further insistence by the owner can make him subject to contempt of court penalties.

If a tenant advises the owner to use freedom of choice, the long arm can reach the tenant with the same penalties.

In the matter of giving advice, even the neighbor must beware. That same long arm can put the neighbor in the same penalty box as the tenant!

14 SALES AND RENTALS OF RESIDENTIAL REAL PROPERTY. INITIATIVE CONSTITUTIONAL AMENDMENT. Prohibits State, subdivision, or agency thereof from denying, limiting, or abridging right of any person to decline to sell, lease, or rent residential real property to any person as he chooses. Prohibition not applicable to property owned by State or its subdivisions; property acquired by eminent domain; or transient lodging accommodations by hotels, motels, and similar public places.   **YES** ✗

OWNERS! TENANTS! NEIGHBORS!

GET BACK YOUR RIGHTS!

VOTE "YES" ON PROPOSITION #14

Figure 2. "Get Back Your Rights," Committee for Home Protection flyer in favor of Proposition 14, 1964. Courtesy of Max Mont Papers, Urban Archives Center, Oviatt Library, California State University, Northridge.

and you have another government encroachment on your freedom as an individual."[72] Reacting to Governor Brown's public appeals for voters not to sign the initiative petition, another Realtor explained that the "opposition has begun to express itself. . . . And I am not referring to the Civil Rights organizations as the opposition but rather the political organizations and other groups that are opposing this action."[73]

WHITE PROPERTY RIGHTS

While the CHP carefully avoided explicit references to race during the campaign, as another article in the *Los Angeles Times* put it, "Anyone who thinks that [Proposition 14] doesn't have anything to do with the racial issue just hasn't been paying attention."[74] An NAACP lawsuit seeking to prevent the initiative from qualifying for the ballot because it violated the Fourteenth Amendment captured the issue clearly. In response to the argument advanced in the Proposition 14 statement of purpose that the initiative would restore a constitutionally guaranteed right, an NAACP attorney argued: "If the asserted right is already 'constitutionally guaranteed' the Legislature could not take it away. . . . The [initiative's] statement of purpose is but a disguised appeal to racial prejudice, because the only part of the right to decline to sell or rent real property abridged by 'recently enacted laws' is that based on race, color, creed or religion."[75]

In other words, Proposition 14's backers were in fact referring to a historically specific *racial* right, a white right to discriminate against and exclude people of color in general and Black people in particular. The rights and freedoms voters were being exhorted to defend were not generic or abstract—they referenced specific historical constructions and narratives recognizable to white voters even when asserted in the language of individual rights and opportunities. They were unmistakable appeals to political whiteness. In fact, restrictive covenants, corporate agreements, and homeowner associations in general abridged the rights of individual property owners to sell, rent, or make use of their dwellings much more significantly than the Rumford Act. Moreover, covenants and corporate agreements, which restrict and restrain free competition between buyers and sellers, were hardly the pillars of an open and free market.

Critical race theorist Cheryl Harris explains how whiteness in this discourse becomes understood as a form of property—"an aspect of identity" converted or reified "into an external object of property" itself dependent on an "absolute right to exclude."[76] The CHP sought to frame the Rumford Act as an assault on the very foundations of this privilege, asserting that the right to discriminate by race was not only rooted in "natural law" and guaranteed by the U.S. Constitution but that it was a cornerstone of American prosperity writ large. Proposition 14, they argued, would simply return the state to a "neutral" position of protecting this right.[77] This racial proposition essentially restated the argument Los Angeles Realtors made in their 1948 bid to enshrine racial covenants in the Constitution: that a central dimension of what made property valuable was the prerogative of (white) property owners to discriminate by race.

In addition, if proponents declared that Proposition 14 had nothing to do with race or civil rights, they also clearly signaled that the Rumford Act would implicitly and necessarily dispossess white homeowners. A CREA pamphlet explained, "The Rumford Act, by granting one group of citizens' rights for reason of race, color, religion, national origin or ancestry, necessarily takes equivalent rights away from the rest of the citizenry. This is denying equal protection under the law."[78] Another Realtor argued that "the issue is not one of property rights versus human rights, but of the human rights of one person in the community versus the rights of another."[79] References to the Rumford "*Forced* Housing" Act, racialized a prevailing antistatist discourse: innocent white families would be *compelled* to cede their neighborhoods and homes, and the status and value they embodied, against their wishes. These references to the dispossession of "one group" reveal that it was a specific "racial right" that was being asserted. The claims naturalized the proposition that such a racial right was foundational and beyond any state action. CHP spokesperson L.H. Wilson argued that "forced housing is like forced religion. An apartment owner may be honestly afraid of members of some particular race. Such a person should have the right to be a conscientious objector to people who he fears."[80]

The message the Realtors brought to voters built on the same ethos and discourse of "neighborhood defense," which they had used in the 1940s and 1950s to organize restrictive community associations and oppose public housing, without direct references to exclusion and property values. They framed the Rumford Act as an unjustified, heavy-handed, and self-aggrandizing attempt on the part of white elites to promote an idealistic and unnecessary scheme at the expense of innocent homeowners. This discourse fashioned an identity position that would prove enormously appealing to white voters: it legitimated a historical "right to discriminate" as beyond the regulation of the state while disavowing any complicity in or responsibility for prevailing inequalities, an unapologetic racial innocence.

CHALLENGES FACING THE PROPOSITION 14 CAMPAIGN

The CHP's campaign initially won few endorsements, even among recognized conservative groups and opinion leaders. Other than the realty boards, only a handful of organizations and individuals formally supported Proposition 14. The initiative split the Republican Party, reflecting a growing divide between backers of the contending candidates for the GOP presidential ticket in 1964, Senator Barry Goldwater and New York governor Nelson Rockefeller. The Republican State Central Committee refused to endorse Proposition 14, as did George Murphy, the Republican candidate for the U.S. Senate. Caspar Weinberger, a former GOP chairman of California and future member of Ronald Reagan's cabinet, declared that the issues at stake had been "settled 100 years ago by a civil war."[81] Rockefeller suggested that the Rumford Act was a "start in the right direction for civil rights and a step ahead for us all."[82]

The initiative did receive enthusiastic support from a growing cadre of activist conservatives, including the California Republican Assembly, the Young Republicans, and many smaller churches and conservative political groups concentrated in Southern California.[83] Both Barry Goldwater and Ronald Reagan, the co-chairman of Goldwater's California campaign, endorsed the measure. Even the Goldwater campaign, however, did not make Proposition 14 a central part of its California strategy. Reagan did not mention Proposition 14, the Rumford Act, or "homeowner's rights" in his famous "A Time for Choosing" speech at the 1964 Republican National Convention in San Francisco, and it was not until Reagan's gubernatorial bid two years later that the term became a central part of his political vocabulary.[84]

Other than these deeply conservative organizations, the large majority of the state's political, civic, and religious organizations opposed the initiative. The debate that unfolded within the Los Angeles County Chamber of Commerce reveals the apprehension evinced by many traditionally conservative groups. Staunch and reliable foes of almost every piece of civil rights legislation in the postwar period, the chamber's twelve-member board of directors took months to study and deliberate over Proposition 14 during the summer of 1964. Some board members concurred with a subcommittee report that cited the threat the Rumford Act posed to property values and property rights, the potential negative impact it could have on the business climate, and the fallacy of government intervention into the realm of personal sentiments.

An equally strident opposition countered with serious concern that the chamber risked assuming a morally dubious position. As one board member explained, "The right we are giving up is the right to discriminate on the basis of race. Is that a right we want to bat for? I don't think this is a thing we should do a lot of breast-beating about. It is not a laudable right in the first place." Another inquired, "I wonder if we are not in favor of this type of legislation because we are men of property and men who have not ever been discriminated against?" Other members cited opposition to the initiative within their church and worried that the chamber would be going against "the so-called official moral leaders in the community." The group remained deadlocked as the election approached, and Proposition 14 was the only measure among the seventeen statewide initiatives that appeared on the November ballot that the chamber did not endorse or oppose.[85]

Even some CREA members sounded similar sentiments. At least ten local realty boards, including those in San Francisco and Ventura, voted to oppose the measure. Floyd Lowe, the president of the CREA in 1955, thanked the anti-14 campaign for "saving the Realtor's profession from its leadership" and insisted that Realtors "are not now and never have been recognized as spokesmen for property owners' rights." In Oakland, Realtors committed to the fair housing law organized a League for Decency in Real Estate to persuade other Realtors to publish nondiscriminatory listings and oppose Proposition 14.[86] Earle Vaughan asked his fellow apartment owners in an article in the trade magazine, *The Apartment Journal*, "If all other types of business can prosper under integration, why can't we?"[87]

Lacking elite endorsements, the Committee for Home Protection continued to organize through its vast network of local Realtors and neighborhood activists around a framework of property owners' rights and home protection. This grassroots approach urged supporters to hold "coffee klatches" in their homes, talk to their friends and neighbors about the dangers the Rumford Act posed, and to monitor news, radio, and television coverage of the initiative and write letters to the editor when appropriate. Apartment owners distributed pro-14 literature to their tenants signed "Your Landlady."[88] A letter delivered to renters in Belford Gardens, a Los Angeles apartment complex, asked, "ARE YOU PARTICULAR WHO YOUR NEIGHBORS ARE?" The letter implored tenants to sign the petition so that the apartment management could continue to ensure the complex would not "become filled with undesirables" to whom "all Belford residents would violently object."[89]

ORGANIZING THE CAMPAIGN TO DEFEAT
PROPOSITION 14

At the end of the legislative session in June 1963, supporters of the Rumford Act were well aware of the CREA's intentions to launch an initiative campaign to roll back open housing legislation and they began to plot their own organizing strategy. The influential grassroots California Democratic Council declared defeat of the "segregation initiative" to be the top civil rights priority for 1964.[90] In December, the California Committee for Fair Practices (the statewide civil rights formation headed by labor leader C. L. Dellums in order to pass the FEPC legislation) convened an emergency meeting to develop a response. Civil rights groups such as CORE and the NAACP conducted regular pickets at CREA events and local realty board offices, demanding the withdrawal of the initiative petition. Once the signature-collecting phase began in February 1964, Governor Brown asked voters not to sign the CHP's petitions, and activists circulated form letters for people who had already signed the initiative to withdraw their signature.

The groundswell of support the CHP engendered during the signature-gathering phase clearly alarmed Proposition 14's opponents. After the secretary of state assigned the measure a ballot number in June, civil rights, labor, religious, and Democratic activists, along with elected officials, formed Californians against Proposition 14 (CAP 14) as an umbrella group to defeat the initiative. Governor Brown dispatched some of the leading figures in his administration to work on the campaign. Richard Kline, the deputy director of the Department of Motor Vehicles, resigned from the Brown administration to run CAP 14's day-to-day operations. Max Mont, a longtime organizer affiliated with the Jewish Labor Committee and a veteran of the campaigns to win a statewide FEPC, signed on to coordinate the activities in Southern California. Lucien Haas, who helped develop the Unruh Civil Rights Act in the late 1950s as an assistant to the assembly leader before becoming Brown's press secretary, assumed responsibility for media relations. Marvin Holden, another stalwart in the Brown administration, became the campaign's treasurer. William Becker, a longtime organizer who worked on farmworker and fair employment issues and had joined the Brown administration as a human relations assistant, kept close track of the campaign's daily progress on behalf of the governor. Brown made the defeat of Proposition 14 a leading priority for the November election and appointed a blue ribbon commission of other high-profile officials to lend their names to the anti-14 campaign.[91]

Collectively, the leadership of the newly formed CAP 14 brought decades of experience in California politics to the campaign. All of the central figures appointed by Brown played a critical role in the landmark 1958 Democratic takeover of the legislature and governor's office, as well as in the subsequent passage of several important pieces of antidiscrimination legislation during Brown's first five years in office. They had a clear-cut mandate: persuade Brown's Democratic base to reject Proposition 14 as an illiberal assault on the state's progressive ideals.[92]

In the 1958 and 1962 elections, Brown successfully stigmatized his Republican opponents as out of step with the state's progressive and forward-minded electorate. The team put in place to defeat Proposition 14 plotted a similar strategy. CAP 14 sought to portray the proposition as a bigoted and extremist measure designed to serve the narrow concerns of Realtors over the best interests of all Californians. In its communications with voters, CAP 14 framed the initiative as a contest between Realtors, Birch Society members, and other racial extremists on the one hand and a broad range of labor, civic, businesses, religious, and civil rights groups and elected officials—the authentic protectors and representatives of the Californian populace—on the other. As Haas would later describe, the campaign was intended to be "based pretty much on organizing the liberal and moral base of the state of California."[93]

The main image and logo selected to represent the No on 14 campaign signified these intentions clearly. Conceptualized by Martha Holden, the wife of the CAP 14 treasurer, it featured stately sketches of Abraham Lincoln and John Kennedy. The tagline read, "Don't Legalize Hate: Vote No on 14." The California Democratic Council used this image to launch a statewide Bucks for Billboards campaign to secure grassroots contributions that would pay for a series of hand-painted billboards in prominent locations. The billboards added an American flag in the background and were eventually placed in fifty-one locations across the state. A CDC memo explained that "the symbolism of the flag was chosen by the artist to reflect the basic nature of a vote against Proposition 14 as being in the American tradition of equal rights for all citizens."[94]

Governor Brown repeatedly emphasized this theme in a series of speeches he delivered before the election. Addressing a Jewish women's group in August, he explained that the initiative represented the voices of "a minority of the angry, the frustrated, the fearful. They do not represent California or its people." He predicted that as "Americans we will heed our great Judeo-Christian heritage . . . we will choose love over hate and concern over indifference." At another Los Angeles rally in October, he announced that the "issue here is not legislating morality; it is the control-

Figure 3. "Don't Legalize Hate," Californians against Proposition 14 flyer, 1964. The image on this brochure was also featured on billboards across the state. Courtesy of Max Mont Papers, Urban Archives Center, Oviatt Library, California State University, Northridge.

ling of anti-social behavior."[95] The ballot argument against Proposition 14 expressed the dividing line clearly: "For generations Californians have fought *for* a tolerant society and *against* the extremist forces of the ultra-right who actively are behind Proposition 14."[96]

Anti-14 forces often used the perceived baseness and bigotry of the South as a foil to contrast the high-minded ideals that Proposition 14 threatened to undermine. Lieutenant Governor Glenn Anderson addressed Mar Vista–Westside Citizens against Proposition 14 before the election and explained that, if the amendment was adopted, California would "be accepting the leadership of states like Mississippi, the poorest, most badly educated and in my opinion, amongst the most badly governed states in the nation." He continued, "If we now ally ourselves with the south in the civil rights struggle, the future of this state will be in serious jeopardy. California did not achieve her present wealth and importance by becoming a symbol of fear and hate."[97] Even highly visible national civil rights leaders like Martin Luther King Jr. often described the conflict in similarly personal, individualistic terms. When King arrived in Los Angeles at an anti-14 rally in late October, he declared, "Men hate each other because they fear, they fear because they do not know one another, and they do not know one another because they are separated."[98]

The mainstream CAP 14 message, which emphasized tolerance and open-mindedness, resonated deeply with a core set of religious, labor, Democratic Party, and other liberal activists, and the campaign mobilized thousands of volunteers among these groups. By late August, CAP 14 had secured dozens of high-profile commitments to oppose the initiative, and its endorsement list was a who's who of California public life. The list included every significant Democratic official in the state, the California Council of Churches and the liberal Protestant denominations it represented, the American Jewish Congress, the California Teachers Association, the State Federation of Labor, the State Bar of California, and every major African American, Asian American, and Mexican American civil rights organization.[99] A Performing Arts Division of CAP 14 won the support of stars, including Richard Burton, Lucille Ball, Dinah Shore, Carl Reiner, Joan Baez, Nat King Cole, Burt Lancaster, Gregory Peck, James Garner, and Elizabeth Taylor, among others. Taylor and Burton headlined a "Night of Stars" fund-raiser for CAP 14 in early October at the Hollywood Bowl; Baez and Pete Seeger led a fundraising concert in the same venue a week earlier.[100]

CAP 14 also began proliferating dozens of identity-based and geographically designated affinity groups to demonstrate the breadth of opposition to the measure on endless grounds: Lawyers against Proposition 14 challenged the constitutionality of the measure; Clergy against Proposition 14 cited the moral contradictions; Orange County Realtors against Proposition 14 suggested the measure would destabilize housing markets; Oriental-Americans against Proposition 14 tied the measure to the state's history of Asian exclusion; Doctors against 14 warned of the serious public health consequences of confining people to "slums and ghettos." Hundreds of neighborhood and locally based groups formed against the measure, organizing their own events, publishing local newsletters, and raising small contributions to defeat the measure. While CAP 14 leadership retained a bird's-eye view of the larger campaign strategy, and coordinated some large-scale efforts such as television and radio advertising in Los Angeles and the Bay Area, it was through these local groups that the campaign to defeat Proposition 14 was carried out.

In seeking to bring together like-minded volunteers who could mobilize a wide range of arguments, CAP 14 hoped to disarm the Realtors' accusations that Proposition 14 was a reasonable response to the extremism of the Rumford Act and reclaim the fair-minded center. But the strategy had profound limitations. In early 1964, William Becker asked Robert Coate, a CDC member and former president of the Fair Play Council of Southern Alameda County, for advice on how to defeat Proposition 14. Coate's prescient reply explained that while raising and spending money for advertisements could be accomplished, the most important obstacle lay in organizing the volunteers of the campaign, whom he described as a "mixture of church groups, civil rights groups, and random collections of citizens with good intentions." He warned Becker, "The interested people enjoy talking to themselves more than tackling jobs which can have any real effect on an election." Coate recommended that volunteers be given a shared task to accomplish, such as circulating and collecting pledge cards against the measure, which would force them to talk to voters outside of their political circles.[101]

Ultimately, the campaign to defeat Proposition 14 realized Coate's worst fears. The anti-14 campaign raised almost $600,000 statewide, nearly matching the amount raised by the Realtors. The CAP 14 campaign sponsored an array of social activities in the name of fighting the initiative. Volunteers organized bike rides, swim-a-thons, two Hollywood Bowl events, a large art auction, folk-song hootenannies, fund-raising and award dinners, and many similar events. The Realtors, by contrast, devoted almost all of their campaign expenditures and energies to direct voter contact, especially advertising and campaign literature. CAP 14 held the vast majority of their frequent rallies and meetings in the Los Angeles and Bay Area communities where their volunteer base was already concentrated. While small groups of anti-14 volunteers could be found in other regions of the state, many replicated these same activities on a smaller scale. This strategy had the deceptive effect of suggesting to volunteers that the opposition to the initiative was enthusiastic and broad-based, a realization of Coate's warning about "interested people . . . talking to themselves."[102]

CAP 14's decision to focus on the white voters that made up Pat Brown's electoral base also meant that groups such as the NAACP, the Los Angeles–based United Civil Rights Committee, and the Mexican American Political Association (MAPA) would only play a marginal role in the official anti-14 campaign. CAP 14 steered some funding to these groups to join in voter outreach and education efforts; the United Civil Rights Committee mobilized 2,000 volunteers to register some 40,000 voters in heavily African American and Mexican American precincts in Los Angeles, and MAPA distributed more than 100,000 bilingual anti-14 materials in the Bay Area alone.[103] In many Black communities in particular, mobilizing to defeat Proposition 14 was the singular political issue of the day, with opposition to the measure expressed in forceful, often outraged tones.

[Whereas the majority of CAP 14's materials emphasized the ideals of tolerance and fairness, civil rights groups tended to focus on the concrete experiences of discrimination and segregation] An NAACP flyer circulated during a protest outside a CREA meeting in September 1963 declared, "We will no longer tolerate segregated housing as a way of life, and demand that housing in California be made available immediately without discrimination because of race, color or religion."[104] Materials produced by CORE similarly urged voters to "Register and Vote against this Jim Crow Amendment! Don't let our hard-won progress go down the drain!"[105]

Mexican American and Japanese American civil rights groups set out to inform their constituencies that housing discrimination was not confined to African Americans alone. Though both groups were often specifically named and excluded by restrictive covenants before the 1950s, by the early 1960s organized efforts to exclude Mexican Americans and Asian Americans had subsided in some neighborhoods, especially in comparison to African Americans, attesting to the multiple axes of racialization at work during this period.[106] Proposition 14 opponent Sal Montenegro, a Realtor from the Los Angeles suburb of Monterey Park, noted in a March 1964 address to the Council on Mexican American Affairs, "Today we find that Mexican-Americans have become complacent because they have been able to purchase homes. They feel that the Rumford bill is only to protect Negroes." To challenge this assumption, Montenegro recounted several recent examples of Mexican American home seekers he represented being told by sellers to "go back where you came from" and of a Realtor who informed a recent client, "If you are light-skinned, we have several homes available, but if you are dark-skinned, don't waste my time."[107] Mexican American activists opposing the measure distributed examples of descriptions of housing for sale listed with local realty boards that specified "owner requests that property not be shown to Mexicans" and "owner reserves right to qualify Mexican American families." A common flyer distributed by Mexican Americans organizing against Proposition 14 thus declared "It's YOUR fight, too!"[108]

Civil rights groups expressed some frustration about their exclusion

from the CAP 14 campaign. Education and mobilization efforts targeting Black voters in Los Angeles funded by CAP 14 only provided for a
single part-time staff person working with the NAACP who had to furnish and supply the campaign office using his own money. The organizer
complained bitterly to CAP 14 coordinator Max Mont about the lack of
resources he received. Another African American lawyer organizing
against Proposition 14 cut his ties with the CAP 14 organization because
of its refusal to bring Hollywood stars opposed to the initiative into the
Black community for fund-raising events.[109]

MAPA noted its displeasure that CAP 14 coordinator Max Mont claimed
he could not find any "'eligible' Mexican-American to do full time staff
work for Californians Against Proposition 14." When CAP 14 finally hired
an organizer to do fieldwork among Mexican American voters in August,
MAPA informed its members sarcastically that "someone finally passed
Max Mont's acceptability test."[110] MAPA leaders were particularly irritated
by CAP 14's decision not to spend money on Spanish-language radio advertisements, especially in comparison to the "thousands spent by the Real
Estate interest for Spanish radio coverage." It noted in a newsletter that "as
the vote draws to a close, the gravity of this mistake becomes more evident.
Spanish radio, throughout the State of California, including Los Angeles,
has been virtually bought out by the proponents of the Proposition. Up and
down the San Joaquin Valley, all that is heard is Yes on 14, and the same is
true for Los Angeles." As a result, only "a few valiant voices" were left on
the airwaves to explain "the real meaning of the Proposition."[111]

AMBIVALENT ALLIES: THE CASE AGAINST
PROPOSITION 14

Why would CAP 14 leaders so committed to defeating Proposition 14
distance the campaign from the communities, organizations, and leadership that bore the brunt of segregated and inferior housing? The omission
was largely intentional. Early in the campaign, CAP 14 leaders made a
strategic decision to attack the abstract ideas and extremist actors animating Proposition 14 rather than to defend the Rumford Act or assert
the widespread prevalence of housing discrimination and segregation.
As an organizing manual prepared in February 1964 by the California
Committee for Fair Practices explained, "it would be a mistake to gear
our campaign primarily to a defense of the Rumford Act. This is what the
amendment's proponents desire." It continued, "Of course, we will speak
for anti-discrimination legislation, but the issue at hand is the constitu-

tional amendment. We are defending the American system of representative government." The committee also counseled against demonstrations or pickets against Realtors, which might suggest Proposition 14 was a "minority rights" issue alone.[112]

Indeed, CAP 14 leaders became convinced that specific references to the existence or prevalence of racism would only hurt the campaign's fortunes among the white voters who dominated the electorate. In April 1964, Bill Becker, the human relations assistant for Governor Brown, came upon a flyer produced by an unidentified group that criticized Proposition 14 in strident antiracist terms, declaring that "HUMAN RIGHTS are NOT subject to a VOTE." It asked, "Shall tax dollars be spent for Jim Crow housing? Shall de facto segregation in schools be constitutionalized?" Fearful of the reaction the flyer might cause among white voters, Becker wrote to Max Mont and Black assembly member Mervyn Dymally asking if they knew who was behind the "frightening movement" that produced the materials with such a "negative approach."[113] Becker, like many CAP 14 leaders, concluded that white voters would not respond to a direct appeal to defend the Rumford Act or the specific protections it provided. That is, anti-14 organizers comported their political claims to meet with the "settled expectations" of political whiteness.

Most CAP 14 leaders and activists also proved deeply ambivalent about asserting the importance of antidiscrimination laws or highlighting the crisis in housing faced by hundreds of thousands of Californians. Many opponents of Proposition 14 placed a repeated emphasis on assuaging the fears of white voters that the Rumford Act would not upset the character of their neighborhoods or violate their "property rights" in any significant way. A memo to Episcopal lay leaders in Los Angeles insisted that the "Rumford law is *not* a 'special privilege' law for the minorities. It does *not* give minorities any special claim on housing in any way, shape, or form. It merely attempts to give them an equal chance for housing if they are fully qualified." The memo declared that the "law was *not* passed for the benefit of the minorities, but for the benefit of the health, welfare, prosperity and peace of the whole community. Delinquency, slums, social welfare programs, reduced community business and income, bitterness and strife—all of which are destructive to total community life—are at stake."[114]

A brochure against Proposition 14 produced by the liberal Council of Churches offered similar reassurances, explaining to parishioners who feared that the fair housing laws might upset the composition of their neighborhood that "economic inequalities over our long history of discrimination make it impossible for most minority citizens to buy homes of their choice." The council assured its audience that among the relatively small Black population in California, "probably not more than 1% or 2% . . . can afford to buy houses in all-white areas. Of those who can afford to do so, experience shows only a small percentage choose to do so, even though they should have this right." The fair housing act, they promised with approval, would not "basically change racial housing patterns."[115]

Similar public education materials produced by groups like the Los Angeles County Commission on Human Relations sought to reassure white voters that the Rumford Act was unlikely to change the composition of their neighborhoods, as the small number of minority home seekers that might move in would not cause their neighborhood to "deteriorate" or lower the "standards of teaching and discipline" in neighborhood schools. Again, the Rumford Act was never defended on its own terms as a solution to the problems facing homebuyers or renters. Indeed, the notion that white Californians had any communal obligations other than to themselves and their neighbors was anathema to this entire discourse.[116]

When CAP 14 and its affiliated groups did mount a defense of the Rumford Act, it was also framed within the expectations of political whiteness. Brown warned that "the ancient problems of segregation and discrimination" would be "settled in the streets, with blood and violence" if Proposition 14 passed.[117] A fund-raising letter to support anti-14 work, from the American Civil Liberties Union (ACLU), asked that if Proposition 14 were to become law "how much will California's spreading slums and their accompanying evils cost us and our children in the interim?" It warned ominously, "What will the minority ghettos do to the newly-planted hopes and the age-old angers of their chief residents?"[118] Opponents also frequently sought to downplay the impact of the Rumford Act itself, pointing out that during its first year of implementation no fines had been issued by the FEPC and that only one of the complaints filed had led to an administrative hearing. Thus, when the Rumford Act was referenced, it was either to emphasize its limitations and feebleness or to argue that its repeal risked inciting explosions in the "ghetto" that might spill into white communities.[119]

In focusing almost entirely on the contradictions and dangers of Proposition 14, CAP 14 declined to endorse or defend the original purpose of the Rumford Act in any meaningful way. Liberal activists rarely mentioned the housing crisis that had driven civil rights organizations to demand the passage of the legislation in the first place; nor did they reference the overwhelming levels of discrimination many home buyers and renters still faced. Only when the housing crisis might erupt beyond the "walls of the ghetto" was the necessity of the Rumford Act invoked. Whereas civil rights groups intentionally sought to link Proposition 14 to a longer history of racial subjugation, the CAP 14 campaign asserted a much different position, largely suggesting that no such tradition of discrimination had existed in the state until the arrival of Proposition 14. Like the CHP, CAP 14 affirmed the basic privileges white homeowners had come to expect as natural and unassailable—they simply argued that Proposition 14 itself represented a greater attack on those interests than the Rumford Act. Their underlying racial propositions shared important ground. Ultimately, the campaign to defeat Proposition 14 was itself segregated, subordinating and marginalizing the claims of those facing housing discrimination in favor of addressing and validating the perceived needs and interests of white voters.

VOTERS RESPOND

CAP 14 mobilized at a furious pace in the two months leading up to the election, organizing endless press conferences and fund-raising events, participating in televised debates and community forums, and running a series of television and radio advertisements. Campaign materials from both sides inundated voters, and the measure received extensive media coverage. At the same time, many property-owner associations took up the issue aggressively, continuing their door-to-door organizing on behalf of Proposition 14 in suburban subdivisions across the state.[120]

Polls conducted throughout the campaign identified two trends. First, contrary to the claims of CAP 14 that the ballot language was deceptive and misleading, voters seemed to increasingly understand that a vote for Proposition 14 meant the evisceration of the Rumford Act. Second, as the campaign wore on and both sides had an opportunity to present their case, support for Proposition 14 grew.[121]

Voters ultimately approved Proposition 14 by a margin of 65 to 35 percent. Nearly 85 percent of registered voters in the state cast their ballots on the measure, the highest number for any proposition on the ballot and just below the number cast in the presidential contest. While President Johnson secured almost 4.2 million California votes in his landslide defeat of Barry Goldwater, only 2.4 million votes were cast against Proposition 14. The California Poll conducted a week before the election suggested that white voters supported the measure by a three-to-one margin—Black voters rejected it nine to one—and that union voters and Protestant voters favored Proposition 14 by more than 60 percent.[122] In Los Angeles County,

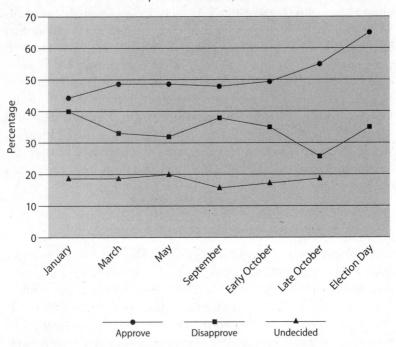

Proposition 14
Comparison of Trends in California Poll

Figure 4.   Comparison of trends in California Poll for Proposition 14, 1964. From California Polls as cited in Casstevens, *Politics, Housing and Race Relations.*

where registered Democrats outnumbered Republicans by three to two and cast ballots for Johnson by the same margin, Proposition 14 won by thirty-five percentage points and nearly a million votes.[123]

ASSESSING THE IMPACT OF PROPOSITION 14

It would be difficult to overstate the profound sense of defeat and anguish that gripped the anti-14 forces after the election. In retrospective assessments, many of the CAP 14 leaders candidly acknowledged that they had simply been out-organized. Richard Kline, the Pat Brown aide assigned to head CAP 14 campaign, confessed, "I made a huge strategic misjudgment which was, in my naiveté, that if you could only explain this issue to people, raise enough money, have enough good media campaigns, organization and everything, if you'd explain the issue to people, people in the goodness of their hearts would vote no on 14."[124]

Lucien Haas, the press secretary dispatched by the Brown administration to work on the campaign, suggested that the outcome of the election shattered his understanding of race relations in the state. Before the initiative, he imagined that "we had Mexicans, we had blacks, everything like that and we were all mixing it up and getting along fine. Everybody was working and happy and so on." Proposition 14, he said, "shattered [the myth] for me" as he realized, "My God, we're facing racism in the state of California."[125] Part of the reason that many leaders and supporters of the CAP 14 campaign likely shared Haas's lack of knowledge of the housing crisis and discriminatory barriers facing so many other Californians was because they also lived in segregated white communities. Indeed, the West Los Angeles communities that voted strongly against Proposition 14 were as deeply segregated as the pro-14 areas in the San Fernando Valley.[126]

An internal memo written by Edward Rutledge, head of the National Committee against Discrimination in Housing (NCADH), based on interviews with people involved in both sides of the campaign, offered the most candid and self-critical assessment of the campaign. He conveyed the deep sense of despair experienced by many activists at the results of the election in observing that "even the most cautious and pessimistic had not anticipated such a major defeat."[127]

On the positive side, Rutledge described the anti-14 campaign as a broad-based, pathbreaking, and heroic defense of civil rights, contending that in "no state had ever before marshaled so many diverse forces in local communities and on a statewide basis to do battle in support of a civil rights issue; nor had any other state developed such intensive activity among citizens of good will in local communities as well as big cities and the suburbs."[128]

But Rutledge also noted a series of tensions that might have limited the campaign's impact. Some in the campaign complained of "foot-dragging by many local union officials and the lack of discussion and active communication" with their members. Though the State Federation of Labor contributed funding, the intense effort devoted to defeating the Right to Work initiative in 1958 was not in effect for Proposition 14. Others noted that religious leaders did "a great deal of 'preaching'" but that there was very little communication or discussion with members of their congregations. A postelection meeting of the California Democratic Council also noted the "lack of contact between the CDC and the Civil Rights Movement, especially the absence of active participation in the . . . UCRC [United Civil Rights Committee]."[129]

Ultimately, Rutledge decided that even if the campaign had addressed these shortcomings, the margin might have been narrowed, but the outcome would have been the same. He concluded that "the overriding reason for the impressive YES vote for Proposition 14 can be attributed to latent and overt anti-Negro racial prejudice (especially as related to integration in housing) of most of the white California voters."[130]

Rutledge's assessment, echoed by Governor Brown and many of his colleagues, overlapped with much of the sentiment expressed by the CREA itself. It was the populace, the Realtors claimed, who insisted on living among "their own kind"; Realtors were responding to this preference and protecting the right of homeowners to make such decisions. While this posture disavowed the indisputable role of Realtors and developers historically in sustaining racially segregated housing, it did point to an important convergence witnessed among both the supporters and opponents of Proposition 14. In the end, both sides affirmed the pronouncement of CREA's Charles Shattuck when he argued that the "present racial tensions will diminish in direct ratio to . . . the determined effort on the part of all to increase the flow of understanding."[131] Here, no large gulf existed between so-called racial liberalism and racial conservatism. Both understood white racial power as an individual rather than structural and historical phenomenon, which would only dissipate in the face of mutual understanding and "tolerance" of difference between free-thinking individuals. In both accounts, political whiteness not only went unchallenged, it became further naturalized. This discourse renovated a powerful political identity, renewing and recasting the idea that the social authority and status of white homeowners was rooted in and premised upon their ability to exclude.[132]

CAP 14 never offered a forceful defense of the Rumford Act or attempted to tie the legislation to the broader vision that animated the Brown administration's other policy commitments during the period—such as the expansion of the state infrastructure and higher-education system—which drew on shared aspirations for a society with greater possibilities and opportunities for all Californians. CAP 14 sought to paint neighborhood Realtors and their organizations as racial extremists, a strategy that hardly resonated with the sensibilities and experiences of most white homeowners. These homeowners might not trust Barry Goldwater's finger on the atomic button, but that did not mean they were ready to believe that their local Realtor was shilling for the Ku Klux Klan. Following the dominant logics embedded in the postwar liberal civil rights discourse, CAP 14 attacked Proposition 14 on the grounds that it used race to justify inequality, a violation of the civic creed. This discourse, largely unchanged since the

1940s when it first came into popular usage, drew simple contrasts between tolerance and bigotry and asserted that racism was a matter of individual belief and mind-set. The Realtors demonstrated, however, that the civic creed might already be racialized and that no bright line existed between racial nationalism and American civic nationalism. Moreover, inequality itself was defended as a natural and inevitable condition under both social visions—racial hierarchy buttressed by racial innocence.

THE AFTERMATH OF PROPOSITION 14

Ten months after the passage of Proposition 14, a massive civil uprising in Watts shattered the idealizations rehearsed by both sides during the initiative debate that figured California as the paragon of racial harmony and unity. While the causes of the uprising were complex—police harassment, joblessness, and the yoke of poverty in general—Loren Miller pointed out that the curfew area put into effect after the uprising began almost exactly traced the boundaries of residential exclusions imposed on the city's Black communities. The immense population density resulting from seven decades of persistent housing segregation—and the segregated schools, workplaces, and social settings it produced and naturalized—fueled the fires of Watts.[133]

As a matter of law and public policy, Proposition 14 had only a fleeting impact. In May 1966, the California Supreme Court ruled in *Mulkey v. Reitman* that Proposition 14 was unconstitutional because it involved the state in encouraging discrimination by "making it at least a partner in the instant act of discrimination."[134] The court rejected the claims of the Realtors, as represented by future Reagan attorney general William French Smith, that "the People" had determined it "in the public interest" to protect a private right to discriminate.[135]

In affirming the ruling the next year, the U.S. Supreme Court noted in a 5–4 decision authored by Justice White that, after Proposition 14 was adopted, "private discriminations in housing enjoyed a far different status than was true before the passage" of the fair housing statues that the measure sought to repeal. In other words, an instrument of the state (a ballot measure) had valorized the right to discriminate by race. Justice Douglas's concurring opinion asserted that "Proposition 14 is a form of sophisticated discrimination whereby the people of California harness the energies of private groups to do indirectly what they cannot under our decisions allow their government to do."[136]

The most enduring impact of the Proposition 14 contest was not the policy it enacted during the two years between the election and the state supreme court's ruling, but the way it helped valorize a set of racial propositions about the "rights" particular homeowners possessed. If, before the election, the large majority of elected officials were unwilling to assert that a right to discriminate existed, in the wake of Proposition 14's overwhelming passage they eagerly embraced this position. During the 1966 election, multiple Republican candidates for the state assembly attacked their incumbent opponents simply as "Rumford Act supporters," a designation that operated as racial shorthand for a politician who failed to champion "homeowner's rights."[137] Los Angeles mayor Sam Yorty similarly condemned Governor Brown during the Democratic gubernatorial primary in 1966 for his continued opposition to Proposition 14, though Yorty also had opposed the measure. Yorty's attack anticipated relentless criticisms made by Republican gubernatorial candidate Ronald Reagan in the general election. Reagan had supported Proposition 14 in 1964, but the majority of his attention in that election had been devoted to Goldwater's candidacy and to a broader criticism of the excesses of liberal government. In his successful campaign against Brown, Reagan used the ideas animating the Proposition 14 campaign to bring these themes together, declaring that "the right of an individual to the ownership and disposition of property is inseparable from his right to freedom itself."[138] Even Governor Brown began to genuflect before the altar of homeowner's rights. In the wake of the state supreme court's ruling against Proposition 14, Brown maintained that the FEPC should utilize conciliation rather than strictly enforce the fair housing laws recently restored by the court. Brown also created a citizen's commission to consider amendments or substitutions for the Rumford Act, prompting newly elected Assemblyman Willie Brown to remark that the governor was beginning to "sound like Reagan."[139]

Like the leaders of the CREA, Reagan also steadfastly maintained his own racial innocence. During the 1966 gubernatorial campaign, Reagan identified civil rights as "one of the three or four most important issues," labeled "bigots" as "sick people," and vociferously objected whenever he was accused of supporting or tolerating bigotry (he stormed out of one campaign event during his first gubernatorial bid when such an insinuation was made). Yet Reagan also depicted a political environment in which hard-working and independent white Californians had to remain vigilant against the ominous and conceited attempts of the liberal state and its racialized clients to undermine their way of life. Like the Realtors, he insisted that significant housing discrimination did not exist, telling an audience in South Carolina, "There is no law saying the Negro has to live in Harlem or Watts." And he, too, <u>mastered the subtle vocabulary of political whiteness</u>: "We all have the responsibility to work to end discrimination and insure equal opportunities for all. . . . But I am opposed to trying to get this with legislation that violates basic tenets of individual freedom."[140]

After winning office, Reagan continued to sustain and address this political identity even as he quietly ended his support for future legislative action to repeal the Rumford Act. While the signifiers "Rumford Act supporter" and "homeowner's rights" became deeply influential in California political discourse, and many Rumford opponents denounced the state supreme court decision invalidating Proposition 14, voter response to the future of the Rumford Act itself was more ambivalent. Reagan spent little political energy on trying to repeal the Rumford Act through the legislature, and the CREA was forced to end its support for such a repeal by 1967.[141]

Proposition 14 also shaped the ways in which advocacy groups organized to defend or challenge patterns of housing segregation, value, and exclusion in the aftermath of the election. An important dimension of the principles advanced by the Realtors during the Proposition 14 campaign was carried on by the neighborhood associations that proved so critical in defining the measure as a natural, populist response to an unlawful government incursion on property rights. Neighborhood and homeowner organizations continued to grow in influence and power, nourished by the experience of "defending their homes" during the Proposition 14 campaign. These associations would play a large role in the 1970s struggles over school busing and property taxes detailed in chapter 4, employing much of the same political grammar in these campaigns. Twenty-six years after Proposition 14, Mike Davis would argue that the "most powerful 'social movement' in contemporary Southern California is that of affluent homeowners, organized by notional community designations or tract names, engaged in the defense of home values and neighborhood exclusivity."[142]

On the other hand, while fair housing organizations continued to grow, their work assumed a far less oppositional stance. Groups such as CORE largely stopped organizing direct-action confrontations with discriminatory developers and Realtors, silenced in part by the verdict pronounced by the Proposition 14 outcome. Instead, dozens of locally based fair housing groups, largely led by sympathetic white activists, took on the task of attempting to open up segregated communities through mainly voluntary methods, as the Realtors had prescribed.[143] A 1966 Los Angeles County survey found that 57 percent of landlords conceded they would not rent to

Black tenants, even as the courts were moving to overturn Proposition 14. Fair housing groups adopted slogans such as "good neighbors come in all colors" and "brotherhood in the neighborhood" and had modest success on an individual level; a group in West Los Angeles, for example, used its listings to find housing for UCLA basketball stars Lew Alcindor (later Kareem Abdul-Jabbar) and Henry Bibby in the early 1970s.[144]

These groups ultimately accepted the proposition that housing segregation and inequality was a product of individual bigotry and volition and focused their efforts on "enlightening" Realtors and apartment managers about the irrationality of intolerance. Erased from this discourse was any engagement with the decades of systematic investments—both material and symbolic—in the racial exclusivity of the state's most desirable housing. By 1970, the large coalition of advocacy groups working on low-income housing in the state did not even include racial desegregation as one of its six policy priorities.[145] In addition, some fair housing groups were accused by critics within their own organizations of "inadvertently reinforcing racism" for only welcoming middle-class and professional home seekers into their communities.[146] These tensions anticipated a growing rift between predominantly white organizations—like fair housing groups and the ACLU—and the Black and Mexican American communities they often sought to represent, divisions that would sharpen during struggles over busing and school desegregation.

Ultimately, while many communities across the state experienced some modest integration in the decade after Proposition 14, the naturalized notions of inequality and restrictive notions of collective responsibility embraced by so many white Californians only grew in power. Proposition 14 valorized a sensibility that would prove enormously influential in state politics for decades to come.

4. "We Love All Kids"

*School Desegregation, Busing, and
the Triumph of Racial Innocence,
1972-1982*

On first glance, the two ballot initiatives adopted by large majorities of California voters in the 1970s to halt mandatory school desegregation seem to be products of the same political imagination. Both the 1972 Wakefield Amendment (Proposition 21) and the 1979 Robbins Amendment (Proposition 1) were sponsored by controversial, sometimes combative Southern California lawmakers determined to stop the progress of court-ordered school desegregation that relied upon student reassignment and busing. Both measures were implicitly grounded in assertions of "racial innocence"—the claim that because white parents and students did not create the second-class schools to which most nonwhite students were consigned, nor explicitly support segregated schools, they could not be compelled to participate in their improvement. And finally, both initiatives raised the hackles of traditional civil rights advocates, including the NAACP and the ACLU, which along with a handful of elected officials attempted to convince voters that the measures endorsed Jim Crow schooling by another name—a direct assault on the modest progress that had been made during the 1960s and 1970s in challenging the prevailing system of apartheid in California public schools.

We learn more, however, about the critical renovations and renewals in political debates over the meaning of race and racism during this period by attending to the significant differences that marked the two initiatives than by dwelling on their similarities. The 1972 Wakefield Amendment, championed by a fiery conservative Republican from the Los Angeles suburb of South Gate, was a legislative sledgehammer; it prohibited all race-based assignments in public school, effectively outlawing any systematic desegregation efforts. Its sponsor, Assemblyman Floyd Wakefield, railed against the yoke of "forced integration" and sounded a thinly veiled call to defend white rights and "freedoms of association." Though the measure passed by a wide margin, it was soon invalidated by the courts as a violation of the Fourteenth Amendment's Equal Protection Clause.

By contrast, the 1979 Robbins Amendment was brought to the ballot by a Democratic lawmaker who supported fair housing laws and declared himself a faithful champion of civil rights and racial integration. He carefully recruited several prominent Black and Chicano figures to promote his ballot measure—deftly incorporating their emerging nationalist critiques of desegregation—even as he incited white voters in his San Fernando Valley district to defend their segregated neighborhood schools. And unlike Wakefield, Robbins meticulously drafted his measure to withstand equal protection challenges. Proposition 1 did not prohibit school desegregation entirely; instead, it carefully specified the limited conditions under which such orders could be given. In 1982, the U.S. Supreme Court upheld Proposition 1 as a race-neutral act that complied with the Equal Protection Clause. The Robbins Amendment effectively ended the twenty-year *Crawford v. Los Angeles School Board* case, which sought to desegregate the largest school district in the state.[1]

Why did Alan Robbins succeed where Floyd Wakefield did not? Or perhaps more accurately, what did Robbins understand about the terrain of racial politics in the 1970s that Wakefield did not? To be sure, by the late 1970s much of the public stood fundamentally opposed to mandatory desegregation and busing. The images of white antibusing mobs in Pontiac, Michigan, Boston, and other cities indexed the rapid decline in white support over the pace and trajectory of racial justice efforts outside the South after the mid-1960s. While civil rights advocates frequently pointed out that 95 percent of student busing nationally (and within California) took place for reasons other than desegregation and argued that the school bus had for at least a generation been regarded as a positive symbol, busing soon became synonymous with many of the ills of the 1970s in general: physically dangerous to students, a drain on taxpayers, a contributor to traffic and smog, educationally irrelevant, and responsible for removing children from the protection and security of their parents.[2]

We must certainly also take seriously the critical transformations underway in the broader terrain of race politics within California and the nation during the 1970s. These transformations include the rise of what economist William Fischel terms "homevoters"—homeowners whose political behavior is shaped largely by their concern over property values—as well as the ongoing residential and fiscal abandonment of the urban core and the emergence of the suburb as a center of political power in local and national politics.[3] These regional dynamics, together with the fracture and defeat of many of the most visible elements of the civil rights coalition that rose to power during the 1960s, unquestionably shaped and obstructed the prospects for systematic school desegregation.

All of these dynamics, however, unfolded within a broader struggle to define the causes, meaning, and consequences of the widespread racial segregation and hierarchy that marked public schools across California. How did the opponents of mandatory desegregation and busing effectively stigmatize these programs as unworkable and intolerable, or as one critic called them, the "neutron bomb of education?"[4] How did their claims resonate with other political narratives and currents, such as the growing antitax movement that was sweeping California at the same time? Why did prevailing desegregation proposals fail to sustain any popular support? The conflicting responses to these questions evident in the campaigns for Proposition 21 and Proposition 1 offer important insights into the transformation of political whiteness during this contentious period.

FLOYD WAKEFIELD AND THE STRUGGLE AGAINST "FORCED INTEGRATION"

Proposition 21 banned school districts from explicitly using race to assign students to schools and passed with 61 percent of the vote in the November 1972 election. Twenty months later, the state supreme court ruled that the initiative's operating language violated the Equal Protection Clauses of the state and federal constitutions.[5] To understand the rise and fall of Proposition 21, we have to travel back at least a decade earlier to the political debates that nourished its creation and the figure responsible for bringing it to the statewide ballot.

Floyd Wakefield was the standard-bearer of postwar white backlash politics, "the unequivocal voice of South Gate's 'silent majority.'"[6] Born in Oklahoma in 1919, Wakefield moved at a young age to the suburbs south of Los Angeles. After serving in the Second World War, Wakefield and his family settled in South Gate, a working-class city of fifty-seven thousand residents that, through the use of racial covenants and other restrictive practices, remained deeply segregated well into the 1960s. Its border with neighboring Watts along Alameda Street was famously described as "The Wall," an unmistakable Mason-Dixon Line marking distinctly separate and unequal territories.[7]

In the early 1960s, South Gate became a flashpoint for initial efforts to desegregate the Los Angeles Unified School District (LAUSD), which included schools in South Gate and twenty-one other cities adjacent to Los Angeles. Groups such as the NAACP and the United Civil Rights Committee seized on South Gate High School as a particularly egregious example of the school board's racial gerrymandering of attendance boundaries: the attendance areas for South Gate High and nearby Jordan High School in Watts were regularly adjusted as Black families in Watts moved closer to the South Gate border. South Gate High remained nearly 100 percent white and was kept in far better condition, while Jordan High was almost entirely Black and badly in need of repair.[8]

The school board maintained that such patterns of racial imbalance were unintentional and that the district operated in a "colorblind" fashion. Indeed, the formal segregation of African American students was effectively outlawed by the California Supreme Court in 1890.[9] The segregation of Mexican American students—which was widespread in most parts of Southern California well into World War II—succumbed to a legal challenge by a group of parents in Orange County. In 1947, the year after the *Mendez v. Westminster* verdict was delivered, Governor Earl Warren repealed all legislative provisions allowing for the segregation of racial minorities in public schools.[10] Thus, when first confronted with evidence of racial imbalance and segregation in South Gate, the majority of the Los Angeles school board simply recited the official prevailing position: colorblind innocence. In response to NAACP charges that racially gerrymandered attendance areas sustained segregated schools, school board member Georgina Hardy insisted that the school staff "counts noses, not color."[11]

To civil rights activists, such responses were not convincing. When the school board voted to rebuild and expand Jordan High as a segregated campus rather than integrate students with nearby South Gate High, it provoked this wry retort from NAACP leader Marnesba Tackett: "You are accidentally spending over a million dollars to accidentally rebuild Jordan in its same location. Hence it will accidentally remain a segregated school. You have accidentally bought two new school sites in areas that are rapidly becoming solidly Negro. In accidental anticipation of this ethnic change you have accidentally named one of these proposed schools after a noted Negro author."[12]

Tackett's testimony demonstrates how the distinction between de facto versus de jure segregation provides so little purchase toward understanding the causes of segregation in Los Angeles and elsewhere in California.[13] As desegregation lawsuits made their way through California courts in the

1960s and early 1970s, case after case revealed that decisions to set attendance zones, locate new school sites, and arrange feeder patterns between
elementary, middle, and high schools were often based on maintaining
and enforcing patterns of racial segregation. As the civil rights attorney
Loren Miller explained in a 1960 public address, "There was a time in Los
Angeles when I could have traced the growth of Negro residence in my city
if I had known nothing else than the manner in which the boundary lines
of one of our high schools expanded." He continued, "As Negroes moved
south that boundary line moved south; when they moved west it moved
west; when they moved east it moved east." Miller called on the school
board to be "color-conscious rather than color blind" and to deliberately
shape attendance boundaries to create integrated schools. The board, he
insisted, had "no business blundering into a situation which will produce
a segregated school."[14]

In Los Angeles, funding formulas for campus maintenance were also
based on the square footage of school facilities, systematically favoring
the sprawling, newly constructed campuses in the San Fernando Valley
over the aging, more compact buildings in older parts of the city. School
boards did not make these decisions unilaterally; parents often lobbied the
board to ensure they adopted policies that would use race to assign students
and allocate resources. Thus, the highly segregated school systems that
developed across the state in the postwar era were driven in large part by a
self-reinforcing dynamic that treated racially determined attendance and
assignment patterns as "natural" and funneled disproportionate amounts
of resources and opportunities to schools serving white students.[15]

Among their other demands for political representation and additional
resources, Tackett and the civil rights groups insisted that attendance
boundaries be redrawn to desegregate both South Gate and Jordan high
schools, a policy that would have required minimal district-provided busing, since the schools were less than a mile apart.[16] The ACLU also filed
a lawsuit to compel this change. *Crawford v. Los Angeles School Board*
(1963) was eventually expanded to include the entire LAUSD and all Black
and Mexican American students; it would be nearly two decades before the
case was resolved.

Wakefield arose to the forefront of the grassroots effort within South
Gate to repel the proposed changes. To Wakefield, the parents and students
of Watts were the authors of their own failures; they had no right to make
claims on the innocent bystanders of South Gate. In crafting his opposition
to "forced integration" and "social experiments" threatening South Gate
schools, Wakefield drew from the same thinly veiled discourse of "white

rights" animating the Realtors' Proposition 14, an initiative Wakefield also enthusiastically championed. As fervently as civil rights groups organized marches, sit-ins, press conferences, and hunger strikes at the school board during late 1963 and early 1964, Wakefield and his supporters counter-mobilized with their own rallies, petitions, and other collective actions.[17] While they disavowed any racist intentions, they nonetheless posed their interests and concerns in direct opposition to the "integrationists." To Wakefield, the struggle was between those who "believed in integration and swapping kids [and those who] didn't."[18] Moreover, while Wakefield asserted at different times that Black students would not benefit from learning in a desegregated setting, the white activists of South Gate never sought any common ground with African American or Chicano political leaders who might also oppose prevailing desegregation proposals. Their political vocabulary was defined by straightforward calls for local control and (white) parents' rights, and they made little effort to conceal their contempt for civil rights proponents.

Such claims had contradictory effects. On the one hand, they effectively aroused the passions and anxieties of large numbers of white parents and voters who felt that preserving segregated schools and communities was essential to protecting their own standing. Hundreds of South Gates residents joined Wakefield at school board meetings, denouncing the proponents of desegregation and pressuring the school board to preserve the existing school attendance boundaries. South Gate voters passed Proposition 14 in 1964 by a ratio of nearly nine to one, among the highest rates in the entire state.[19] Floyd Wakefield rode the same political currents to a victory in the state assembly race in 1966, even though he ran as a Republican in a Democratic-leaning district.

Wakefield's unapologetic defense of white rights also had significant political and legal liabilities. The California Real Estate Association learned these limits when the U.S. Supreme Court ruled that Proposition 14 violated the federal Equal Protection Clause, holding that the measure's blanket prohibition on antidiscrimination remedies demonstrated discriminatory intent.[20] In addition, as a political discourse, demands for white rights failed to offer any solution or response to the growing crisis facing highly segregated Black and Mexican American schools beyond the token support it offered for the principle of "equal education." Finally, by marking itself as opposed to "forced integration," white rights claims ran against a growing public consensus, shaped largely by the work of the southern civil rights movement but reflected in opinion polls nationally, that segregated schools were anathema to a pluralist democracy.[21]

THE EMERGING CHALLENGE TO SEGREGATED SCHOOLS

Indeed, by the late 1960s, Wakefield and his South Gate constituents increasingly found they could no longer claim to represent an unassailable public consensus against the desegregation of public schools. In 1963 the state supreme court ruled in *Jackson v. Pasadena City School District* that where residential segregation existed it was "not enough for a school board to refrain from affirmative discriminatory conduct. The harmful influence on the children will be reflected and intensified in the classroom if school attendance is determined on a geographic basis without corrective measures." The court offered an expansive interpretation of the state Equal Protection Clause in determining that the "right to an equal opportunity for education and the harmful consequences of segregation require that school boards take steps, insofar as reasonably feasible, to alleviate racial imbalance in schools regardless of its cause."[22] The decision essentially made the distinction between de jure and de facto discrimination irrelevant, foregrounding the principle of equal educational opportunity and giving local desegregation advocates a potent tool in their negotiations with school boards.

The state board of education, with pressure from the NAACP, also adopted a series of administrative directives beginning in 1962, urging school districts to "exert all effort to avoid and eliminate segregation of children on account of race or color."[23] Four years later, even with Reagan appointees comprising a majority, the board adopted an advisory policy declaring that any school whose enrollment of minority students differed by more than 15 percent from the percentage of students in the district as a whole would be considered "racially imbalanced" and would require the school district to take corrective action.

To Wakefield's dismay, many local school boards began responding to these mandates. In May 1968, Los Angeles school board president Georgina Hardy, who five years earlier equivocated when faced with demands to desegregate South Gate High School, now chastised San Fernando Valley residents for turning their backs on the problem of overcrowded and deteriorated schools in the central city. She told an audience at the Van Nuys Chamber of Commerce that when the Valley needed money for schools during its period of expansion in the 1950s, voters eagerly supported bond issues. But "once you had it made" she told the group, "you didn't give a damn what was happening in other parts of the city." Hardy called opposition among "white, middle class parents" to a modest, voluntary program designed to bring students from overcrowded schools elsewhere in the city to empty classrooms in the Valley "ridiculous."[24]

To be sure, other than the Berkeley district's unprecedented mandatory desegregation plan (which was adopted in the late 1960s without a court order), most of these efforts were uneven and partial rather than comprehensive or resolute. In cities such as Richmond and Pasadena, the opposition of some parents and district officials plagued desegregation efforts from the start; in other cases, the reticence of local leadership to act decisively only contributed to the perception that desegregation was unworkable and excessively burdensome. But the transformations afoot during the 1960s should not be underestimated. California schools had become segregated over the course of many decades through a complex set of forces and relationships, and it was logical that the remedies would have to be locally tailored and implemented.[25]

In addition, contrary to Wakefield's contentions, white parents and students did not uniformly oppose or flee mandatory desegregation. Their actions and assessments were often contradictory, and we must balance the tension between examining the prosegregationist expressions of many white parents seriously without treating them as historically inevitable. On the one hand, because local school districts often funneled the most resources—the newest buildings, the most experienced teachers, and the most comprehensive curricular offerings—to the schools serving white students, it is unsurprising that many parents would infer that maintaining a white-dominant student body and teaching staff was critical to "protecting" the quality of their schools. In many cases, they eagerly pursued and embraced the relative opportunities and privileges afforded to them by segregated school systems.[26]

On the other hand, the doomsday admonitions that white parents would never participate in desegregated schools also proved spurious. When the Berkeley and Riverside school districts voluntarily inaugurated a districtwide busing program in the late 1960s, and when districts in San Francisco, Pasadena, Santa Barbara, and other cities instituted court-ordered programs in the 1970s, the highly vocal opposition they faced typically gave way to rapid adjustment and acceptance among the majority of parents and students. Nor were desegregation opponents ever able to conclusively establish that mandatory desegregation programs singularly drove patterns of "white flight" to private or parochial schools and other school districts.[27] Some clear defections occurred; a series of private academies serving white families opened in the San Fernando Valley as the desegregation plans advanced in the late 1970s. But most of the evidence suggested that an objection to busing and desegregation was only one among several factors contributing to the exodus of white students from urban public school systems, a trend that had been underway for many years prior to busing proposals.[28]

If the desegregation plans had a significant liability, it was that by focusing almost exclusively on rectifying rigidly determined racial imbalances they often left other questions of equity involving teacher and personnel hiring, "ability tracking," inadequate resources, parental involvement, curriculum, and language policy unaddressed. Many of these issues animated the largest student-led protest in the history of California public education—the Chicano student "blowouts" involving twenty-two thousand students centered in East Los Angeles in the spring of 1968. The students' complaints—a curriculum that ignored Mexican American history and steered students away from college and toward vocational training, the paucity of Mexican American teachers, the continued use of corporal punishment, overcrowded campuses—reflected many of the same desires for justice and opportunity pursued by desegregation advocates. But the Chicano students made little mention of desegregation as a political imperative; their priority was the immediate improvement of conditions in East Los Angeles schools.[29] The desegregation remedies proposed in Los Angeles and elsewhere made little commitment to address these issues or the forms of cultural domination that fueled the walkouts. The inability of desegregation advocates and the student protestors to find common ground would eventually be exploited by opponents of both groups.

BRINGING PROPOSITION 21 TO THE BALLOT

In 1970, the San Francisco Unified School District became the largest district in the country to desegregate its elementary school system. The same year, in the *Crawford v. Los Angles* case, California Superior Court judge Alfred Gitelson found the state's largest school district to be deliberately segregated and ordered the board to devise a far-reaching districtwide desegregation plan.[30] Soon after, the legislature adopted a bill sponsored by Marin County Republican assemblyman William Bagley that formally established school desegregation as a policy goal of the state. Bagley's modest legislation required the collection of race and ethnicity data to determine patterns of imbalance, but it gave broad discretion to local boards to alleviate these patterns without any specific mandates or penalties for noncompliance. Indeed, the bill was backed by Republicans such as Governor Reagan in large part because of the perception that providing local districts with an administrative framework to address racial imbalance was preferable to becoming subject to a more far-reaching court order.[31]

From Wakefield's perspective, however, such considerations were irrelevant; the Bagley Act was an invitation to "massive busing." All efforts at "forced integration" were equally untenable, a position he felt would be vindicated at the ballot. If the courts and lawmakers would not agree, he would take his case directly to voters.

Wakefield's proposed initiative statute added a provision to the state Education Code that declared, "No public school student shall, because of his race, creed, or color, be assigned to or be required to attend a particular school." The Wakefield Amendment, as it came to be known, also repealed the Bagley Act's mandate for school districts to correct racial and ethnic imbalances within student enrollment.

A fund-raising appeal that Wakefield sent to his supporters two weeks before the election revealed the ways the assemblyman sought to construct Proposition 21 as an unambiguous defense of white rights. Asserting that the busing agenda pursued by "liberals" was being masked by "press suppression" and the "pro-busing news-media," Wakefield's appeal included a ten-panel photo storyboard for a television commercial he hoped to begin airing immediately. The storyboard showed a terrified young white girl being forced to board a school bus as her mother stood by helplessly, explaining, "The government says you and your little friends can't go to school anymore in the neighborhood, honey." The girl's forlorn and bewildered response, "Aren't we people too?" implicitly set the rights of white viewers—the "we"—against a racialized other receiving unwarranted advantages from, as the ad described, "that old government." The storyboard's concluding panel, "Restore Freedom of Choice," was again explicitly racialized, for such a "freedom" was only available to white parents—minority students assigned to inferior and segregated schools had no such choice.[32] The ad unmistakably cast busing as an abrogation of the prerogatives of political whiteness. The ad and Wakefield's larger defense of segregated schools defended a set of racially specific white rights as natural and inalienable.

Wakefield continually emphasized the racialized dimensions of his critique. He referred to the Bagley Act as the "forced integration law," announcing that the "courts have said we are not going to tolerate segregated (by law) schools. Now we're turning around and saying we're not going to tolerate integrating them by law either."[33] The brief ballot argument and rebuttal in favor of Proposition 21 used the phrase "forced integration" nine times, making Wakefield's proposition clear: segregation was natural and a matter of choice, while integration was artificial and required coercion.[34]

Undoubtedly, Wakefield hoped to tap the antibusing currents that seemed to be rapidly accelerating in other parts of the country. In March 1972, 74 percent of Florida voters supported a straw-ballot resolution in support of a constitutional amendment prohibiting "forced busing." Soon after, President Nixon called for a national moratorium on busing for desegregation and Congress adopted legislation declaring that such busing must be a remedy of last resort. The busing controversy loomed as a major issue in the 1972 presidential contest and dominated local politics in cities such as Detroit, Boston, and Charlotte.[35]

Yet Wakefield's measure failed to catalyze the same response in California and fell far short of triggering the outpouring of grassroots support witnessed in the Proposition 14 campaign. His campaign collected only 329,675 signatures, barely enough to qualify the measure for the ballot, and attracted only minor attention from the news media. Only a handful of conservative school boards and individual school board members endorsed the measure.[36] Wakefield raised a modest forty-five thousand dollars for the entire effort, including money he donated from his own campaign fund. Most of the donations came in small amounts from a handful of supporters scattered across Southern California, in addition to a few organizational contributions from local Republican clubs.[37] While the measure clearly garnered the approval of voters, it did not ignite the populist outcry Wakefield predicted.

THE CAMPAIGN TO DEFEAT PROPOSITION 21

As the campaign season for the November election kicked off in early September, Floyd Wakefield's opponents hastily mobilized to defeat the measure. The ACLU of Southern California, which had taken the lead in the *Crawford v. Los Angeles* case, formed Californians against Unequal Schools and Education (CAUSE) to coordinate the effort against Proposition 21, appointing ACLU board member Joyce Fiske director. Fiske promised a determined campaign that would incorporate lessons learned in the failed effort to defeat Proposition 14 eight years earlier. Many volunteers with the campaign against Proposition 14 had been shocked at the overwhelming passage of the anti–fair housing measure, as "No on 14" bumper stickers seemed to be ubiquitous in many parts of Los Angles and the San Francisco Bay Area before the election. Fiske declared they would not be similarly lured into a false sense of confidence.[38]

But their efforts to expand support for school desegregation among the electorate proved just as difficult in 1972 as the fair housing campaign had been in 1964, registering several challenges that desegregation advocates faced in building a broad-based constituency. After the initial burst of grassroots mobilization in 1963 and 1964 around the South Gate controversy, groups in favor of desegregation focused their efforts almost entirely on litigation and lobbying. This emphasis made some tactical sense. The state courts in particular had become increasingly supportive of local desegregation mandates. As long as the legislature did not obstruct these interpretations, the courts seemed to be the most promising avenue of redress. The grassroots organizing that did occur—such as the 1968 student walkouts and some parent activism at local school sites—had little formal connection with the advocacy led by the NAACP and ACLU. Thus, when the ACLU established CAUSE in order to defeat Proposition 21, it had no meaningful grassroots base to mobilize.

Instead, CAUSE turned to a handful of like-minded organizations for support, securing the endorsement of many of the groups that had opposed Proposition 14: the NAACP, the California Teachers Association, the State Federation of Labor, the League of Women Voters, and several faith-based groups that CAUSE briefly organized into an Interfaith Committee.[39] Yet because the 1972 general election ballot was crowded with other controversial initiatives, including a death penalty measure, a marijuana legalization initiative, and a controversial tax reform measure, CAUSE's efforts attracted few resources or attention from these allies. Working out of a rented office on West Pico Avenue in Los Angeles, the campaign raised only seventeen thousand dollars, more than half of which came from the ACLU. While Wakefield also had difficulty arousing a critical mass of interest in his initiative, his opponents' organized constituency was even smaller.[40]

Lacking any meaningful grassroots base, CAUSE mobilized a tepid, almost apologetic defense of the antidiscrimination measures it sought to defend and failed to offer any affirmative vision of the benefits of desegregated or integrated schools. Proposition 21 opponents accused Wakefield of "raising scare words and horror stories" such as "'forced integration,' 'forced busing,' [and] 'destruction of public schools,'" hoping to prevent Wakefield from using the menace of busing to frighten voters. At the same time, CAUSE also sought to mobilize these fears. CAUSE repeatedly warned that without the "calm and deliberative progress" provided for by the Bagley Act's modest requirements, the courts would be forced to intervene with a far worse prescription. The first line of the ballot argument against Proposition 21 read, "Passage of this proposition will encourage Court-ordered 'busing' in California! Please vote 'no.'"[41] In other words, if voters wanted to minimize the reach and pace of desegregation, the limited remedies of the Bagley Act were their best guarantee, essentially restating Governor Reagan's position.

Just as Proposition 14 opponents argued that the protection of fair housing was necessary to avoid unleashing the "anger of the ghetto," CAUSE hoped to frame its appeals within the expectations of political whiteness. And while they repeatedly contended that Proposition 21 would be overturned by the courts if passed, they made few moral claims about the imperative to desegregate or the advantages an integrated education might present. No mention was made of the growing and unmistakable patterns of segregation in districts such as the LAUSD, where 95 percent of Black students and 80 percent of white students were enrolled in highly segregated schools by 1972.[42] In addition, in the public debate, school desegregation and remedying "racial isolation" seemed completely divorced from most other concerns for the state of public education—the overcrowding beginning to face some schools, buildings in need of repair, and growing concerns about learning and achievement.

Black and Chicano leaders and organizations played a minimal role in the anti–Proposition 21 campaign, indexing both their marginal role within these advocacy coalitions and their own ambivalence toward the meek solutions implied by legislation like the Bagley Act.[43] In short-term tactical calculations seeking to win blocs of voters, the failure to include Black and Chicano leaders perhaps seemed unimportant; white voters easily constituted 90 percent of the California electorate. Yet it was precisely the schism between desegregation advocates and the grassroots communities they sought to represent that opponents would eventually exploit in order to naturalize and defend the status quo.

THE PROPOSITION 21 VOTE AND ITS AFTERMATH

Given the limited reach and effectiveness of both campaigns, it is unsurprising that a week before the election, a Field Poll found that more than one in three voters remained undecided about Proposition 21; 36 percent said they intended to vote in favor of the initiative, while 27 percent intended to vote against it.[44]

Ultimately, 63 percent of voters favored the measure, which passed by more than two million votes.[45] The strongest opposition recorded to the measure occurred in several Bay Area cities, including Oakland and San

Francisco, which had voted in favor of Proposition 14 eight years earlier but voted against Proposition 21. The San Francisco vote was particularly revealing because the city was in the midst of a mandatory desegregation program and, only a year earlier, a local referendum on a policy urging that no busing would be "compelled" without parental permission passed by more than three to one.[46]

As promised, immediately after the election both the NAACP and the ACLU filed suit to overturn Proposition 21. The cases became attached to desegregation litigation already pending in San Bernardino, Sacramento, and Santa Barbara.[47] In January 1975, the state supreme court found the operative portion of Proposition 21, which prohibited student assignment based on race, color, or creed, to be in violation of the state and federal constitutions. Associate Justice Raymond Sullivan argued that, like Proposition 14, Proposition 21 involved the "state in racial discrimination" and that the measure could not abrogate "the school district's constitutional duty not to segregate." Citing the U.S. Supreme Court's recent decision in *Swann v. Charlotte-Mecklenburg Board* (1971). Sullivan further asserted that "to forbid all assignments made on the basis of race would deprive school authorities of the one tool absolutely essential to fulfillment of their constitutional obligation to eliminate dual school systems." Wakefield's proposition that white parents and students bore no responsibility to address prevailing conditions of inequality failed to pass the court's muster.[48]

Though it was only in effect for two years, Proposition 21 did have a chilling effect on many local school desegregation efforts. The Inglewood and Pasadena school boards immediately attempted to appeal their own desegregation orders, and in cities such as Whittier and Santa Ana planned desegregation measures were never put into effect. At the same time, the state auditor began monitoring whether school districts were complying with Proposition 21's mandates. One state education official observed that "things have come to a dead halt in the area of desegregation since Proposition 21 passed . . . we have lost ground." Indeed, in early 1974, the state census revealed that 192,000 more students attended segregated schools in comparison to five years earlier.[49]

THE DECLINE OF FLOYD WAKEFIELD

By the time the state supreme court overturned the operative portion of Proposition 21, Floyd Wakefield had left public office and returned to South Gate, working as a house painter with minor real estate investments. His

South Gate assembly district was eliminated in a redistricting plan, and he moved in early 1974 to Anaheim to run in a newly created district. Wakefield lost the Republican primary there and promptly moved back to South Gate and resumed life as a private citizen, "just picking up odd jobs from other people."[50]

The decline of Wakefield's eight-year career in the state assembly paralleled important transformations in the political landscape of Southern California during the 1970s. Wakefield never tempered his ardent conservative postures. In the last months of his final term in the assembly, he sought to qualify a ballot measure to rescind the California Legislature's 1972 ratification of the Equal Rights Act and sat at the head table of a John Birch Society political banquet where founder Robert Welch called for President Nixon's impeachment.[51] But Wakefield could no longer count on a constituency in South Gate to reliably support such appeals. The white working-class residents that a decade earlier had rallied behind Wakefield's defense of Proposition 14 and segregated South Gate High School were rapidly abandoning the inner suburbs south of Los Angeles for new residential developments in the San Fernando Valley and Orange County. Wakefield was no innocent bystander in this retreat. By insisting that cities such as South Gate could never prosper if they became racially integrated, he implicitly endorsed the exodus of white residents that ultimately led to his own political demise. Wakefield's uncompromising assertion of white rights anchored in the white working-class suburbs of South Los Angeles would give way to a more subtle and sophisticated defense of racial inequality and segregation centered in the burgeoning San Fernando Valley.

ALAN ROBBINS AND PROPOSITION 1

Alan Robbins was an unlikely candidate to succeed Floyd Wakefield as California's leading crusader against mandatory school desegregation. Twenty-four years Wakefield's junior, Robbins grew up in an integrated area in North Hollywood, earning his undergraduate and law degrees at UCLA. He became politically involved at a young age, volunteering frequently at a Democratic Party office to register the legions of new arrivals to the San Fernando Valley. Like many other young Jewish political activists, Robbins supported the early southern civil rights movement and campaigned locally against Proposition 14. Robbins profited handsomely from early investments in real estate and by his late twenties had grown wealthy enough to return to politics and finance much of his successful

1973 campaign, which was supported by the liberal California Democratic Council.[52] Where Wakefield often appeared combative and curmudgeonly, Robbins fashioned himself as young, energetic, and optimistic, a favorite son of the San Fernando Valley and a booster of leading Democratic causes: he spoke alongside Jane Fonda in support of the Equal Rights Amendment (ERA) and championed the United Farm Workers.[53]

Deeply ambitious, Robbins quickly ingratiated himself within the local politics of the Valley. He became an early and enduring legislative advocate of "rape laws"—increased criminal penalties for sexual assault crimes— and other "victims' rights" legislation. Robbins also courted support from boosters for a plan to see the San Fernando Valley secede from the City of Los Angeles, a political project that constantly drew contrasts between a corrupt, free-spending, racially polyglot city and its exploited, innocent, white suburbs. Robbins demonstrated how these themes could be brought together when he kicked off his campaign to challenge Los Angeles mayor Tom Bradley at a dinner in the Valley in December 1976; he passed out rape whistles printed with his name to symbolize his defense against the rape of the city.[54]

During the mayoral campaign, Robbins met with a group of parent activists from BUSTOP, a fledgling organization with roots in the Valley community of Encino. The group had started organizing over the last year in anticipation of a districtwide desegregation plan stemming from the *Crawford* case that could include their schools. Bobbi Fiedler, an Encino parent and one of the early leaders of BUSTOP, attracted considerable attention for her insurgent school board candidacy and her uncompromising stand against mandatory busing. Like Robbins, Fiedler was Jewish, grew up in an integrated Santa Monica neighborhood, and supported fair housing laws. Indeed, many BUSTOP leaders felt little affinity with figures like Wakefield; Fiedler was not, as one later profile put it, a conservative in the mold of Phyllis Schlafly. She also supported the ERA and condemned the "deliberate segregation" that characterized the South.[55] But Fiedler asserted that Los Angeles schools were free of such intentional actions (in spite of court findings to the contrary) and that desegregation plans must be limited to voluntary programs that preserved the rights of parents to keep their children in their current schools, however racially imbalanced they might be. As the Los Angeles school board appeared close to exhausting its legal challenges in the now thirteen-year-old *Crawford* desegregation suit, Fiedler recited apocalyptic scenarios of a mammoth busing order that would destroy neighborhood schools, arousing enormous support from anxious Valley parents. By attacking desegregation remedies, rather than the principle of "forced integration" (as Wakefield had done), Fiedler and BUSTOP helped recast the defense of white innocence on new terms.[56]

Robbins initially decided against making busing an issue in his campaign for mayor, telling BUSTOP that he was convinced he could win the election on "crime and taxes" alone.[57] But while Robbins was trounced in the mayoral election the following year, Bobbi Fiedler cruised to an easy victory, as did antibusing incumbent Richard Ferraro. As the debate over mandatory desegregation began to dominate Valley politics, Robbins found the issue that would keep him in the public spotlight for the next five years.[58]

THE LEGAL AND POLITICAL INNOVATIONS
OF THE ROBBINS AMENDMENT

As Robbins contemplated a ballot initiative to halt the desegregation orders facing the Los Angeles and other California school districts, he confronted two challenges—one legal, the other political—that turned on questions of intentionality and racial innocence. State courts ruled that previous efforts to halt desegregation orders, including Wakefield's Proposition 21, violated the state constitution's Equal Protection Clause. The courts determined that this twenty-three word passage in Article I, Section 7(a)—"A person may not be deprived of life, liberty, or property without due process of law or denied equal protection of the laws"—required school boards "to alleviate racial imbalance in schools regardless of its cause," thus dismissing the distinction between de facto and de jure segregation.[59] In addition, any ballot initiative to limit desegregation orders also had to adhere to the Fourteenth Amendment of the U.S. Constitution. In lawsuits challenging the anti–fair housing Proposition 14 (1964) and Proposition 21, plaintiffs successfully argued that the blanket prohibitions on civil rights protections included in these initiatives demonstrated discriminatory intent on the part of the electorate. Any challenge to the desegregation order facing the LAUSD or other California school district would have to withstand similar scrutiny.[60]

On June 1, 1977, less than two months after his defeat to Mayor Bradley, Robbins unveiled a proposed constitutional amendment that cleverly addressed this dilemma. Robbins proposed to amend the nearly hundred-year-old state Equal Protection Clause with a lengthy (176 word) exemption. It held that "with respect to the use of pupil school assignment or pupil transportation" the state constitution could not be interpreted to impose "obligations or responsibilities which exceed those imposed by the Equal Protection Clause of the 14th Amendment to the United States Constitution."[61] In other words, as long as the U.S. Supreme Court interpreted the federal Equal Protection Clause as only prohibiting de jure school segregation, California courts would have to do the same.[62] A lesser provision of the Robbins Amendment also affirmed the right of school districts to pursue voluntary desegregation programs at their discretion, an exception that Wakefield never proffered.

The Robbins Amendment thus addressed a legal bind that had stymied opponents of desegregation in California for fifteen years. Robbins's legislation precluded state courts from vigorously applying the state's equal protection guarantees. At the same time, by affirming the Fourteenth Amendment standard, the initiative also seemed immune from challenges on these grounds. Robbins's opponents understood the gravity of this legal innovation. NAACP West Coast secretary Virna Canson, one of Robbins's most astute and uncompromising adversaries, later accused the senator of mandating "a course of action which places the State Court off limits to NAACP and other petitioners on behalf of school desegregation. . . . Your effort to constitutionally restrict our access to certain courts and your determination to take away what we have gained through legal methods is insidious."[63]

In addition to this legal move, Robbins embraced a political strategy markedly different from Wakefield. When the South Gate lawmaker qualified Proposition 21, he primarily sought support from his existing base of white conservatives: Republican clubs, a handful of school board members, and individual voters in his own district. Robbins, by comparison, was alert to the growing criticism of prevailing desegregation plans within many minority communities and actively courted African American and Chicano figures to take visible, active roles in his initiative campaign. Robbins recruited state senator Alex Garcia, a prominent East Los Angeles Democrat who had opposed Proposition 21 five years earlier, to be the principal cosponsor of his legislation. Garcia contended that mandatory busing and student reassignment would undermine the tenuous status of newly established bilingual education programs. At Robbins's request, Garcia circulated a letter to colleagues urging support of the bill: "Compulsory busing in most California cities would mean the virtual end of bilingual education as we know it today. Where will you find sufficient bilingual instructors if you spread the Chicano students all over the school district? . . . Please don't force us to try it 'for our own good': Thank you, but no thanks."[64]

Similar arguments for community self-determination were sounded by another leading Chicano figure recruited by Robbins, East Los Angeles social worker and parent activist John Serrano. Serrano served as the lead plaintiff in a groundbreaking lawsuit to equalize school funding supported by the ACLU. Serrano became one of the leading backers of the Robbins Amendment over the next two years, writing in the ballot argument that as the plaintiff in the funding lawsuit, he "worked to insure equal educational opportunity for all California children. The excessive use of court-ordered forced busing will not guarantee this result."[65]

While Serrano and Garcia claimed to be representing a uniform position among Chicanos toward busing and desegregation, their comments indicated the presence of contentious debate more than a fully formed consensus. To be sure, Chicano education activists in Los Angeles and elsewhere were suspicious of desegregation proposals that threatened the future of emerging bilingual education programs. Asian American and Mexican American advocates had only recently won the funding and legal mandate for bilingual education in the late 1960s and early 1970s, and a lack of qualified bilingual teachers raised issues about how such programs could be staffed if the students who needed them were reassigned across a large school district. No one wanted a return to the days when Mexican American students were punished for speaking Spanish on school grounds, even during recess.[66]

In addition, the 1968 Chicano walkouts heightened attention to issues of cultural domination within public education. Indeed, many proponents of the Los Angeles desegregation plan, such as ACLU leader and UCLA professor John Caughey, spoke openly of identifying and distinguishing "unassimilated" Mexican Americans who would be prioritized in reassignment plans.[67] Such comments resonated uneasily with a long history of "Americanization" programs in the state, rooted in allegations of cultural pathology. An editorial in the left-oriented newspaper *Sin Fronteras* lambasted a judge's endorsement of the desegregation proposal and the notion that a court official would scrutinize individual Chicanos to determine their degree of "assimilation."[68]

Chicano members of a committee set up to advise the Los Angeles school board on its desegregation policies sounded its trepidation toward "an integration policy that is totally assimilationist in nature—one that does not respect the rights and needs of the culturally different." They argued repeatedly that student reassignment and desegregation were necessary but not sufficient: they demanded parity in resources, culturally relevant instruction and curriculum, and attention to racial discrimination in teacher staffing and hiring.[69] And they expressed continued frustration at being left out of the larger debate over desegregation. One member of the committee, an East Los Angeles parent activist, complained that when she tried to explain bilingual education issues to ACLU officials handling the *Crawford* litigation, she was rebuffed: "They didn't know what we were talking about."[70]

Many established Mexican American civil rights organizations, however, felt that support for bilingual education did not require opposition to desegregation. Indeed, Chicano parents in both Oxnard and San Jose filed lawsuits seeking desegregation remedies as a component of improving the educational opportunities for Chicano students.[71] In testifying against the Robbins bill at a Sacramento hearing in January 1978, Peter Roos, speaking on behalf of League of United Latin American Citizens, the Mexican American Political Association, the Mexican American Legal Defense and Education Fund, and National La Raza Lawyers, asserted, "The concept that bilingual education and desegregation are incompatible precedes from the false premise that desegregation cannot be sensitive to the unique educational needs of those children integrated."[72] Vahac Mardirosian, director of the Hispanic Urban Center, argued that "if parents are convinced that sending their children twenty-five to thirty miles will result in exactly the same education that child had when he was in the school next door, logically there really isn't a good reason for that parent to want to cooperate with a desegregation program." But, he added, "if parents understand that this process of desegregation ultimately will result in a better future for their children . . . most . . . would be willing to live with the additional anxiety."[73]

Robbins had less success securing support among the state's recognized African American leadership. While Mayor Bradley was never a strong supporter of a citywide desegregation program, leading figures in the state legislature such as Diane Watson (a former Los Angeles school board member), Maxine Waters, and Yvonne Braithwaite Burke were strong advocates of mandatory desegregation. But Robbins found enough backing to support his claim that opposition to busing was not a "white rights" issue but represented a multiracial consensus. Soon after introducing his initiative, he secured the endorsement of Rev. William Jackson of the Beth-Ezel Baptist Church in Watts. Jackson did not necessarily represent or influence a large bloc of African American voters, but when he campaigned on behalf of the Robbins initiative he spoke as a Black community representative, claiming widespread support. At an early 1978 press conference, he explained, "I am here representing all those Black people who are terribly distraught about busing. . . . We know what is best for our people."[74]

In making these claims, Jackson placed himself squarely within the civil rights tradition. He asked at an assembly committee hearing on the bill, "How brutal can we be to impose this action (compulsory busing) on little children? We'd rather have $100 million spent on books and teaching aids than $100 million spent on busing." Similarly, another Black parent recruited by Robbins to testify before the assembly committee described the "humiliation and psychological damage done to the child" by busing, reciting the central themes of Dr. Kenneth Clarke's famous testimony in the *Brown* case about the deleterious psychological effects of segregation on Black children.[75]

The antibusing stance of Rev. Jackson, Senator Garcia, and others had complex origins. While it did not represent a unanimous position within African American, Chicano, and Asian American communities, it did reflect a deep ambivalence toward nominal desegregation efforts that seemed unable to deliver significant changes in opportunity or equity. The comments also reflected the growing demands for "community control" on the part of Black and Chicano students and parents, who had grown apprehensive about a desegregation debate that rarely seemed to include their participation or perspective; most of the desegregation plans ordered by the courts gave little attention to such issues.[76]

Robbins's own antiracist claims must be viewed with more suspicion. While he carefully developed his ties to visible Black and Chicano leaders, he was unafraid of addressing and cultivating the reactionary populist sensibilities of white voters. That is, Robbins modified and adapted, rather than abandoned, Floyd Wakefield's appeals to "white rights." These actions are brought into sharp relief in a strategy memo for a direct-mail effort to raise money for the antibusing campaign in the summer of 1978, an effort developed by consultants hired by Robbins. The memo suggested targeting particular middle-class white communities across the state by referencing the nearby "undesirable areas" to which their children might be bused. In Contra Costa County, for example, the memo identified the "City of Richmond—in total better than 50% black—W Richmond probably the worst." Twelve other predominantly Black neighborhoods were listed as next to an adjoining white neighborhood or city whose residents could be targeted for an antibusing direct-mail appeal.[77]

Evidence such as this suggests the tenuous basis on which antibusing campaigns sought to include Black and Chicano spokespersons. While their participation was made possible by a deep-seated apprehension toward prevailing desegregation proposals, their inclusion was mainly sought to legitimate assertions of white racial innocence. Fiedler later said that in preparing BUSTOP's legal challenge to the desegregation order the group "focus[ed] heavily on minority children, because we knew that the charge of racism would be made in the minute that we started trying to go to court."[78]

The intent of this approach was not lost upon Robbins's opponents. The NAACP's Canson testified at a state assembly hearing on the Robbins Amendment that "one of the strategies of our opposition is to seek to project individual black spokesmen, exploit their individual points of view, and trade it off as a massive departure of NAACP from our historic goal of full integration." Canson directly attacked the antiracist claims made by Robbins and his allies: "The proponents of segregation have taken great comfort in a simplistic campaign phrase 'A black child does not need to sit beside a white child to learn.' Education in isolation is not an effective way to end this dismal record. . . . Not only does a black child need to sit beside a white child, or a white teacher needs to work in a class room with non-whites to learn, but a white child desperately needs to sit beside a black child to learn and be prepared to be a citizen of this colored world."[79]

Robbins putative incorporation of antiracist themes and tactics was still effective. Calls among busing opponents for the protection of "majority rights" quickly waned in favor of arguments that represented the interests of "all children." The *Los Angeles Herald Examiner* explained that the antibusing movement "is not (and should not) be racist in either intent or effect. The goal of the movement is not to deny minority students a quality education, but to deny the state the power to wreck neighborhoods and lives."[80] Robbins affirmatively embraced "integration carried out in an orderly fashion" as a desirable goal but asserted that "compulsory busing, where it has been mandated by the courts against the will of local residents, has caused not only racial tension, but actual racial strife, an unfortunate ingredient that we ought not to weave into the social fabric of our society."[81] Robbins's claim that mandatory school desegregation was the cause rather than the solution to "racial strife" recited a theme that was familiar in postwar debates about antiracism. Yet when sounded with populist, pluralist accents, it seemed more like a pragmatic assessment rather than a racist disavowal.

In addition, Robbins's support for "voluntary" rather than "mandatory" desegregation had important racial dimensions. Since 1968, Los Angeles had operated a voluntary busing program that gave parents the option of sending their children to another school in the district on a space-available basis, with district-provided transportation, if it led to increased racial balance in the "receiving" school. But the only students who would need to take advantage of such a program were Black and Chicano students confined to overcrowded schools in South, Central, and East Los Angeles. A 1979 report confirmed that only 2 percent of the nearly ten thousand students enrolled in the program were white and that travel times for students going to white-majority schools in the Valley and West Los Angeles averaged nearly an hour.[82] Experts also predicted that such voluntary programs alone would never deal with the pervasive levels of segregation across the district, which a federal study in 1978 described as being "among the most segregated in the entire country."[83] Thus the debate over busing in the late 1970s was primarily a debate over whether white students could be compelled to participate in desegregation programs, or whether that burden would fall exclusively on nonwhite students under a "voluntary" system.

THE MOVEMENT AGAINST MANDATORY BUSING AND DESEGREGATION

In California political lore, the grassroots opposition to mandatory desegregation has often been described as a powerful antibusing political machine forged over kitchen table meetings across the San Fernando Valley. Busing as a campaign issue certainly launched the careers of numerous local politicians: BUSTOP leader Bobbi Fiedler parlayed her opposition to busing first to a spot on the school board and eventually to a seat in Congress; other BUSTOP leaders, including Tom Bartman and Roberta Weintraub, also won spots on the Los Angeles school board. And at various points in the late 1970s, antibusing meetings and rallies in the Valley drew hundreds and sometimes thousands of participants. The controversy was not simply manufactured by opportunistic leaders.[84]

Yet these accounts overstate the levels of organization and stability that typified antibusing groups while eliding the role of professional campaign consultants in constructing and popularizing their message. For example, when Robbins failed to win the endorsement of the state assembly to place his constitutional amendment on the June 1978 ballot—Democratic lawmakers controlling the body voted it down—he was forced to qualify the measure by petition. Robbins recruited BUSTOP leader Roberta Weintraub to head a new organization, Californians Helping to Obtain Individual Choices in Education (CHOICE), to gather the roughly five hundred thousand signatures necessary. Robbins and Weintraub confidently declared their goal would be met; the public's antibusing fervor and opposition to the pending Los Angeles plan could not be suppressed. CHOICE set up petition-collection stations at elementary schools across the Valley, hoping

Figure 5.   Rev. William Jackson and Alan Robbins deliver
petitions for antibusing initiative to the county registrar,
Los Angeles, June 5, 1978. The campaign ultimately failed
to submit enough signatures to qualify for the ballot. Many
of the boxes contained photocopied signatures. Courtesy of
Los Angeles Times Photo Archives, Department of Special
Collections, Charles E. Young Research Library, University
of California, Los Angeles.

to replicate the all-volunteer effort that had qualified Proposition 13 with
more than a million signatures a few months earlier.[85]

When the filing deadline arrived, however, CHOICE found itself roughly
three hundred thousand signatures short of its goal; some boxes had been
filled with tens of thousands of forged petitions produced by a printer,
which Robbins's blamed on an errant staffer. CHOICE apparently had few
records of the number of signatures it was collecting, and even if the forged
petitions had been legitimate the effort would have come up short. The
organization soon disbanded.[86] Other antibusing efforts in the Valley and
Orange County met similar fates, with promises of school boycotts or
statewide initiatives ending in failure.[87]

These challenges even brought the mighty BUSTOP to the brink of collapse. BUSTOP had been founded in 1976 by Weintraub, Fiedler, and other parent activists involved in Valley parent-teacher associations, quickly claiming a membership of sixty thousand parents. A year and a half later, hobbled by a financial crisis and internal discord, it abandoned its model of grassroots parent activism and turned over its management and leadership to professional fund-raisers and administrators, including Paul Clarke and Arnold Steinberg, a thirty-year-old campaign consultant who would become a rising star in electing Republican candidates statewide and would eventually help guide the anti–affirmative action measure, Proposition 209, to victory in 1996.[88]

Steinberg and Clarke turned BUSTOP's attention almost entirely to raising funds through direct-mail solicitations, primarily to support its legal efforts as a newly recognized intervener in the *Crawford v. Los Angeles* suit. Over the next three years, BUSTOP's continuous stream of appeals to carefully targeted voters across Southern California yielded more than $550,000 in tax-free contributions.[89] These appeals were usually signed by school board members Fiedler or Weintraub (who was elected in 1979) and often tied the antibusing campaign to the antitax fervor sweeping the state in the wake of Proposition 13's passage. A typical letter began, "Are you willing to pay *higher property taxes* to finance the forced busing of over *100,000* Los Angeles schoolchildren?" The mailings included "Official Reply Ballots" and other "surveys" that allowed voters to register their antibusing sentiments. Following Robbins, the BUSTOP mailers counseled the use of "constructive proposals for voluntary, *not*, mandatory, integration."[90] These appeals were expanded to Beverly Hills, Orange County, and other outlying areas in early 1979 as rumors grew over a potential metropolitan desegregation plan that would reassign students between adjacent school districts.[91] Steinberg would later explain that the mailers and solicitations served two purposes: they helped raise money, often in small donations, but also allowed the group to "accumulate a list [of supporters], involve people and motivate them to keep the issue alive."[92]

After the failure of CHOICE, Robbins also turned over much of his grassroots organizing to professional campaign consultants. Butcher-Forde, the self-proclaimed "Darth Vader of direct mail," was an Orange County–based consultancy that managed much of the Proposition 13 direct-mail campaign on behalf of Howard Jarvis and took on the Robbins initiative as a client. The coveted lists of voters and campaign donors Butcher-Forde developed through the antitax campaign provided an ideal audience for the Robbins antibusing effort. While the return from these fund-raising appeals was never lucrative—the campaign raised approximately $250,000 between mid-1978 and late 1979, a reported 50 percent of which was kept by Butcher-Forde—the direct-mail strategy allowed Robbins to send out over a million pieces of campaign literature across the state during this period.[93] While political campaigns had relied on direct mail for decades in California, it was through the busing and tax controversies that these efforts reached unprecedented levels of sophistication, scale, and impact.[94]

Thus, even though Robbins and BUSTOP failed to sustain ongoing grassroots organizations, their strategic and continuous use of targeted mail appeals and their ability to make busing a central issue within many electoral races paid enormous benefits. They persistently primed the electorate with a singular characterization of busing as an expensive, half-baked bureaucratic scheme that failed all children and accelerated the decline of public education. On one side within this discourse stood a handful of deep-pocket ACLU and NAACP attorneys, insular politicians, self-aggrandizing judges, and their academic advisors who found great pleasure in raising taxes to advance their own "social experiments." On the other side stood the vast majority of "innocent" taxpayers, parents and children of all racial and ethnic backgrounds who would be forced to shoulder the burden of this preposterous scheme. They were a silent majority perhaps, but not in the revanchist mode of George Wallace, for they professed to value the education of all children. For civil rights advocates, what began as an effort to challenge racial hierarchy and expand educational resources and opportunity had become increasingly tarnished by their opponents as a disastrous folly of bureaucratic elites emptied of any antiracist ethics.

PROPOSITION 1 REACHES THE BALLOT

Gary Orfield, a leading scholar on school desegregation issues, who served as an expert witness in the *Crawford* case and many similar lawsuits around the nation during this period, has argued that in nearly every city where a mandatory desegregation order was issued, strident opposition typically gave way to gradual acceptance among most parents and students.[95] Even districts that went on to develop highly regarded desegregation programs, such as in Charlotte, North Carolina, initially faced significant opposition. In such cases, the mandatory court order provided school districts and desegregation supporters with the legal authority necessary to withstand this initial opposition. As a Woodland Hills pastor and desegregation supporter testified at a California Assembly hearing in 1978, "I think everyone knows that voluntary integration would be about as successful as voluntary taxation."[96] This was as true for California schools as it was for those in Alabama. By 1980, thirteen California school districts faced some sort of mandatory desegregation order from state courts.[97]

After Robbins failed to qualify his ballot measure by petition in the summer of 1978, the possibility remained that a similar process might unfold in Los Angeles. Indeed, efforts to organize a school boycott at the start of the LAUSD's mandatory desegregation program in September 1978 failed; antibusing rallies organized by Robbins and others a few months later were poorly attended.[98] Many parents were certainly frustrated at the uncertainty surrounding the new student reassignment and busing plans, and concern about long bus rides worried even desegregation supporters.[99] But the mandatory desegregation program begun in the 1978–79 school year, which involved approximately 40,000 students in grades 4 through 8, including 16,000 who were bussed, progressed without any major conflicts or disruptions. While the plans certainly faced continued denunciation in some quarters, the program did not "self-destruct" from parent rebellion as BUSTOP had predicted. The opposition encountered did not differ dramatically with what occurred in other cities. Letters to the editor published in the *Los Angeles Times* certainly included condemnations of the program, but also testimonies from desegregation supporters, including a white PTA president from the wealthy Valley suburb of Woodland Hills, who wrote that her nine-year-old daughter faced a long bus ride each day without "fear or resentment." She suggested her daughter "seems to understand that children have been racially isolated and it falls to her lot to help remedy this situation."[100]

To be sure, if given the option, most white parents from middle-class neighborhoods would certainly have chosen to remain in their previous schools (as would have parents in Little Rock). But when the desegregation program began for a second year in 1979, the *Los Angeles Times* reporter who had been covering the story for several years described student experiences with the program as having "become almost routine."[101] The school district had achieved some success in reducing travel times and had begun implementing training initiatives to address questions of classroom climate and culture with teachers, parents, and schools staff.[102] And Robbins's critics pointed out that even if white student enrollment was declining in the LAUSD, as table 2 suggests, (a pattern witnessed in nearly every other large city in the state and the nation), such developments should not exempt the school district from constitutional imperatives to desegregate.[103]

Robbins's assertions, however, that there were "families in this state going through a living hell," came to dominate the political debate, obscuring the full range of experiences with the desegregation program.[104]

TABLE 2 Segregation Trends in Select California School Districts,
1968–1980

District	White			Total % change, 1968–1980	Black			Total % change, 1968–1980
	1968	1974	1980		1968	1974	1980	
Los Angeles	44	31	26	–18	31	38	38	7
San Diego	76	72	56	–20	12	14	15	3
Long Beach	85	74	53	–32	8	13	19	11
San Francisco	41	28	17	–24	28	30	27	–1
Oakland	31	20	14	–17	55	66	66	11
Fresno	70	66	54	–16	9	10	12	3
Sacramento	66	59	46	–20	14	18	22	8
Garden Grove	89	84	69	–20	0	1	1	0
San Jose	68	71	64	–4	1	2	2	1
Santa Ana	63	—	21	–42	7	—	6	–1

SOURCE: Data compiled from Orfield, *Public School Desegregation in the United States, 1968–1980.*

Ultimately, it was Robbins's Democratic colleagues in the state legislature, rather than parents themselves, that paved the way for the end of
mandatory desegregation in Los Angeles and elsewhere in the state. As
BUSTOP and other desegregation opponents continued to warn voters
about the specter of a "massive" metropolitan desegregation program, and
as antibusing candidates prevailed in several key local and state campaigns,
Democratic lawmakers increasingly became concerned over the liabilities
the issue posed. Assembly majority leader Howard Berman of West Los
Angeles, a prominent liberal, signaled in early 1979 that he was ready to
back the Robbins Amendment and support only voluntary desegregation
efforts, citing white flight from the Los Angeles Unified School District.
Other Democratic lawmakers soon followed, no longer willing to defend
the policy before their own constituencies. In the legislature, the remaining opposition to the Robbins Amendment came almost entirely from the
handful of Black representatives, who continued to denounce the measure
as racist.[105] Assemblyman Willie Brown of San Francisco dismissed what
he called "that phony freedom [of choice] argument" offered by opponents,
saying, "The issue is a question of whether or not you get reelected—pure

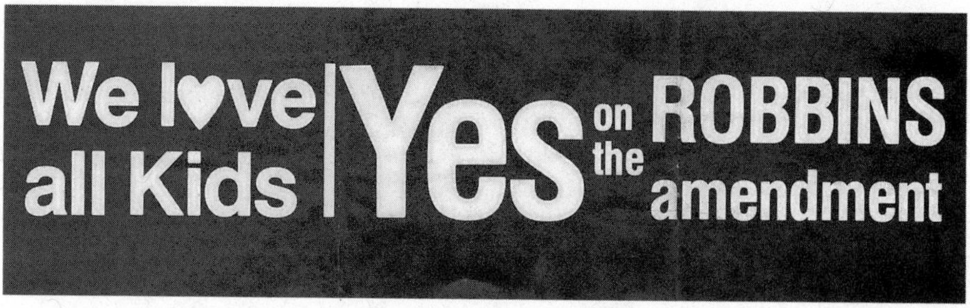

We l♥ve all Kids | Yes on the **ROBBINS amendment**

Figure 6. "We Love All Kids," bumper sticker for Proposition 1, 1979. Courtesy of Alan Robbins Collection, Urban Archives Center, Oviatt Library, California State University, Northridge.

and simple."[106] The *Los Angeles Sentinel* editorialized to its predominantly Black readership about the changes taking place: "Whether we like it or not, it is about time we recognize the climate of the times. No longer will some of our so-called liberal 'friends' help us wage the kinds of fights we need if we are to break down the doors of racism."[107]

By March 1979, both the assembly and the state senate voted overwhelmingly to place the Robbins Amendment on the next ballot, scheduled for June 1980. According to the *Sacramento Bee*, Assemblyman Leo McCarthy, the liberal Assembly Speaker who earlier had managed to prevent his Democratic colleagues from supporting Robbins, now "sat glumly at his desk like a stone figure" as the measure was approved, frustrated that the political winds had changed so rapidly.[108] Robbins pressed this advantage fully. He quickly sponsored another bill calling for a special election in November. Such an action was almost unprecedented in the history of California elections; special elections were always reserved either to fill vacancies or recall incumbents from office. But in addition to Robbins's legislation, antitax leader Paul Gann had already qualified his own "Spirit of 13" initiative to restrict the growth of state and local spending. An ad hoc coalition of desegregation advocates mobilized to prevent approval of the special election proposal, but few legislators would risk being tagged as obstructionists by antitax and antibusing leaders. Governor Jerry Brown agreed to call the special election, placing both the Robbins Amendment (Proposition 1) and the Gann initiative (Proposition 4) on a special November 1979 ballot.[109]

As the election approached, the aura of an antibusing machine based in the San Fernando Valley continued to grow. While the relationships between Robbins, Fiedler, and others involved in the antidesegregation project were always strained and subject to the pressures of their personal ambitions, there was little doubt that they had succeeded in making any public defense or endorsement of busing an act of political suicide. A poll conducted in August found that while less than one in three respondents were aware of Proposition 1, nearly 80 percent registered their opposition toward "busing designed to achieve racial balance."[110]

At the same time, Robbins and other Proposition 1 leaders increasingly moved to identify their campaign more closely with the antitax currents that propelled Proposition 13. Fiedler was appointed to co-chair a Los Angeles Nonpartisan Committee for Yes on 4. Gann announced that he was "against busing for anything but educational purposes" and Jarvis declared that "throwing money at the problem is not the answer. . . . Forced busing does not work." Indeed, much of Jarvis and Gann's attack on excessive property taxes drew from the same claims of suburban innocence that drove the antibusing movement: just as liberal politicians were wasting tax dollars on overly generous welfare payments to Black and Brown families in the central city, so to were irresponsible politicians and judges sacrificing the education of students in the Valley in pursuit of their own self-aggrandizing visions. Fiedler asserted that "between the anti-busing and Proposition 13 movements we have one of the strongest grass-roots movements that has ever come together."[111]

Robbins continued to strike a balance between emphasizing the common fiscal concerns that drove his Proposition 1 and Gann's Proposition 4—he told supporters that busing would cost every household an additional $352 per year in taxes—while ensuring the campaign did not become too publicly identified with white San Fernando Valley homeowners. John Serrano and Rev. William Jackson joined Robbins in signing the official Proposition 1 ballot argument, which repeatedly emphasized the negative impact of busing on all children. But in personal fundraising appeals to his Valley supporters Robbins continued to associate busing with the dangers that lurked beyond their suburban communities; busing outside one's own neighborhood would inevitably lead to tragedy: "Children in strange, unfamiliar neighborhoods are much more prone to violence than they would be in their own neighborhood, close to the safety of their own home, family and friends. And there's always the danger of a child missing the bus, becoming terrified and getting lost—which again multiplies the opportunity for some sick person to make your child a victim of violence."[112]

These comments resonated strongly with a political affect, quite dominant in the white enclaves of the San Fernando Valley, which came to

Figure 7.   Alan Robbins and Howard Jarvis at a press conference against
Proposition 1, Los Angeles, October 26, 1979. Courtesy of Los Angeles
Times Photo Archives, Department of Special Collections, Charles E. Young
Research Library, University of California, Los Angeles.

understand low property taxes and racially homogonous schools and neighborhoods as, not only unassailable prerogatives, but conditions that had no
connection to or culpability for the widening social and racial inequalities
in neighboring urban areas. As in housing, racial segregation in education
was explained entirely through neutral market forces. As one mother from
the Sunland-Tujunga neighborhood in the Valley explained, "Our husbands work hard so we can live in a decent neighborhood and send our kids
to decent schools and it isn't fair for them to be bused someplace else."[113]

To be sure, it would be inaccurate to describe all BUSTOP members
and opponents of mandatory desegregation as unreconstructed bigots or
to suggest that their professed support for racial equality was always dis-
ingenuous. As Arnold Steinberg recalls, BUSTOP was not an exclusively
white organization, and the group's leadership took care to distance itself
from more extreme desegregation critics.[114] But BUSTOP's contention that
the state lacked the authority to remedy clear racial disparities that were
the direct result of long-standing public policies, and that any such interventions were destined to fail, in many ways mirrored earlier criticisms
of fair employment and fair housing laws. Indeed, it was the assertion
that mandatory desegregation could ultimately succeed in Los Angeles

and that white parents could be compelled to participate in such a process that always raised the greatest ire among BUSTOP activists. The Robbins measure was in many ways a proposition about their racial innocence.

After the legislature agreed to place the Robbins Amendment on the ballot, the familiar coalition of civil rights groups, faith-based organizations, and labor unions scrambled once again to offer some nominal resistance. The Southern California ACLU helped launch Californians against Proposition 1 (CAP 1) and lent the group temporary office space in its Los Angeles headquarters. State senator Diane Watson and television producer Norman Lear served as honorary co-chairs of the effort, which raised a miniscule fifteen thousand dollars; CAP 1 lacked the fund-raising and voter-contact capacities that antibusing advocates had spent the last few years cultivating. While CAP 1 secured a predictable set of endorsements—the State Federation of Labor, League of Women Voters, California Teachers Association, California Democratic Council—even these groups offered little concrete support to the campaign.[115] Some progressive Jewish activists and leaders also criticized Bobbi Fiedler and Roberta Weintraub in particular for creating the impression that the city's Jewish community stood unanimously opposed to school desegregation.[116]

The NAACP's Virna Canson, who was in the midst of attempting to reinvigorate the grassroots base of the organization, sent a memo to local NAACP branch leaders in July warning that if "we NAACP-ers allow [the Robbins Amendment] to happen without a fight, we might as well close up shop."[117] In August, she reported to Watson an inventory of how the campaign against Proposition 1 was shaping up. While she tried to remain optimistic, the activities she identified revealed how limited their capacity was: organizers anticipated some outreach to college campuses and a few volunteer groups and a one hour spot on a local radio show. No references were made to any of the capacities needed to seriously compete in a statewide political campaign, such as organized precinct work, paid media, or the active involvement of organizations with large constituencies.[118]

Canson publicly promised that the campaign against Proposition 1 would "open voter schools in communities throughout California . . . in store fronts, basements of churches, homes and other places where people can come to learn about the issues, the records of candidates and the importance of voting." But such activities never came to fruition; it was far too late in the desegregation struggle to begin constituting a large enough audience to seriously challenge Robbins. A late October rally in an African American church in a South Los Angeles church against Propositions 1 and 4 drew only one hundred participants, a turnout Watson described as "really sad."[119] But lacking any recent history of sustained grassroots organizing or contact with parents and voters about the importance of desegregation or the stakes of the current busing debate, this turnout was hardly surprising. The day had long passed when civil rights organizers could simply post and circulate a few flyers and expect an audience to materialize or presume that they were the only ones who could lay claim to the civil rights tradition.

Equally as damaging, the campaign against Proposition 1 made few inroads in winning endorsements among Asian American and Latino political leaders or organizations. Canson made the case for a multiracial, interdependent defense of education rights, arguing that "Chinese, Japanese, Chicanos, Filipinos have all been discriminated against in their pursuit of public education in California." She insisted that while this "time the educational opportunities of Blacks is the target, the next time the target will be employment opportunities, the next attack will be on bi-lingulism, the next attack on rights of women, the next on abortion and so on down the line."[120]

Her pleas fell on deaf ears. Most of the desegregation proposals under consideration by the court offered only vague support for bilingual education and other compensatory programs. Robbins, by contrast, promised that once mandatory busing was ended money would be freed up to directly fund such programs. Other than the Los Angeles–based Hispanic Urban Center, which had taken an active role in the *Crawford* case, the anti–Proposition 1 effort secured little formal support from Latino organizations or elected officials, and none from Asian American organizations. Moreover, three of the most powerful Mexican American elected officials—Senators Alex Garcia, Ruben Ayala, and Joseph Montoya—endorsed the Robbins measure, reasoning that bilingual education would not weather a large-scale desegregation plan.

As the election approached and Robbins's momentum showed no signs of abating, the campaign against Proposition 1 opened a final, desperate attempt to derail support for the measure. In communications with predominantly Black parents and voters, CAP 1 described the measure as a "racist attack on education" and described opponents like BUSTOP as seeking to impose "forced segregation."[121] Similarly, activists with the Integration Project, a predominantly white organization of educators and activists that championed a systematic desegregation plan, described the measure as "racist and segregationist."[122] But when forced to communicate to the electorate through ballot arguments, the expectations of political whiteness once again restrained their political vocabulary. The ballot argument against Proposition 1 insisted that "neither desegregation in Los Angeles, nor the busing used as a tool to achieve it, would come to a halt with the passage of this measure." It further explained that recent Supreme Court decisions meant that "federal standards may impose broader rather than narrower duties to desegregate," hoping to press the same antibusing anxieties fanned by Robbins into service against the initiative.[123]

Proposition 1 opponents' concession that mandatory desegregation and busing were unpopular and undesirable spoke to their broader inability to advance any affirmative argument for the benefits of a desegregated or integrated education. While the ACLU and the NAACP made reference to the need to improve funding, repair dilapidated buildings, or reduce class size, they largely failed to link their desegregation proposals to such broader imperatives and needs.[124] And because the overwhelming attention of the courts, desegregation opponents, and the media was focused on issues of busing and student reassignment, they were effectively painted as being obsessed with busing at the expense of any other concerns. Thus while Robbins, Jackson, and Serrano suggested that the end of "forced busing" would bring new resources to teachers, classrooms, and buildings, their opponents could only counter that while busing may be undesirable, it was inevitable.[125]

THE ELECTION AND ITS AFTERMATH

In the days before the election, as Robbins continued to campaign aggressively across Southern California, Watson conceded that the best opponents could hope for was to limit Proposition 1's margin of victory. Even that modest goal proved unattainable. Proposition 1 passed statewide by thirty-eight percentage points, twelve points higher than the margin of victory for Proposition 21, and received majorities in all fifty-eight counties. Los Angeles County passed the measure by 74 percent. In the city of Los Angeles, the west San Fernando Valley communities that formed the nucleus of the antibusing movement voted nine to one in favor of Proposition 1, with a 43 percent turnout rate. In the three South Los Angeles city council districts represented by African Americans, the measure was defeated by a two-to-one margin, but turnout lagged at 25 percent. It passed by almost 70 percent in the generally liberal Westside and was approved by smaller majorities in the heavily Latino Eastside district.[126] Table 3 demonstrates that Proposition 1 passed at a higher rate than Proposition 21 in almost every city statewide, though turnout in the 1979 special election was markedly lower.

TABLE 3 Proposition 21 (1972) and Proposition 1 (1979) Vote in Select Cities

City	Proposition 21			Proposition 1		
	Yes (%)	No (%)	Total Votes	Yes (%)	No (%)	Total Votes
Statewide	63	37	7,870,196	69	31	3,546,295
Oakland	43	57	133,857	57	43	36,578
San Francisco	49	51	250,761	56	44	173,691
Los Angeles City	58	42	998,699	73	27	390,743
Compton	43	57	18,005	36	64	5,475
South Gate	75	25	20,013	82	18	5,908
Pico Rivera	59	41	16,531	63	37	5,573
Santa Ana	70	30	50,944	74	26	16,872

SOURCE: *Statement of Vote: 1972 General Election* (Sacramento: California Secretary of State, 1972); *California Ballot Pamphlet: Special Statewide Election, November 6, 1979* (Sacramento: California Secretary of State, 1979).

In its December 1980 decision upholding the constitutionality of the measure, the California Court of Appeals ruled, "We do not believe a state constitutional amendment can be said to violate the Fourteenth Amendment by specifically embracing it." The court also determined that the electorate had not acted with discriminatory intent in adopting the measure, calling the charge "pure speculation." At one hearing, Associate Justice Lynn Compton told ACLU attorney Fred Okrand, "I just think you're being very unfair in imputing sinister motives to the people who adopted Proposition 1."[127] The three-judge panel also rejected the ACLU's assertion that the markedly inferior conditions in predominantly Black and Latino schools demonstrated a pattern of intentional discrimination. The court held that "the two problems (unequal facilities and discrimination) frequently parallel one another but they are distinct and different problems."[128]

When the state supreme court refused to review the appellate decision in March 1981, it opened the door for the faction of the Los Angeles school board opposed to desegregation to immediately end the district's mandatory busing program. The state supreme court's decision not to review the case surprised both sides and led superior court judge Paul Egly to remove himself from the *Crawford* case after four years, charging that the school board had "failed to even meet the [separate but equal] standard of *Plessy v. Ferguson*." Critics noted it was the first time in U.S. history that a court ruling resulted in the reassignment of minority students from desegregated schools to segregated ones.[129]

The ACLU and NAACP were granted one last opportunity to present their arguments when the U.S. Supreme Court agreed to hear the case in 1982. Almost the entire legal case of the Los Angeles school board and other supporters of Proposition 1 rested on the professed racial neutrality and innocence of the measure. Attorneys for the board noted that Proposition 1 passed by 75 percent in Los Angeles County, where racial minorities constituted half of the population, but only got 53 to 55 percent of the vote in nearly all-white Humboldt and Marin counties, the lowest margin of victory in the state. Furthermore, one of Proposition 1's main supporters was "Rev Jackson, [who] is a black parent and the pastor of the Beth Ezel Baptist Church in Watts, a minority neighborhood in South Central Los Angeles."[130]

Most of the amicus briefs submitted in the case supporting the ballot measure also raised the banner of racial innocence. Bobbi Fiedler, by then a member of Congress, averred that "Proposition 1 is racially neutral" and that "Californians of every race and ethnic background" had determined that "the experiment" of mandatory desegregation was not working.[131] Solicitor General Rex Lee asserted that "the motivating purposes behind the enactment of Proposition 1 . . . provide no basis for inferring racial animus" and that "no appeals to racist sentiments" were made in the public campaign to pass the initiative.[132] Robbins's brief drew from his own biography to establish the innocence of the measure: "The author of Proposition 1 is a Democrat, a 20-year supporter of Rev. Martin Luther King, the elected representative of a district where half of the school children are members of minority groups, and a strong committed advocate of achieving integration through open housing in the community" and various voluntary means.[133]

Opponents of Proposition 1 challenged such claims of innocence. As one amicus brief from a plaintiff in an ongoing desegregation suit in Palo Alto contended, Proposition 1 "stigmatizes minority children and their parents" by declaring that "desegregation must stop and resegregation must occur to preserve racial 'harmony and tranquility' in public schools. . . . This language necessarily will be understood by minority children (and their parents) to mean *they* cause such strife and turmoil." The brief called Proposition 1 "a modern day affirmation of Dred Scott" because, like that infamous 1856 court decision denying citizenship rights to African Americans, the ballot measure relied on a contention that integration was "dangerous to the peace and safety" of the polity and that Black people were "altogether unfit to associate with the white race." The brief concluded forcefully, "Proposition 1 is a *racial law* and as such discriminatory intent should be conclusively presumed."[134]

In June 1982, the Supreme Court affirmed the appellate court's decision by an eight-to-one vote; Justice Thurgood Marshall offered the lone dissent. Writing for the majority, Justice Lewis Powell asserted, "It would be paradoxical to conclude that by adopting the Equal Protection Clause of the Fourteenth Amendment, the voters of the State thereby had violated it." The measure "neither says nor implies that persons are to be treated differently on account of their race." Moreover, because school boards could be ordered to relieve segregation in other ways that did not require mandatory busing, the initiative could not be construed as favoring segregation. In his dissent, Marshall concluded that "the fact that California attempts to cloak its discrimination in the mantle of the Fourteenth Amendment does not alter this result."[135]

The Supreme Court's ruling was a death knell for mandatory desegregation programs across the state. Local school boards were still free to craft their own programs, but without the threat of a court order these programs were largely feeble. Pasadena ended its mandatory programs in late 1981. Participation in San Diego's voluntary program grew much more anemic after the Proposition 1 ruling. In San Mateo, a local school district successfully used Proposition 1 to reject an intradistrict desegregation plan that would have required minimal busing, allowing wealthy Palo Alto schools to remain segregated from a neighboring district that was 95 percent Black.[136] While these changes reflected a number of forces, especially the declining enrollment of white students in nearly every urban school district in the state, it was Proposition 1 that provided a populist, even antiracist imprimatur to the movement to halt systematic desegregation of California schools.

In Los Angeles, after their court victory, Robbins and other antibusing activists vowed to make full use of "voluntary measures" to achieve desegregation, including magnet schools and voluntary busing programs that provided students transportation to attend schools outside of their neighborhood. In reality, most of these voluntary efforts were "one-way" programs, requiring Black and Chicano students from Central, East, and South Los Angeles to be bused from their neighborhood schools to attend better-resourced schools in West Los Angeles and in the Valley. By 1985, the district was busing fifty-seven thousand students each day—more than at the height of the mandatory desegregation program—for voluntary programs and to relieve overcrowding.[137] Some students in South Gate High

School, which by the early 1980s was predominantly Latino, were forced to ride a bus thirty-five miles each way to the Valley community of Tujunga in order to relieve overcrowding.[138] The end of mandatory desegregation meant that the burden of busing had fallen almost exclusively on students of color. One East Los Angeles high school teacher demanded, "Where is BUSTOP now? Where are all the antibusing activists who assured us that the issue was not racism or integration but busing itself? If busing was wrong for children from the San Fernando Valley, then it follows that busing should be wrong for children from the inner city."[139]

By 1980, Black students in California would be more likely to attend a segregated school than students in any state in the South except Mississippi.[140] Latino students, who made up nearly one-third of the total population of Latino students in the country, had also become significantly more segregated from white students during the previous twelve years. Voluntary measures did almost nothing to alleviate these patterns of segregation, which in turn reinforced disparities in resources and educational quality. Twenty-five years after the passage of the Robbins Amendment, patterns of racial isolation and segregation in the nation's second-largest school district were at all-time highs, especially with regard to white students' isolation from Black students.[141]

Yet the fallout from the struggles over school desegregation did not exempt all white, middle-class communities. Robbins and other Proposition 1 supporters claimed that once mandatory busing was abolished, white parents would return in droves to public schools. Robbins was wrong. Years of pillorying the public school system and undermining its funding base through property tax cuts had taken a toll. The problem compounded because, as more parents abandoned the public schools, state funding for those schools (which was determined by attendance) also declined. One Reseda couple who left the public school system for a Christian school explained what they discovered after visiting their neighborhood school in hopes of reenrolling their children: "[At the visit] we learned the following: (1) The school library is no longer operated due to a lack of funds (2) The music teacher is assigned to the campus every other year (if that often) (3) There are no cultural enrichment programs due to a lack of funds (4) Maintenance on the campus has been curtailed due to a lack of funds."[142]

The couple decided they had no choice but to keep their children in private school, though the cost and long travel time to the school was burdensome. Indeed, Robbins and Weintraub could offer little comfort to parents when the school district was forced in 1982 to close ten Valley schools with low enrollment in order to save money.[143] The school closures and program cancellations augured the steady decline in taxpayer support for the state's once vaunted public education system; over the next decade, California would fall to the bottom 20 percent nationally among states in per pupil spending.[144]

Nor could Robbins offer much support to those politicians and activists he had recruited to join the Proposition 1 campaign in the name of preserving bilingual education programs. As chapter 5 reveals, the attacks on bilingual education and language rights began almost immediately after the busing debate subsided. By the mid-1990s, when ballot initiatives were launched seeking to bar undocumented immigrants from public schools and to ban bilingual education entirely, Robbins was already out of politics. In November 1991, he pled guilty to federal racketeering charges after accepting bribes from insurance companies while serving as chair of the Senate Insurance Committee. He served two years in prison.

5. "How Can You Help Unite California?"

English Only and the Politics of Exclusion, 1982-1990

The leaders of the organization U.S. English could barely contain their excitement following their meeting in the spring of 1983 with Paul Gann. Gann's reputation as one of the state's foremost ballot-initiative strategists rose quickly after his role in passing Proposition 13, the 1978 property tax–slashing measure. The following year, he qualified and passed a measure to limit government-spending growth, and in 1982 he won approval for a Victim's Bill of Rights initiative to toughen criminal sentencing guidelines. To U.S. English's delight, the seventy-one-year-old Gann offered to counsel the group in qualifying an "English Only" initiative for an upcoming California ballot. Upon returning to her office in Washington, D.C., U.S. English executive director Gerda Bikales wrote to Gann, "I am absolutely elated to know that you'll be working with us on the English Language Initiative next year. With the Master himself guiding the course, we are sure of victory!" John Tanton, the group's founder, told Gann, "[I want to] apprentice myself to you for this campaign. . . . I'm interested in spreading the practice to other states and in the development of a model initiative and referendum statute." Tanton passed along to Gann a well-known quote from Supreme Court justice Louis Brandeis about the important role states played as "laboratories of democracy" for the nation, providing opportunities to "try novel social and economic experiments without risk to the rest of the country." Above the passage Tanton scribbled, "Paul—Thought you'd like this. I've long thought of the initiative process as playing this important laboratory role."[1]

Though U.S. English had only been in formation since mid-1982, it enjoyed several important advantages. Samuel I. Hayakawa, recently retired from his single term as California senator, had agreed to be the organization's main spokesperson. Hayakawa had introduced his own constitutional amendment to declare English the nation's official language in 1981, arguing that the legislation would prevent the country from replicating the linguistic conflict and separatism fracturing his native Canada. But the amendment attracted little public attention or legislative traction. For his part, Tanton had significant nonprofit and policy advocacy experience. He worked with local chapters of the Sierra Club and Planned Parenthood before serving as national president of Zero Population Growth in the mid-1970s; he then went on to establish the Federation for American Immigration Reform (FAIR), a group that would soon play a leading role in the national effort to restrict immigration. Funding was not a problem; Tanton could count on several deep-pocketed (though unidentified) donors to help bankroll his initiative. What U.S. English needed was an audience.

Gann's invitation to learn the ropes of the California ballot initiative process provided the opportunity Tanton and his colleagues had been seeking. Within three years of meeting with Gann, U.S. English bankrolled two state ballot initiatives that passed by wide margins, launching the upstart organization into national prominence. Proposition 38, approved in November 1984, required Governor George Deukmejian to write a letter to the president and Congress requesting that "federal law be amended so that ballots, voters' pamphlets, and all other official voting materials shall be printed in English only." Proposition 63, passed in 1986, declared "English is the official language of the State of California," though it provided only vague provisions for enforcement. The fact that both ballot measures did not result in any substantive policy changes seemed to matter little to Tanton. As he wrote in a 1986 memo to other FAIR leaders, "Ideas will win out in the end, or so I believe."[2] The initiatives were more a platform to circulate and raise such ideas—"to make immigration a subject of conversation among thinking people"—than an arena to enact particular legislation.[3]

But what type of "conversation" was Tanton seeking to have and with which particular groups of "thinking people?" Given the long history in California of movements for immigrant exclusion, we might expect the English Only project to operate in a similar register: casting the growing numbers of immigrants from Asia and Latin America as threats to the nation and demanding their exclusion.[4] Indeed, scholars who have examined the English Only initiatives in California and other states have understood support for such measures as relatively transparent expressions of nativism and have sought to distinguish the specific factors—negative perceptions about the economy, large increases in migration levels, proximity to new immigrant communities, attitudes about American identity—that explain or motivate such a position.[5] In these accounts, nativism is regarded an aberration from the commitments of liberal democracy, because racial or ethnic political attachments trump liberalism's promise of formal equality.[6]

The debates inaugurated by the English Only ballot measures in California, however, suggest a more complicated relationship between the forces of nativism, race, and liberal democracy. These initiatives operated as processes of both exclusion *and* inclusion, not only limiting access to rights, resources, and opportunities (the more familiar story), but also conditioning the terms on which acceptable claims to these goods could be made. Within a political culture increasingly attentive to determinations of "innocence" and "guilt," these distinctions proved critical. English Only ballot initiatives became a generative location to establish and make visible those members of the populace whose innocence had been extinguished and who had thus forfeited their right to make claims on the polity.[7] While it would later be revealed that U.S. English founder Tanton had clear ties to white supremacist organizations, the English Only project incorporated, rather than rejected, key narratives of racial liberalism, celebrating the incorporation, empowerment, and assimilation of some immigrants even as it disavowed others. While these ballot measures were largely symbolic, with no direct impact on public policy, they rehearsed the language through which far more punitive attacks on immigrant rights would be made in the future. The measures again reveal how the racialized gaze on politics I describe as political whiteness became renovated and renewed at a time of considerable social, economic, and political change.

THE SYMBOLIC CHARACTER OF
ENGLISH ONLY LEGISLATION

Samuel I. Hayakawa was nearing the end of a single term in the U.S. Senate in 1981 when he first introduced a constitutional amendment declaring English to be the nation's official language. Compared to the accolades he earned for staring down student protestors as president of San Francisco State University in the late 1960s, Hayakawa's tenure in the Senate was largely undistinguished; a lapse of drowsiness at a Harvard conference on the eve of his arrival to Washington had earned him the name Sleepy Sam.[8] A semanticist by training, Hayakawa was a reliable conservative on most issues, but his legislative projects rarely attracted great public attention. Such was the case when Hayakawa first brought his English Only amendment to the Senate floor in April 1981. He secured a handful of sym-

Figure 8.   Samuel I. Hayakawa, August 28, 1981. A single-
term Republican senator from California, Hayakawa
nominally headed two Official English ballot measures
in the mid-1980s. Courtesy of Los Angeles Times Photo
Archives, Department of Special Collections, Charles E.
Young Research Library, University of California, Los
Angeles.

pathetic op-ed columns but found few colleagues or advocacy organizations
interested in the effort. Indeed, not since the 1920s, in a time of significant
anti-German sentiment and growing calls to restrict immigration, had
there been a national debate of any note on official language legislation.
His interest in the issue stemmed primarily from his preoccupation with

language as an obligation of citizenship and his frequent accusations that demands for minority language rights were the work of radical political projects. He blamed the upsurge in separatist sentiments in Quebec, for example, on the destructive influences of the "American Civil Rights movement" and an "aggrieved black minority." He insisted that "pressure from ambitious politicians" promised to do the same for the "influx of Hispanics" entering the United States.[9]

To broaden awareness of his amendment, Hayakawa turned to the Orange County political consultancy Butcher-Forde, which as described in chapter 4 had been instrumental in building a grassroots funding and voter base for Howard Jarvis and Proposition 13 as well as for Alan Robbins's crusade against mandatory school desegregation and busing. Butcher-Forde consultants prepared for Hayakawa a detailed "Communication Assessment and Action Plan" in order to "build a constituency for the issue and proposed legislation." The consultants described the numerous challenges his proposal would face, including "suspicion of anti-minority intentions," "suspicion of extreme Right activity," "lack of funding," and "possible infringement upon due process of law." Yet one challenge stood above all the others. Noting the central importance of identifying and mobilizing a political base to fight for the measure, Butcher-Forde pointed out to Hayakawa, "AT THIS POINT THE NATURAL CONSTITUENCY for the Amendment is not clear."[10]

What Butcher-Forde laid bare to Hayakawa was a challenge that would follow English Only advocates for the next two decades: they seemed to have a solution in search of a problem. English Only supporters were challenged to describe a specific set of rights and privileges that their legislation sought to protect. Proponents certainly attempted to express the "material" stakes of their proposals, pointing to the fiscal burdens imposed by printing multilingual ballots and election materials. Yet those costs, even when exaggerated, never attracted great attention, as they comprised only a small fraction of overall election expenditures.[11] Other arguments about a loss of entitlements—to jobs or public services—were made but never circulated widely.

Indeed, as one analysis has observed, "symbolic attitudes rather than material concerns are the predominant influence on mass preferences" for English Only policies.[12] That is, we should be cautious about assuming a particular instrumentality or coherence within the English Only effort and remain alert to the contradictions and ambivalence articulated by the diverse range of people who came to vote for English Only measures. Ultimately, Hayakawa and other U.S. English leaders were never able to answer many of the questions posed by Butcher-Forde. But they soon learned that, in qualifying a ballot measure, they did not have to.

MULTILINGUAL BALLOTS AND THE RISE OF U.S. ENGLISH

The first project U.S. English backed after its 1983 meeting with Paul Gann was an advisory ballot measure in San Francisco. Proposition O, which appeared on the November 1983 ballot, required city officials to urge the federal government to repeal legislation mandating that local jurisdictions publish election materials in languages other than English. In the mid-1970s Texas congresswoman Barbara Jordan and civil rights groups including the Mexican American Legal Defense and Education Fund led a successful effort to extend the protections of the Voting Rights Act (VRA) of 1965 to "language minority groups." In adopting the legislation, Congress clearly acknowledged the historical dimensions of language discrimination as a tool of disenfranchisement, determining that "citizens of language minorities have been effectively excluded from participation in the electoral process." The provisions were passed "in order to enforce the guarantees of the fourteenth and fifteenth amendments to the United States Constitution" by outlawing such discriminatory practices "and prescribing other remedial devices" such as bilingual ballots.[13]

Thus, as originally articulated, the VRA was a direct outgrowth of postwar civil rights efforts to secure the franchise on the part of rights-bearing citizens. The legislation specifically identified particular groups—"American Indians, Asian Americans, Alaskan Natives, and Spanish-heritage citizens"—that had been systematically excluded from the electoral process and specified the conditions under which political subdivisions had to make election materials available in particular languages. While it was also true that many proponents viewed multilingual ballots as a form of remedial assistance for voters unable to understand election materials in English—one study noted that the average readability of California ballot measures in the 1970s was the eighteenth grade level (a bachelor's degree plus two additional years)—this was not the main rationale for the VRA's language minority protections.[14] They were enacted as a response to historical patterns and practices of discrimination and disenfranchisement, akin to the literacy tests imposed on African American voters in the South.

In the late 1970s, census figures identified San Francisco as one of thirty-nine California counties that was required to furnish election materials—including registration forms, ballots, and voter information pamphlets—in languages other than English. (In San Francisco, materials were required in Spanish and Chinese; in most other jurisdictions they were only required in Spanish.)[15]

Why would English Only forces test their initiative on what was arguably the most liberal electorate in the state, and where civil rights groups had a long history of activism? The decision was partly pragmatic. Quentin Kopp, a conservative member of the San Francisco Board of Supervisors who had been active in earlier debates over bilingual education, was an outspoken opponent of the multilingual ballot requirements and was eager to take the lead on a local referendum. In addition, Stanley Diamond, a one-time Hayakawa staff member who was among the founding members of U.S. English, was also based in San Francisco.[16]

In many ways though, San Francisco was a logical place for U.S. English to launch its nascent effort. The group's strategy to popularize English Only measures centered on turning the claims that multilingual voting materials empowered language minorities against the civil rights groups that made such arguments. In these representations, it was not English-language ballots that restricted the political participation of language minorities, as civil rights groups alleged. Instead it was the multilingual ballots that marginalized language minorities by inhibiting them from learning English. U.S. English sought to represent its legislation as an attempt to free language minorities from the "illusion" that they could become fully empowered citizens without learning English, rather than as an attack on minority rights.[17]

Hayakawa continually employed such claims when he first introduced his constitutional amendment in the Senate in 1981, often with reference to his own experiences as an immigrant. He told his Senate colleagues that, as a "son of an immigrant to an English-speaking country," he believed that "we are being dishonest with linguistic minority groups if we tell them they can take full part in American life without learning the English language." The purpose of his English Only legislation, he promised, was "to insure that American democracy always strives to include in its mainstream everyone who aspires to citizenship, to insure that no one gets locked out by permanent language barriers."[18]

The campaign for Proposition O in San Francisco recited many of these themes. Sociologist Kathryn Woolard explains that proponents "recast . . . the bilingual ballot as a means of robbing minority voters of their voice." This argument "gave the referendum a meaning that was not only acceptable in polite public talk but was laudable even by progressive and pluralistic standards. . . . Removing the offending languages from the ballot [was] presented symbolically as a move toward freeing the minority language citizens." In addition, because proponents demonized "ethnic bosses," "ward-type manipulators," and "political scoundrels" who allegedly defended bilingual ballots to maintain their own base of power, "any minority leader who spoke in favor of bilingual ballots was effectively discredited, since the very act of speaking out for bilingual ballots could be interpreted as providing positive evidence of the Pro-'O' allegations of self-interest."[19]

In characterizing those who relied on multilingual ballots as "poorly informed and incompetent voters" trapped in "linguistic ghettos," proponents implicitly delegitimized their right to participate in elections while simultaneously naturalizing "English [as] a vehicle of pure information."[20] In this discourse, the voting process becomes degraded and sullied by uninformed and corruptible voters who can only prove their fitness for civic recognition and participation by renouncing their reliance on any language other than English.

In spite of opposition from Mayor Diane Feinstein, most of Kopp's colleagues on the board of supervisors, and from all of the city's Democratic clubs, San Francisco voters approved Proposition O by a margin of 62 to 38 percent. The measure passed in normally liberal-leaning areas such as Eureka Valley and Potrero Hill, as well as in the neighborhoods with the highest concentrations of African American and gay voters; it was only barely defeated in heavily Asian American and Latino areas of the city.[21] Proposition O was nonbinding—local voters did not have the authority to override a federal mandate. But the outcome affirmed U.S. English's belief that English Only campaigns could succeed without seeming to resort to strident nativist appeals; they too could command the pluralist language of minority empowerment. For many years, U.S. English leaders would remind observers that their proposal first won widespread backing in "perhaps the most liberal and ethnically diverse city in the country."[22]

Buoyed by this success, U.S. English leaders quickly established the California Committee for Ballots in English—with Stanley Diamond and Samuel Hayakawa as co-chairs—to qualify an advisory ballot measure nearly identical to Proposition O for the statewide ballot in 1984. John Tanton had established a series of nonprofit entities based in Michigan to funnel money to the projects he championed, including FAIR and U.S. English. Though the network of organizations shared many of the same consultants, staff, and funding sources, their public faces were entirely distinct. For the 1984 English Only effort, Tanton used the U.S. English Legislative Task Force to direct more than $185,000 to the California ballot initiative, which comprised more than 90 percent of the campaign's entire budget.[23] The funding allowed the California group to hire signature gatherers to circulate petitions. By June 1984, with 626,321 signatures collected, the measure was certified for the November ballot as Proposition 38.[24]

Like the San Francisco measure, Proposition 38 was purely advisory; it required the governor to write a letter to the secretary of state, Congress, and the U.S. attorney general stating that "the People of the State of California recognizing the importance of a common language in unifying our diverse nation hereby urge that Federal law be amended so that ballots, voters' pamphlets and all other official voting materials shall be printed in English only." The measure also included a "Findings" section that affirmed many of the pluralist themes tested in the Proposition O campaign. The proposition's first finding asserted that "the United States has been and will continue to be enriched by the cultural contributions of immigrants from many countries with many different traditions." It further declared that while the English language "permits interchange of ideas at many levels and encourages societal integration," multilingual ballots were "divisive, costly and often delay or prevent our immigrant citizens from moving into the economic, political, educational and social mainstream of our country."[25]

Again, U.S. English embraced the rhetoric of diversity and inclusion for specific strategic reasons. The California electorate had not even voted on a ballot initiative related to immigration or language since 1946, when it rejected a measure to extend the provisions of the anti–Japanese Alien Land Law. While the intervening period had been marked by some attempts to systematically exclude or remove large groups of immigrants—such as the Immigration and Naturalization Service's "Operation Wetback" deportations of the early 1950s and the surveillance and expulsions authorized by the McCarran-Walter Act of 1952—the state had not witnessed any significant populist or grassroots political projects aimed at immigrant exclusion or control during this time. Immigrants certainly continued to face a broad range of restrictions during this period, but a sustained anti-immigrant political project had yet to coalesce. Well into the 1980s, for example, then-senator Pete Wilson aggressively supported guestworker programs to meet the labor needs of California agribusiness.[26] Even conservative commentator Pat Buchanan denounced the proposed Simpson-Mazzoli Act in 1984 (which included increased penalties against employers for hiring undocumented workers) as an unfair attack on immigrant workers.[27]

In the early 1980s, Tanton's attempts to build a local membership base and organization in Southern California to support FAIR's goals of sharply curtailing immigration into the United States failed completely. In 1982, amid a growing recession and rising unemployment rates, Tanton took ten months away from his ophthalmology practice to work full-time on expanding local chapters of FAIR. During this period, he contracted the services of Marie Koenig, a well-connected conservative and freelance publicist based in Pasadena who was active in many right-wing issues for years, to help build a membership and donor base for FAIR. Koenig helped FAIR publicize ten billboards raised along Los Angeles area freeways, which read, "HELP US STOP ILLEGAL IMMIGRATION. The job you save may be your own," and to sponsor a press conference at the Los Angeles Press Club promoting FAIR's local work. Koenig also wrote more than a dozen personal letters on Tanton's behalf to conservative associates and friends asking them to host fund-raisers in their homes to help FAIR "become better known to the area's community leaders who are in a position to support a concerted campaign" against "illegal immigration." The press conference received little attention and Koenig failed to secure any commitments for fund-raisers or meetings with Tanton; the issue held little interest for these conservatives. FAIR eventually abandoned its strategy of growing local chapters, focusing almost exclusively on lobbying Congress and continuing its direct-mail funding appeals.[28]

FAIR's inability to ignite a local political movement around immigrant exclusion was not exceptional. The lack of a broad restrictionist movement during this time can be traced to a number of countervailing forces: the United States' geopolitical interests in cold war Asia (and to a lesser extent, Latin America); the labor needs of domestic employers in a wide range of sectors; and, as chapter 2 explores, the rise of cultural pluralism as a central current within both California and national political culture. After the passage of the Immigration and Nationality Act of 1965, which resulted in large net increases in immigration to the United States from Asia and Latin America in particular, California became the leading destination for this generation of new arrivals.[29] A 1983 *Time* magazine cover story on immigration to Los Angeles described the "exotic multitudes . . . altering the collective beat and bop of L.A., the city's smells and colors," resulting from more than two million foreign-born immigrants arriving in the metropolitan region since 1970, and ninety thousand in 1982 alone. In spite of some alarmist references to the "invasion" of the city, the magazine christened Los Angeles "the New Ellis Island," suggesting that the waves of newcomers, including "60,000 Samoans and 30,000 Thais, 200,000 Salvadorans and 175,000 Armenians," were infusing the sprawling metropolis with new life and vibrancy.[30] While there were certainly efforts to restrict immigration levels nationally and to curtail rights and benefits to various categories of immigrants, those forces had yet to coalesce.[31]

From the perspective of John Tanton, rising levels of foreign immigration to the United States posed a threat, yet there was little space for meaningful public debate over immigration policy. He claimed in a 1986 interview that "too often when you bring up the subject of immigration, you just get Emma Lazarus' poem (which appears on the Statue of Liberty) back, and that's the end of the conversation."[32] As one of Tanton's early colleagues on the board of FAIR explained, the prevailing popular assumption when the organization began was that "restrictionist ideas [against immigration] must somehow derive from the reactionary side of the national character," harkening back to an earlier era of eugenics and a concern with "racial purity."[33] Tanton and others understood that they would gain little traction in their attempts to force debate on immigration policy if they employed the harsh tones associated with the earlier era of nativism. As Tanton's colleague explained, "The restrictionist case can and must be articulated from centrist, and even liberal or radical, perspectives." Many of FAIR's early leaders met through environmental, reproductive rights, and population-control organizations in the 1970s, viewing the efforts to restrict immigration from non-European countries in particular as fully commensurate with their environmental-protection sensibilities.[34] U.S. English's Gerda Bikales, who like Tanton had strong connections to conservation organizations, explained in a 1977 essay in *National Parks and Conservation* magazine why environmentalists should take immigration restriction seriously: "The continued degradation of our environment, a growing national awareness of the adverse effects of increased population pressures upon our natural resources and of the ensuing decline of the quality of life, the swelling stream of immigrants landing on our shores and crossing our borders, and an immigration policy incapable of coping with this invasion have changed our perspective during the past decade."[35]

FAIR focused on addressing the "economic and political impact of immigration on average Americans" while generally avoiding questions of "assimilation and pluralism."[36] James Crawford, a leading critic of the English Only effort argues that the decision to establish U.S. English as a separate entity from FAIR was primarily a tactical measure: "To charge linguistic minorities with refusing to assimilate and simultaneously to propose limiting their numbers smacked of ethnic intolerance, a return to the old nativism. It would reveal an impolitic analysis . . . that the problem was not merely the quantity of new immigrants, but the *quality:* too many Hispanics."[37] It was thus entirely deliberate that U.S. English's first foray into a statewide ballot initiative was an advisory measure fused with references to "the enriching experience of living with and learning from other cultures." U.S. English had no intention of being painted as the Workingman's Party of its era.[38]

The campaign for Proposition 38 was a low-key affair. Nominally led by Samuel Hayakawa, Stanley Diamond, and Republican assemblyman Frank Hill of Whittier, another former Hayakawa staff member, the campaign contended that multilingual ballots would impose a "burden" on both taxpayers and those "earlier immigrants [who] . . . learned English in their new country in order to participate fully in American life." At the same time, the campaigners insisted that multilingual measures were a disservice to immigrants themselves, as a bilingual ballot "demean[s] . . . Hispanics and Asians" and "classifies them as 'different.'" Abolishing such ballots, they promised, would help restore, a national "unity" to a fragmented society.[39] The Proposition 38 ballot argument concluded, "The United States, as a country of immigrants from other lands with different languages and cultures, has had the enriching experience of living with and learning from other cultures. We learn from each other because we are unified by a common language, English."[40]

Collectively, these arguments demonstrate the subtle play between representations of the "worthy" and "unworthy" immigrant subjects described by political theorist Bonnie Honig.[41] In Honig's account, nativist political projects must be examined in connection to (rather than as an aberration from) the familiar and celebrated claims that the United States is a nation founded by immigrants. These accounts of xenophilia are continually rehearsed in representations of immigrants as redemptive and idealized economic, civic, and familial subjects—the "supercitizen" who is committed to national ideals of citizenship and democracy, who contributes to the national economy, and who obeys conservative, often patriarchic social norms. Through these practices, the good immigrant thus affirms foundational narratives of exceptionalism and choiceworthiness in a moment when such ideals and practices seem increasingly out of reach for much of the populace. This redemptive figure is contrasted to the "bad" immigrant—the menacing newcomer who takes jobs, welfare, and other goods from the nation; disregards prevailing social norms; and remains ambivalent or even hostile toward national ideals of patriotism and citizenship—the subject of intense xenophobia.[42]

Honig's work helps to explain the contradictory representation of immigrants within the debate over Proposition 38. On the one hand, immigrants were characterized as a threat to the integrity of the democratic system—uninformed and easily "led into block [sic] voting by opportunistic political leaders" as well as potential perpetrators of voter "abuse" and fraud. And they were explicitly racialized: the Proposition 38 ballot argument asserted, "Only Hispanic, Asian American, American Indian and Alaskan native languages are targeted for special treatment in the law." Finally, by making continual references to "foreign language ballots," the measure suggested that the nation's linguistic heritage and character was defined by English alone and that the quality of American exceptionalism extended from this tradition of a "unified common language."[43] Erased in this account is California's own history of official bilingualism—the state's first constitution in 1849 was written in both English and Spanish, and the Treaty of Guadalupe Hidalgo ceding California from Mexico to the United State has been interpreted by many as providing Spanish and English equal standing in government and education.[44] Absent this history, these xenophobic narratives figure the immigrant as the "taker"—the "free-rider" who drains the nation of social, political, and economic resources.

On the other hand, the narrative offered by Proposition 38 proponents left open, and even celebrated, the possibility of immigrant redemption and inclusion. By fetishizing a mythical earlier generation of newcomers who learned English as a matter of course and contributed to the nation-building project, these narratives instruct the current generation of immigrants on their obligation to do the same. Honig points to the figure of the "immigrant supercitizen" in such claims—exemplified by the ubiquitous photos of large groups of proud newcomers participating in citizenship swearing-in ceremonies; in sustaining and reproducing a "nationalist narrative of choiceworthiness." Here we have the figure of the foreigner as the "giver"—dutifully contributing to the economy, modeling traditional relations of family, and reperforming the ritual of consent and choice central to the founding myths of the country. Yet as Honig points out, this iconic characterization is hardly innocuous: "Since the presumed test of both a good and a bad foreigner is the measure of her contribution to the restoration of the nation rather than, say, to the nation's transformation or attenuation, nationalist xenophilia tends to feed and (re)produce nationalist xenophobia as its partner."[45]

Following Honig's analysis, we can understand the ideological work embodied in even an advisory measure such as Proposition 38. The initiative's proponents rehearsed the terms by which a renewed public debate over immigration as a "problem" might be conducted. Even opponents would have to frame their arguments in these terms, celebrating the "good immigrant" narrative in order to discredit the attacks implicit in the proposed measure. The *Los Angeles Times* editorial against Proposition 38 concluded, "Thousands of Latinos and Asians have found California a hospitable state in which to live. They strive for good jobs, they look for a good place to raise their children, they seek economic opportunity and political tolerance." The ballot argument against Proposition 38 similarly asserted that "Hispanics and Asian Americans want very much to learn English. It is one of the keys to economic advancement and social integration. . . . In fact, bilingual ballots encourage assimilation by encouraging all citizens to participate in their government." Here, the consenting, productive, and loyal immigrant is deployed to undermine representations of the immigrant as "taker." Yet as Honig points out, "xenophilic insistence that immigrants are givers to the nation itself feeds the xenophobic anxiety that they might really be takers from it."[46] In both representations, immigrants are charged with an obligation to perform and reproduce a host of practices and relations necessary to sustain the nation.

The organized opposition to Proposition 38 was extremely limited—it consisted of a few ad hoc groups spread across the state. Cesar Chavez organized several press conferences and rallies in conjunction with a voter-education mobilization designed to defeat the proposition and several other Republican-backed initiatives on the same ballot. Chavez offered a different analysis of the problem presented by Proposition 38, arguing that proponents were attempting to block the rights of farmworkers to vote in order to "do something about racism in the schools, how the police treat . . . kids, and the way Anglo politicians take our people for granted."[47] Indeed, for the most part, the original vision animating the campaign to win multilingual ballots in the 1970s—the historical disenfranchisement of language minority voters by the state—was almost completely lost in the debates initiated by Proposition 38.[48] More often, bilingual ballots were defended as a regrettable but necessary form of remedial assistance, described by one Proposition 38 opponent in Los Angeles as a small concession to "allow 9,300 elderly Latinos to read voting materials in their own language."[49]

Proposition 38 was approved by more than 70 percent of the statewide electorate and passed in all fifty-eight counties. In San Francisco, 56 percent of voters favored the measure, a slight decrease from the 62 percent that had approved of Proposition O twelve months earlier. It is interesting to note that while the measure passed in liberal, predominantly white cities such as Santa Monica, it was defeated soundly in Inglewood and Compton, two cities bordering Los Angeles with large numbers of African American voters.[50] Relative to the other five initiatives on the ballot, which

TABLE 4 Polling Trends for Proposition 38, 1984

Response	Early Sept. (%)	Early Oct. (%)	Late Oct. (%)
Have not seen/heard	50	40	27
Have seen/heard	50	60	73
Favor	68	59	61
Oppose	27	35	26
Undecided	5	5	12

SOURCE: California Poll, nos. 84–05, 84–06, 84–07, http://ucdata
.berkeley.edu (accessed April 1, 2007).

collectively drew more than $32 million in campaign expenditures, only
$120,000 was spent on the Proposition 38 campaign, all of it by propo-
nents.[51] In spite of these relatively small expenditures, as table 4 demonstrates, three polls taken in the two months before the elections suggested
that voters were widely familiar with the measure by Election Day.

U.S. English again secured the outcome it sought. As Stanley Diamond
argued just before the election, "California is the first test in the nation. . . .
We think if we win and it is overwhelming, Congress is going to have to
pay very close attention to this."[52]

PROPOSITION 63: THE OFFICIAL ENGLISH MEASURE

Within two months after the passage of Proposition 38, Assemblyman
Frank Hill introduced a bill in the state legislature to declare English
the state's official language. Hill's legislation mirrored much of Samuel
Hayakawa's 1981 proposed federal constitutional amendment; its primary
enforcement mechanism required the legislature to "endorse" the official
language "by appropriate legislation." Hill suggested that the measure was
in large part symbolic: "Keep in mind that we have an official state bird
(the valley quail) and an official state flower (the California poppy). . . .
There is no reason we shouldn't have an official state language."[53]

At the same time, emboldened by the passage of Proposition 38, U.S.
English began positioning the legislation as a response to the state's burgeoning Spanish-speaking population. Hill claimed that the overwhelming
passage of Proposition 38 demonstrated that Californians did not want a
bilingual society. Hayakawa explained that what proponents called the
Official English bill was "an Hispanic issue. . . . Many [Latino] students

go to transitional classes in which they are taught in Spanish year after year . . . [and] graduate from the sixth or eighth grade without knowing English worth a damn."[54]

Hill's legislation did not make it out of the assembly's Democratic-controlled Government Organization Committee. While other Republicans expressed support for the measure, no one could suggest that their constituents were specifically clamoring for an Official English law. Only six states carried similar legislation on their books; several were relics of World War I–era policies adopted in a time of considerable anti-German sentiment. Hill's legislation was quickly put to a vote and lost. When Stanley Diamond asked the committee chair, Richard Alatorre, for the debate to be extended, the Los Angeles assemblyman replied, "I'm from Mexico and bilingual. I find your bill offensive."[55]

Hayakawa and Diamond immediately promised another statewide ballot initiative to carry their Official English legislation. Alatorre's snub soon found its way into U.S. English's steady stream of direct-mail fundraising solicitations. Always signed by Hayakawa, the appeals described a looming crisis that required the reader's immediate attention: "In recent years, something has been going on that concerns me deeply. Some ethnic leaders seem to have a goal of creating several bilingual and bicultural states. . . . Foremost among the states marked for bilingualism is California." Quoting Alatorre's stern rebuke to Diamond, Hayakawa asked, "Have any other ethnic leaders, in all our history, ever made such statements! I think not." A call to action always followed: "I hope I can depend on you. It's *not too late*. We must save our common language before the erosion becomes irreversible."[56] Readers who lived in California were urged to circulate and return petitions in order to get the measure on the ballot. Other mailings typically included surveys for readers to complete and return to U.S. English, posing questions such as "Do you favor providing election materials in foreign languages?" The envelopes, with a photo of Hayakawa, similarly asked, "I need your opinion. . . . Should *English* be designated the Official Language of the United States?" Devices such as these not only brought tens of thousands of new members into U.S. English, they reinforced the organization's populist image—while the government ignored the people, U.S. English solicited their opinions.[57]

U.S. English's use of the ballot initiative and its heavy reliance on direct mail registered the influence that Paul Gann's and Howard Jarvis's antitax efforts had on issue-based advocacy organizations nationally. While some liberally oriented groups working on issues such as environmental protection and the nuclear freeze made use of similar tactics, they were taken up most widely by conservative-leaning organizations.[58] Five of the six measures on the 1984 ballot—including Proposition 38, a Jarvis tax-limitation measure, and a proposal to drastically cut the state's welfare program—were sponsored by Republican politicians or conservative activists.[59] Gann's Sacramento-based People's Advocate organization in particular had refined a systematic process for using both direct mail and paid petitioners to meet signature-collection goals. In this way, the organization could claim a wide base of "members" and "volunteers" while still maintaining tight control over the signature-gathering process.[60]

Even before Hill's proposal was rejected by the state legislature, U.S. English established the California English Campaign to begin qualifying the legislation for the 1986 ballot. The campaign received nearly all of its financial support over the next twenty-two months—about $800,000 all together—from U.S. English and its related subsidiaries. U.S. English claimed that half of its two hundred thousand nationwide members in 1986 resided in California, and Diamond always painted the organization as a volunteer-driven operation operating on a shoestring budget. Yet because the organization, like the Gann group, did not rely on rallies, meetings or other collective actions, its grassroots involvement and activity could never be evaluated. Only Diamond, Hayakawa, Hill, and a handful of others made public statements on behalf of the campaign.[61]

For its purposes, U.S. English's model of armchair membership was highly effective. The group utilized mailing lists from other organizations supported by John Tanton, such as Californians for Population Control, to send blank petitions and fund-raising appeals, and it paid American Petition Consultants nearly $350,000 to collect signatures.[62] In July 1986, Hayakawa announced that the effort had collected more than one million signatures to qualify the proposed constitutional amendment for the ballot, the third-highest total in the history of the state.

The language of Proposition 63 struck an effective balance between symbolic declarations of state efforts "to preserve, protect and strengthen the English language" without mentioning any specific policies or programs that would be subject to repeal. Proponents could thus gesture toward the types of programs they viewed with mistrust—"governmental bilingual activities [that] cost millions of taxpayers' dollars each year"—without giving opponents fodder to claim the measure would harm essential services. In addition, proponents took great pains to clarify that the measure only applied to government business. Hayakawa explained that "in unofficial, private or religious or other circumstances, you can use any language you like. You can have a prayer meeting, a crap game or a bingo tournament in any language you like, but English is to be the language of government."[63]

Such exemptions were dictated by tactics more than principle. Indeed, in 1985, Diamond organized a letter-writing campaign to the local phone company, protesting the decision to publish a Spanish-language Yellow Pages, declaring in a letter to local U.S. English supporters that "Pacific Bell needs to be made aware of the American public's concern about the erosion of English and its conviction that the Spanish Yellow Pages further reduce the incentive to learn our language." Diamond also attacked the Philip Morris corporation the same year, suggesting its advertising in Spanish was promoting "dangerous divisiveness."[64]

• Diamond renounced all such claims in the effort to pass Proposition 63. The campaign repeatedly emphasized "languages in the home, church, private affairs, and private businesses are not affected." Diamond and others even objected whenever the measure was characterized as English Only legislation (they insisted on the title "Official English"), even though it was U.S. English leaders who first introduced the term "English Only" in the campaign for Proposition 38.[65] In addition, while the implementation mechanisms were vague, Proposition 63 did contain a section that gave citizens a standing right to sue the state in order to enforce the measure's findings, a provision that Official English measures in other states did not include.

• In the public debate that followed, Proposition 63's endorsers never tired of declaring the antiracist commitments of the measure. The *San Francisco Examiner* editorialized that the measure would "work to the vast benefit of immigrants and others in our society whose prospects for livelihood too often are crippled by deficiency in the language that propels this country's economic life." The paper declared that "majority that favors this proposition is not racist or xenophobic, but simply realistic. We think the California majority wants to help immigrants to assimilate and succeed, rather than to raise a barrier against them. This is a law to help improve the melting pot, not interfere with it.[66]

U.S. English similarly contended that it operated "squarely within the American political mainstream, and reject[ed] all manifestations of cultural or linguistic chauvinism."[67] In a mailer titled, "How Can You Help Unite California?" Hayakawa confronted the issue directly, stating that "the racist argument is the argument of desperation by the opposition. The amendment encourages all immigrants to become fluent and literate in English. . . . Racist slurs usually come from ethnic political leaders who attempt to maintain political leadership with fear statements and distorted information."[68]

These arguments illustrate how the very debate over Official English legislation articulated and naturalized several propositions about the relationship between language, race, and political power. First, the campaign figured opposition to multilingualism in government as a race-neutral position disembodied from any relations of power or authority. From this perspective, the history of language discrimination and disenfranchisement that animated the efforts in the 1960s and 1970s to win multilingual ballots, bilingual education, and other public programs became cast as a narrow debate over language acquisition and assimilation strategies. Originally, the provision of multilingual services and programs implicitly recognized the claims-making rights of historically excluded language minorities. In the English Only debate, it was these very claims-making rights that were negated; multilingual services were unjustified because they were an accommodation to those who lacked standing to make such demands.

Second, Proposition 63 proponents represented those whose primary language was not English—always immigrants from Mexico, Latin America, and Asia—as having a disability and problem that Official English legislation sought to cure. References to "sending a message" that English fluency was a prerequisite for social mobility characterized these same groups as unmotivated and lacking in an ambition shared by earlier generations of immigrants. As Hayakawa commented, "The problem of California is that it is very often oversensitive to linguistic minorities and, in effect, encourages many not to learn English at all by making life too easy for people who don't speak English."[69] Here, the rewards of citizenship and recognition before the polity become tied to a particular behavior—learning English, joining the mainstream, and fulfilling the historical obligation of the newcomer to celebrate the nation's exception and promise. Implicitly, those who chose not to obey these expectations forfeited their rights to political recognition and standing.

Third, Proposition 63 proponents posited that English alone was the language of enterprise, education, and, most importantly, progress. "Ethnic enclaves" were pathologized as marginal sites of public life. Other languages (and cultures) could be used in private settings, but they must be excluded from the public sphere in order to safeguard the common good. As University of Southern California journalism professor Felix Gutierrez pointed out in an essay published in the *Los Angeles Herald Examiner*, most large corporations would not agree with this contention: "Spanish is fast becoming a language of commerce in the state. . . . The amendment, if it passes, is unlikely to stop companies from telling Latinos 'Coke Lo

Es,' or urging them to ask for 'Otra fria, otra Coors.'" Gutierrez argued that while Spanish speakers would still get targeted for their consumer dollars and taxes, they would receive fewer "services than their English-speaking neighbors." Thus, "the existing social, economic and educational gaps between Anglos and Latinos would grow, not diminish."[70] By characterizing English as the privileged medium of citizenry and progress, the measure naturalized the claim that English speakers were entitled to benefits and rights to which non-English speakers were not.

Finally, Official English proponents invited observers to recognize in the measure a problem that went well beyond language acquisition and effective citizenry. Caltech political scientist Bruce Cain gave voice to such a proposition when he observed that "there are a lot of reasonable people out there who are worried about what's going to happen to California society if we have too many people who don't speak English, who have a genuine concern about whether the fabric of society can absorb so many new people."[71] That is, in staging a public debate over a relatively innocuous advisory measure, English Only proponents depicted and framed a much larger political question in racial terms: In an era of fiscal limitations and austerity, who was "fit for citizenship?" What limitations could the "innocent" members of the populace—the native-born, dutiful citizens who worked hard, spoke English, and paid taxes—place on those who were clearly not innocent? And what must newcomers, especially from Asia and Mexico and other parts of Latin America, do in order to prove their fitness to the other members of the populace?[72]

Indeed, connections between language debates and immigration levels were precisely what Tanton and others at U.S. English hoped to kindle. Tanton explained in an interview that the "language question is derivative of immigration policy. Large numbers of immigrants are coming from the same (non-English) language backgrounds. They create communities where English is not spoken . . . [leading to] institutional segregation and a gradual loss of national unity."[73] Provoking a public debate on language policy created space for longer-term political efforts to "to make immigration a subject of conversation among thinking people."

OPPOSITION TO PROPOSITION 63

In mid-August, Californians United against Proposition 63 launched their campaign, almost a month and a half after the measure qualified for the ballot. An ACLU leader quickly conceded that the opposition should have begun organizing soon after the passage of Proposition 38; U.S. English already had a fifteen-month head start in framing its issue, raising funds, and constituting an audience for the measure through the signature-gathering process and direct-mail appeals.[74]

A coalition of unions, civil rights, and advocacy organizations led the opposition, including the ACLU, the California Teachers Association, the Service Employees International Union, the Mexican American Political Association, the Japanese American Citizens League, and at least eighteen other Latino and Asian American advocacy groups.[75] Support from prominent African American organizations was less forthcoming; the NAACP, a faithful opponent of all of the earlier anti–civil rights ballot initiatives addressed in this book, did not formally join the coalition, perhaps still frustrated by the lack of support it had received in the school-desegregation struggles a few years earlier. The campaign raised only $120,000, securing minor donations from groups such as the Bank of Canton, the Chinese Chamber of Commerce, and Phillip Morris, which had been the target of earlier criticism by U.S. English for its Spanish-language advertising.[76]

With no funds for television or radio advertising and only a limited budget for voter mailings and other printed materials, the opposition focused on securing endorsements and disseminating information to its members. It developed and distributed a hefty information kit filled with a detailed analysis of the measure's faults and offered a wide range of factual evidence to counter the proponents' arguments. Like the opponents of Proposition 14 in 1964 and the antibusing initiatives of the 1970s, the anti–Proposition 63 coalition won the battle over official endorsements. Only a handful of groups and elected officials, including the California Republican Party, the American Legion, and Senator Pete Wilson, endorsed the measure. Even several members of U.S. English's advisory board—high-profile figures whom the organization listed on its letterhead and in most of its official communications—withdrew their support for the organization because of Proposition 63. Norman Cousins, the former editor of the *Saturday Review*, resigned from his board position during the campaign, stating that while he was sympathetic to the "original concern of the sponsors" of Proposition 63, he feared "a momentum may have been created that is carrying us in an unwise and unhealthy direction" because of the "negative symbolic significance" of the measure. Others listed as advisory board members, including newsman Walter Cronkite and authors Gore Vidal and Saul Bellow, claimed they were either unaware of the measure or opposed it.[77]

By contrast, many of the state's most recognizable political leaders came out strongly against the measure. Republican governor George Deukmejian issued a statement calling Proposition 63 an "unnecessary, confusing and counterproductive way to emphasize the importance of a common language" that would "cause fear, confusion and resentment among many minority Californians, who see the measure as an effort to legislate the cultural superiority of native English-speaking people."[78] The ballot arguments against Proposition 63 were signed by Attorney General John Van de Kamp, San Francisco mayor Diane Feinstein, Assembly Speaker Willie Brown, and Los Angeles police chief Daryl Gates. Most of the state's leading newspapers, including the *San Diego Tribune, Stockton Register, San Francisco Chronicle,* and *Los Angeles Times* editorialized against the initiative.[79] The *Sacramento Bee,* which had endorsed Proposition 38, called the Official English measure "unnecessary and therefore gratuitously insulting to the millions of Californians who come from other nations and have totally committed themselves to this country."[80]

The arguments advanced by the campaign against Proposition 63 largely worked within the framework established by the proponents. The anti-63 campaign sought to challenge the claim that recent immigrants were reluctant to learn English or to participate in the mainstream of California society. Samuel Hayakawa had argued that Proposition 63 would "protect California against Hispanic leaders who say America must become a bilingual nation," while Frank Hill had testified at a legislative hearing that Latino civil rights groups sought to keep Latino immigrants in "a language ghetto, a language barrio, where they're out of touch with the common language of this country."[81] To discredit such charges, opponents offered an alternative account, one of hardworking immigrants anxious to "contribute to and enter the mainstream of American life." The ballot argument against Proposition 63 asserted that "the overwhelming majority of immigrants *want* to learn English . . . a recent study shows that 98% of Latin [sic] parents say it is essential for their children to read and write English well. Asians, Latinos and other recent immigrants fill long waiting lists for English courses at community colleges and adult schools." It was legislation such as Proposition 63, opponents charged, that would "*discourage* rather than encourage the assimilation of new citizens," thus "preventing them from becoming better, more involved citizens while making the transition into American society."[82] Opponents frequently cited a RAND study that reported that 90 percent of first-generation Mexican Americans born in the U.S. were proficient in English and that by the second generation the majority spoke English only. They also pointed to the tens of thousands of people on waiting lists for spaces in English as a second language (ESL) classes across the state.[83]

While celebrating the civic commitment and determination of recent immigrants, Proposition 63's opponents also implicitly conceded that new immigrants might well pose a problem to other Californians. The anti-63 ballot argument quoted from a resolution passed by the Los Angeles County Board of Supervisors against the measure, which stated: "In many areas . . . non-English-speaking persons have sometimes represented a problem for schoolteachers, service providers, law enforcement officers, who are unable to understand them. The problem will be solved over time as newcomers learn English. It has happened many times before in our history. In the meanwhile . . . common sense . . . good will, sensitivity, and humor will help us through this challenging period."[84]

Another main argument made by Proposition 63 opponents was that the measure violated American traditions of fair play, tolerance, and respect for difference. An anti-63 flyer charged that "by legally sanctioning the punishment of those with limited language ability, Proposition 63 breeds intolerance and bigotry." The cover of one of the pamphlets published by the campaign read, "America! Where people come from all over the world seeking freedom," and included an image of the Statue of Liberty. Another publication labeled the measure an "un-American idea" that threatened to "tarnish California's proud history of tolerance and diversity." The ballot argument similarly contrasted the recent centennial anniversary of the Statue of Liberty—"that glorious 4th of July brought all Americans together"—against Proposition 63's intention to "divide us and tarnish our proud heritage of tolerance and diversity."[85] Thus, according to Irvin R. Lai, national president of the Chinese-American Citizens Alliance, Proposition 63's proponents were "anti-minority, anti-immigration and anti–foreign language."[86]

It would be folly to suggest that a different set of ballot arguments or messages would have reversed the outcome of the election. Not only did the measure's proponents have an enormous advantage in terms of resources and preparation, the very framing of an Official English ballot question left little ground for dissent. In the brief amount of time most voters dedicate to deliberating any particular ballot initiative, offering another account of Proposition 63's consequences was almost impossible. The measure's ambiguity was its strength. It effectively invoked the spectacle of a problem—a menacing, racially marked other bent on fracturing the cultural unity of the populace—while reciting familiar pluralist shibboleths.

Though the measure's overwhelming success on Election Day suggests its passage was inevitable, the opposition's arguments and strategy are critical to examine for several reasons. First, the campaign's late start and limited base of grassroots support registered an important restriction in the reach and capacity of immigrant rights organizations during this period. U.S. English spent years in the early 1980s contemplating, testing, and refining approaches to shaping the public debate over language policy and (by implication) immigration. The group effectively constituted an audience for its arguments and adopted a long-term strategy to influence public perceptions. The legal advocacy and policy organizations that led much of the resistance to Proposition 63 had little experience or capacity in communicating directly to the electorate; their strengths and talents lay elsewhere. Once the measure reached the ballot, they became almost spectators to the process.

Second, opponents of Proposition 63 echoed many of the arguments of the measure's backers. The narratives animating both campaigns were remarkably similar, tailored as they were to the expectations of political whiteness. Indeed, after the election, Stanley Diamond declared the result "a victory for all of us, including our opposition. In a fundamental sense, we have the same goals."[87] Both sides celebrated the nation's traditions of diversity and inclusion in the most exceptionalist terms. Because questions of power and structure were rendered unintelligible in such accounts, language-policy debates become *depoliticized*, disembodied from any relations of hierarchy or authority. The campaign against Proposition 63 valorized the same representation of the "good immigrant" committed to rapid assimilation, patriotism, and national belonging—the iconic supercitizen—while begging "good will, sensitivity, and humor" for those struggling with this charge. Yet as Bonnie Honig suggests, this celebrated figure always summons and even requires its opposite—the "bad immigrant" who takes rather than gives and who must be excluded from the body politic.

Finally, in raising the specters of extremism and catastrophe, the anti-63 campaign actually provided a reliable foil against which the measure's proponents could define their own innocence. That is, every time the initiative's opponents accused the measure's sponsors of ethnocentrism or intolerance—invoking the figure of the narrow-minded bigot incapable of accepting difference—it gave proponents an opportunity to assert their own pluralist commitments and values. It was not *all* immigrants they opposed—only those whose behavior threatened the polity. These immigrants, in fact, did not have rights that could be violated; they had forfeited such rights by refusing to assume the proper values and conduct. In largely ceding this point, opponents' charges of racism seemed unfounded. Racism, as defined in this discourse, involves the denial of recognition or power based on ascriptive characteristics—ethnicity, race, nationality, and so forth. Here, because it was (allegedly) behavior or conduct rather than such ascriptive characteristics that served as the basis of exclusion, racism could not be charged.

The rationale in crafting such arguments in order to defeat the measure was clear. If the white electorate could be convinced of the benign, even positive intentions and aspirations of most immigrants, their antipathies might not be aroused. As Senator Art Torres insisted, "We're not here to take over the state, but to contribute to it and make it the best in the nation."[88] But by accepting and even endorsing the position that some immigrants might be less than worthy of the benefits of citizenship and political recognition, anti-63 activists did little to contest the larger purpose of this project, which was to naturalize and nourish an articulation between language, nationality, race, and political power. That is, in extolling the exemplary citizenship practices of immigrants—hardworking, taxpaying, law-abiding subjects who simply want to purse the American Dream—English Only proponents implicitly acknowledged both the presence and the threat of those newcomers who did not seem to fulfill these expectations.

THE PROPOSITION 63 ELECTION AND ITS AFTERMATH

Voter awareness of Proposition 63 was extremely high; by early September, more than 90 percent of respondents to one poll had heard of the measure, and more than two-thirds stated they intended to vote yes.[89] Indeed the measure ultimately passed in all fifty-eight counties and by 73 percent statewide. The California Poll suggested that support tended to be higher among conservatives, Republicans, and white voters, though the proposition was also backed among Democrats and the small samples of Black and Asian voters polled. It even passed in heavily Democratic cities such as San Francisco (53 percent yes), Oakland (51 percent yes), and Santa Monica (58 percent yes).[90] Only among Latinos (who according to one estimate voted against the measure by a margin of 60 to 40 percent) and moderate to strong liberals was the measure rejected.[91]

Immediately after the election, U.S. English leaders went on the offensive. Stanley Diamond told the *Oakland Tribune*, "I believe that we tapped into deep, deep feelings of resentment that voters have against immigrants who they perceive as being unwilling to learn English."[92] Assemblyman Hill declared he would sponsor legislation to curtail bilingual education programs as well as multilingual welfare services and driver's license tests.[93] J. William Orozco, a Southern California spokesman for the campaign, called for the elimination of school notices sent home in languages other than English, adding "if you continue to put crutches under people, they're never going to learn English."[94] U.S. English soon announced the creation of a Center for the Implementation of Proposition 63 to coordinate potential legal actions and other activities aimed at implementing the measure.[95] Jessica Fiske, director of the ACLU of Southern California, declared that she was "expecting an avalanche" of litigation and other actions.[96]

In early 1987, Diamond filed a complaint under Proposition 63's enforcement provisions, which allowed individuals the right to sue the state to enforce the legislation. Diamond sought to compel San Francisco and two other municipalities to stop providing multilingual election materials, claiming such materials violated the initiative. Attorney General John Van de Kamp issued a nonbinding determination that interpreted the law as only requiring voting materials to be made available in English, rather than prohibiting such materials from being available in languages other than English. The legislature, for its part, also refused to enact any of the bills proposed by Hill and others to specifically ban particular multilingual materials or programs.[97]

Diamond was furious and promised an overwhelming backlash. He excoriated lawmakers for seeking to "cripple, gut, and emasculate the Amendment that was the Will of THE PEOPLE." Diamond declared, "THE PEOPLE are stirring, blood pressures are moving up. There is a whisper out there on the way to a relentless, irreversible roar. Can you get away with this one? It's HELL, HELL, no."[98]

Diamond soon promised a $200,000 fund-raising drive to support lawsuits against school districts or local government entities in Los Angeles, San Francisco, Alameda County, and San Diego.[99] His threats echoed Frank Hill's earlier promise that if lawmakers refused to implement the measure, the California English Campaign would return to "its network of 60,000 volunteers, put it on the ballot and pass it over the heads of the Legislature."[100]

Yet over the next five years, only six lawsuits (all by private individuals) were filed under the enforcement provisions of the measure; five dealt with English Only rules in the workplace.[101] No significant individual or collective challenges emerged to force implementation of the measure. Part of this inaction stemmed from the tactical interests of U.S. English in other states. Aggressive litigation or enforcement of Proposition 63 might have compromised the prospects of English Only ballot initiatives and legislation the group was backing in other states, including Florida, Colorado, and

Arizona. Indeed, by mid-1987, leaders such as Samuel Hayakawa seemed content with realizing the symbolic intentions of the ballot measure without ending any particular programs.[102]

But even if U.S. English decided against bringing such actions, why did the "relentless, irreversible roar" promised by Diamond fail to materialize? After all, the initiative provided any individual or citizen's group the standing to sue in state court if they felt a state or local agency was violating the initiative. And there was no shortage of programs in California that employed and provided multilingual materials and services: about one in eight of California's four million public school students were enrolled in some sort of program for English-language learners, and the state government had established at least 3,300 positions for bilingual workers to assist members of the public in accessing motor-vehicle, unemployment, and other services.[103] Given the overwhelming passage of the measure, why did no effort emerge to challenge such programs?

Here, we must be cautious in interpreting the widespread endorsement of Proposition 63 in singular or unequivocal terms. Most polls conducted on English Only measures suggest a more complicated perspective. On the one hand, in nearly every poll conducted, respondents endorsed the concept of declaring English the official language (in fact, large majorities assumed that it already was) and agreed with statements that speaking and writing in English was important in "making someone a true American" and that "if you live in the U.S. you should be able to speak English."[104]

On the other hand, contrary to the interpretation offered not only by Hill and Diamond, but often by their opponents, support for measures such as Proposition 63 did not express a monolithic stance against multilingualism or immigrants not fluent in English. In a 1988 California Poll, only 18 percent of Anglo respondents stated they were "very worried" that the growth of Latino and Asian communities would threaten the "American way of life."[105] A survey conducted by a UCLA graduate student found that respondents offered wide-ranging and sometimes contradictory understandings of the legislation. Only a small percentage of respondents to the California Poll found that support for the measure stemmed from an instrumental concern such as reducing the costs imposed by providing multilingual services and materials.[106] Other state and national polls consistently evidenced support for non-English-speaking immigrants to maintain their native language and customs. As political scientist Jack Citrin and colleagues concluded, "public opinion data suggest that attitudes towards immigrants are ambivalent." The success of Proposition 63 and other Official English measures, they argued, reflected the way groups such as U.S. English "won the battle over how to define the symbolic meaning of language policy" by "infusing this stance with patriotic overtones" and nationalist affirmations.[107] The decision not to enforce Proposition 63 did not trigger a popular backlash because voters did not share or express a singular consensus on the initiative's meaning, purpose, or intentions.

Yet as a statement of ideological commitment and consensus, the measure largely rendered such ambivalences imperceptible. Proposition 63 instead suggested—even performed—the conclusion that a vast majority of the electorate stood unwaveringly opposed to a multilingual society. As important, its widespread passage reinforced the proponents' claims that the measure had "nothing to do with race." As one pollster concluded, "I don't think anybody is prepared to say in excess of 70 percent of the voters in California are racist."[108]

These two seemingly paradoxical conclusions—that the electorate was strongly and perhaps unalterably hostile toward multilingualism (and by extension toward many immigrants) and that this hostility was racially innocent—increasingly became treated as unassailable within statewide political culture. This effect would soon embolden other political actors to launch more aggressive, populist assaults targeting the so-called bad immigrants and their elite protectors. In addition, the Official English initiatives helped reinforce the perspective that making forceful antiracist claims before the electorate was self-defeating. Official English opponents concluded that the majority of voters viewed most immigrants with suspicion and antagonism, and it was futile to counter this innate hostility. As the ACLU's Jessica Fiske commented, the Proposition 63 outcome had "an undertone of fear—people have looked at the changing demographics and they have voted . . . out of a sense of panic."[109]

THE RISE AND FALL OF U.S. ENGLISH

For the first two years after the Proposition 63 triumph, U.S. English continued its rapid ascent. In 1987 alone, thirty-seven state legislatures deliberated Official English measures, primarily at the behest of U.S. English. Five states—Arkansas, Mississippi, North Carolina, North Dakota, and South Carolina—adopted the legislation. The following November, the organization replicated the California initiative campaign with equal success in Arizona, Colorado, and Florida; sixteen states now had official English policies. In addition, the organization hired as president Linda Chavez, who won acclaim in conservative circles for her opposition to affirmative action as a Reagan-appointed director of the U.S. Commission on Civil Rights. While Chavez had few admirers among other Latinos, she helped burnish U.S. English's image as an inclusive organization free of racial enmity.[110]

But a month before the November 1988 presidential election, the *Arizona Republic* printed portions of a confidential memo written by John Tanton two years earlier. The memo—prepared for a close-knit group of Tanton's colleagues from FAIR, U.S. English, and allied organizations—contemplated hypothetical and largely apocalyptic scenarios that might result if immigration from Mexico and Latin America continued unabated. He warned of "ill-educated people" who would bring "the tradition of the *mordida* (bribe)" and a corrupt Catholicism into U.S. politics. Tanton asked, "Will the present majority peaceably hand over its political power to a group that is simply more fertile? . . . As Whites see their power and control over their lives declining, will they simply go quietly into the night? . . . Perhaps this is the first instance in which those with their pants up are going to get caught by those with their pants down!"[111]

A torrent of negative publicity unfolded after the memo's disclosure. Chavez quickly resigned in protest, and Tanton soon quit his own position as board chair. The scandal also focused new attention on U.S. English's financial sponsors. Proposition 63 opponents had attempted to challenge the large amounts of cash proponents had received from a variety of Michigan-based funding sources. All of this funding, it turned out, was connected to a single corporate entity, U.S. Inc., used by Tanton to channel money from several ultraconservative foundations and donors, including the secretive Pioneer Fund, a longtime supporter of eugenicist and other "race betterment" projects. A subsequent series of investigative articles published by James Crawford revealed several figures with connections to white supremacist and neo-Nazi formations within Tanton's circles. Tanton steadfastly maintained his own racial innocence, declaring in a letter to supporters, "No, I am not a racist. I want to bring all members of the American family together to share in our Thanksgiving feast—but I want us to be able to speak to each other when we're gathered around the table. Make no mistake, my desire for national unity is my real sin."[112]

THE IMPACT OF CALIFORNIA'S ENGLISH ONLY MEASURES

How can Tanton's use of the California initiative process as a political laboratory to test his vision for national unity best be evaluated? As policy measures, the initiatives carried no weight. Today, the state and many local governments conduct a wide range of business in multiple languages, including the publication of multiracial ballots, with little objection from the public. Moreover, the Official English movement has no significant presence in state politics; its agenda seems quite removed from the immediate concerns of most Californians.[113]

Yet the debates inaugurated by Propositions 38 and 63 are still worthy of attention. These initiatives did not simply give voice to a preexisting, fully formed nativist identity that was unleashed by a large wave of newcomers. Instead, the debates reveal the ways in which a set of political actors attempted to shape contradictory, often ambivalent ideas about immigration and language in service of their own deeply hierarchical social vision. At a time when no clear public consensus existed over the role and meaning of the many newcomers arriving in California during this time, the measures helped to stage a public debate over the obligations of citizenship and the grounds on which exclusion from particular rights and recognition might be made acceptable, forging and articulating the terms of a public consensus amid deeply ambivalent and contradictory currents of opinion. The symbolic politics of English Only legislation would soon give way to a ballot measure over immigration policy with far more violent and dehumanizing undertones, but be built upon the same claims of incorporation and innocence.

6. "They Keep Coming!"

The Tangled Roots of Proposition 187

On January 5, 1994, readers of the *Los Angeles Times* opened their morning paper to a front-page article on the status of several initiative petitions attempting to qualify for the upcoming primary and general elections. A lagging economy, reticent donors, and the lack of substantive issues, experts agreed, had slowed the number of initiatives likely to qualify to a trickle. While some twenty initiative petitions were still in circulation, the *Times* explained, "virtually all of them appear to lack significant political and financial support." "It's a bleak year," declared Mike Arno, of American Petition Consultants. His firm's effort to qualify a measure that would sentence repeat felony offenders to life in prison had been forced to suspend its paid signature gathering after proponents ran out of cash a month earlier. A measure sponsored by former Los Angeles County supervisor Pete Schabarum to eliminate medical care for undocumented immigrants was receiving only "questionable enthusiasm." Schabarum conceded that his fundraising and political support was floundering. Buried in the article's closing paragraphs was a two-sentence mention of an initiative petition sponsored by two former high-ranking Immigration and Naturalization Service (INS) officials, Alan Nelson and Harold Ezell, to "expel illegal immigrants from public schools." Unrelated to the Schabarum effort, it also had not received any large donations. California Republican Party strategists, activists, and donors seemed to be paying little attention to these initiatives, focusing instead on the upcoming gubernatorial election—Republican incumbent Pete Wilson's approval ratings had hovered in the midthirties for the last two years—as well as trying to pry a few seats away from the Democrats' solid hold on the state assembly and senate. As Tony Miller, the chief deputy secretary of state observed, as far as initiative issues were concerned, 1994 seemed to be "a light year in terms of substantive and weighty measures."[1]

The political developments that erupted over the next ten months confounded nearly every one of these predictions. While the measure sponsored by Schabarum never reached the ballot, the more far-reaching immigration restriction measure by Ezell and Nelson qualified for the November election as Proposition 187. The initiative passed by eighteen percentage points after a tumultuous and deeply polarizing campaign. Proposition 187's far-reaching mandate—to make alleged violations of federal immigration status grounds for denying all public benefits, education, and health services and to require all public employees to report anyone *suspected* of such violations to federal authorities—immediately reordered the landscape for immigration policy debates nationally. Though the courts eventually ruled that most of the measure's operating provisions were unlawful, many of the initiative's animating ideas found their way into the overhaul of federal welfare and immigration policies over the next two years. On the same ballot as Proposition 187, the criminal-sentencing initiative, Proposition 184, dubbed "Three Strikes and You're Out" won 72 percent of the vote.[2] The legislation would extend the sentences of tens of thousands of Californians over the next fifteen years, including at least 8,200 condemned to spend the rest of their lives inside one of the state's eighteen maximum-security prisons, and it further heightened enormous racial disparities within the criminal justice system.[3]

To be sure, much about California was rapidly changing as Proposition 187 marched toward the ballot: the state's job and tax base shrunk dramatically, housing values in many neighborhoods plummeted, poverty rates and income inequality skyrocketed, and the state's demographic profile changed considerably. Immigration from Latin America and Asia helped drive a 25 percent increase in the California's overall population during the 1980s, while the non-Hispanic white proportion fell from 71 to 59 percent.[4] The conflagration and turmoil in May 1992 following the acquittal of the Los Angeles police officers accused of beating motorist Rodney King and the trial of O.J. Simpson in early 1994 sharpened the sense that divisions of race, class, and opportunity in California ran deep.[5]

While a souring economy may have legitimated the resolutions offered by Proposition 187 in particular ways, these circumstances alone did not produce the measure. Nor did the initiative pass solely because of an inexorable reaction to demographic transformations. Specific political actors and institutions, armed with evolving and often contradictory ideas and political objectives, labored for many years to make immigration restriction the subject of popular debate. To be sure, many of these actors, like the proponents of the English Only ballot measures explored in chapter 5, marshaled long-standing constructions of Mexican immigrants in particular as racially and culturally subordinate. But the effort also incorporated ideas about individual worthiness and national belonging embraced by a broad range of political figures, including many self-identified liberals.[6]

As much as any measure in this book, the Proposition 187 contest reveals how an issue shaped by an array of contradictory and ambivalent attitudes became almost singularly framed by the expectations of political whiteness through an initiative campaign. This effect was evident in remarks made by Governor Wilson in his press conference the morning after the election. Triumphantly celebrating his fifteen-point victory over Democratic challenger Kathleen Brown, but mindful of the accusations of racism and xenophobia he and other Proposition 187 supporters faced during the campaign, Wilson proclaimed, "There is no room in California for bigotry or discrimination. . . . California remains a state of compassion and tolerance. . . . This is a state of opportunity." Wilson then announced he was suspending a program that provided prenatal care for low-income women without regard to their immigration status because it violated the exclusions promised by Proposition 187.[7] How did it come to be that a state that had just declared a significant portion of its residents to be civically dead—void of any publicly recognizable rights to food, education, shelter, or medicine—could simultaneously celebrate its own "compassion and tolerance"? What social, cultural, and political forces permitted this seeming paradox to be embraced by such a wide portion of the state's body politic?

THE BIRTH OF PROPOSITION 187

The group that met on October 5, 1993, at the opulent members-only Center Club in the Orange County city of Costa Mesa to draft what would become Proposition 187 could not be easily described as a coherent or well-developed political movement. Some of the participants had long-standing relationships, but the group as a whole did not have a history of working together, nor did they share a common organizational base or even a common political affiliation, though several had ties to the state and county GOP. In fact, the group largely disbanded soon after the initiative was drafted and then publicly feuded with one another in the weeks before the election, eventually leaving the campaign more than $200,000 in debt.

The October meeting was convened by Robert Kielty, a forty-six-year-old Republican political consultant and a former chair of the Orange County Republican Party, along with his wife, Barbara Kielty, age forty-seven and the mayor of the wealthy enclave of Yorba Linda. Also at the table were Ronald Prince, a forty-six-year-old accountant from nearby Tustin who had been a registered voter for only three years; Barbara Coe, sixty, another political neophyte, who published an immigrant-restrictionist newsletter from her home in Huntington Beach; Alan Nelson and Harold Ezell, two high-ranking INS officials under President Reagan; and Richard Mountjoy, a Republican assemblyman from Monrovia, a suburb east of Los Angeles.

Prince had approached the Kieltys a few months earlier after claiming he had been defrauded of $500,000 by a business partner he contended was an "illegal alien from Canada." (Court records would later reveal that the man in question had been a legal U.S. resident since 1961.) Prince had drafted his own homespun petition, asking, "Do you believe illegal immigration is a problem in California?" and stood outside a Von's supermarket near his home in the small Orange County city of Tustin to collect signatures. Prince found the response to be overwhelming, explaining that "with each signature came a story" about how "illegal immigration" was "affecting California just about everywhere they could see."[8]

Robert Kielty, sensing a potential opportunity for his consultancy, eventually contacted Ezell, a Newport Beach businessman who had parlayed his role as a Republican fund-raiser into an appointment as the INS's western commissioner, overseeing the nation's busiest ports of entry, though he lacked any experience related to immigration policy. Ezell brought in Nelson, his former boss at the INS, who was currently working for the Federation for American Immigration Reform as a lobbyist in Sacramento, and Coe, a civilian employee of the Anaheim Police Department. Coe, described in one account as possessing "an apocalyptic vision of the world that is all exclamation points and question marks," was connected to an expanding network of grassroots immigration-restriction organizations in the area.[9]

After extensive discussions at the October 5 meeting, the group decided that a ballot initiative would be the most promising avenue for their multiple legislative priorities. A ballot measure had the advantage of generating the kind of "massive public attention" that a legislative effort could not, and it would not be subject to the same sort of compromises.[10] In addition, a ballot measure could incorporate a broader set of policies reflecting the varying priorities of those in the group. For example, Mountjoy wanted a provision regarding criminal penalties for the fraudulent use of social security cards, drivers' licenses, and other government documents. Coe insisted that the grassroots immigration-restriction activists she represented would only circulate the measure if it mandated the exclusion of undocumented children from public schools. Coe and others hoped this controversial clause would provoke a legal challenge to the 1982 Supreme Court ruling in *Plyer v. Doe*, which invalidated a Texas school district effort to enact a similar ban. Nelson, a long-standing fiscal conservative, viewed the elimination of public benefits as the top priority.[11]

Once the committee gave its final approval to the language in early November, Nelson and Ezell assumed the public face of the campaign as the authors and sponsors of the petition, though Ezell in particular contributed only a few words to the measure. The final text of the measure incorporated an ambitious set of policy proposals that just a few years earlier could only be found in the communications of FAIR and other stridently restrictionist organizations. It included additions to the state's Penal Code, Welfare and Institutions Code, Health and Safety Code, Education Code, and Government Code that would implement the specified bans on public education (including postsecondary education), health services, and public benefits, along with the new criminal penalties for document forgery. In addition, the measure required all law enforcement officers to fully cooperate with the INS and state attorney general in reporting persons suspected of immigration violations, and it required all public entities or those receiving state funding, including hospitals, schools, and social service programs, to similarly verify the immigration status of anyone attempting to use their services. Public schools were additionally obligated to check the immigration status of all students who were enrolled or were attempting to enroll, as well as the status of each of their parents or guardians; the measure required the expulsion within ninety days of any student whose status (or that of the their parents or guardians) could not be verified or who was "reasonably suspected" of being in violation of federal immigration laws. Finally, every school in the University of California, California State University, and the 109-campus California Community College systems would be required to verify the immigration or citizenship status of every student enrolled; the institutions would have to repeat such verification for all three million students at the beginning of every term or semester and prohibit any student who did not comply. No due process or appeals provisions were included; a determination of suspicion alone was adequate grounds for the denial of services and referral to state and federal authorities.[12]

The formal title of the initiative conferred by the secretary of state when it was approved for circulation in January 1994—"Illegal Aliens. Ineligibility for Public Services. Verification and Reporting"—sounded a bureaucratic tone. The proponents, however, announced their effort as the

Save Our State, or S.O.S., initiative, a moniker reinforced by the opening paragraphs of the measure:

The People of California find and declare as follows:

That they have suffered and are suffering economic hardship caused by the presence of illegal aliens in this state.

That they have suffered and are suffering personal injury and damage caused by the criminal conduct of illegal aliens in this state.

That they have a right to the protection of their government from any person or persons entering this country unlawfully.[13]

This central narrative—the "suffering" and "hardship" of an innocent populace at the hands of lawbreaking intruders—came to singularly define the campaign over the next twelve months. It was a message that resonated powerfully and immediately with the electorate; the first polling done on the measure in late March 1994, in the midst of the signature-gathering effort, found that 62 percent of registered voters declared they would support the initiative, while only 32 percent said they would oppose it, a margin that would persist for most of the campaign.[14]

Before Proposition 187, an immigration-restriction measure had not appeared on the California ballot since 1920, when voters approved a measure to restrict "aliens ineligible for citizenship" from owning land, primarily targeting Japanese American farmers.[15] Indeed, even as the number of both authorized and unauthorized immigrants in California grew dramatically during the late 1980s and early 1990s—including an estimated 42 percent jump in the number of unauthorized residents between 1988 and 1992 alone—public opinion polls consistently found that immigration ranked relatively low in comparison to other public policy concerns. In six statewide polls conducted between May 1991 and August 1993, for example, immigration was never cited by more than 5 percent of respondents as the most important problem facing the state, far below issues such as crime, the economy, and education.[16] Yet by the November 1994 election, some 48 percent of Orange County voters would identify immigration as the most important issue shaping their voting preferences, far outpacing any other option.[17]

Restrictionist organizations like FAIR had labored since the late 1970s to find the public language, frameworks, and policy demands that would allow immigration to become a source of legitimate public debate, failing much more often than they triumphed. In Congress during the 1980s, as immigration scholar Daniel Tichenor explains, "the political processes favoring a decidedly pro-immigration regime were overwhelming."[18]

Political pressure from agribusiness and manufacturing interests in the West and Southwest and from civil rights activists nationally—including a growing Latino advocacy community—rebuffed any attempts to lower aggregate immigration levels. In signing the 1986 Immigration Reform and Control Act—which implemented a limited battery of sanctions targeting employers who failed to verify the legal status of their workforce and also provided amnesty to more than two million undocumented persons already in the country—President Reagan praised the newly secured opportunities "to improve the lives of a class of individuals who now must hide in the shadows, without access to many of the benefits of a free and open society."[19] While there was certainly national media coverage focused on "illegal aliens" as a political, cultural, and economic threat, and prominent figures inside and outside Washington called for greater restriction, these efforts did not culminate in any decisive policy victories.[20]

IMMIGRATION-CONTROL GROUPS READY FOR BATTLE

During this period, it was a series of grassroots restrictionist organizations that emerged in Southern California that helped incubate the unflinching criticism of immigration that animated Proposition 187. Since Harold Ezell's and Alan Nelson's tenures at the INS in the late 1980s, these groups had become increasingly active in the white suburban communities of San Diego, Orange, and Los Angeles counties and often had loose affiliations with FAIR or other national restrictionist groups.[21] Fueled by their relative proximity to the border and long-standing commitments to "taxpayer" and "homeowner" rights, they were the first to denounce new entrants as deviant and criminal, the proverbial "bad immigrant" subjects discussed in chapter 5.

In early 1992, Bill King, who had retired from his position as Border Patrol chief under Ezell, a political ally, set out to find like-minded champions for immigration restriction. He soon met Barbara Coe, who like many early activists cited "billions of tax dollars . . . being put out to illegal aliens" in explaining her motivation. Coe and King decided to convene a meeting in nearby Costa Mesa and placed a classified ad in the *National Review* to recruit people who had "been victims of crimes either financial (welfare, unemployment, food stamps, etc.), educational (overcrowding, forced bilingual classes, etc.) or physical (rape, robbery, assault, infectious disease, etc.) committed by illegal aliens."[22]

The meetings that followed established the membership base of Citizens for Action Now. Participants, primarily white, middle-aged residents of Orange County, echoed Coe's accounts of fiscal decline elaborated through cultural alienation. Their testimonies connected stories of personal loss and injury—of medical and education benefits denied, fear of crime and violence, neighborhoods lost to "marauders"—to the racial transformation of their communities. They focused relentlessly on the suffering of law-abiding, hardworking, taxpaying citizens who were "literally being inundated" by a lawbreaking class of "illegals" whose degraded and criminal behavior they were forced to subsidize.[23] Often expressed in gendered terms, they fixated on Latina women as rogue reproducers and deviants whose presence threatened the cultural stability of the nation. Indeed, many of FAIR's founders emerged out of the reproductive rights and population-control movements of the 1970s and 1980s.[24] While Coe and her fellow activists were always quick to deny any racist motivations, the collective identity they invoked in framing their injury had unmistakable racial dimensions. Coe explained that the group "decided that the only way we are literally going to save our heritage is to put the focus on the illegal alien problem."[25] In this setting, political whiteness sutured a range of identities—taxpayer, homeowner, American—which made the distinctions between worthy and unworthy subjects recognizable.

Scholar Lisa Cacho suggests that these collective narratives of "white injury"—captured powerfully in Proposition 187's opening declaration that "The People of California . . . are suffering"—rely on individual stories of victimhood that disavow racist intent while constructing a population of "illegals" as existing beyond the pale of civil society. From Coe's perspective, racism, defined as the illegitimate and unlawful subjugation of an otherwise rights-bearing subject, could not be fairly charged. Here, a *civil offense*, technically defined by the INS as "entry without inspection," becomes a *racial offense*, an affront to a civilization and a people and thus grounds to impeach a racialized population, evident in the transformation of the term "illegal" from an adjective to a noun. Linguist Otto Santa Ana's extensive study of the language, metaphors, and imagery used to characterize Mexican immigrants within public discourse during the Proposition 187 campaign documents the violent and dehumanizing dimensions of this collective racial project: such immigrants were metaphorically represented as animals, invaders, and vectors of degeneracy.[26]

Provocative and incendiary attacks such as these were certainly connected to a much longer history of subordination forced upon the Mexican-origin population of Southern California, rationalized by implicit and explicit claims of inevitable racial, cultural, and national hierarchies.[27]

This history played a constitutive role in the region's development, evident in the formative acts of violence during and after the U.S. War against Mexico, the simultaneous importation and segregation of Mexican labor that followed, the multiple rounds of deportation launched throughout the twentieth century amid economic downturns, and the history of forced sterilizations of Mexican American women that did not end until the 1970s. The steady increase in migration from Mexico during the 1980s corresponded directly to periods of high demand for low-wage labor; uniform national quotas imposed by federal immigration law (which afforded the same number of visas to Mexico as for almost every other country in the world) necessitated that authorized immigration alone would not meet this demand.[28] As some Proposition 187 critics would point out, when the logics of this hierarchy were obeyed—as when low-wage manufacturing workers, landscapers, and domestics dutifully assumed their roles—the suburban enclaves of Southern California eagerly welcomed a Latino immigrant presence, legally authorized or not. But when those underlying logics became disturbed—through perceptions that immigrants were making claims for public goods, political power, or cultural autonomy—they were met in some corners with seething anger and resentment. Here again, an underlying and largely unstated notion of apartheid—a natural understanding of social position and division mediated by race—served to rationalize acerbic group-based claims of domination and subordination.[29]

CHALLENGES FACING RESTRICTIONISTS MOVEMENTS

In the early 1990s, immigration restrictionists still had few prominent supporters, even within conservative ranks. The most recent bipartisan reform to federal immigration policy, the 1990 Immigration Act signed by President Bush, actually raised the annual ceiling on visas by 40 percent.[30] Those championing greater restrictions, such as Peter Brimelow, a senior editor at *Forbes*, excoriated fellow conservatives for their participation in a "conspiracy of silence" regarding immigration policy.[31] Among national Republicans, only far-right presidential candidate Pat Buchanan attempted to make immigration an issue in the 1992 presidential election. In the midst of the Republican primary, Buchanan held a news conference along the border in San Diego and called for doubling the size of the Border Patrol, further fortifying and militarizing border crossing areas, and charging a two-dollar toll on legal crossings to fund border enforcement.[32]

Lacking support among leading conservatives, Bill King and Barbara Coe moved to expand their network among other grassroots activists. In

May 1992 they announced the formation of the California Coalition for Immigration Reform (CCIR) to bring together a dozen similar groups, immediately claiming a collective membership of four thousand activists.[33] Most of the concrete initiatives they pursued failed. A proposed statewide ballot initiative requiring cities to enforce immigration law and to study the impact of immigration on the state's economy and quality of life (modest goals to be sure in comparison to Proposition 187) was entirely ignored by elected officials from both parties.[34] Alan Nelson's legislative proposals on behalf of FAIR to eliminate all social services, public benefits, and public education for undocumented immigrants were roundly defeated, and FAIR continued to complain about the marginal status afforded to immigration issues.[35]

None of these efforts reaped any tangible policy reforms. But even these failed attempts helped Coe, King, and other grassroots activists refine the narratives, symbols, and story lines they would deploy within future public debates and allowed them to assemble a set of policy proposals that would be ready when the opportunity arose. These activities also enabled them to broaden their base of support, recruiting more volunteers and developing relationships with a number of Republican elected officials willing to promote their demands in the legislative arena.

THE AMBIVALENT IMMIGRATION POLITICS OF PETE WILSON

Most accounts of Proposition 187's development and passage give Governor Pete Wilson almost singular credit for raising the profile and salience of immigration politics within the state during this period. Immigration, together with crime, indeed rose to the top of Wilson's political agenda as the ballot initiative was beginning to emerge in the fall of 1993, and his 1994 campaign for governor took up many of the ideas animating the measure. But Wilson's full embrace of immigration occurred *after* many other public officials, including nearly all of the state's prominent Democratic leaders, signaled that they were willing to make immigration restriction and enforcement a leading political priority.

To understand these seemingly contradictory developments, it is helpful to understand Wilson's own history regarding immigration politics. In California in the 1980s, few political-opinion leaders spoke in favor of drastically reducing immigration levels or public benefits to immigrants, certainly not Senator Pete Wilson. Wilson's almost singular focus with regard to immigration policy was guaranteeing access to migrant labor for agribusiness. He cosponsored legislation that required judges to sign warrants before the INS could conduct sweeps targeting undocumented farmworkers, arguing that such protections would ensure that "timely harvests" would not be jeopardized. And he was instrumental in the passage of a provision within the 1986 legislation to ensure that some 350,000 temporary workers would be admitted annually. Agricultural lobbies rewarded Wilson with nearly $520,000 in political contributions during the 1980s.[36] In commenting on immigration policy during his 1990 campaign for U.S. Senate, he reminded voters that "a state cannot limit immigration" and suggested that "we should celebrate our diversity as a strength and distinct cultural asset" while bearing in mind the "limit on the financial burden the federal government can equitably impose through allocation of refugees."[37]

Wilson did not imagine the Mexican workers he lobbied to admit to have rights and claims once the crops were harvested. As he was championing an expansive guest-worker program on behalf of the agricultural lobby, he announced his support for Proposition 63, U.S. English's 1986 Official English ballot proposition (see chapter 5). He also described the border region as "out of control" and suggested that migrants crossed the border not for employment but because they "want their babies born here" and sought access to public services available in the United States. He suggested that "closing (the border physically) . . . with some sort of physical barrier or with armed guards" was a harsh but necessary solution to this problem.[38]

Even in the early 1990s, however, Wilson's embrace of more restrictionist and racially charged attacks against immigrants unfolded unevenly and with considerable assistance and support from Democratic leaders; his initial overtures were not considered particularly nativist or restrictionist. In 1991, as the state's economic downturn headed into its second year and the state budget forecast looked grim, Wilson released a report claiming that California's large population of authorized and unauthorized immigrants and refugees was straining the state's fiscal capacity. Alan Nelson seized on the report to call on the governor to stop providing all employment, public benefits, college education, tax refunds, and driving privileges to unauthorized immigrants.[39]

Wilson ignored Nelson's plea and instead announced that he would travel to Washington to lobby for more than $200 million he claimed the state was owed by the federal government for providing services to immigrants and refugees. While some critics accused Wilson of blaming immigrants for the state's budget woes, most Democratic leaders wholeheartedly endorsed the plan, including Assembly Speaker Willie Brown, who insisted that the "federal government should appropriate more money and assign that money to where the problems are. He (Wilson) has got to go get the money. We need it. And we are entitled to it."[40] When Wilson continued to press these claims in 1992 and 1993, for even more money, he again did so with the support of a large majority of Democrats. San Jose congressman Don Edwards, the senior member of the California delegation, declared that in seeking the funds from Washington the "governor made a point on which there is no disagreement."[41] The *San Francisco Chronicle* reported that Wilson's efforts to recover the funds "cheered immigrant rights advocates and city financing experts."[42]

During this period, only a year and a half before Proposition 187 was drafted, Wilson focused far more attention on allegedly high levels of spending on welfare programs than he did on immigration restrictions or benefits. In 1992, Wilson faced a budget stalemate that forced the state to issue IOUs, sending Wilson's approval ratings plummeting. In response, Wilson drafted a ballot measure to reform the state's welfare programs and budgeting process and funded a petition drive to qualify it for the November election. The measure, Proposition 165, denied cash benefits to children born to mothers already receiving welfare, restricted the amount that could be paid to applicants who had moved from other states, and implemented a 23 percent reduction in cash benefits paid to most other recipients.[43]

Thus, as the state's budget crisis was peaking and as voter frustration was heightening, Wilson believed that welfare reform, rather than immigration, was the issue that would arouse the greatest public anger. That is, at least for Wilson and his strategists and allies, immigration was not yet regarded as an issue that offered much political advantage. In addition, in spite of conditions that seemed quite encouraging for its passage—a budget stalemate, attacks on a program often regarded as unpopular with the electorate, and a well-funded statewide media campaign—Proposition 165 failed at the polls by nearly one million votes, losing 53.4 to 46.6 percent. An opposing coalition of Democratic leaders and labor unions poured more than $1.5 million into television ads of their own, depicting the measure as a power grab by the governor at the expense of vulnerable children, seniors, and families. While their campaign largely focused on portraying Wilson as an ineffective and power-hungry leader, they did not reproduce or reiterate any of the stigmatizing caricatures of welfare recipients in their campaign.[44]

Proposition 165's failure in 1992 suggests that conditions assumed favorable to a ballot initiative's success—taxpayer anger, budget shortfalls, and racially stigmatized social programs—did not guarantee passage. The electorate may have indeed harbored many misgivings towards welfare programs and frustration over the state's economic decline, but Proposition 165's opponents successfully defended the families targeted by the measure while challenging the intentions and credibility of the measure's proponents. When the public debate turned to immigration policy, however, the same coalition of Democratic and union leaders employed a dramatically different strategy.[45]

When the legislative session opened in January 1993 following Wilson's Proposition 165 defeat, immigration restriction still did not garner the support of many lawmakers beyond a group of Southern California conservatives who represented districts where the grassroots restrictionist groups were most active. Assemblyman Mountjoy failed in his legislative efforts to press FAIR-endorsed measures to bar unauthorized immigrants from all public schools, colleges, and universities and to restrict medical care.[46] Mountjoy, according to one account, regularly got "hooted down as a right-wing kook whenever he attempt[ed] to advocate one of his proposals on the Assembly floor."[47]

IMMIGRATION COMES OUT OF THE CLOSET

Rather than Governor Wilson, it was Senator Diane Feinstein, who won the seat vacated by Wilson in 1992 but had to stand for reelection at the expiration of the term in 1994, who made the first public move to take "immigration out of the closet," as one newspaper columnist described it. In an op-ed piece in the *Los Angeles Times* in June 1993, Feinstein detailed the growing hardships that "illegal residents" and the lack of enforcement at the border were imposing on California: drug smuggling, increased crime, and nearly two billion dollars in school, medical, and corrections costs. Feinstein insisted that she was raising the issue in order "to avoid a serious backlash against all immigrants" and to forestall more extreme proposals emanating from the "far right." But her policy prescriptions were largely taken from those same groups—her solutions mirrored those made by Pat Buchanan just one year earlier—and focused almost entirely on punitive measures. The proposals included an expansion of the Border Patrol's personnel and budget paid for in part by a new border-crossing fee, increased federal penalties for smuggling, new policies to restrict newcomer access to Medicaid, and a crackdown on unauthorized immigrants who committed federal crimes. FAIR executive director Dan Stein was thrilled, noting that Feinstein "is in a position to be a defining figure" and calling on FAIR supporters to rally "a lot of positive reinforcement" on her behalf. Stein and other observers commented that Feinstein was the first California senator in decades to take a hard-nosed stand on immigration policy, a telling comment considering that Pete Wilson and Samuel Hayakawa occupied the seat before her. Feinstein publicized her proposals aggressively, appearing on national news talk shows.[48]

Other prominent Democrats, including Senator Barbara Boxer, President Clinton, State Treasurer Kathleen Brown, and Attorney General Janet Reno, announced their own intentions to toughen border enforcement and deal with the fiscal costs associated with immigration.[49] Longtime Democratic congressman Anthony Beilenson endorsed a proposal to revoke automatic birthright citizenship to children of unauthorized immigrants and called for a tamperproof national identification card to limit unauthorized access to public benefits. Referencing his background as an environmentalist, Beilenson explained that the reason he had "long been sensitive to immigration issues of all kinds [was that he had] long been concerned about population problems" in other countries.[50] Beilenson, representing an affluent Santa Barbara district that relied heavily on low-wage immigrant labor, was a central figure in the effort to link immigration restriction to environmental concerns, eventually becoming a member of the FAIR Board of Directors.[51]

It was not until August 1993, after considerable debate within his administration, that Pete Wilson decided to add his voice to the restrictionist chorus. Continuing to face dismal approval ratings, the governor abandoned his previous restraint and joined his Democratic counterparts in championing a new restrictionist regime. On August 9, 1993, he issued an "open letter on behalf of the people of California" to President Clinton, reproduced in full-page ads in the *New York Times, USA Today,* and the conservative-leaning *Washington Times,* declaring that "massive illegal immigration will continue as long as the federal government continues to reward it . . . [by] providing incentives to illegal immigrants" and leaving California "under siege." Wilson's demands included the denial of public education and health care services to unauthorized residents; the creation of a new tamper-resistant identification card for legal immigrants; the end of the country's long-standing birthright citizenship policy; and using negotiations over NAFTA to win commitments from the Mexican government to deter unauthorized border crossings. He also suggested that all legal migration be temporarily halted to reduce the demand for state services. These policies virtually replicated the demands made by Alan Nelson and FAIR two years earlier, when few politicians, Democrat or Republican, took them seriously. Now, the incumbent governor of California had decided to base his reelection campaign on the very same agenda.[52]

Though Wilson's proposals were denounced by many Latino civil rights groups as trading in "the politics of racial polarization," they were received cordially by high-profile Democratic leaders. Senator Boxer suggested that "the proposals Gov. Wilson has outlined warrant serious consideration," and Senator Feinstein thought the national identification card merited particular attention. FAIR's Orange County representative said her group was "delighted to see the governor . . . beginning to deal with this issue."[53] Wilson's approval ratings shot up immediately, with one opinion poll finding that more than 80 percent of respondents now believed that "illegal immigration" had become a major problem.[54]

With Wilson moving to take more aggressive restrictionist positions and with leading Democrats like Feinstein, Boxer, and Clinton all endorsing the idea that unauthorized immigration posed a serious threat to the state's well-being, it became almost impossible for Democrats to offer legitimate opposition to Wilson's policies. In late August, the California Democratic Party attempted to undercut some of the momentum Wilson seemed to have built after his announcements; the party ran television ads attacking the governor for "flip-flopping" on immigration, charging him with "opening our borders to cheap labor" during his tenure in the Senate. State Democratic political director Bob Mulholland declared that Wilson's actions "made it easier for criminal migrant networks to bring their foot soldiers into the country."[55] But once immigration became framed through the language of criminality and fiscal austerity—a move that Democrats played no small part in facilitating—"toughness" increasingly became the singular standard around which positions on immigration would be measured.

Political pragmatism alone, however, did not fully explain why various Democratic figures joined the alarmist chorus around immigration. Calls for strident restriction and law enforcement did not necessarily violate long-standing liberal positions around immigration policy. Since 1965, federal immigration policy had been structured broadly within the Hart-Cellar Act, which eliminated discriminatory national immigration quotas that had long favored northern European immigrants. Passed by a Democratic Congress and signed by President Johnson in the shadows of the Statute of Liberty, the 1965 act brought the liberal commitments of equality of opportunity and nondiscrimination driving much civil rights legislation to bear on federal immigration policy. While supporters emphasized the traditions of inclusion and American exceptionalism on which the act was founded, the legislation did not disavow the ideals of restriction altogether. Nearly all of the proponents of the 1965 act eagerly insisted that only those newcomers whose presence could be justified as beneficial to the nation would be welcomed. As Senator Ted Kennedy, a forceful champion of the 1965 law explained, "Favoritism based on nationality will disappear. Favoritism based on individual worth and qualifications will take its place." He specifically assured his colleagues "that the people who comprise the new immigration—the type which this bill would give preference to—are relatively well educated and well to do. . . . They share our ideals."[56]

While public discourse over immigration changed noticeably in the aftermath of the Hart-Cellar Act, stigmatizing some restrictionist demands as nativist and bigoted, the legislation also remained heavily invested in the principle that individual contribution, merit, and worthiness were defensible tests of admissibility and inclusion. Immigrants (or their advocates) had to be prepared to justify and explain how their presence benefited the nation economically, culturally, and politically. This distinction, between worthy and unworthy immigrant subjects, rehearsed in the English Only initiatives of the mid-1980s, operated powerfully within the emerging debate over immigration enforcement, allowing actors from across the political spectrum to insist that restrictionist policies were necessary to defend and protect the nation's inclusionary traditions. Thus, when President Clinton announced an effort in late 1994 to further militarize and fortify the border, he explained that the nation would "not surrender our borders to those who wish to exploit our history of compassion and justice."[57] Though the 1965 law disavowed official policies that placed immigrants from different nations into a hierarchy, race could still operate as a silent referent within this framework, helping to distinguish those who did and did not meet the criteria for worthiness. Proposition 187 would be debated within, rather than beyond, the framework of liberal immigration policy, as its proponents insisted that the nation was justified in excluding those immigrants who failed to meet these tests.

Even Democratic assemblyman Richard G. Polanco of Los Angeles, who as head of the state Latino Caucus led the legislative fights against the proposals backed by Mountjoy and FAIR earlier in 1993, felt compelled to publicly distinguish between worthy and unworthy immigrants. His *Los Angeles Times* opinion piece on August 13, 1993, endorsed Feinstein's border-crossing toll, a proposal by the Clinton administration to limit preventive and emergency health care for undocumented immigrants, and echoed Wilson's long-standing demand for Washington to reimburse the state for expenses related to immigration. Polanco described his position as "a get-tough but humane policy to tighten up our borders, while ensuring that legal immigrants are allowed to reach their potential." He also stated at a press conference with other Latino legislators and Assemblyman Willie Brown that the "Latino caucus believes we need to take a tough stance on illegal immigration."[58]

Thus, as Ronald Prince, Barbara Coe, Harold Ezell, Alan Nelson, Richard Mountjoy, Robert Kielty, Barbara Kielty, and their supporters met in Orange County to draft their ballot initiative in the fall of 1993, the bulwark that had prevented ardent restrictionists for nearly three decades from shaping the public debate over immigration had been breached. By this point, much of the taboo over addressing immigration that had long frustrated groups like FAIR had been diminished. Feinstein, Clinton, and other Democrats had faced some criticism from Latino elected officials and advocacy groups for their positions, but they proved it was possible to take openly restrictionist positions without being altogether dismissed as a racist or extremist.[59] And with the head of the Latino Caucus now adopting a "get-tough" posture, there was little to obstruct the floodwaters that would become Proposition 187.

GETTING S.O.S. ON THE BALLOT

The preliminary period of coalition building, activist recruitment, and assorted campaigns that grassroots restrictionist groups embarked upon in the early 1990s failed to yield any concrete policy reforms. But they succeeded in expanding the groups' memberships and organizing capacity, transformations that proved crucial in qualifying S.O.S. for the ballot.[60] Without a budget to hire paid signature gatherers or even funding to print and mail petitions, their prospects for qualifying initially seemed dim. The effort was sustained at first by small contributions from individual supporters and the volunteer time of local activists, drawn from the growing network of Bill King and Barbara Coe's California Coalition for Immigration Reform. The upsurge in activism eventually convinced state GOP leaders that the initiative was worth sustaining, and the state Republican Party soon provided some $86,500 worth of nonmonetary contributions to the S.O.S. petition drive.[61] Additional contributions from individual Republicans late in the qualification period finally allowed the campaign to retain paid signature gathers to collect some three hundred thousand signatures in the final two months of petitioning. Together with the three hundred thousand signatures collected by volunteers, the campaign met its mid-May qualification deadline and earned a spot on the November ballot.[62]

As the initiative circulated, Pete Wilson continued to frame his own attacks on immigration strategically. On the one hand, during the petition phase, Wilson insiders were cautious about how the S.O.S. effort would play out. Wilson did not participate in drafting the initiative nor did he contribute funding to the effort or use his campaign organization to help collect signatures. To be clear, Wilson did not harbor substantive ethical or moral concerns about the measure. Instead, it is important to remember that even a growling critic of undocumented immigration like Wilson had early doubts about how Proposition 187 would play in the arena of public opinion. Though Wilson would ultimately announce his support of the measure six weeks before the election, and tether much of his reelection campaign to the initiative's passage, at these preliminary stages his official support was measured rather than unqualified.[63]

At the same time, Wilson sharpened and explicitly racialized his own attacks on immigration. In mid-May, almost at the exact time that S.O.S. proponents submitted their signatures to the secretary of state for verification, Wilson's gubernatorial campaign released a highly controversial and inflammatory television spot. Over grainy footage of a group of figures running past cars identified by an on-screen graphic as a "Border Crossing . . . San Diego County" an ominous voice warned, "They keep coming. Two-million illegal immigrants in California. The federal government won't stop them at the border, yet requires us to pay billions to take care of them."[64] The ad rehearsed the same distinctions animating the S.O.S. initiative—a beleaguered body of hardworking taxpayers under siege by lawbreaking foreign invaders. Like the S.O.S. backers, Wilson made the racial and spatial dimensions of the threat easy to comprehend— the invasion was coming from Mexico, and the invaders were beyond the pale of civil society. Here, race and national identity again helped signify which potential immigrants failed to meet the test of worthiness. Wilson's concluding line, "Enough is enough," suggested that the taxpayers' tolerance and compassion had been exhausted and that only muscular and punitive action could resolve the crisis.[65]

Wilson's position on the S.O.S. initiative converged powerfully with his support for a "Three Strikes" criminal-sentencing initiative that would also appear on the November 1994 ballot, and there were strong resonances between the two measures. California had been in the midst of a historic prison boom since the early 1980s, with the Department of Corrections' budget swelling from $728 million to $3.1 billion between 1984 and 1994.[66] Since voters had adopted a death-penalty measure in 1972, sixteen subsequent criminal-sentencing enhancements or prison-construction measures had been approved by the electorate, many driven by the same political forces (and actors) implicated in the antitax, antidesegregation, and home-owner's rights initiatives.[67] But the high-profile abduction and murder of twelve-year-old Polly Klass from a slumber party in Marin County in October 1993, and the media frenzy that followed, paved the way for more. Mike Reynolds, a photographer whose own eighteen-year-old daughter had been murdered at a Fresno restaurant the year before, was waiting in the wings with a legislative proposal to dramatically increase prison sentences for repeat felony offenders, including those convicted of nonviolent crimes. Wilson, who had ignored the Reynolds measure before the Klass murder, now became a loud defender of the far-reaching legislation. Wilson signed the law in March 1994, inaugurating what one analyst described as "the largest penal experiment in American history."[68] Wilson then joined Reynolds in championing identical legislation as a ballot measure, in order to ensure that their quest to place "career criminals, who rape women, molest innocent children and commit murder, behind bars where they belong," could not be undone by a simple majority vote of the legislature.[69] As in the Proposition 187 conflict, the Three Strikes debate depicted an angry and vulnerable populace drawing the line against an incorrigible criminal class that lay beyond the pale of society. Both the Three Strikes measure (Proposition 184) and eventually Proposition 187 helped Wilson establish himself as the singular figure defending "Californians who work hard, pay taxes, and obey the law."[70]

THE OPPOSITION BEGINS TO ORGANIZE

Throughout the qualification period in the first half of 1994, civil rights groups, immigrant rights organizations, union and Democratic leaders, and other opponents of the measure were reluctant to call public attention to the petition, fearing that such publicity might inadvertently help proponents to further announce their effort. They regarded the initiative's sponsors as fringe organizations drawn from the most reactionary corners of Orange County politics, and they remained unconvinced that such groups had the capacity or sophistication to bring their agenda before a statewide electorate. Indeed, the signature-gathering effort received relatively little attention from the press, much to the chagrin of Ronald Prince and Barbara Coe.[71] The opponents of S.O.S mostly hoped the petition would go away.

On June 23, 1994, when the secretary of state announced that the S.O.S. initiative had qualified for the November ballot, all such illusions were shattered.[72] Only then did a coalition of leading Democratic elected officials and organizations announce the formation of a No on S.O.S. fund-raising committee. The group included representatives from the Service Employees International Union, California Federation of Teachers, State Federation of Labor, and the California Medical Association as well as Assembly Speaker Willie Brown and Assemblyman Richard Polanco. All sophisticated and experienced players in state politics, they soon realized they faced a daunting task. A *Los Angeles Times* poll in late May revealed that the measure was favored by 59 percent of registered voters and opposed by only 27 percent. In addition, public denunciations of the "illegal alien" crisis had escalated dramatically during the last twelve months, culminating in Wilson's fuming "They Keep Coming" spot. Funding prospects for the opposition were not encouraging; the state Democratic Party remained officially undecided about the issue, withholding any funding until a statewide meeting in September. At the same time, the state GOP formally endorsed Proposition 187, and both the party and individual Republican candidates began to aggressively promote it. And while Proposition 187's proponents had been developing a network of grassroots supporters and refining their populist rhetoric for many years, the opponents were forced to build a fund-raising and public messaging strategy from scratch, with the election only four months away.[73]

THE TAXPAYERS AGAINST 187 CAMPAIGN

In early July, the No on S.O.S. committee turned to the political consulting firm of Woodward and McDowell, a veteran ballot initiative consultancy, to develop a strategy to defeat Proposition 187. Based in the tony San Francisco peninsula suburb of Burlingame, the firm's two principals, Richard Woodward and Jack McDowell, were Republicans who specialized in defeating heavily favored ballot measures, most famously two 1990 pro-environmental measures, nicknamed Big Green and Forests Forever, opposed by corporate interests. The decision by a Democratic–civil rights–labor coalition to retain a Republican consultancy to derail a deeply racialized ballot initiative spoke volumes about the limited confidence they had in their own ability to communicate with the electorate about this issue.

Woodward and McDowell quickly undertook its own survey and convened focus groups to gauge public opinion on the initiative and to test potential messages and arguments. In mid-July, the consultants produced a memo for their clients summarizing their findings. The "bad news," the memo began, was that "without a doubt, voters are eager to do something (anything) to address what they perceive to be an illegal immigration problem" and would vote yes on any measure that seemed to represent a solution. Anticipating what would become a major cleavage in the campaign, the consultants acknowledged that while "diverse groups and individuals opposing Proposition 187 differ in their views on illegal immigration," the imperative was to "make the most salient arguments necessary to move *public opinion*" and there was "no time to undertake any 'general education' on the issue." The consultants argued that it was fruitless to challenge voters' beliefs that "'our illegal immigration problem' [is caused by] . . . the flow of people coming across our southern border." "You can't change that," the memo insisted. "Don't try."[74]

The good news the consultants contended, was that the measure could be defeated if the campaign obeyed a basic imperative: "RECOGNIZE THERE IS A PROBLEM AND POINT OUT HOW PROPOSITION 187 DOES NOTHING TO FIX THE PROBLEM . . . [and] WOULD CAUSE A HOST OF NEW PROBLEMS." As Scott Macdonald, a Woodward and McDowell staff member who became the campaign's communications director later explained, the campaign was "trying to talk to white middle-class voters with messages that resonated with them, because they are the people who vote." Macdonald conceded that while it would certainly be better if the electorate were more diverse and broad-minded, "when you're trying to win an election campaign, you have to deal with the realities of it."[75]

Woodward and McDowell soon established Taxpayers against 187 (hereafter Taxpayers) as the statewide organization to carry this message out to the electorate, attempting to connote a reasoned, centrist profile that would persuade the proverbial median voter, and the firm pledged to raise up to $4 million in order to purchase the television and radio time necessary to do so.[76] A campaign spokesperson declared that the issue was "much deeper than the Hispanic vote" because the "real battleground will be in the San Fernando Valley and Orange County—in the white, middle-class suburban communities," where voters must be convinced that the measure would undermine their interests. And these interests were defined in subtle but unmistakable racial terms; that is, the Taxpayers campaign would seek to affirm the notion of collective white injury proposed by Proposition 187 supporters but would argue that the measure failed to effectively resolve such injuries as promised.[77]

One of the first tasks of the campaign was to draft the ballot argument for the official guide distributed by the secretary of state to all voters. The Taxpayers argument exemplified its basic assumptions and strategy. It began, "Something must be done to stop the flow of illegal immigrants coming across the border. . . . Illegal Immigration is a REAL problem, but

Proposition 187 is NOT A REAL SOLUTION." It warned that the measure would "kick 400,000 kids out of school and onto the streets" but "WON'T result in their deportation" and would certainly create more "CRIME and GRAFFITI." It declared that "every day, hundreds of thousands of undocumented workers HANDLE OUR FOOD SUPPLY in the fields and restaurants. Denying them basic health care would only SPREAD COMMUNICABLE DISEASES THROUGHOUT OUR COMMUNITIES and place us ALL at risk." The argument concluded with an unambiguous declaration: "Illegal immigration is ILLEGAL. Isn't it time we enforce the law?" It called for more enforcement at the border and the punishment of "employers who continue to hire illegal immigrants." The argument was signed by Los Angeles County sheriff Sherman Block and the heads of the California Medical Association and California Teachers Association.[78]

During the next four months, Taxpayers continued to appeal to the same sense of political whiteness—a shared understanding of political community, interests, and opposition—that Proposition 187 supporters had painstakingly constructed in the years leading up to the campaign. Woodward himself criticized the education ban as folly because the students would "have free time and [be] on the streets. It doesn't take too much imagination to see that it will lead to more gang activity, and more graffiti." He pledged that the Taxpayers campaign would not try "to argue that illegal immigration is good" but would instead make the case that more aggressive law enforcement was the real solution. He explained that Proposition 187 "does nothing to beef up the Border Patrol. This doesn't deport one single illegal alien. This doesn't touch the thousands of illegal aliens in prison."[79]

From one perspective, the logic of the Taxpayers campaign followed the conventional wisdom about how to defeat a controversial initiative that starts out with a sizable lead among voters: frame arguments in terms of the perceived self-interests of frequent and persuadable voters; give voters concrete reasons to reject the measure and suggest troubling unintended consequences if the measure passes; and use credible, recognizable public figures to deliver the message through mainstream television and radio advertising.[80] To be sure, the consultants at Woodward and McDowell were not the only figures insisting upon such a strategy. Many of the labor, health, and education leaders that formed the leadership of the campaign similarly believed that if the goal of the campaign was to win on Election Day, they could not afford to rehearse wide-eyed claims about immigrant rights and social justice.[81]

This line of reasoning even proved highly influential to one of the leading Washington, D.C.–based advocates for immigrant rights. Frank Sharry, the executive director of the National Immigration Forum, a leading advocacy coalition supporting immigrant rights and liberal immigration reforms, took a leave of absence from his job to work on the Taxpayers campaign as deputy campaign manager. Sharry became convinced that the strategy advised by Woodward and McDowell provided the only realistic possibility for defeating the measure; what mattered in the end was "the goal of winning 50% plus 1 of the votes on election day" and that "actions and decisions made need[ed] to flow from the priority of winning."[82]

Other seasoned advocacy organizations agreed. The Service Employees International Union, which was in the midst of its groundbreaking Justice for Janitors campaign to organize tens of thousands of immigrant workers who cleaned downtown office buildings in Los Angeles, San Jose, and other western cities, also joined the Taxpayers effort. The union loaned an organizer to serve as the campaign's deputy manager in the newly opened Los Angles office.[83]

IMMIGRANTS RIGHTS GROUPS ORGANIZE

To other opponents of Proposition 187, however, the "pragmatic" decision to rehearse the most stigmatizing and degrading caricatures of immigrants was appalling. Since the passage of the Immigration Reform and Control Act (IRCA) in 1986, dozens of service and advocacy groups had formed across the state, especially in Los Angeles and the San Francisco Bay Area, to assist immigrants in taking advantage of the amnesty provisions and to help them access various social and legal services. Groups like the Northern California Coalition for Immigrant and Refugee Rights (NCCIRR), which included some sixty affiliated organizations in the Bay Area that operated such programs, also lobbied in Sacramento and Washington, D.C., in favor of inclusive public benefit programs and other immigrant rights issues. From their perspective, one of the main imperatives of immigrant rights advocacy was to challenge the demeaning language and assaults that immigrants, particularly those from Mexico and Central America, often faced in the political arena.[84]

Many local immigrant rights advocates were thus outraged when informed of the Taxpayers strategy. They were particularly mortified that the first line of the No on 187 ballot argument was an explicit attack on undocumented immigrants, essentially endorsing the proponents' claim that "illegal immigration is out of control." Ignatius Bau, an immigrant rights attorney for the Lawyers Committee for Civil Rights in San Francisco, saw in the argument "all the 'racial specters' of undocumented kids running around causing crime, undocumented immigrants spreading disease, [and] all the fear" that the Taxpayers campaign hoped to use to motivate voters. "All of us said there's absolutely no way we're going to sign off on this," Bau said in an interview. It was inconceivable to try and defeat a measure attacking immigrants by joining the attacks.[85]

Bau and other California-based immigrant rights advocates quickly concluded that there was little they could say or do to deter Taxpayers from its message or strategy. These immigrant rights groups, however, faced a severe limitation. Unlike the consultants and the unions who made up the mainstream campaign, the immigrant rights organizations had little experience organizing around a ballot initiative or participating in electoral politics more generally. "Groups interacting the most with undocumented folks [didn't] historically play in the electoral arena," explained Bau. To fight a ballot initiative meant that it was "no longer a conversation about organizing in the Mission District" of San Francisco and other immigrant-rich neighborhoods but about "what do you say in San Bernardino or Orange County to voters." A group—including Bau, NCCIRR executive director Emily Goldfarb, and others—realized they needed help to navigate this unfamiliar terrain.

They quickly turned to Jan Adams, a veteran organizer who cut her political teeth during the Berkeley antiwar movement in the late 1960s before doing Central America solidarity work in the 1980s. Adams also had important electoral experience; she had been a field organizer in her hometown of San Francisco for a campaign to defeat a 1989 ballot proposition that would have repealed the city's first domestic-partnership ordinance. Adams's employer, the Applied Research Center, an Oakland-based nonprofit focusing on racial justice issues, agreed to allow her to help establish and organize a grassroots response to Proposition 187 centered on immigrant communities in particular. Together with Goldfarb and Bau, Adams helped launch what would be one of the main grassroots efforts against the measure, Californians United against 187.[86]

Working out of a small office provided by the teachers union in San Francisco, Adams, Goldfarb, Bau, and other Californians United organizers began their work with the election only four months away. They had no difficulty generating interest or passion in the issue among their own constituents. As word spread of Proposition 187's qualification during the late summer, particularly in immigrant Latino communities, small groups in dozens of cities began to meet and organize on their own. Sometimes the groups were simply comprised of parents seeking to share and disseminate information about the measure; other groups were convened by activists based in local community organizations or college campuses. Adams later described the effort as "probably one of the most intense campaign experiences" she had ever had in more than three decades of organizing: "The quality of emotion of the people who were against it was greater than anything I've ever seen before or since. . . . The notion that somebody would put to a vote whether their kids should enjoy the benefits of living in this country, should be able to go to school, should be able to get health care was a moral outrage of the sort that people don't usually feel."[87]

The challenge that Adams and others faced was trying to provide basic organization and infrastructure to this upsurge of activism. To be sure, there was already deep and sophisticated political experience within many of these communities. Many immigrants and refugees who arrived from Mexico and Central America in the 1980s were politicized during the often violent civil and military struggles that raged within their countries of origin; they needed no tutoring in political analysis, the operation of power, or the importance of civil and human rights. But the nonprofit and civic organizations that had been built in these communities during the last decade had focused most of their energies on direct service and legislative advocacy rather than on overt political conflicts. Proposition 187 would be a baptism by fire.

Over the next three months, Adams and other Californians United organizers attempted to support, enhance, and expand this upsurge of activity. The San Francisco campaign eventually trained and organized more than a thousand volunteers to take on specific tasks to reach voters directly. During the weekend before the election alone, a group of more than seven hundred activists delivered some sixty thousand door hangers across the city and made more than thirty thousand calls. Phone banks were conducted in English, Chinese, and Spanish—an innovation at the time—and flyers and other publicity materials were translated into as many as eight languages.[88]

Californians United eventually expanded its work beyond San Francisco and affiliated with several other anti-187 local efforts across the state. By early September, a loose coalition of anti-187 groups based in immigrant communities was beginning to take shape, with groups actively organizing in Los Angeles, Sacramento, San Diego, Marin County, the San Francisco East Bay, Orange County, and San Diego.[89] As in San Francisco, many were built out of the emerging network of immigrant rights advocacy organizations. In Los Angeles, advocates and organizers based in nonprofit organizations such as the Central American Resource Center, One

Stop Immigration, and the Coalition for Humane Immigrant Rights of Los Angeles coordinated various anti-187 activities, focusing most of their efforts in immigrant communities.[90] A coalition of Asian American groups called Asian Pacific Americans Opposed to Proposition 187 also joined the statewide alliance, though as Ignatius Bau later pointed out, "no major contributions from Asian Pacific American organizations, businesses, or individuals were made" to the opposition campaign.[91] Other groups, such as the newly founded Latino Civil Rights Network and various student organizers based at different campuses within the University of California and California State University systems, also eschewed the Taxpayers strategy of focusing solely on high-frequency white voters by affirming anti-immigrant sentiments. But the grassroots strategy also had its limitations.

CHALLENGES FACING THE GRASSROOTS CAMPAIGNS AGAINST PROPOSITION 187

Three critical challenges faced the grassroots campaigns, which operated independently of the Taxpayers campaign. First, the assertion by the Woodward and McDowell consultants that white voters dominated the electorate was entirely accurate. In 1994, Latinos constituted 29 percent of the California population, 26 percent of the adult population, 14 percent of the eligible voter population, and only 11 percent of registered voters. In the June 1994 primary, white voters cast 83 percent of the total ballots, compared to just 8 percent for Latinos and 4 percent each for African Americans and Asian Americans. On this point, there could be no dispute; the fate of most statewide elections was largely in the hands of the collective white electorate.[92]

The reasons that white voters dominated the electorate, and that Proposition 187 opponents lacked a political vocabulary to discuss immigration politics, however, were more complex. Historian and union organizer Kenneth Burt suggests that as the Chicano movement of the late 1960s and 1970s demobilized, an emerging bloc of Latino leaders focused attention on political incorporation within the electoral system rather than building grassroots organizations. "In the general absence of grassroots social movements," he explains, "liberal Latinos utilized the court system or formed alliances with Democratic legislative leaders. While these moves produced tactical victories in an increasingly hostile political environment, the failure to invest resources in naturalization and citizenship classes, voter registration, and get-out-the vote drives served to depress Latino working class participation in politics. It also failed to incorporate new voters among the millions of immigrants and their children who arrived in the state from Mexico and Central America during the seventies and eighties."[93]

In addition, the provisions within IRCA for obtaining citizenship were not instantaneous, and naturalization rates among Latinos in California eligible to become citizens were relatively low. And unlike restrictionist groups such as FAIR, which were constantly developing and promoting a *public* language through which to contest immigration policy, these advocates had no such experience or capacity, confining their work almost exclusively to service delivery or occasional legislative lobbying. Groups that had historically served as the repository for more robust political claims on behalf of the undocumented, such as the leftist Centros de Accion Social Autonomos (CASA), went into decline by the late 1970s.[94] As a result, even immigrant rights advocates affiliated with Californians United against 187 had little experience in making forceful demands for the rights of immigrants in general and the undocumented in particular.[95] They understood clearly what they opposed—the derogatory racial propositions that fueled both the S.O.S. and Taxpayers campaigns—but they struggled to articulate a more proactive and unified framework on behalf of immigrant rights. Even among social justice organizations, there were vigorous disputes about the most effective way to respond to Proposition 187.[96]

A second major challenge facing the various grassroots efforts against Proposition 187 involved the rapid expansion of a political discourse shaped by often violent claims that undocumented immigrants lacked any standing to assert political rights or demand civic recognition. The emergence of these dynamics was at least two decades in the making; public opinion about immigration had always been contradictory and paradoxical rather than unified and coherent.[97] But as a growing number of elected officials and opinion leaders from across the political spectrum affirmed the notion that unlawful immigration was the central policy crisis of the day—and as grassroots restrictionist groups grew in size, recognition, and influence (accelerated through the process of qualifying Proposition 187)—claims for immigrant rights became increasingly stigmatized and ridiculed within public debates. The restrictionist claim that unauthorized immigrants—constructed in racialized terms as undeserving, criminal, and degenerate—lacked any claims-making authority now moved to the center of California political culture.

This shift did not exempt the standard-bearers of the Democratic Party. While gubernatorial candidate Kathleen Brown, Senators Boxers and Feinstein, and President Clinton all eventually came out against Proposition 187 by late October, their stance was hardly unequivocal. Feinstein continued to conduct tours of the California-Mexico border accompanied by the press to spotlight her call for greater enforcement. In July, a Feinstein campaign ad accused her Republican challenger, Congressman Michael Huffington, of failing to vote for additional border guards while declaring that Feinstein herself "led the fight to stop illegal immigration." The ad included footage similar to that used by Wilson's "They Keep Coming" ad of a shadowy mass of border crossers and a voice-over by Feinstein declaring that "three thousand illegal immigrants try to cross the border many nights." Even when Feinstein came out against Proposition 187 in late October, she championed her alternative plan of 2,100 additional Border Patrol agents, a dollar-per-person border-crossing fee, and a tamperproof work permit.[98] At a September press conference in Los Angeles, Attorney General Janet Reno announced the inauguration of Operation Gatekeeper to further fortify the San Diego sector of the Border Patrol with new agents and resources.[99] In short, while leading Democrats did not endorse Proposition 187, they fully participated in constructing unauthorized immigration as a political and economic crisis that required uncompromising action, essentially affirming the rationale that fueled Proposition 187.

Grassroots immigrant rights advocates struggled with these sentiments in their daily work. In the midst of the election in 1994, the *Orange County Register* carried a story about the nascent anti-187 organizing efforts of a group affiliated with the Delhi Community Center and the Sisters of St. Joseph in Anaheim. Rigoberto Rodriguez, a recent graduate of University of California, Irvine, who worked for the community center and the newly formed Orange County against 187 campaign, recalled that for two full days after the story ran a barrage of hostile callers tied up the center's phone lines with complaints, demanding to know why the nonprofit organization was supporting lawbreaking "illegals." Overwhelmed by the outrage and response, Rodriguez came to the sinking realization that the callers were probably "the same people calling the elected officials and media" with similar charges, a capacity that Proposition 187 opponents simply did not have.[100]

A final challenge facing the grassroots anti-187 campaigns concerned the ongoing, sometime public disagreements that erupted with the Taxpayers against 187 campaign. These disagreements were rooted in differences over tactics as well as the types of public narratives and messages the campaigns used. The Taxpayers continued to maintain that the framework asserted by Governor Wilson and Proposition 187's proponents, which constructed a fundamental opposition between *them* (unauthorized immigrants) and *us* (the innocent taxpayers) could not be contested; it was a fixed feature of the political landscape. Therefore, the only credible response was to affirm the basic framework but argue that the initiative would cause "us" more problems without doing anything about "them."

Again, it was not only the Republican consultants who embraced the logic of this approach. Many Latino elected officials, Democratic and labor leaders, and even prominent Latino civil rights organizations recited variations of this core message. For example, John Palacio of the Mexican American Legal Defense and Education Fund wrote in an *Orange County Register* op-ed that if three hundred thousand "kids without proper documentation" were thrown "out of our schools and into our streets . . . some of these kids would surely become involved in committing crimes."[101]

Frank Wu, the attorney who volunteered for several months with Californians United against 187, says that he was initially persuaded by this logic, particularly after making public presentations to audiences who were extremely hostile toward any perceived defense of undocumented immigrants. But Wu says that, in retrospect, he might have favored embracing what he describes as the "moral high-ground" argument, foregrounding the human rights of the undocumented and challenging the racist suppositions of the ballot measure. Wu suggests that the attempts to appeal to the notion of self-interest by arguing "we don't like them any more than you do but if we don't provide these services we'll all suffer" might be persuasive if voters somehow considered the measure entirely through a "rational policy discourse" framework and if they employed a "strict cost-benefit analysis." But Wu concludes that if a "racial subtext is there," then voters are not "amenable to these" claims, resulting in the use of "arguments [that] just don't sound good" or ethical, like those used by the Taxpayers campaign.[102]

The grassroots and Taxpayer factions began to clash, often publicly, accusing each other of sabotaging the campaign. Many grassroots organizers felt that the Taxpayers campaign sought to muzzle them before the mainstream press, fearing their strident opposition to the measure would alienate the very voters they were targeting. As one Los Angeles organizer told the *Sacramento Bee*, "We're tired of all this scapegoating. If the people in the suburbs can't deal with it, they can't deal with it. I have my disagreements with Taxpayers Against 187 and some of the arguments they've raised, too."[103]

The Taxpayers campaign was well aware of this friction. Scott Macdonald conceded in an interview after the election that the decision to affirm the idea that undocumented immigration was a problem "drove the people who were supposed to be our allies right through the roof," and the conflict diverted the time and energy of people on both sides of the debate. But he maintained that he and his colleagues at Woodward and McDowell had the expertise regarding "how to evaluate the polling and come up with the messages" and that a campaign like theirs had to "reflect those messages and further the public's understanding of them, or it is a waste." Because grassroots activists like Californians United, he insisted, "did not concentrate on those messages" the Taxpayers campaign had developed, their efforts were a "waste and in fact counterproductive."[104]

Disputes over tactics were another main difference between the two anti-187 campaigns. The Taxpayers campaign believed the best way to reach the high-frequency voters was to use recognizable centrist or even conservative spokespersons. Los Angeles County sheriff Sherman Block thus became one of the main spokespersons for the Taxpayers campaign, in the hopes that he could credibly make the case that Proposition 187 risked increasing the threat of street crime. In addition, there was an unspoken but well-understood rule within the campaign that Latino immigrants themselves would not be persuasive representatives before the white electorate.[105]

Groups like Californians United, by contrast, felt that the initiative provided an important opportunity for immigrants themselves to get involved in political activity. Even those who could not vote could still speak to the ethnic media and join phone banks and precinct walks in their communities. And whereas Macdonald felt that any imperative other than winning on Election Day was a distraction and a waste, organizers like Jan Adams with Californians United held the opposite view. According to Adams, when she looked at the initial polling data and realized the tenor of the political debate that was unfolding, it became "clear absolutely from the get-go that we could not defeat this thing." Adams and many of her colleagues hoped to use the campaign to build the political capacity of immigrant communities beyond the election by developing networks, relationships, and skills. To focus exclusively on the (unattainable) task of winning a majority of the votes statewide while neglecting the very communities being targeted made little sense.[106]

This dispute erupted most forcefully a few weeks before the election when anti-187 activists called for a large march in downtown Los Angeles. On October 16, an estimated crowd of seventy thousand to one hundred thousand people marched from East Los Angeles to city hall, a four-mile trek through the heart of the city's Latino community. Newspaper coverage of the crowds fixated on the thousands of Mexican flags carried by the marchers and their strident denunciations of Pete Wilson and Propo-

Figure 9.   March against Proposition 187, Los Angeles, October 16, 1994. Estimates put the crowd at between 70,000 and 100,000 people. Photo by Andy Scott courtesy of the *Los Angeles Times*.

sition 187. Over the next two weeks, students at dozens of high schools across the state followed by organizing their own walkouts and marches; thousands of students, mostly Latino, participated in the loosely coordinated actions.[107]

For some, these marches represented a breathtaking display of political energy—a rejection of a deeply abusive and racist political culture that constructed Latino immigrants as fit for low-wage labor but not for basic human rights or civic recognition. Californians United, which did not organize the marches formally but attempted to channel some of the energy into the election, felt that the marches and walkouts represented an outpouring of political anger and expression that could not and should not be suppressed. As Californians United's Irma Munoz explained, "Students are extremely frustrated. They're worrying about whether their friends and neighbors are going to be able to attend school, and they want to do something about it. But they can't vote, and they don't know how to make an impact."[108] Adams believed it was pointless for organizers to fret over the impact the marches would have on broader public opinion; they were going to happen regardless of whether the organized campaigns thought they were tactically effective. Californians United tried to recruit some of the students participating in the walkouts to join phone-banking and precinct-walking efforts before the election.

The Taxpayers campaign, however, regarded the marches and walkouts as a huge tactical blunder that sabotaged much of their work during the last three months. Their entire campaign strategy had been based on avoiding explicit discussions about race, immigration, and the political status of Latinos while largely affirming the anti-immigrant sensibilities of white voters. The march represented an outright rejection of such a strategy—a refusal to remain politically invisible and silent in the midst of venomous attacks or to apologize for one's presence. From the perspective of the Taxpayers campaign, the images of thousands of Latino students marching in the streets waving Mexican flags undercut any progress made by affirming the deepest fears of white voters. Taxpayers consultant Jack McDowell described the marches and walkout as a "tragedy. [The marchers] were trying to help. But the result was, I believe, they hurt."[109] As one letter in the *Los Angeles Times* put it, "Why should Californians support a foreign welfare state on its own soil? I would like to see all those Mexican flag-wavers go back to Mexico and demand free health care, education aid to dependent children and welfare."[110]

RACIAL LIBERALISM AND PROPOSITION 187

Just as the marches were erupting in mid-October, the Taxpayers campaign opened up a second front in their attack on Proposition 187. The Taxpayers launched a series of radio ads charging that the measure was tainted by extremism through its associations with the controversial Pioneer Fund, a New York–based foundation with a long history of funding eugenic and often explicitly racist social science research. Since 1988, the Pioneer Fund had contributed at least $600,000 to FAIR, which was employing Alan Nelson as a part-time consultant when he helped draft Proposition 187. The Taxpayer ads charged that "white supremacists are behind 187" and suggested that indiscriminate profiling would result if the measure were passed.[111]

The Taxpayers decision to affirm the racialized anxieties of the electorate, while simultaneously charging that Proposition 187 was a measure that went "too far," was a familiar tactic. The same approach was used by fair employment proponents in 1946 and continued with opponents of the anti–fair housing measure in 1964, the antidesegregation measures of the 1970s, and the English Only measures of the 1980s. The Taxpayers campaign similarly argued that Proposition 187 violated the principles of tolerance, fairness, and racial liberalism more generally.

The ballot measure's proponents, however, eagerly refuted such charges, recalling an equally familiar strategy of defending racialized political claims within the same discourse of fairness, tolerance, and liberalism. Disavowing any racist intent and invoking a long tradition of racial innocence, the proponents claimed the measure had nothing to do with race; it was illegal behavior, rather than people, they sought to address. Here, narratives about the environmental and fiscal "carrying capacity" of the state—the regrettable but inevitable limits imposed by nature itself—as well as the distinction between worthy and unworthy immigrants, effectively refuted charges of extremism. Ronald Prince asked, "What is it about the initiative that's racist? It doesn't deal with race. No one is identified in the initiative by race, creed or color." To the contrary, he insisted, "We're doing this out of love; we love our country." Republican congressman Dana Rohrabacher similarly held that "people with love in their hearts and good intentions know we can't afford to take care of everybody that comes here."[112]

Pete Wilson also defended his support of Proposition 187—he finally endorsed the measure on September 18—by rehearsing the distinction between worthy and unworthy immigrants. A television ad Wilson released in late October, which ran extensively during the two weeks before the election, opened with a nighttime view of the Statue of Liberty before cutting to a proud sea of faces at a citizenship ceremony. The warmhearted narration began, "It's how most of us got here. It's how this country was built. American citizenship is a treasure beyond measure." The ad then cut to the same footage of a stampede across a border checkpoint used in the "They Keep Coming" advertisement from the spring. Turning more stern and alarmist, the narrator intoned, "But now the rules are being broken." Alternating between these two images—proud new citizens affirming their loyalty and ominous figures streaming across the border—the narration concluded, "There's a right way, and there's a wrong way. To reward the wrong way, is not the American way."[113]

Some Proposition 187 supporters did certainly embrace the measure as a deliberate expression of racial nationalism and nativist exclusion. For example, Glen Spencer, head of a San Fernando Valley–based restrictionist group, Voices of Citizens Together, declared that "illegal immigration" was a "part of a reconquest of the American Southwest by foreign Hispanics." He added, "Someone is going to be leaving the state. It will either be them or us." Another bombastic Long Beach–based activist within the California Coalition for Immigration Reform similarly declared, "I have no intention of being the object of 'conquest,' peaceful or otherwise, by Latinos, Asians, blacks, Arabs or any other group of individuals who have claimed my country."[114]

But political scientist Robin Dale Jacobson, who conducted interviews with Proposition 187 supporters after the election, concluded that her respondents dismissed any notion that they were motivated by racism or cultural chauvinism.[115] From their perspective, pragmatic notions of fiscal limitations and the rule of law motivated their support for the measure, which they believed adhered to the basic principles of tolerance, fairness, and indeed racial liberalism as they understood them. Heavy-handed restrictions on unauthorized immigrants could not be regarded as racist because unauthorized immigrants remained legally outside of the nation's protections; they were not recognized as rights-bearing subjects.

This critique and disavowal worked on the terms and terrain of a liberal national political imagination. As legal scholar Linda Bosniak has perceptively argued, even progressive critics of Proposition 187 had difficulty establishing the normative grounds on which the measure could be opposed. For such progressives, the nation-state still functioned as the arbiter of rights for disenfranchised or subordinated groups. Because a nationally defined conception of political community seemed by definition to exclude unauthorized persons from its protections, progressives lacked a political vocabulary and imagination to summon a bold defense of the rights of the unauthorized. Bosniak argues that, as a result, even progressive critics of the measure primarily emphasized the *collateral* damage the measure would cause—such as violations of the rights of U.S.-born Latinos through racial profiling—rather than defending the rights of the undocumented as such.[116]

In the imagination of many Proposition 187 supporters, nationally defined ideals of rights and protections similarly exempted them from any charge of racism or an unwarranted denial of rights. Race could still function as an absent referent in this discourse, an unstated proxy for those who resided beyond the protections of the nation. And race, gender, and nation still mediated conceptions of worthiness and unworthiness through distinctions drawn between taxpayers and "illegals." But the normative ideals of rights, equality, and nondiscrimination not only failed to offer any resources or protection against such equivalences, they actually nurtured them, supplying Proposition 187 proponents with a liberal vocabulary through which to narrate and legitimize their claims.

While I describe the political subjectivity shaping this process as political whiteness, support for Proposition 187 extended beyond white voters. The distinctions between "good" and "bad" immigrants were also embraced by some African American, Asian American, and even Latino voters. A Latina in East Los Angeles fumed in a television interview that undocumented immigrants "know if they come over here, everything is going to be for free. They have more babies . . . they have it made."[117] While scholars have cited various factors for the support Proposition 187 garnered among some Latinos, the comment reveals that the gaze of political whiteness, which relies on race to help signify the boundaries of exclusion and the grounds of inclusion, can be inhabited by those who do not identify as white.[118]

COUNTDOWN TO THE ELECTION

As the election approached, Proposition 187 was still only endorsed by the California Republican Party, some individual Republicans, and a network of grassroots restrictionist organizations.[119] The opposition, by contrast, won endorsements from nearly every leading news organization in the state; dozens of prominent law enforcement, health care, and religious officials; numerous corporate representatives and various chambers of commerce; and even several prominent Republicans, including Jack Kemp, President Bush's secretary of housing and urban development, and William Bennett, who served as secretary of education under President Reagan. Kemp and Bennett, summoning the figure of the good immigrant argued that the "vast majority of immigrants hold principles which the Republican Party warmly embraces: an entrepreneurial spirit and self-reliance, hostility to government intervention, strong family values, and deeply-rooted religious faith."[120]

In addition, the original proponents of the measure began openly feuding, as grassroots activists like Barbara Coe and Ronald Prince faced off with more prominent figures like Harold Ezell and Alan Nelson. The sponsoring committee largely abandoned fund-raising and waged no organized campaign. Several proponents, including Ezell and Prince, stopped talking to the media altogether, wary of the increasingly strident tone and tactics of their critics.[121]

These developments, ordinarily disastrous for an initiative effort, mattered little in the campaign's final weeks, as the terms of the debate had already been firmly set. During the preceding year, Democrats had reasoned that by taking a tough posture on some restrictionist reforms—especially increased border enforcement and limiting access to public benefits—they would forestall demands for more sweeping changes. The opposite occurred. With Democrats now fully endorsing the claim that immigrants were indeed responsible for many of the state's crises, the rationale for limiting far-reaching policy prescriptions, such as those within Proposition

187, had largely dissipated. The state GOP never directly involved itself in the racialized ballot measures discussed in previous chapters in this book, and its support of Proposition 187 was uneven during the qualification period, as party operatives waited to see how the initiative would play. But with Democrats also advocating a crackdown on unauthorized entrants and with polls suggesting that voters believed the measure to be reasonable rather than extremist, the risks of backing the measure seemed small. The California Republican Party decided to make the ballot measure the central issue of its voter mobilization efforts, distributing slate mailers, coordinating volunteer phone banks, and delivering more than two million door hangers to mobilize voters. Wilson also aggressively promoted and backed the measure with millions of dollars after also deciding in late September that the potential benefits outweighed the risks of backlash. Wilson's focus on the measure in the weeks leading up to the campaign was relentless. According to one Wilson critic, "by the time the election rolled around, Wilson's internal tracking polls showed that more than 90% of voters knew Wilson's position on Proposition 187, more than the number of people who could identify Sacramento as the state capital." Wilson's own pollster conceded the recognition number was "amazing."[122]

The Taxpayers against 187 campaign, which fell well short of its $4 million fund-raising goal, continued attempting to convince voters that while their hostilities toward undocumented immigrants were legitimate, the unintended consequences the measure would produce would outweigh any benefits. But opinion polls taken in the closing weeks before the election seemed to confirm that many voters cared less about the specific components of Proposition 187—and their relative benefit or harm—and more about the message it would send to lawmakers and immigrants themselves that, as Wilson declared, "Enough is enough."[123] That is, they responded affirmatively to the first part of the Taxpayers message—that "illegal immigration" was indeed a problem—and remained ambivalent toward the second part—that Proposition 187 only made a bad problem worse. As Frank Wu of Californians United against 187 suggested, the effort to reach the rational and utilitarian voter who would be amenable to a "right idea, wrong solution" message was futile. With both sides affirming the proposition that there were indeed worthy and unworthy immigrants, the dispute mainly focused on the best method of containing or expelling the bad ones.[124]

A troubling irony also undergirded this strategy. Though the Taxpayers consultants concluded that the campaign must endorse the idea that many immigrants posed a somber threat to the welfare of the state, they also implicitly participated in wildly exaggerating the scale and impact of this alleged threat. As scholar David Hayes-Bautista later pointed out, beginning in the early 1990s immigration to the state had dropped considerably; in 1994 and 1995 more Latino immigrants left California than arrived, a pattern that continued for much of the decade. California's rapidly contracting labor market dimmed the prospects facing new arrivals. Yet even Senator Feinstein's reelection ads, depicting shadowy border crossings at night, insisted, "And they keep coming! Three thousand each night." Hayes-Bautista argues that if Feinstein's figures were correct, by the end of 1994 one in three California residents would have been an undocumented Mexican immigrants, and eight out of ten Latinos in Los Angeles County would have been undocumented.[125]

Hayes-Bautista also notes the flaws in the alarmist charges that "our children's classrooms" had become "over-crowded by those who are ILLE-GALLY in our country."[126] In fact, the overall enrollment in the Los Angeles Unified School District was actually 2.7 percent lower in 1994 than it was in 1969, and most school overcrowding could be traced to the district's decision in the early 1980s (in the wake of the ballot measures slashing property taxes and fanning public discontent over busing) to close many schools. Roughly 95 percent of Latino students in Los Angeles public schools were U.S. citizens or legal permanent residents; the "flood" of undocumented students was entirely imaginary, yet it was a problem affirmed by Proposition 187's proponents and opponents alike. Similarly, the large-scale cutbacks in public services that fueled so much of the animosity driving Proposition 187, nearly all of which could be traced to the wave of property tax–slashing measures in the late 1970s and early 1980s as well as to the increase in state prison spending, became almost singularly understood as a result of the impact of undocumented immigration.[127] But these points became largely inadmissible in the debate over Proposition 187.

THE OUTCOME OF THE ELECTION AND BEYOND

Proposition 187 was approved by 59 percent of the California electorate, receiving more than five million votes (see table 5). Exit polls suggested that the Taxpayers strategy of targeting white moderate and suburban voters largely failed. Sixty-three percent of white voters supported the measure, along with 62 percent of independent voters and 55 percent of self-described moderates.

Proposition 187 spawned multiple and contradictory legacies. Immediately after the election, a coalition of civil rights groups, backed by an

TABLE 5 Proposition 187 Exit Poll Data by Race/
Ethnicity, 1994

Group (% of electorate)	Yes (%)	No (%)
All (100%)	59	41
White (81%)	63	37
Black (5%)	47	53
Latino (8%)	23	77
Asian American (4%)	47	53

SOURCE: *LAT* exit poll, California General Election, November 8, 1994.

array of unions, school boards, city councils, and religious and medical groups, filed successful legal challenges before the California Superior Court and U.S. District Court to block implementation of the measure; the suits had been readied well before election day by attorneys in anticipation of the measure's passage. Multiple legal cases were ultimately consolidated as the *League of United Latin American Citizens et al. v. Wilson.* The case took more than four years to finally adjudicate; not until activists groups pressured Democratic Governor Gray Davis, who succeeded Pete Wilson in 1998, did the state formally drop its appeal and accept the judge's ruling blocking implementation of nearly all provisions of the measure. Only the section providing for penalties for document forgery were permitted to stand, and even those had a contradictory impact, as errors in the phrasing of the initiative language meant that the new provisions actually lowered criminal penalties for some forgery infractions.[128]

Though the courts prevented the state from implementing most of Proposition 187's provisions, several of the key tenets of the measure provided the blueprint for sweeping and more far-reaching federal reforms. The Republicans' 1994 Contract with America included no mention of immigration policy reforms. But after Proposition 187, a newly organized Congressional Task Force on Immigration Reform, chaired by Republican Elton Gallegly of California, essentially recommended federalizing much of Proposition 187. California Democrats, including Anthony Beilenson, Howard Berman, and Jane Harmon, expressed "strong support" for many of the proposals.[129] Major revisions to federal welfare law through the 1996 Personal Responsibility and Work Opportunity Reconciliation Act and immigration law through the 1996 Illegal Immigration Reform and

Immigration Act prohibited undocumented immigrants from receiving most public health services and benefits. The laws further prescribed a five-year waiting period even for lawful permanent residents to receive many of these services.[130]

For their part, the grassroots restrictionist organizations responsible for bringing Proposition 187 to the ballot failed to grow significantly in size or authority after the election. Proponents like Barbara Coe promised they would successfully recall many of the elected officials who supported the court's ruling against the measure. None of these efforts were successful. Nor did these organizations succeed in multiple subsequent attempts to qualify a Son of 187 measure for the ballot after the initial court rulings. Indeed, between 1994 and 1999, restrictionist groups attempted to qualify seven different statewide measures barring unauthorized immigrants from receiving different public services or benefits; Proposition 187 was the only one to even reach the ballot. Attempts to qualify measures in 2004 and 2006 also failed to meet the signature threshold. The populist ire claimed by Proposition 187 supporters proved less reliable and enduring than imagined.[131] But the boundaries of legitimate discourse over immigration control had been firmly established; political actors who did not make their claims through appeals to an aggrieved California populace risked swift dismissal. And as the next chapter explains, Democratic Party leaders in particular would come to view such boundaries as unassailable.

For many California Latinos, both immigrant and nonimmigrant, Proposition 187 represented a singularly important political event. During and after the election, advocacy organizations noted a swift upsurge in reported incidents of anti-Latino violence and aggression; one Los Angeles group set up a hotline that recorded more than one thousand incidents in the eleven months following the measure's passage.[132] In time however, analysts would conclude that the measure would help bring about a dramatic increase in naturalization, voting, and political participation rates among many Latinos, producing a cohort of deeply politicized voters that would begin transforming the composition of the California electorate.[133] Nonprofit organizations serving immigrant communities would also increasingly come to appreciate the role of political participation in asserting the rights of their constituents.[134]

For Proposition 187's organized opponents, response to the measure's passage fell into two distinct camps. The groups affiliated with the mainstream Taxpayers against 187 reiterated their contention that the crisis posed by undocumented, largely Latino immigrants could not be fundamentally altered, at least within the cycle of any election. The Taxpayers strategists insisted that pragmatism alone should govern the messaging and framing strategies for future public debates and ballot measures over immigration policy. A postmortem memo authored by Frank Sharry, head of the Washington, D.C.–based National Immigration Forum who worked for the Taxpayers campaign, made these points forcefully. Sharry declared that the "goal of winning 50% plus 1 of the votes on election day" was the only imperative that mattered with regard to such initiatives. Sharry emphasized that he "strongly endorse[d] the kind of messages" used by the Taxpayers campaign and that these themes should serve as the blueprint for future initiative campaigns.[135]

Organizers aligned with the Californians United against 187 effort sharply disagreed with this assessment. A postelection memo written by two of the main Californians United organizers and leaders, Ignatius Bau and Emily Goldfarb, challenged the fundamental assumption that the Taxpayers campaign strategy had any impact on the electorate or that a winning campaign must start with the concession that "something must be done to stop illegal immigration." They insisted that their "pro-immigrant/immigrant rights messages [were] sound" and that "Proposition 187 was a pretext for racism, for fear and anger about the demographic changes in California." Goldfarb and Bau conceded that their groups were "totally unprepared for an initiative campaign. . . . We didn't have the experience, expertise, or resources to respond."[136]

Jan Adams of Californians United also rejected the "50% plus 1" criteria asserted by Sharry. From her perspective, the anti-187 campaign had already arrived too late and with too few resources or electoral expertise to have any realistic hope of defeating the measure. She agreed that the various grassroots efforts to defeat Proposition 187 all "suffered from lack of electoral experience." In particular, the challenge of how to compete for votes within an electorate that was older, whiter, and more conservative than the populace as a whole was much different than shaping public opinion within the constituencies the groups behind Californians United typically engaged. In this Adams largely agreed with Sharry's assertion that marches and walkouts could not win elections, though she did contend that "this kind of activism was an important way for threatened communities to express perfectly justifiable outrage" and to "raise the visibility of the threat of the groups under attack."[137] However, as long as the electorate remained overwhelmingly white and expertise in electoral organizing remained the sole province of high-priced consultants who frowned upon grassroots involvement, the Proposition 187 outcome would likely be repeated in future electoral cycles.

For Adams, Goldfarb, and Bau, building the capacity to contest state-wide elections and expanding the electorate more generally constituted the long-term imperative. In this regard, the Californians United campaign in San Francisco seemed to hold some promise.[138] In San Francisco County, 71 percent of voters rejected Proposition 187. Adams would insist that this outcome was not simply the bias of the state's most liberal electorate, pointing out that other liberal campaigns—including the effort to approve a single-payer health insurance initiative (Proposition 186) and to reject the Three Strikes criminal-sentencing law (Proposition 184)—did not achieve similar results. Even the most conservative districts in San Francisco rejected Proposition 187, and margins in solidly immigrant and progressive areas exceeded 80 percent.[139]

The San Francisco outcome and experience, Adams reasoned, gestured toward a new model of electoral organizing. What if, rather than ceding the capacity to run successful electoral campaigns to consultants, community organizations developed these skills and abilities themselves? What if, rather than focusing almost exclusively on the mythical white, middle of the road voter, such a project grounded itself precisely within the communities that were most often marginalized by the electoral process? And finally, what if such a project placed the battle over ideas and interests—especially regarding race and racial oppression—at the center of its aspirations and tactics, refusing to subordinate itself to the "50% plus 1" mantra?

Adams and her colleagues soon began drafting a concept paper for a new framework for electoral organizing. Their plan, they soon realized, would face an immediate test: sponsors of a sweeping proposal to abolish all public affirmative action programs promised to qualify their own ballot measure within the next eighteen months.

7. "Special Interests Hijacked the Civil Rights Movement"

Affirmative Action and Bilingual Education on the Ballot, 1996-2000

In 1997, on the thirty-fourth anniversary of the 1963 March on Washington, where Rev. Martin Luther King Jr. had delivered his famed "I Have a Dream" speech, a smaller but similarly spirited crowd joined Rev. Jesse Jackson in a procession across the Golden Gate Bridge. This March to Save the Dream also coincided with the first day of the implementation of Proposition 209, a ballot measure approved the previous November banning public affirmative action programs in California. Together with the 1994 passage of Proposition 187 and the Three Strikes initiative, and with a signature-gathering effort underway to ban public bilingual education programs, a disturbing pattern seemed to be taking shape. Jackson implored the marchers to initiate a new civil rights movement in the Golden State in response to Proposition 209's "bludgeoning the dreams of this generation."[1]

Much of the crowd's ire was directed toward Republican governor Pete Wilson and University of California regent Ward Connerly, the African American businessman and Wilson ally who led the Proposition 209 campaign. Particularly infuriating to opponents was the use of the language and imagery associated with King—the ballot measure was dubbed the California Civil Rights Initiative. Jackson told the crowd, "Those who did not march with [King], who did not support him, cannot be the interpreters of the dream. I can interpret the dream. I marched with him. I walked with him and talked with him."[2] Similar charges would soon be directed at Ron Unz, the conservative Silicon Valley entrepreneur who would name his 1998 anti–bilingual education initiative English for the Children.

Jackson's charge echoed not only a common sentiment among many of the activists who labored to defeat these ballot measures but also pointed to something of an unfulfilled desire. If the opponents of civil rights would simply end their ideological charade and reveal their true racists intentions, none of these bitter debates would have erupted. The regularly sounded accusation that Connerly, Wilson, and others *stole* the language of the civil rights movement spoke to a particular understanding of the proprietary character of political ideas. From this perspective, the main signifiers of civil rights—empowerment, opportunity, justice, and equality—*belonged* to Jackson and his supporters in a way they did not belong to Connerly and Wilson.

But the debates over Proposition 209 in 1996 and the anti–bilingual education Proposition 227 in 1998 suggest a more complex relationship between language, ideology, and political transformation. The campaigns demonstrated that the prevailing language of civil rights was far more contradictory and polyvalent than many activists hoped, permitting Connerly to insist that it was affirmative action supporters who were the "special interests" who "hijacked the civil rights movement."[3]

These two landmark initiatives of the 1990s thus raised important questions about the relationship between racial liberalism and political whiteness: Would an electorate dominated by voters who were older, whiter, and more conservative than the state as a whole inevitably remain hostile to claims about the endurance of racism and racial inequality? What role would the political parties play in accentuating, engaging, or avoiding these questions? And could grassroots organizations that lacked the resources or capacity to wage expensive media campaigns still play a role in shaping the terms and outcome of ballot initiative elections?

THE PARADOXES OF AFFIRMATIVE ACTION

"The tide has turned," Thomas Wood told the *Washington Post.* "There is an anti-affirmative action issue coming down the pike in California that is going to make 187 look like kindergarten."[4] In December 1994, as Proposition 187 opponents raucously debated which faction of the campaign bore the greatest blame for the defeat, Thomas Wood and Glynn Custred were buoyed with optimism.

Since they first met in 1991, the two Bay Area academics had been toiling in relative obscurity to qualify a ballot measure to end public race- and gender-based affirmative action programs in the state. Though they called their measure the California Civil Rights Initiative (CCRI), arguing that a ban on race and gender "preferences" was consistent with the landmark 1964 Civil Rights Act, their grounds for opposing affirmative action programs were hardly novel. Wood and Custred were both self-identified conservatives who had grown frustrated in debates over multiculturalism, curricular reforms, and initiatives seeking to diversify the race and gender of college faculty in the state's universities. As a professor of anthropology at California State University, Hayward, Custred asserted that he observed "large numbers of under-prepared students" admitted through affirmative action programs. He asked, "Are we going to be a remedial institution or an institution of higher education?"[5]

Custred's claims expressed a familiar criticism of race- and gender-based affirmative action programs. These programs, their critics howled, benefited unqualified women and people of color at the expense of hard-working individuals who were penalized simply for their skin color or gender. Such charges emerged as soon as affirmative action programs became institutionalized in the early 1970s. In 1972, Pat Buchanan, a young speechwriter for Richard Nixon, authored a passage in the president's address at the Republican National Convention that warned of "the specter of a quota democracy—where men and women are advanced not on the basis of merit or ability, but solely on the basis of race, or sex, or color, or creed," threatening the "American dream." "You do not correct an ancient injustice by committing a new one," Buchanan wrote. "You do not remove the vestiges of past discrimination by committing a deliberate [act] of present discrimination."[6] For Buchanan, such instigations were a component of a wider partisan strategy to cast Democrats as "the party of the Blacks" in order to draw more white voters into the Republican fold.[7] The most notable controversies over affirmative action since then, including the 1978 *Bakke* decision of the U.S. Supreme Court overturning the affirmative action policies of the University of California, Davis, medical school and the infamous "Hands" television ad run by Senator Jesse Helms against challenger Harvey Gant in 1990, followed a similar narrative, one that could be traced back to the days of Reconstruction: an overreaching government rewarding an undeserving and shiftless Black population at the expense of the industrious white worker.[8]

These attacks stigmatized any signs of Black advancement in education or employment as undeserved and unwarranted while also erasing from consideration a much longer and deeper history of preferences benefiting white men.[9] The charges demonstrate political scientist Jennifer Hochschild's assertion that affirmative action often enters the public debate as a proxy for other racialized sentiments, a kind of cultural and political weapon largely untethered to empirical claims or experiences.[10] Thus data suggesting that white men filed a miniscule portion of the total employment discrimination complaints nationally or that women were far more likely to believe they were subject to discrimination on the basis of gender than men mattered little in the face of such claims.[11]

The possibility of firing an affirmative action arrow from the quiver of racialized issues led Buchanan to become one of the earliest and most prominent supporters of CCRI. Looking to the 1996 presidential election, Buchanan declared in a February 1994 syndicated column, "To win back California, the [Republican] party must win back the Perot vote, that vast middle-class constituency, alienated and populist, that felt itself abandoned by the Beltway." He suggested that the initiative proposed by Custred and Wood provided a "populist issue to reunite its old coalition and to slice Bill Clinton's new coalition asunder."[12]

Yet beyond right-wing activists like Buchanan and conservative publications like the *National Review,* Wood and Custred received little attention or support well into 1994. Their attempts to qualify their measure in 1992 and 1994 were quickly aborted. The state Republican Party passed a resolution endorsing the CCRI but did little to help it reach the ballot. In the midst of the California recession in the early 1990s, affirmative action garnered almost no mention in polls of pressing public concerns; education, crime, jobs, and eventually immigration garnered the lion's share of the attention.[13] In August 1994, a bill introduced by Republican assemblyman Bernie Richter to ban race- and gender-based affirmative action programs attracted little public notice; it died in the Democratic-controlled legislative committee.[14] The 1994 Republican Contract with America, while animated by provocative racialized attacks on crime and welfare, made no mention of the issue.[15] Many prominent Republican leaders, including Governor Pete Wilson, Senator Bob Dole, Congressman Jack Kemp, and others had historically backed modest race- and gender-based affirmative action programs. In September 1994, only six months before he announced his support for CCRI, Wilson declared, "I have long supported set-asides as a means to assist traditionally underrepresented businesses."[16]

Indeed, in spite of appeals from the likes of Buchanan and Helms, most extant affirmative action programs were in many ways compatible with conservative political commitments. They allowed for modest rather than sweeping desegregation in particular fields or industries. They did not require extensive commitments of government spending or oversight. They helped stave off broader and more disruptive antidiscrimination lawsuits and political advocacy. They were supported by many private employers seeking to diversify their workforces (and customer bases) in order to remain competitive. And they often traded in a language of individual deficit, compensation, development, opportunity, and competition, which comported well within an atomized and market-based analysis of racial or gender inequality.

THE DEMOCRATIC DISAVOWAL OF AFFIRMATIVE ACTION

Indeed, given the repeated failures that Wood and Custred had experienced during the previous three years and the limited support they garnered, one might wonder why Wood declared so confidently in late 1994 that "the tide has turned" regarding affirmative action. The shift he was asserting was less evident among Republicans, whose historical ambivalence toward affirmative action had not become suddenly transformed. Instead, the change Wood was describing was most apparent among the standard-bearers of the Democratic Party.[17] In 1993, a friend of Custred and Wood advised the pair to read the Democratic Leadership Conference's (DLC) "New Orleans Declaration," a 1990 document that outlined the policy vision of the Democratic alliance for the coming decade and their intentions to move the party away from traditional civil rights concerns. Chaired at the time by then Governor Bill Clinton of Arkansas, the declaration proclaimed, "We endorse [Andrew] Jackson's credo of equal opportunity for all and special privileges for none. . . . We believe the promise of America is equal opportunity, not equal outcomes." A year later, the DLC's platform specifically condemned "quotas that create racial, gender or ethnic preference."[18]

The language of the New Orleans Declaration resonated with Custred and Wood, who were pleased to see the obvious convergence between the central propositions of CCRI and the DLC position. The pair soon contacted the DLC leadership, which initially welcomed the opportunity to engage in some affirmative action warfare of its own.[19] The DLC had been launched in large part to move the Democratic Party toward the right, and through much of the early 1990s the DLC and Clinton actively sought out public opportunities to attack programs, figures, and politics that implied an allegiance to civil rights concerns traditionally identified with African Americans. In 1992 Clinton used an address to Rev. Jesse Jackson's National Rainbow Coalition to upbraid rapper Sista Souljah, comparing comments she made to those of former Louisiana Klan leader David Duke; the provocation was designed to make evident Jackson's diminished status within the "New Democrat Party." Indeed, the 1992 Democratic platform was the first in the post–World War II era "to make no mention of redressing racial injustice." Cheered on by a bevy of liberal strategists, journalists, and political leaders for neutralizing the kind of race-baiting attacks Democrats had endured during for the previous two decades, Clinton and the DLC eagerly sought opportunities to demonstrate their commitments to political whiteness.[20]

For much of 1995, even before CCRI qualified for the ballot, Democratic leaders from California indicated they would be open to endorsing the anti–affirmative action measure. Wood and Custred met DLC leaders Al From and Will Marshall early that year, and Wood contributed a short essay to the DLC journal *The New Democrat* on the future of affirmative action. State Democratic Party chairman Bill Press, who also met with Wood and Custred, publicly signaled his acquiesce in early 1995, before CCRI proponents even began collecting signatures. "Not only is this area where there's a possibility of compromise," Press told the *Los Angles Times,* "we have to be aggressive in seeking compromise in order to avoid a bloodbath in 1996." Press echoed Custred and Wood's refrain that many affirmative action programs had outlived their usefulness, perpetuated discrimination, and were subject to abuse. In a revealing metaphor, Press described the anti–affirmative action measure as "another Proposition 187 or worse, and I don't want another 187. I was mugged once. I don't want to be mugged again."[21] Prevailing wisdom held that the racialized currents that had buoyed Proposition 187 and sunk Kathleen Brown were unassailable. The party had little to gain from becoming embroiled in a contentious battle over affirmative action. Only after a showdown at the April 1995 state Democratic Convention, in which a coalition of CCRI opponents organized a group of delegates to carry "No Retreat on Affirmative Action" signs on the convention floor, did the prospect of the party's formal endorsement for CCRI finally fade.[22]

THE ALTERNATIVE MEASURE

Though state Democratic Party leaders decided not to endorse the CCRI, they were still not inclined to confront the initiative directly. In the middle of 1995, a group that included several Sacramento-based union strategists, Democratic consultants, and Bay Area legal advocacy groups concluded that, based on initial polling, support for CCRI was so high that an outright campaign to defeat the measure would lose. They decided instead to develop a competing initiative to put before voters that seemed to comport to pollster findings that a slim majority of voters would support affirmative action, provided that such programs explicitly disavowed numerical quotas and so-called preferential treatment. Rather than face an all or nothing vote against CCRI, the consultants argued that a debate between two competing measures—one that would altogether eliminate affirmative action and another that would modify it—was more favorable. The consultants and a group of attorneys soon drafted an Equal Opportunity without Quotas measure that revised the state constitution to explicitly outlaw quotas, even though quotas had already been banned by the U.S. Supreme Court eighteen years earlier and no state program made use of them. The draft measure also prohibited the hiring of "unqualified applicants" and levied fines against anyone found to have improperly benefited from an affirmative action program.[23]

Other CCRI opponents, particularly groups based in Los Angeles, including the Feminist Majority Foundation, the California chapter of the National Organization of Women (NOW), and the NAACP Legal Defense Fund (LDF), were adamantly opposed to the alternative initiative strategy. One critic argued that the alternative measure was actually "worse than CCRI," as it "gave into the premises and the assumptions of the right wing."[24] A poll conducted by Louis Harris of the Harris Poll for the Feminist Majority suggested that voters' support of CCRI remained high only when respondents were under the impression that the measure banned "preferential treatment." But when told the measure banned nearly all forms of affirmative action, polling suggested that support for the measure dropped to 31 percent, and opposition rose to 56 percent. This finding formed the basis of a different interpretation for pollster Harris and his clients.[25] They concluded that most voters believed that some race and gender discrimination still existed and were willing to support programs designed to remedy such discrimination. The dispute reveals the extent to which polling data and electoral patterns in general become relevant through the stories fashioned to interpret them. Where the group supporting the alternative Equal Opportunities without Quotas measure crafted a story about an unstoppable tidal wave of white opposition to race- and gender-based affirmative action, the other group offered an account of a more sympathetic electorate that could be mobilized to defend antidiscrimination protections for women and people of color.

Ultimately, the debate over the alternative initiative ended before a single signature was gathered. In December 1995, the nonpartisan legislative analyst concluded that the measure as written would require the state to end roughly $38 million in payments to magnet schools and "racially isolated minority school programs" that had developed during the desegregation struggles of the 1970s and 1980s that even most busing opponents had championed (see chapter 5).[26] Against the hopes of many Democratic and labor strategists and their consultants, CCRI would have to be opposed directly.

CALIFORNIANS FOR JUSTICE

Where Democratic leaders and many of their allies saw a nearly hopeless quandary, Jan Adams saw an opportunity. "Contrary to many people's despairing thoughts in the wake of the Prop. 187 experience, there is a 'progressive' majority which can be won in November 1996, if we do the work to win it." So began the brief memo she prepared for her colleagues at the Applied Research Center (ARC), an Oakland-based policy and advocacy nonprofit founded to highlight the endurance of racism and racial disparities in public policy. After reflecting on her experiences as one of the central organizers with Californians United against 187, the grassroots coalition that worked to defeat the measure within San Francisco and seven other Northern California counties, Adams saw a narrow window of opportunity to defeat CCRI. It was true, she conceded, that the eight to ten million people who regularly voted in California did not reflect the diversity of the state. The electorate continued to be older, wealthier, and more formally educated than California's thirty million residents as a whole. Most striking and salient in relation to CCRI was the continued racial imbalance: *"though nearly half the state's residents are members of the various communities of color, the electorate in 1994 was 81% white."* In 1994, 63 percent of these white voters cast ballots in favor of Proposition 187, which provided more than enough margin of victory for the measure to pass statewide, regardless of how Latinos, Asian Americans, and African Americans voted. It was this bloc of voters, and their entanglements with political whiteness, that seemed to make CCRI a guaranteed winner.[27]

Adams reasoned that the anti–affirmative action measure could be narrowly defeated if two conditions were met. First, an intensive education and mobilization campaign targeting Black, Latino, Asian American, and progressive white voters—those most receptive to an unapologetic defense of affirmative action—would have to take place. If voters of color could collectively raise their share of the electorate from roughly 19 percent in 1994 to 25 percent in 1996, and if they could be persuaded to vote against CCRI by a margin of at least three to one, it would help mitigate the broader racial imbalance within the electorate.

To meet this first condition, Adams and her colleagues would launch a new organization in an attempt to "break with the notion, supported by both political parties, that the way to win elections is to influence the swing sector of the already existing electorate," which "forces the less experienced and less resourced groups to play on the other side's terrain."[28] Where most electoral campaigns began in earnest a few months before the election, this effort would start immediately, nearly eighteen months before the November 1996 election. The campaign would eschew the expensive radio and television advertising that dominated statewide politics and instead rely on direct contact with voters in more than a thousand precincts across the state. While traditional campaigns often paid little attention to voters in low-income African American, Latino, and Asian American neighborhoods, reasoning that relatively low turnout levels did not justify the return, this campaign would be focused almost entirely on such communities. Finally, while nearly all electoral campaigns pulled up stakes immediately after an election, this project would not only identify, register, educate, and turn out tens of thousands of voters for the election, it would build the capacity to contest future electoral contests.

The long-term goal would be to change the overall composition of the California electorate by building power for what Adams referred to as "the emerging majority" in California politics—progressives, people of color, low-income people, and young people. As Adams later explained, the hope was "to speed up the incorporation of people who would eventually make up the majority."[29] ARC executive director and longtime community organizer Gary Delgado suggested a simple but compelling moniker— Californians for Justice (CFJ)—and a local artist, Kristen Zimmerman, designed a vivid logo for the new formation, which incorporated a quote from a 1972 open letter to Angela Davis from James Baldwin: "If they take you in the morning, they will be coming for us that night."[30]

The incorporation of the Baldwin quote expressed another significant aspiration of the proposed project. Traditionally, most electoral organizing was either explicitly nonpartisan, such as voter-registration efforts launched by independent organizations, or narrowly partisan, such as turnout efforts on behalf of an individual candidate. CFJ's premise was different. Voting and electoral activity alone carried little relevance or significance unless it was tied to a broader political vision, one that explicitly laid out the competing ideological stakes confronting voters and their communities.

This ideological emphasis became one of the clearest and sharpest priorities of the new group. Several of the trainings CFJ would soon develop specifically focused on educating the group's staff, volunteers, and other organizations about the importance of projecting a strong and uncompromising defense of affirmative action, in contrast to the compromise strategy preferred by Democratic and labor strategists. An internal CFJ memo sought to explain why these groups would likely use "infuriating and racist messages" in their effort to defeat the initiative. Their campaign messages, developed through focus groups and carefully vetted by cautious professional strategists, would lead mainstream opponents of CCRI "to adopt messages which conciliate centrist white voters and are likely to infuriate many people in the communities of color and among white progressives." CFJ insisted that campaign messages had consequences beyond short-term voter persuasion: they valorized or stigmatized particular ideas about racism and sexism, fairness, and equality and what society could and should do about patterns of inequity. CFJ remained critical of such apologetic messages because they "pander[ed] to the racism and sexism of centrist voters, validating their concerns, fears and anger with affirmative action and people of color" without acknowledging "that racism and sexism exist." That is, these groups would "concede upfront what many of us defend as a matter of principle. . . . We would say they give away in advance what we are trying to defend."[31]

The second condition that Adams believed had to be met to defeat CCRI was to limit the margin of support among white voters for the initiative to no more than 55 percent. Adams reasoned that if a meaningful gender gap could be secured by "making a no vote the vehicle by which women express their distress about sexism, especially in the workplace (the Anita Hill believers)," then the "angry white male" vote seeming to animate the measure could be neutralized. Here, paradoxically, the fate of the initiative would rest with the very organizations that CFJ viewed with such suspicion—labor unions, Democratic Party leaders, and mainstream civil rights and women's rights organizations—as they had the capacity and resources to reach such voters, even if they relied on messages that undermined a full-throated defense of affirmative action.[32]

CFJ's goal of significantly expanding the electorate in a state with thirty million people was wildly ambitious. But they would not go it alone. In Los Angeles, another organization, Action for Grassroots Empowerment and Neighborhood Development Alternatives (AGENDA), was hatching a wide-eyed campaign of its own to mobilize a citywide coalition of voters to defeat CCRI. By August 1995, AGENDA helped launch the Greater South Los Angeles Affirmative Action Project (GSLAAP), which would spend the next year doing intensive precinct-based organizing to educate voters about the initiative and to mobilize them on Election Day. The effort brought together scores of political leaders as well as dozens of local unions, churches, and other community organizations. While the project targeted the Black voters, who for decades constituted the political backbone of South Los Angeles area, it made deliberate efforts to reach out to the rapidly expanding bloc of Latino voters as well. AGENDA also set out to both defeat the measure within the city and to build the capacity of organized South Los Angeles residents to influence future elections.[33]

QUALIFYING CCRI FOR THE BALLOT

The great fear of Democratic leaders like state chairman Bill Press, who hoped to avoid having to make any public defense of affirmative action (which might trigger, in his words "Armageddon"), was that Republicans would follow Pat Buchanan's call to use CCRI to break apart Bill Clinton's base of white voters.[34] This was certainly the motivation of some CCRI supporters. In early 1995, Governor Wilson, who had historically supported modest affirmative action programs, concluded that a shift in his position could help boost his chances for winning the GOP presidential nomination in 1996. In mid-February, he announced his support for CCRI, and in early June issued an executive order to "End Preferential Treatment and to Promote Individual Opportunity Based on Merit." In July 1995, he worked with University of California (UC) regent Ward Connerly, to bring a resolution to the upcoming board of regents meeting in San Francisco banning the UC system from using "race, religion, sex, color, ethnicity or national origin as a criteria for admission." More than 250 news reporters from across the country descended on the meeting, as did Rev. Jesse Jackson and hundreds of protestors. It was exactly the kind of political theater that Wilson sought. Over the strident objections of the chancellors, faculty senates, and student associations at all nine UC campuses as well as the UC president and provost, the resolution passed by a fourteen-to-ten vote, making the UC system the first public university in the country to adopt such a restriction. Their efforts to explain how affirmative action actually worked in the UC system—that all students had to meet exceptionally rigorous admissions criteria and that the policy's main impact was to ensure that individual campuses did not become rigidly segregated by race and class—had little traction in the face of Wilson's charges that skin color rather than merit determined who was admitted to the prestigious system. More important to Wilson, he received national attention for staring down Jackson and rejuvenating his campaign promise to stand up for those people that "worked hard, paid taxes, and obeyed the law."[35]

Wilson did not hesitate to express the shrill and aggrieved tones that were the currency of racial propositions favored by Pat Buchanan. He told CBS's *Face the Nation* that ending affirmative action would return the focus to more pressing problems: the "children growing up in fatherless homes producing the next generation of unwed mothers and the next

Figure 10.   Gathering signatures for the California Civil Rights Initiative,
Proposition 209, at a San Francisco gun show, October 1995. Photo by
Scott Braley.

generation of thugs."[36] Wilson also proved quite willing to promote the
CCRI for partisan gain. During a conference call with GOP House Speaker
Newt Gingrich and several California businessmen in the fall of 1996,
Wilson argued explicitly that Republicans should use the measure to help
"wedge" Democrats and defeat Bill Clinton by forcing him to take a stand
on the issue.[37]

Wilson's attacks on affirmative action certainly resonated with a portion of the electorate and appealed to a certain base of CCRI supporters.
The CCRI campaign began its signature-gathering drive in the fall of
1995 and specifically targeted gun shows in search of such audiences.[38]
But ultimately, a self-proclaimed base of "angry white males" alone could
not sustain the CCRI campaign or even Wilson's presidential ambitions.
Though Wilson's bid for the GOP nomination received a temporary bump
from the UC controversy, his campaign soon faltered, failing to trigger
the enormous backlash against affirmative action predicted at the time by
many pundits. Indeed, heading into the fall, other Republicans, including Gingrich and Senator Bob Dole, proved reluctant to enter the fray
over affirmative action. The CCRI campaign soon found itself in desperate
straits. In October, the loose committee of early proponents who had been
coordinating the petitioning effort, including political consultant Arnold

Steinberg and conservative San Diego businessman Darrel Issa, was forced to suspend gathering signatures; contributions for the effort had slowed to a trickle. Unlike the Proposition 187 effort, which could rely on a legion of volunteers to collect a significant proportion of the necessary signatures, the CCRI effort had no such support.[39]

Ultimately, it was not a Pat Buchanan or Jesse Helms backlash figure that saved CCRI's fortunes. It was instead Ward Connerly, who announced on December 1, 1995, that he would serve as chairman of the campaign, almost certainly preventing the demise of the measure.[40] The Sacramento-based housing-development consultant had been a political ally of Wilson for more than two decades when the governor nominated him to the UC Board of Regents in 1994. Born in Louisiana and raised in Sacramento, Connerly was best described as a moderate Republican who secured his spot as a regent because of his longtime financial support for Wilson and because, as his critics noted with irony, the governor was under pressure at the time to diversify his appointments to the board.[41]

Connerly's announcement instantly rejuvenated the campaign. In less than three months, he and Wilson raised more than $900,000 for the measure, primarily from the Republican Party and conservative donors, who were much more confident about the initiative's fate under Connerly's leadership. Signature gathering quickly resumed, as the campaign now paid top dollar to petitioners in a frantic attempt to meet the deadline.[42] At a February 21 press event, Connerly and Wilson delivered boxes containing some of the 1.1 million signatures collected to a Sacramento elections office, assuring the measure a place on the November ballot as Proposition 209.[43]

Connerly proved to be devastatingly effective over the next ten months as the leading voice of CCRI. While Thomas Wood and Glynn Custred had authored the ballot measure and bequeathed it a shrewd title, the two academics, and the early circle of conservative supporters who championed their cause, narrated the attack on affirmative action in familiar ways—appealing to abstract notions of fairness, individual rights, and equality before the law and railing against the sins of reverse discrimination. Connerly did not substantially depart from these arguments. But the claims took on a completely different resonance when articulated through Connerly's self-fashioned narrative of personal uplift and post-racial triumph.

Connerly insisted that CCRI expressed a high-minded and unifying commitment to fairness and equality rather than a racist revolt against the promise of civil rights. He deliberately distanced himself and the campaign from more extremist figures such as Buchanan. During the week

Figure 11.   Ward Connerly and Governor Pete Wilson deliver signatures for the California Civil Rights Initiative, Proposition 209, to Sacramento County registrar, February 1996. Photo by Scott Braley.

before the March 1996 presidential primary, Connerly refused to appear anywhere with Buchanan, who was again seeking the GOP nomination.[44] Buchanan's right-wing populism conflicted with Connerly's professed commitments to fairness and equality.

At the same time, Connerly staunchly defended the racial innocence of the CCRI's supporters.[45] Connerly insisted that Californians were "outraged by bigotry. Whether it is in the '60s, garbed in hoods and sheets, or in the '90s, garbed in the guise of racial solidarity."[46] "Bigotry," Connerly declared, was "an equal opportunity disease. Anybody can get it."[47] And while he described his personal encounters with racism—"'colored only' bathrooms and drinking fountains in the South"—he insisted that those experiences did not define his racial world. "I've seen racism" he said. "But I've seen people who've helped me without there being an affirmative action gun to their heads."[48]

Even as Connerly endorsed the triumph of white racial innocence, he also emphasized the supplementary narrative of white racial injury, championing the cause of those wounded by allegedly spurious quotas and preferences. "There is no such thing as victimless affirmative action," he warned. "At some point, we must say we are going to stop redressing past sins."[49] He could testify to the "humiliation of drinking from a fountain that says 'colored only,'" but he insisted equally "with every fiber of my being that what we're doing is inequitable to certain people. . . . I want something in its place that is fair."[50] And he did not hesitate to confront those who would give comfort to the perpetrators of white injury. When Pacific Gas and Electric (PG&E) announced that it would oppose CCRI, Connerly led a picket in front of a company site in San Francisco, wielding a "PG&E Discriminates" sign.[51] Connerly thus asserted familiar appeals to political whiteness, rejecting, as he euphemistically described it, "discriminat[ion] against non-affirmative action eligible students."[52] But these arguments had little of the revanchist tinge associated with Buchanan when offered by Connerly.

Connerly also constantly recounted personal stories of struggle and triumph in ways that allowed him to recite familiar allegations of Black failure and dependency while still proclaiming his unqualified commitment to Black uplift and prosperity. "I walked to school with holes in my shoes" and returned to a dinner of "a couple slices of sweet potato" and "a glass of milk," he told the *Sacramento Bee*. "I know what it's like to struggle."[53] Indeed, he offered himself as a racial martyr of sorts, willing to endure sharp-tongued criticism and ridicule in order to deliver the candid, even empathetic admonition to fellow African Americans that reliance on state-sponsored programs like affirmative action was a cause rather than an effect of racial inequities. Dozens of profiles of Connerly drew on the same stock story: a "black, self-made businessman" who braved derision from his own community to stand up to racial preferences and quotas.[54]

If his story offered a lesson in the values of self-discipline and individual uplift, he contended that those who did not share in his prosperity did so because they lacked such traits: "What are the forces causing blacks not to be competitive? Lack of family, lack of values, black kids not appreciating the importance of education." And it was his opponents, he insisted, who were ultimately responsible for enduring racial inequities. "The other side is implanting in these kids minds that they can't survive without affirmative action, that there is some white racist society holding them down. As a result they don't work as hard as their talents would allow. It's not healthy for blacks to be perceived as a permanent underclass."[55] Affirmative action programs had produced "quota addicts" who developed a "slavish reliance" to the myth of their own dependency.[56]

With Connerly at the helm, efforts to brand CCRI as a crass expression of racial animus became extremely difficult. Defending the campaign's claim to the "civil rights" moniker unapologetically, Connerly deployed this signifier as largely commensurate with, rather than in opposition to, appeals to political whiteness. After a generation's worth of effort to publicly cast Martin Luther King Jr. as a distinctly American hero and a champion of individual rights and liberty (evident in standard portrayals of the civil rights leader during most King Day celebrations), Connerly's claims were not without precedent. The 1963 Washington, D.C., address where King offered his vision of a society that would someday judge his children by the "content of their character" rather than the "color of their skin" was organized as the March on Washington for Jobs and Freedom. But the wider demands animating the march—claims for economic justice and a broad condemnation of racial subordination—had for many years been erased from popular memory, replaced with a vision of a civil rights movement committed narrowly to individual rights, opportunity, and a condemnation of overt discrimination, the familiar shibboleths of racial liberalism. Nearly thirty years after King's death, the groundwork had long been laid for Connerly to argue that he too was committed to King's dream.

CCRI backers readily conceded that the 1964 Civil Rights Act provided the moral and legal warrants to punish individual perpetrators of discrimination. Erol Smith, an African American businessman, former conservative talk show radio host, and a vice chair of the Yes on 209 campaign, explained on a Los Angeles television program that "when we find cases of discrimination, we [should] punish them on a case by case basis. This is a good thing and we should continue to do that. What we should stop doing is to operating with blanket policies that assume that to be white is to be advantaged and to be a minority or woman is to be disadvantaged." Smith's proposition, then, was that a commitment to civil rights did not warrant any broad, group-based efforts to remedy racial hierarchies, a contention that followed rather than contradicted the main commitments of racial liberalism. Indeed, most of the enabling legislation of the civil rights period—fair employment and fair housing laws and other antidiscrimination protections—addressed intentional and individual expressions of racial animus and adjudicated them through individual complaints and remedies; the legislation did not seek to resolve entrenched forms of group power, privilege, and advantage. Those contending that racism functioned through collective rather than individual actions had difficulty summoning the "civil rights movement" signifier to their cause. Connerly did not.[57]

It was these claims that ultimately confounded CCRI opponents more than the racialized "mugging" long feared by Democratic leaders. After CCRI qualified for the ballot with a large contribution from the state Republican Party, most national Republican leaders kept their distance from the measure. GOP presidential nominee Bob Dole eventually endorsed Proposition 209 but failed to champion it with any great enthusiasm. In June, House Speaker Newt Gingrich publicly urged Dole to move away from the issue, charging it would be a "strategic mistake" for him to endorse CCRI, particularly when there was no alternative program in place.[58] Other influential Republican figures, including General Colin Powell and Congressman Jack Kemp, Dole's running mate, made clear that they viewed affirmative action as positive. Corporate contributors sympathetic to Republican causes also stayed out of the fray; several, including ARCO and Bank of America, signed on to a statement circulated by the California Business Roundtable reaffirming a commitment to affirmative action.[59]

THE GRASSROOTS CAMPAIGNS AGAINST PROPOSITION 209

While both the national Democratic and Republican parties vacillated in their respective positions on Proposition 209, Californians for Justice continued mounting a statewide field campaign to register and turn out the hundreds of thousands of new voters it would take to defeat CCRI. Since the early summer of 1995, the organization had been recruiting the legion of volunteers it would need to accomplish this task. CFJ organizers began fanning out at public fairs, college campuses, and busy street corners asking passerby to sign a Million Voices for Justice petition declaring their support for affirmative action. The petition was not a legal document, but a tool to give organizers a reason to begin talking about CCRI and the attack on affirmative action within their emerging majority constituency and to recruit volunteers at follow-up phone banks. Over many months, this process brought hundreds of new activists through the group's Oakland and Los Angeles offices, preparing for the approaching campaign.

CFJ also organized boisterous protests and actions targeting a series of donors to CCRI. The group's Youth for Justice arm organized a series of demonstrations outside local branches of Home Savings and Loan, the bank owned by wealthy CCRI supporter Howard Ahmanson. These actions never attracted overwhelming media attention or more than a hundred participants, but they modeled and exemplified the explicitly political and activist orientation of CFJ that distinguished the organization from mainstream CCRI opponents. As CFJ organizer Mimi Ho explained, "If we miss the opportunity to make the analytic connections" between affirmative action and other political debates, "we will lose the battle and the war."[60] Jan Adams noted that this approach sought to influence the "the ideological

Figure 12. Million Voices for Justice petitioning, 1996.
Mike Chavez of Californians for Justice gathers signatures
for a petition in support of affirmative action at a Pasadena
supermarket. Photo by Scott Braley.

context" of the anti-CCRI effort, thus "deepening resistance to the anti-ideological counter initiative strategy" that was being championed by most Democratic strategists, consultants, and legal advocacy groups.[61]

By the summer of 1996, one year into the effort, CFJ had collected nearly eight hundred thousand signatures on its petitions, identified eight thousand potential volunteers, and collectively trained more than two thousand people about the initiative and electoral organizing. Other organizations interested in supporting the campaign sent staff, members, and

Figure 13. Student activists with Californians for Justice confront a representative of Home Savings and Loan Bank, 1996. The bank's majority shareholder, Howard Ahmanson, had contributed heavily to the campaign to pass Proposition 209. Photo by Scott Braley.

interns to the volunteer opportunities CFJ offered each week in locations across the Bay Area and Los Angeles. CFJ also convened a twenty-six-member steering committee of representatives from various faith, labor, and community-based organizations to involve them in the effort.[62]

As the final campaign push began in early September 1996, the painstaking work of the previous fourteen months raised high expectations among CFJ's leaders that the organization could indeed help tip the scales against Proposition 209. While the group survived its first year on a shoestring budget, relying on a combination of volunteers, staff, and resources donated by other organizations and on grassroots donations, it eventually cobbled together enough support from progressive foundations, individual donors, and allied community-based organizations to increase its capacity substantially. It developed a series of detailed training modules covering the basics of CCRI, affirmative action, petitioning, volunteer recruitment, and other aspects of electoral organizing. By September the group claimed twenty-five paid organizers in some thirteen offices—some no larger than a desk, phone, and fax borrowed from a local union—across the state.[63]

As the fall campaign unfolded, however, the limitations of the effort also became apparent. The group faced difficulty expanding beyond its base in the Bay Area and some parts of Los Angeles; it had no presence in the Central Valley, Inland Empire, or other Southern California counties. Thin resources and staffing limited the rate at which the group could expand. In addition, even in those areas where volunteers had been successfully recruited, the labor required to register, educate, and mobilize voters in communities with historically low-turnout rates was time-consuming and exacting. Residents in such areas tend to move frequently, so official voter-registration lists quickly become outdated. Volunteer teams often need to be multilingual, especially in many parts of Oakland, San Francisco, and Los Angeles. Within such constraints, progress was measured slowly. Even though hundreds of volunteers were passing through the group's various offices, and the goal of working in fifteen hundred precincts across the state seemed within reach, it was clear that the CFJ effort alone was not going to reach the hundreds of thousands of new voters Adams projected would be necessary to defeat CCRI. And while there were other field-organizing efforts in the state—most notably the Greater South Los Angeles Affirmative Action Project and a group of college students brought together by an initiative sponsored by the Feminist Majority—those groups also faced similar constraints.[64]

The issue of affirmative action itself also proved challenging. Adams and other CFJ leaders concluded they had no choice but to confront the CCRI effort directly, lest the conservative backers of the measure would become further emboldened and "kick us again, and harder" and use the victories in California over affirmative action and immigration to launch national campaigns. But Adams conceded that the issue was not of their choosing: "Clearly, if we had a choice about where to draw the line, affirmative action might not be at the top of the list."[65] While affirmative action was important to defend—both as a set of policies and as a symbolic commitment—there was no widespread constituency or group invested in the issue. To be sure, among some groups—especially college students, older African Americans, and some progressives—the issue had a strong resonance. Many of CFJ's staff and core volunteers were college students and recent graduates already energized by struggles over multiculturalism and diversity issues on their campuses, and they interpreted CCRI as a similar attack. But for the majority of those contacted on precinct walks or during petitioning, recognition of the issue was not automatic, and other connections had to be made.

Maritza Madrigal, a UC Berkeley student and CFJ volunteer explained that when walking in a predominantly Latino precinct in the East Oakland neighborhood where she grew up, it was the sting of Proposition 187 that provided an opening to talk about CCRI: "You ask someone if they've heard about 209, they say 'No,' but you say 'Pete Wilson' and it's 'Oh, yeah.'"[66] Most volunteers shared similar experiences; mentioning Wilson's support of Proposition 209 alone was enough to convince the vast majority of Latino voters to oppose the measure, even if they had no direct experiences with affirmative action programs. But Proposition 187 had provoked a march of some seventy-five thousand people in Los Angeles and dozens of school walkouts across the state; except for among some students, Proposition 209 simply did not arouse the same intensity of reaction.

Even among African American voters, awareness about the issue was often limited. As Anthony Thigpen, organizer with Action for Grassroots Empowerment and Neighborhood Development Alternatives, told journalist Lydia Chavez, "First we had to convince people that affirmative action was something that had to do with them . . . I'd ask [at a community meeting], 'Who knows anyone working for the post office or police,' and hands would go up. That was affirmative action. And then I'd talk about their children in schools. Still the degree that it touches them in their daily lives is small." Thigpen's examples illustrated that, contrary to the claims of some critics, working-class communities did benefit from many affirmative action programs. But as he and many other Proposition 209 opponents came to realize, it was an issue that often demanded intensive one-on-one conversations.[67]

For both CFJ and AGENDA, the energy unleashed by their campaigns suggested that these emerging efforts—the first in more than two decades that sought to involve large numbers of grassroots volunteers in an electoral drive in defense of racial justice—seemed rich with possibility. But even CFJ's extensive grassroots fund-raising efforts yielded only $364,352 for the entire campaign—enough to keep the field operation going but not enough to take to the airwaves in a week before the election.[68] It was labor unions, Democratic Party leaders, and traditional civil rights and women's rights groups who were positioned to raise the millions of dollars necessary to reach the predominantly white Democratic and middle of the road voters through an expensive television, radio, and direct-mail campaign. The measure's fate would ultimately be in their hands.

THE MAINSTREAM CAMPAIGN
AGAINST PROPOSITION 209

Since they first began meeting to plot a response to CCRI in January 1995, the more established organizations opposing the measure often found themselves in bitter internal disputes over strategy, messaging, and resources. As the election approached, the groups remained mired in rancorous internal clashes as they struggled to find a persuasive narrative for their campaign. On one side of this divide stood groups like the Feminist Majority and the National Organization for Women, which insisted that the campaign against Proposition 209 should center on a bold defense of women's rights. As a NOW strategy memo explained, "The attack on affirmative action—much like the current attacks on reproductive rights, welfare rights, family law—must be placed in the context of a broader attack on women's fundamental civil rights."[69] Bill Clinton won the 1992 presidential election on the strength of a seven-percentage-point advantage among women voters, and groups like NOW reasoned that these voters could similarly help swing the Proposition 209 election. The 1995 Harris Poll commissioned by the Feminist Majority suggested that moderate white women in particular could be persuaded to recognize CCRI as a gendered attack on their rights, as opposed to an appeal to their racial privilege; the Feminist Majority and NOW set out to reframe the debate on those terms. Their strategy focused on what they described as CCRI's "skeleton clause," or Clause C, which stipulated that "bona fide qualifications based on sex" could not be prohibited if they were "reasonably necessary." The term "reasonably necessary," they argued, lowered the prevailing legal standard of protection against gender discrimination, potentially paving the way for the elimination of girls' sports and education programs, sealing cracks in the glass ceiling, and forcing women into "low-paying, low status jobs."[70]

NOW and the Feminist Majority set out to raise $5 million in support of a major media campaign to defeat the measure; their leaders were well connected to liberal Hollywood donors who supported many Democratic candidates. NOW made the defeat of CCRI a leading priority of its national Fight the Right rally in San Francisco in March 1996 and at its national conference in Las Vegas in June, and the group developed an ambitious plan to target a bloc of nearly one million white women voters whom polls suggested were undecided about CCRI.[71]

A second faction of the group based in Northern California, which had earlier supported the attempt to qualify an alternative initiative, was less convinced that a strategy singularly focused on a gender gap could win the election. An October 1995 poll commissioned by this group suggested that 74 percent of white women initially supported the measure, a rate marginally higher than for white men. Pollster Diane Feldman interpreted the results of her firm's findings: "White women, with the exception of those who are college educated and in professional positions, seemed to identify

with the economic stresses on white men more than with the potential benefits of affirmative action." The Northern California group favored a more
moderate and broad-based message, emphasizing that the ballot measure
would go "too far" in curtailing "equal opportunity" programs and that it
would foment "racial division," avoiding the more conspiratorial tones that
predicted the end of girls' sports programs and rape crisis centers.[72]

Both factions managed to work together for the first half of 1996, sharing
staff and some resources, but tensions mounted. The campaign's conference
calls and meetings became rife with conflict, and debates over campaign
strategy, staffing, fund-raising, and messaging grew more intense and
debilitating. Fund-raising faltered, as Democratic donors and even benefactors of the Feminist Majority and NOW proved unwilling to support
what they thought would be a losing cause. Personality clashes deepened.
In mid-August, the campaign formally split apart. The faction led by the
Feminist Majority and NOW formed the Stop 209 campaign and remained
headquartered in Los Angeles; the Campaign to Defeat 209, which included
the Democratic strategists and the civil rights organizations, was based in
the Bay Area. (Representatives from CFJ and AGENDA joined the latter
group but devoted their energies to their respective field campaigns.)

While this bitter divorce suggested dramatic differences in political
strategy and ideology, the challenge and liability facing both sides was
the same: how to respond to CCRI's fundamental racial proposition that
California had moved beyond the days of outright bigotry and explicit
racism, rendering affirmative action programs unnecessary, divisive,
and unfair. With Ward Connerly effectively neutralizing claims about
the historical connections between the civil rights era and opposition to
Proposition 209, CCRI's opponents struggled to find a credible language to
characterize or describe how racism might operate beyond the basis of individual rights and injury, especially to moderate white voters. The constituencies targeted by CFJ and AGENDA might recognize the effects of racism
and disadvantage embedded in other institutions—decaying public schools,
restricted job opportunities, or heavy-handed policing. But for most white
voters who did not personally confront such barriers or conditions, it was
difficult to see how those dynamics could be made visible, especially after
decades of investments in the narrow tropes of individual rights and opportunity. The CCRI opponents' challenge was confounded further because the
official summary of the measure, prepared by Republican attorney general
Dan Lungren, failed to note that the measure banned "affirmative action"
programs, instead using the proponents' language that it simply prevented
state and local agencies from "discriminating against or giving preferential

treatment." Polling done by both sides established that when voters understood the measure took aim at "affirmative action" rather than race and gender "preferences," support dropped from between twenty and thirty percentage points.[73] Lungren, a staunch CCRI supporter, won the ensuing court battle over the initiative's summary, meaning that voters with no other information about Proposition 209 would encounter a measure titled "Prohibition against Discrimination and Preferential Treatment" that promised to outlaw "quotas" and "preferences" and a summary that made no mention of the elimination of affirmative action. These portions of the official state guide essentially repeated the proponents' framing of the issue, significantly increasing their opponents' burden to tell a different account of the impact the measure would have.[74]

This dilemma led to two distinct but related responses from CCRI opponents. The gender emphasis in the Stop 209 campaign asserted that the measure was wrong because it violated women's rights, largely leaving CCRI's racial propositions intact. Indeed, their reference to Clause C of CCRI as the "skeleton clause" suggested that while white women voters might find the other (race-based) provisions of the initiative appealing, it was this clandestine provision that made it unacceptable. The campaign's radio ads singularly emphasized this message—a spot featuring Candice Bergen warned that the measure would "cut funding for rape crisis centers" and end maternity benefits—while linking it to a broader conservative assault. The weekend before the election, the Stop 209 group ran its only commercial, which "showed male hands stripping a woman of a diploma, stethoscope, and medical lab coat, a police officer's cap and a hard hat" as a narrator warned that Proposition 209 would keep women out of these male-dominated sectors of the workforce, even preventing young women from "going into math, science, or sports." Stripped of these opportunities, the ad implied, women would be vulnerable to sexual exploitation.[75]

The Campaign to Defeat 209, backed by Democrats, unions, and civil rights advocates, similarly treated CCRI's main racial propositions as unassailable; in fact, the ill-fated alternative "antiquota" measure largely echoed the main racial propositions of this group's opponents. Indeed, Connerly's campaign used the title of the abandoned alternative measure, "Equal Opportunity without Quotas," as the tagline for pro-209 commercials.[76] Again, lacking any compelling language or narratives to persuade voters to support affirmative action programs on their own, the Campaign to Defeat 209 affirmed the core propositions of its opponents, attacking the measure in its ballot argument for making the "current problems [with affirmative action] worse."[77]

In a move recalling the 1964 No on 14 campaign over fair housing, which adopted the slogan "Don't Legalize Hate," the Campaign to Defeat 209 then abruptly shifted its focus and sought to portray CCRI as an unapologetic declaration of racial nationalism, a political effort that was beyond the pale of respectable liberalism. Its lone television ad opened with a shot of David Duke, the former state representative and Ku Klux Klan member from Louisiana who in late September appeared at a debate at California State University, Northridge, to argue in favor of Proposition 209. The debate, which was organized by students who opposed the measure, sought to use Duke's endorsement and appearance to illustrate CCRI's extremist backers and commitments. The ad similarly used Duke's support of Proposition 209, along with that of Newt Gingrich and Pat Buchanan, to argue that the forces of intolerance and bigotry were driving the measure. It closed with an image of Duke in a white robe in front of a burning cross. The ad was roundly condemned in editorial commentaries as desperate and sensationalist, and even members of the steering committee for the Campaign to Defeat 209 wanted the ad pulled. "We pleaded with them," recalls Eva Patterson, who argued that the ad would only alienate swing voters. But the campaign's staff insisted it was too late. The ad was produced by Bob Shrum, a longtime Democratic strategist and Clinton ally based in Washington, D.C., who served as a media consultant to the campaign. While the explosive ad would do little to persuade undecided voters to oppose the measure, Shrum and others in the Democratic National Committee (DNC) predicted the ad would resonate strongly with African American voters, whom the Clinton campaign needed to turn out in high numbers. Money suddenly came in from the DNC to keep the ad on the air.[78]

Thus, while the dueling factions of the mainstream anti-209 campaign signaled significant differences in their strategies, both worked from the shared premise that the racial propositions implicit in Proposition 209 (that racial discrimination had become irrelevant and affirmative action was unfair and unnecessary) were largely irrefutable. The disagreement between the two factions was over how best to move the public debate to a different subject. For the Stop 209 campaign, that meant switching the subject from race to gender. For the Campaign to Defeat 209, it meant focusing on the extremist underpinnings of the measure.

For their part, CCRI proponents keenly understood these attempts to change the subject. CCRI campaign manager Arnold Steinberg advised his colleagues in a memo, "The opposition will try to turn attention from race to gender, in an attempt to appeal to the largely white electorate, especially females. In turn, we would rather, in the limited attention span afforded by a campaign, focus on race, than gender."[79] Connerly responded directly to opponents' claims that women would recognize CCRI as an attack on hard-earned protections against gender discrimination. If CCRI opponents believed that their success depended on having white voters interpret the measure on gendered *rather than* racial terms, Connerly was quick to point out the racial investments also at stake: "The white males they're trying to demonize are husbands, sons, grandsons, relatives. The proponents of preferences are in for a surprise when they pursue their strategy of gender division."[80]

Connerly and Steinberg effectively insulated the CCRI campaign from this gender critique in a number of ways. They brought on as campaign co-chairs Pamela Lewis, a lawyer and Clinton Democrat from the suburbs of Oakland, and Gail Heriot, a professor of law at the University of San Diego, challenging the notion that the measure jeopardized the standing of professional white women.[81] The single television ad produced by Connerly's campaign, which ran in late October, also directly engaged this issue. The ad featured Connerly, Lewis, and Janice Camarena Ingraham, a white college student and mother of two young children in San Bernardino County. Ingraham had recently settled a lawsuit with San Bernardino County Community College because she was barred from attending an introductory English class that she claims had been set aside for Black students. (The college denied the allegation, claiming Ingraham did not meet prerequisite requirements, but settled the suit.) Ingraham described in a voice-over how a group of Black students laughed at her as she was told to leave the class. By foregrounding a struggling working-class white woman who suffered a racial injury, the ad directly refuted the gendered argument of the Stop 209 campaign.[82]

THE PROPOSITION 209 ELECTION

In late October, a Field Poll suggested that the commanding lead once enjoyed by Proposition 209 was tightening, as a fifteen-point advantage from earlier in the month had been whittled to five percentage points.[83] If the gap continued to close, the grassroots campaigns built during the last eighteen months by CFJ and the Greater South Los Angeles Affirmative Action Project might be able to secure the razor thin margin of defeat they predicted was possible. And while opponents were still frustrated at President Clinton and the Democrats' continued refusal to assist the campaign in any meaningful way—Clinton eventually came out against the measure but said little about the issue on the campaign trail, and Democratic donors kept their checkbooks closed to the anti-209 effort—their neglect had less of an impact because the Republican Party was also keeping its distance from the pro-209 campaign.

As the end of October approached, however, the foundering Dole campaign decided to make an eleventh-hour play for California's fifty-four electoral votes. Within a week, a $2 million television buy supporting CCRI and attacking Clinton's endorsement of the measure filled the airwaves. The ads were produced by the state Republican Party and were not coordinated with the official CCRI campaign, to the enormous frustration of Connerly and campaign manager Steinberg; both feared the ads would erode bipartisan support for the measure. The ad promised that Proposition 209 affirmed the simple principle that "we shall not discriminate" and declared that Clinton was "wrong" to oppose the measure.[84]

While CCRI opponents often talked about the measure as a project of the monolithic Right, the dustup over the pro-209 ad revealed that multiple interests and forces championed Proposition 209; it was not the work of a singular conservative bloc or movement. During the last week of the campaign, CCRI campaign manager Steinberg and the chair of the state Republican Party exchanged angry public attacks over the commercials. In addition, though the Republican Party's $2 million advertising blitz undoubtedly benefited the campaign, it resulted from a last-second decision; the GOP followed rather than led on the issue. CCRI author Thomas Wood noted with disdain that the party "kept their mouths shut until the very last minute, then . . . used it as a crass wedge issue."[85] And when the Republican Party did jump into the fray over Proposition 209, the racialized "mugging" that had so frightened Democrats leaders proved to be relatively innocuous. The Republican Party's ad, which simply condemned discrimination and attacked quotas, was largely indistinguishable from the prevailing Democratic position on affirmative action.

By Election Day, as the small armies assembled by CFJ and AGENDA raced to bring Proposition 209 opponents to the polls, the brief window of opportunity that appeared open only a week earlier seemed firmly closed. Statewide, the measure passed by a margin of 54.6 to 45.4 percent, a difference of 879,429 votes (see table 6). Only in six Bay Area counties and Los Angeles County did a majority of voters cast ballots against CCRI. As CFJ and other anti-209 campaigners had hoped, turnout increased significantly among nonwhite voters, who rejected the measure soundly. But the long-anticipated gender gap never materialized. Women, who made up 53 percent of the statewide electorate overall, were 52 percent opposed to

TABLE 6 Proposition 209 Exit Poll Data by Race/
Ethnicity and Gender, 1996

Group (% of electorate)	Yes (%)	No (%)
Statewide (100%)	55	45
White (74%)	63	37
African American (7%)	26	74
Latino (10%)	24	76
Asian American (5%)	39	61
Male (47%)	61	39
Female (53%)	48	52

SOURCE: *LAT* exit poll, Study no. 389, California General
Election, November 5, 1996, www.latimesinteractive.com/pdf
archive/stat_sheets/la-timespoll389ss.pdf (accessed July 3, 2009).

the measure, but 58 percent of white women favored it. Clinton cruised to
a thirteen-point victory in the state over Dole, and exit polls suggested the
measure had little impact on the presidential contest.[86]

More vexing still to some 209 opponents was an exit poll finding that
54 percent of California voters expressed support for "private and public
affirmative action programs designed to help women and minorities get
better jobs and education."[87] Another poll suggested that even 80 percent
of those who voted yes on Proposition 209 agreed with the statement that
"discrimination is still common."[88] Once again, the polling results left
wide room for interpretation: Did the election express the intractable ver-
ity that most white voters were inevitably opposed to claims of ongoing
discrimination against people of color? Or was there room to assert and
popularize such claims within the right political strategy?

REACTIONS TO THE PROPOSITION 209 ELECTION

The grassroots opponents of Proposition 209 did not hide their disgust
for the actions of the Democratic Party. CFJ explained in a newsletter to
supporters immediately after the election that, "all along, we knew that
it would take two things to beat 209—a field campaign in communities
of color and a media campaign directed especially to women of all colors.
We did our part, but while the Republicans paid millions to pass 209, the
Democrats betrayed their own people and put no money into the media

campaign to defeat it."[89] Eva Patterson, the veteran civil rights lawyer from San Francisco, agreed: "I think we were badly used by the national Democratic Party—Bill Clinton and Bob Shrum—because I don't think they really cared about Proposition 209. They wanted us to get our base out to help Clinton get reelected."[90]

For the grassroots organizations like CFJ and AGENDA, the campaign as a whole largely confirmed their belief that a new model of electoral organizing committed to long-term engagement, political education, training, and a deliberate focus on the emerging majority of California voters was possible. By the end of the election, CFJ's electoral organizing had grown to at least fifteen hundred precincts in fourteen cities and six counties. They noted that while the measure initially polled strongly even among Democrats and communities of color, Proposition 209 was soundly defeated in all the precincts the groups had targeted. And statewide, voters of color raised their share of the electorate from 19 percent in 1994 to 25 percent in 1996.

Privately, Jan Adams was less optimistic about the likelihood that Proposition 209 could have been defeated, even with the support of the Democratic Party: "Once they got the civil rights language [attached to the measure] we lost." She was quick to note a broader set of accomplishments, however, that had been a deliberate goal of the anti-CCRI campaign: "What came out of it was a lot of people with a lot more experience" in electoral organizing. From her perspective, the CFJ campaign helped to "spread widely in a lot of nonprofit advocacy organizations the notion that staff could participate in electoral activity" and that community-based nonprofit work in general could and should be politically committed. Moreover, Adams was optimistic that CFJ could serve in the future as a kind of "repository institution" that would help other community organizations and activists develop the skills and analysis necessary to do electoral organizing, which were increasingly difficult to learn in what Adams described as the "depoliticized nonprofit environment of the 1990s."[91]

Patterson also took away a number of sobering lessons that would shape her thinking around future approaches to contesting racialized initiatives on the ballot. When CCRI was first announced, she explained, many civil rights advocates thought it could be addressed head-on: "'This is racism, this is a problem, Californians will get it.' We were naïve and learned a very bitter lesson." They were also mistaken, she believed, to assume that white women would "vote their gender over their skin color." Echoing Connerly's prediction months before the election, she conceded, "We were wrong in a huge way. . . . They think about their sons, their fathers, their husbands. . . . They don't think that affirmative action helps them. They think it's a 'Black thing.'"[92]

Democratic strategists were largely unrepentant for their decision to keep their distance from Proposition 209. Bill Carrick, a senior advisor to the Clinton campaign based in Los Angeles, later explained that with the polling data showing wide support for the measure and with the long shadow cast by Proposition 187, he felt strongly that the Democratic Party had no business opposing the measure: "Why would you expect the Democratic Party organizations whose job it is to elect individuals to office to divert its energies, efforts and treasuries to other fights particularly when they could have a negative impact on the party? Logic tells me you would not do that."[93] Interviewed a year and a half later, Clinton was a little more remorseful, conceding, "I made a couple of statements in California on 209, and maybe I could have done more, and I think if the thing had gone on three more weeks, it would have come out differently."[94]

THE AFTERMATH OF PROPOSITION 209

The morning after the election, opponents of Proposition 209 filed the lawsuit they had been preparing to block implementation of the measure. Though a state superior court judge issued a temporary restraining order, the measure was eventually upheld in 1997 by the state supreme court. Over the next decade, the impact of Proposition 209 would be subject to intense debate. Critics noted that in the five years after the measure passed, the enrollment of Black, Latino, and Native American undergraduate and law students at the most competitive campuses, UCLA and UC Berkeley, plummeted. By 2006, even as the percentage of Black high school graduates in the state who were eligible for UC admission had more than doubled in the prior decade, the percentage of Black freshman admittance offers was dropping to twenty-year lows.[95]

Ward Connerly, for his part, continued to litigate to force the aggressive implementation of the measure. With the backing of a conservative legal foundation, he eventually prevailed in suits against the State of California and City of San Jose over various public contracting programs.[96] In 1998, he led a successful campaign to pass a similar anti–affirmative action measure in the state of Washington.

In explaining the passage of Proposition 209, most scholarly and popular attention has focused on Connerly, Governor Wilson, and the California GOP.[97] All of these figures clearly played leading roles. But the measure's passage was also made possible by a number of other complicated forces:

Democratic leaders intentionally seeking to distance the party from racial justice concerns; the inability of civil rights groups to collaborate and wage an effective campaign; and a longer history of transforming and limiting the meaning of "civil rights" from an expansive vision of social equity toward a narrow set of concerns about individual discrimination. The outcome of the election did not simply reflect a unified position of the white electorate on the question of affirmative action or racial discrimination, nor did it signal the dominating influence of state Republicans.

For groups like CFJ and AGENDA, the election confirmed their belief that in order to change the course of California politics in the long run to reflect the interests and lives of the state's emerging majority of people of color, immigrants, and the working poor, it would be necessary to develop a grassroots base of electoral power independent of the Democratic Party. CFJ leaders spent the six months after the election transitioning the organization from a temporary campaign project into a long-term effort capable of challenging future attacks on the ballot. It would not be long before the new endeavor would be tested. Another ambitious conservative entrepreneur had been watching the CCRI campaign closely and was preparing a ballot foray of his own.

RON UNZ AND THE GENTEEL ATTACK
ON BILINGUAL EDUCATION

In the midst of the campaign against Proposition 187 in mid-1994, Frank Sharry met an unlikely volunteer. Sharry, the executive director of the Washington, D.C.–based National Immigration Forum, had come to California to work with the mainstream Taxpayers against 187 campaign. He soon met Ron Unz, the thirty-four-year-old businessman from Silicon Valley who had just mounted a surprisingly potent conservative challenge to Governor Wilson in the recently concluded GOP primary. Unz had already made a small fortune developing financial-analysis software on Wall Street and had been drawn to conservative and libertarian political causes early on, contributing to groups like the Heritage Foundation and the Manhattan Institute. During his bid for the GOP gubernatorial nomination, he accused Wilson in provocative campaign commercials of "let[ting] the National Guard sit on its hands as mobs of criminals burned and looted my native city for days" during the 1992 Los Angeles unrest. Other ads railed against the prevalence of quotas and affirmative action in California universities.[98] Unz won 34 percent of the vote in the primary, drawing conservative voters long disaffected by Wilson's policies on taxes, the environment, and abortion rights. A few months later, Unz abandoned fellow Republicans and joined the campaign against Proposition 187, believing the measure's harsh tone and far-reaching mandates would ultimately hurt Republican and conservative interests by driving Latinos and Asian Americans into the Democratic Party. He addressed the crowd of seventy-five thousand immigrants and immigrant rights supporters at the momentous anti-187 march and rally in Los Angeles during the heat of the campaign, and he wrote an op-ed against the measure in the *Los Angeles Times*.[99]

A few years after the Proposition 187 election, Unz and Sharry spoke again about a new ballot measure the software developer was drafting. Unz had been an early donor to CCRI and was coming to understand the transformative role that ballot measures could play in changing the terms of public debates around hot-button issues. For several years, Unz had been critical of the state's bilingual education programs. During his gubernatorial bid in 1994, he declared in a campaign newsletter, "Our schools should teach one langue—the English language—and one culture—American culture."[100] Nearly one in four students in California public schools was designated as having Limited English Proficiency (LEP); and about half of these students received some form of instruction in their native languages. Unz's new ballot measure sought to ban native language or bilingual instruction for such students, mandating a uniform English-immersion approach. Sharry attempted to dissuade Unz from pursuing such a sweeping project, fearing it would unleash another wave of harsh Proposition 187–style attacks. But as Unz was clearly determined to press his case, Sharry offered him some advice: "This could get ugly, divisive. If you're going to do it, do it in a way that is pro-Latino and pro-immigrant."[101]

On first glance, Sharry's guidance seems incongruous. The right to bilingual education programs had been won in the late 1960s and early 1970s by parents, activists, and advocates who were championing the needs of immigrant Latino and Asian American students left behind by a system that historically mandated English-only instruction. The U.S. Supreme Court's 1974 *Lau v. Nichols* decision (originating from a case filed by Chinese American parents in San Francisco under the authority of the 1964 Civil Rights Act) held that instruction solely in English violated constitutional guarantees of equal protection on the basis of national origin.[102] As a result, school districts with larger numbers of LEP students began instituting bilingual programs to meet these constitutional guarantees and to ensure that students' broad academic development continued as they were learning English. Demand for the programs had only been expanding.

Between 1982 and 1997 there was a 220 percent increase in LEP students in California schools. Bilingual educators always imagined themselves as defenders of the needs of immigrant students in general and Latino students in particular. While there were active debates among such educators over the effectiveness of different types of programs, there was no body of research that suggested that Unz's singular English-immersion program would bear any results.[103] How could a white conservative businessman with no background in public education advance an initiative to abolish nearly all bilingual programs in a way that was, as Sharry suggested, "pro-Latino and pro-immigrant"?

In many ways, the CCRI campaign had demonstrated how such contradictions could be overcome, and Unz adopted many of its lessons. He gave his initiative a seductive title, "English for the Children," that connoted a sense of empowerment and opportunity. He identified several Latino educators to serve as spokespersons and nominal leaders of the campaign, bolstering his assertion that bilingual programs burdened rather than benefited the students they were serving, paralleling a claim Ward Connerly often made about affirmative action. To co-chair the campaign he recruited Gloria Matta Tuchman, a Mexican American elementary school teacher from Santa Ana. Tuchman had long been critical of bilingual education programs and was a former board member of John Tanton's U.S. English in the late 1980s (see chapter 5). But she also proudly declared, "I love being bilingual. I think it's a true asset," and she insisted her concerns centered on the failure of bilingual education programs to successfully teach English.[104] Jaime Escalante, whose achievements as a high school math teacher in East Los Angeles were celebrated in the 1988 film *Stand and Deliver*, agreed to serve as the campaign's honorary chair.[105] Henry Gradillas, a former principal at Garfield High School in East Los Angeles, also became a campaign spokesperson.

While the large majority of Latino educators, political leaders, and voters ultimately came out against the measure, Unz's efforts to bring Tuchman, Escalante, Gradillas, and others into the campaign reflected his own understanding of the long-standing and deeply symbolic debates around language acquisition, fluency, and social stigma among Latinos— what political scientist Lisa Garcia Bedolla describes as the "internal borders" shaping political relationships among this diverse group.[106] But the participation of even a handful of prominent Latino supporters of the measure raised a compelling question to non-Latino voters: "If they don't back these programs, why should we?"[107]

Unz also developed a simple but devastating critique of bilingual education programs, charging them with a "95% failure rate" while attacking an unscrupulous "bilingual education establishment" that was enriching itself at the expense of poor immigrant children. This charge was actually made earlier by Democratic gubernatorial candidate Kathleen Brown, who in September 1993 called for a uniform and limited time frame for English acquisition and demanded that Governor Wilson overhaul bilingual education programs. Wilson's secretary of education dismissed the attacks as "simplistic" comments that "pandered to a bias"; bilingual educators called Brown's proposal "naïve" and "ridiculous."[108]

Critics would point out that Unz's charges similarly distorted the ways that all programs serving LEP students operated; because students gain English fluency over a period of several years, it is typical that in any given year only 5 to 7 percent of students will be officially redesignated as English proficient, whether they are in a bilingual education program or not. No program could realistically redesignate 100 percent of its students each year. Indeed, only 22 percent of LEP students were even enrolled in fully certified bilingual education programs, as there was an estimated shortage of twenty-seven thousand credentialed teachers. But Unz used this prevailing redesignation figure to substantiate his charge of a 95 percent failure rate. He repeated the line relentlessly throughout the campaign to indict bilingual "profiteers" who were being "financially rewarded for not teaching English" with "as much as $1 billion."[109]

Like affirmative action, bilingual education quickly became portrayed in the media during the ensuing campaign through a stock narrative. As the *Wall Street Journal* put it, what began as a "well-meaning liberal experiment" had grown "to become another bureaucratic entitlement, even as it provided no real benefits to kids."[110] Bilingual education, initially championed as a right to a quality public education, became stigmatized as a rejection of that education—a refusal to participate in an English-dominant society. Author James Crawford noted that this framing established "a false choice in voters' minds: either teach students the language of the country or give them bilingual education." Bilingual education defenders became defined as apologists for the broader crises of California public schools, which by then had sunk to forty-first in the country in per pupil spending, and for the failures of many schools to provide a quality education to immigrant students.[111] And the measure resonated with a familiar story of a failed bureaucracy that coddled and nurtured those who were falling behind rather than demanding that they labor to overcome their own deficiencies.

Unz also effectively insulated himself from charges that he was trading in shrill nativism and xenophobia. He unabashedly described himself as "pro-immigrant"; the campaign's publicity materials centered on Latino parents and children, who, as Unz described in the ballot argument, were "the principal victims of bilingual education."[112] Unz promised early that "nobody prominently associated with Proposition 187 will be allowed any significant role in our campaign." He specifically warned Governor Wilson to keep his distance from the effort, explaining that "Hispanics consider Pete Wilson the devil. He's the kiss of death."[113] Unz repeatedly pointed to early polls that suggested that Latino voters overwhelmingly supported his measure.[114] He specifically insisted that his proposal was "not an English-first initiative. This is English for the children."[115]

For Unz, the decision to position the campaign against Pete Wilson and Proposition 187, not only reflected his shrewd awareness of the antipathies already developing against the governor, but also revealed some important dimensions of the racial propositions guiding his effort. In a 1994 essay in the Heritage Foundation's journal, *Policy Review*, titled "Immigration or the Welfare State?" Unz argued that conservatives should focus their political energies on policies such as welfare, which he charged was "breeding pathological levels of crime and dependency," rather than on immigration restriction.[116] He insisted that "most Hispanics are classic blue-collar Reagan Democrats," while Asians were "much like Jews in their professional and socio-economic profile, but without the liberal guilt." Unz also argued that the "anti-immigrant rhetoric of Senator Barbara Boxer, Representative Tony Beilenson, and other prominent California liberal Democrats" suggested that Democrats were moving rapidly toward "an anti-immigration stance" that could sour some immigrants on the party. At least part of Unz's interest then, was in using the anti–bilingual education measure to demonstrate the possibilities to create a "dominant political alliance of Asians, Hispanics, and conservative Anglos" committed to "a massive rollback of the welfare state and ethnic group policies of the past 20 or 30 years."[117] Unz's measure would show that allegedly egregious state programs such as bilingual education could be challenged without resorting to immigrant bashing, and that many Latinos and Asian Americans would embrace a multiracial antistatism that implicitly attacked African Americans as the embodiment of social pathology and state failure.

THE AMBIVALENT OPPOSITION

If Unz's strategy was to put Latinos in front of the camera and in the center of the debate over his ballot measure, his opponents sought to do the opposite. As early as March 1995, backers of bilingual education acknowledged that in the wake of Proposition 187, an attack on bilingual education was possible.[118] And though Unz filed his measure with the secretary of state in the spring of 1997 and kicked off his campaign in early July, opponents waited until November of that year to formally launch their own campaign, giving Unz a four-month advantage to establish the terms of the debate. As the measure built a four-to-one lead in the polls among registered voters, Harry Pachon, a longtime scholar of Latino politics and public policy, described the "silence of the bilingual education establishment" as "deafening." Pachon suggested that bilingual educators continued to live "in a sheltered world" and believed their programs, won after decades of political struggle in the 1970s and 1980s, were beyond the ambit of political critique. He warned they would soon have "to realize that in California, nothing is sacred."[119]

When leaders of the California Association of Bilingual Educators (CABE) and the California Teachers Association finally organized as Citizens for an Educated America, they hired veteran Democratic consultant Richie Ross, who crafted a familiar strategy to defeat the Unz measure. As James Crawford explains, the focus groups and polling they conducted suggested that "bilingual education" evoked an unsympathetic response among moderate, swing voters. As a result, the campaign declared that the Unz initiative was "not a referendum on bilingual education" (which they feared they would lose) but a vote on an "extreme proposal." The campaign instructed supporters, "DO NOT get into a discussion defending bilingual education." Instead, the campaign would focus on the "unforeseen consequences" that could result from the measure's "extreme" provisions—teachers facing sanctions for refusing to comply or students being placed in dangerous classrooms during the year-long English-immersion classes stipulated by the measure. As Ross explained at the campaign kickoff, "If your 7-year-old girl is in a classroom with a 13-year-old boy, you have no right to appeal as a parent." Such messages were designed to sway one of the main targeted groups of swing voters, Republican women over fifty, who consultants felt would be important to influence. Unz insisted that his opponents' refusal to answer his central charge about the failure of bilingual education programs proved that the programs were "almost indefensible."[120]

There certainly were figures who called for a more forceful defense of bilingual education, insisting that the programs were sound and produced measurable results. In the wake of a recent decision by the school board in Santa Barbara to eliminate the district's bilingual education programs, a group of Latino families organized a three-day boycott and convened an alternative school. Rueben Rey, one of the leaders of the boycott, explained that eliminating bilingual education "has tremendous impact on kids' self-concept, self-growth, self-esteem. It's not just about eliminating the language. . . . By eliminating these programs what you're saying is what you're bringing to the classroom is not good." For Rey and many other bilingual education supporters, the Unz initiative could not be understood outside of a wider history of political efforts to stigmatize the Spanish language and Spanish speakers, particularly those of Mexican or Latin American origin, as subordinate and inferior—Spanish seen as a cultural deficit that burdened its bearers. This history, expressed in literacy tests applied to border crossers in the early twentieth century, the Americanization programs that soon followed, and the prohibitions on speaking Spanish imposed on many Mexican American students in Southern California public schools into the 1960s, was for many bilingual education supporters the absent referent within this debate.[121]

Mara Bommarito, the principal of Woodlawn Avenue Elementary in Bell, south of downtown Los Angeles, also insisted that for the large number of immigrant students in her school bilingual education was "working," and she had "hard data to show it." She explained that only 5 percent of parents in her school exercised their right to opt out of the program and that "participants in bilingual ed are scoring better than English language speakers."[122] And while it was true that questions of English language acquisition, fluency, and bilingualism were real and long-standing sources of debate within Latino immigrant and nonimmigrant communities, some opponents of the Unz measure were quick to challenge his assertion that the measure represented the sentiments of large majorities of Latino parents.[123] Vicky Castro, a Latina member of the Los Angeles Board of Education, insisted that local communities took great pride in such programs, which could not be blamed for the larger crisis in public education.[124]

To emphasize such experiences and perspectives during the campaign, however, ran counter to the strategy of the mainstream opponents of the Unz measure, which became Proposition 227 when it was placed on the June 1998 ballot. While some Republicans, most notably gubernatorial candidate Dan Lungren, came out against the measure, fearing the backlash an endorsement might generate, leading Democrats offered only limited opposition.[125] President Clinton resisted the appeals of various civil rights groups and waited until a month before the election to come out against the measure.[126] The campaign ultimately ended up meeting its fundraising goal of $5 million, buoyed by a $1.5 million contribution from Jerry Perenchio, the majority shareholder of the Spanish-language television network Univision, and another large contribution from the California Teachers Association.[127]

The contributions permitted the anti-227 campaign to purchase some $2.7 million worth of television and radio time in the weeks before the election. Remaining firmly committed to the strategy of avoiding mention of bilingual education, of making any strong defense of the programs that were proving effective, or of highlighting the students who benefited, the ads instead focused on a minor provision of the initiative that would appropriate $50 million annually to adult English learners to help tutor LEP students.[128] Unz included the provision in part to bolster his pro-immigrant credentials. Similar programs promoting language instruction for adults had long been supported by bilingual educators. But the anti-227 ads attacked the provision as "$50 million a year for a new spending program" that would go to "teaching non-English speaking adults who will tutor kids English."[129] The strategy reproduced an assumption, evident in nearly every other ballot measure discussed in this book, that the only way to defuse the appeal of a racialized measure was to affirm its basic premise (here, that bilingual education indeed deserved to be abandoned) and to focus on other extreme or hidden provisions. Even the ads that ran on Spanish-language networks targeting Latino voters made no defense of bilingual education programs or warn of the dangers of a singular English-immersion approach.[130]

As the mainstream anti-227 campaign ran television ads attacking the basis of bilingual education and adult English learners, Californians for Justice set out to reinvigorate the grassroots field campaign that had mobilized thousands of volunteers during the campaign to defeat Proposition 209. The campaign against Proposition 227 proved to be far more modest, though the group did work in roughly 350 precincts in Northern and Southern California and continued to place an emphasis on training and developing youth activists in electoral organizing. As with Propositions 209 and 187, it was high school and college students who proved most willing to confront the ballot measures without equivocation; in February, some two thousand students walked out of dozens of San Francisco Bay Area high schools and converged on the East Bay suburb of Concord, which had just christened a $21.4 million police station that symbolized the increasingly punitive stance taken by state and local governments in recent years.[131] CFJ continued to direct resources to its youth-organizing component and supported a modest precinct-based effort to mobilize voters against both Proposition 227 and Proposition 226, a Wilson-backed measure supported by business interests to restrict the political activity of labor unions.[132]

THE PROPOSITION 227 ELECTION AND ITS AFTERMATH

By the June 2 election, the Unz campaign had been outspent nearly five to one by opponents and had attracted little support from the state Republican Party or leading Republican candidates. The campaign never hired a professional consultant, did not purchase any significant television or radio time, and did little polling. The measure did win the backing of several of the same wealthy conservative donors who contributed to Proposition 209, including Home Savings and Loan mogul Howard Ahmanson, a patron of multiple far-right political projects, and several boosters of the Club for Growth, including Heritage Foundation board member William Hume. An analysis of the funding of the English for the Children Campaign by political scientist Kathryn Miller concluded that the "top five financial contributors . . . totaling about 93% of the . . . funding, [were] wealthy, white, English-speaking men," and all were self-identified conservatives. Several had in fact contributed to groups and individuals who loudly championed immigration restriction. For these backers, the underlying racial proposition of the Unz measure—in which English-language fluency served as a proxy for both whiteness and national belonging—undoubtedly drew them to the campaign.[133]

This proposition, however, when expressed through the English for the Children framework, seemed benevolent rather than malicious. Proposition 227 passed by a resounding 61 to 39 percent (see table 7). A CNN/ *Los Angeles Times* exit poll found that nearly one in four voters cited the measure as the main reason they came to the poll, more than double the number that cited the U.S. Senate primary on the same ballot. The measure was narrowly defeated in the Bay Area but passed by overwhelming margins everywhere else in the state. The Republican women voters targeted by the mainstream anti-227 campaign backed the measure by a 72 to 28 percent. Reflecting the combination of narratives that animated the campaign, the top reasons cited by those who voted for the measure were "If you live in America, you should speak English" and "Bilingual education is not effective."[134]

While leaders of the anti-227 campaign proclaimed that the measure's overwhelming passage was unavoidable and simply expressed the unvarnished racist sentiments of California voters, intense criticism of the opposition campaign began soon after the election. Some faulted the organized group of bilingual educators for believing their programs were beyond political criticism and for failing to respond forcefully when such attacks mounted. Others believed the campaign consultants had made an

TABLE 7 Proposition 227 Exit Poll Data by Race/
Ethnicity, 1998

Group (% of electorate)	Yes (%)	No (%)
Statewide (100%)	61	39
White (69%)	67	33
African American (14%)	48	52
Latino (12%)	37	63
Asian American (3%)	57	43

SOURCE: CNN/*LAT* exit poll, June 2, 1998.

enormous strategic blunder by ordering bilingual teachers, students, and their parents to remain silent, letting Unz's endlessly repeated refrain of "failed programs" go unchallenged.[135] As one analysis put it, "By abandoning any defense of bilingual education, opponents of Proposition 227 allowed proponents to take on the role of children's champions, defending immigrants' right to learn English. That role had previously been filed by bilingual education advocates."[136]

Ron Unz, like Ward Connerly before him, became the subject of glowing media coverage after the election, including a cover story in the *New Republic* titled, "This Man Controls California," which credited him with "scrap[ping] a failed system of bilingual education for 1.4 million California kids, almost certainly improving their life chances."[137] James Crawford noted that reporters covering the campaign almost never questioned Unz's claims about the effectiveness of bilingual programs, in part because the opposition rarely suggested they were effective. While the multiracial coalition of antistate conservatives predicted by Unz failed to materialize—Latinos and Asian Americans were registering as Democrats in unprecedented rates by the end of the decade—the proposition that bilingual programs were failures and their advocates were simply self-interested bureaucrats became widely embraced. Unz demonstrated once again the power of an effectively framed ballot measure to advance such a transformation. For his relatively modest personal investment of $750,000, his measure eviscerated programs that parents, students, and civil rights groups had worked for a generation to secure; and the proposition did so using many of the core narratives of racial liberalism, emphasizing student and parent rights and demands for quality education in the face of a hostile bureaucracy.

Proposition 227 withstood court challenges, and during the first ten years of its implementation the debate continued over whether the legislation improved outcomes for LEP students as Unz promised.[138] With the support of the same coterie of conservative donors, Unz helped finance similarly successful measures in the next four years in Arizona and Massachusetts, though a Colorado measure in 2002 was narrowly defeated.[139]

THE CONFLICTING LEGACY OF PROPOSITIONS 209 AND 227

Propositions 209 and 227 left a conflicting legacy within the state's political culture. For some opponents, especially those closely tied to the Democratic Party, the passage of these measures suggested that the large majority of white voters would remain hostile in the face of any claims for racial justice. They came to regard political whiteness as an unimpeachable force within the state's political culture. Fearful of defending the very premise of affirmative action and bilingual education, Connerly's and Unz's opponents instead attempted in vain to change the subject. Even though there were powerful examples of the role race played in shaping life outcomes and possibilities in the state—the Dickensian conditions differentiating most Black and Brown urban public schools from their predominantly white suburban counterparts and the continued racial disparities in employment, wages, and wealth—liberal opponents lacked an effective political vocabulary to even introduce such cases into the public debate. Constrained as they were by a long-standing discourse fixated on vilifying racist individuals over structural patterns and forces, they ceded much of the ethical high ground to their opponents. To an emerging network of grassroots activists, the experiences with these two ballot measures suggested an alternative possibility. In time, they reasoned, with an adequate combination of resources, organization, and political vision, communities traditionally ignored in statewide elections could be transformed into a potent force that could make forceful calls to address racial inequalities. Motivated by the mostly spontaneous mobilization of Latino immigrants and immigrant rights supporters during the Proposition 187 campaign, these efforts, especially those of Californians for Justice and the Action for Grassroots Empowerment and Neighborhood Development Alternatives, sought to build multiracial formations capable of training new organizers and volunteers to become savvy electoral organizers, while working in conjunction with supportive political leaders, community organizations, faith groups, and unions on shared causes. Yet these projects also faced significant challenges. Even groups like CFJ, which began with an explicit agenda to contest statewide elections from a racial justice perspective, soon found that it was difficult to sustain the thousands of volunteers necessary to build such an effort across multiple election cycles.

Two years after Proposition 227 passed, CFJ and its allies were forced to dust off their precinct maps and voter-registration cards again when they faced Proposition 21, a draconian youth criminal-sentencing measure, and Proposition 22, which effectively banned recognition of same-sex marriage. Both passed by landslide margins in spite of the determined organizing efforts of grassroots organizations, which again found themselves, for the sixth time since 1994, on the losing side of a statewide ballot measure; the emerging majority had yet to arrive.

For Ward Connerly and Ron Unz, the legacies of their respective forays into direct democracy suggested altogether different lessons. Each emerged from political obscurity, with only limited backing among leading Republicans, to demonstrate that even in a state dominated by Democratic voters professing strong commitments to racial tolerance and inclusion, programs like affirmative action and bilingual education could be criticized and politically undermined. Their campaigns incorporated rather than challenged many of the tenets of racial liberalism, leaving opponents with a meager set of counternarratives.

More than just abolishing programs that civil rights groups had fought for many years to institutionalize and advance, the triumph of Propositions 209 and 227 served to naturalize and warrant a broader racial proposition that societal racism had indeed been effectively abolished, its only traces evident in the occasional remark of an unreconstructed bigot. Unz and Connerly adamantly insisted that their efforts were motivated not by a conviction that people of color could not or should not participate in California political and economic life, but that such participation had to be premised on an acceptance of white racial innocence and a disavowal of any historically grounded or group-based claims for racial justice. Those who insisted on claiming that a right to affirmative action or bilingual education was defensible and warranted faced criticism for fanning the flames of racial division. It was a potent racial proposition, and one that Connerly in particular had no intention of abandoning.

8. "Dare We Forget the Lessons of History?"

Ward Connerly's Racial Privacy Initiative, 2001-2003

California's October 2003 gubernatorial recall election will be remembered by most observers for the colorful cast of 135 candidates seeking to unseat incumbent governor Gray Davis and for the ascent of Arnold Schwarzenegger in a campaign that seemed at once riveting and absurd.[1] But a similarly provocative if less spectacular political debate unfolded in the shadows of the recall's drama. Ward Connerly, the Black conservative who led the Proposition 209 campaign to victory in 1996, sponsored the Racial Privacy Initiative, a ballot measure to prevent state and local agencies from collecting or classifying most race and ethnicity data about California's thirty-five million residents. The University of California regent railed against the history of arbitrary and oppressive state-sponsored racial classification systems, denouncing "Jim Crow–era race boxes" that failed to acknowledge the "inherently private and complex nature of racial identity." He described race as a "biologically meaningless" concept and reminded voters of the scientific consensus that "greater genetic variation exists within groups than among them."[2] Indeed, if the measure had appeared on the ballot in the late 1940s or 1950s, it could easily have been the work of the state's network of liberal civil rights and human relations groups, which had led several campaigns during that time to compel state agencies to stop collecting racial data about individuals. But Connerly's Proposition 54 was funded almost entirely by deep-pocketed conservative donors and foundations. Its chief impact would be to eviscerate the data used to enforce antidiscrimination laws and to monitor racial disparities in education, law enforcement, housing, and employment, vastly curtailing civil rights enforcement in the state. More importantly, Connerly's invocation of a "colorblind" society rested on the racial proposition that systemic racism was no longer a meaningful or relevant force in public life and that any enduring focus on racism was unfounded and divisive.

A group of veteran civil rights advocates, whose advisors included David Axelrod, the Chicago-based consultant who in a few years would help guide Barack Obama to the White House, understood clearly the threat posed by Proposition 54. But in an equally striking rhetorical reversal, the coalition of labor, public health, and Democratic Party leaders that assembled to defeat Proposition 54 made little mention of race, civil rights, or discrimination in their campaign. Instead, they largely affirmed Connerly's aspiration for a colorblind society but warned the electorate in a well-funded campaign about the threat the measure could pose to public health, implicitly countering Connerly's assertion that race was a mere biological fiction: "We use this [racial] information to identify groups at risk for infectious disease. If there is an outbreak of disease in one group, we have to be able to identify and contain it before it spreads to the general population."[3]

The paradoxes revealed in this snapshot of California political discourse are remarkable: a Black conservative attempting to roll back antidiscrimination legislation through an account of the historically contingent basis of racial categories while civil rights advocates flirt with notions of genetically conditioned racial differences in their defense. Deepening this complexity, the debate unfolded precisely at the moment when California became the first large state in the nation in which those classified by the state as white constituted a minority of the population. Finally, while polls conducted by both Connerly and his adversaries suggested that the electorate strongly endorsed the vision of a colorblind state and polity which seemed to animate the initiative, voters handed the measure a twenty-six-point defeat; unlike every other initiative examined in this book, on election day, it was civil rights groups celebrating a landslide victory on a racialized ballot measure. Executing a nearly flawless campaign, they effectively halted Connerly's meteoric rise within California politics.

To relieve the analytic vertigo suggested by this account of Proposition 54, this chapter explores the emergence of the Connerly initiative in the context of the ballot measures that emerged in the aftermath of Proposition 187 in 1994. Much of the strategy that informed the civil rights groups' opposition to Proposition 54 was forged by the devastating losses in ballot initiative campaigns during the previous decade. Chapters 6 and 7 explored why these experiences convinced many leading Democrats and their advisors that claims about racial justice could not be effectively made to the majority of voters in California; the gaze of political whiteness was indifferent to such assertions. The Proposition 54 campaign raises an altogether different question: how was it that civil rights groups themselves had come to view almost any mention of racial justice before the overall electorate as an act of political suicide?

THE EMERGENCE OF THE RACIAL PRIVACY INITIATIVE

Proposition 209 launched Ward Connerly into the national spotlight. Profiled on CBS's *60 Minutes* and in the *New York Times*, the *Wall Street Journal, Parade Magazine,* and dozens of other national media outlets, he was even mentioned as a Republican candidate for the U.S. Senate in 1998. Eager to capitalize on these newfound opportunities, in 1997 he launched the American Civil Rights Institute (ACRI) to "educate the American public about racial and gender preferences and the importance of achieving equal opportunity for everyone."[4] Connerly had never identified as a staunch conservative, but during the Proposition 209 campaign he met a number of powerful conservative benefactors, including Dusty Rhodes, the president of the *National Review* who urged Connerly to carry his campaign against affirmative action elsewhere; Rhodes would become a cofounder of ACRI.[5] In the midst of eight years of Democratic control of the White House, and with the Republican revolution of 1994 falling short of its initial promise, the conservative movement seemed to have few stars brighter than Connerly. Between 1995 and 2002, he received at least eleven different awards from conservative political groups and began speaking to conservative organizations nationally. Right-wing funders, including the Bradley Foundation, the Sarah Scaife Foundation, and the John M. Olin Foundation, directed $3 million in contributions and grants to the ACRI between 1997 and 2001. In 2000, a conservative imprint, Encounter Books, published Connerly's memoir, *Creating Equal: My Fight against Race Preferences.*[6]

With a small staff working out of a Sacramento office, the ACRI and Connerly began casting about for other issues. In mid-1997, the ACRI weighed in on the advocacy effort to pressure the federal government to adopt a "multiracial" category in the 2000 U.S. census, arguing that "Americans are tired of being divided and categorized along racial and ethnic lines" and that "the federal government should be advocating for one simple box—American."[7] The argument resonated with one of Connerly's main assertions during the Proposition 209 campaign: that an overreaching government obsessed with outdated notions of race was harming, rather than promoting, the promise of individual rights secured by the civil rights movement.

In early 2000, Connerly commissioned pollster John Zogby to assess the potential of carrying this proposition further by banning government agencies from collecting race and ethnicity data altogether. The national poll suggested the concept had strong public support. More than 80 percent of respondents agreed with the statement that "Americans have a right to racial privacy," and more than 75 percent supported the idea of "eliminating boxes that require race identification"; 58 percent said they would support the elimination of boxes even if it meant losing "evidence of discrimination."[8] Connerly began actively raising money in support of his new project.

THE RACIAL PRIVACY INITIATIVE

At a press conference in Sacramento in April 2001, Connerly unveiled his next foray onto the statewide ballot, the Racial Privacy Initiative (RPI). The one-page constitutional amendment banned the state from classifying "any individual by race, ethnicity, color or national origin in the operation of public education, public contracting or public employment." The initiative included specific exemptions for "medical research subjects and patients" and permitted law enforcement officers to describe "particular persons in otherwise lawful ways." It exempted the Department of Fair Employment and Housing until 2015. Specifically included, however, were "the University of California, California State University, community college district, school district, special district, or any other political subdivision or governmental instrumentality of or within the state."[9]

While some commentators described the RPI as the "son of Proposition 209," the measure actually represented a more complex and contradictory racial proposition than the anti–affirmative action ban.[10] On the one hand, the colorblind polity that Connerly continued to invoke had significant resonances with a long tradition of white supremacist thought that depicted race relations as a private matter beyond the ambit of state intervention. Connerly's assertion that the "government must accept that what 'race' we associate with is a purely private matter" suggested that race was a formal distinction and neutral signifier of skin color or ancestral origin, independent from any historical or social context and hierarchies.[11] Critical race theorist Neil Gotanda suggests that this doctrine maintains structures of racial power by drawing a bright line between the public and private spheres, putatively outlawing the recognition of race in the former while permitting racial hierarchies to go undisturbed in the latter as a matter of a private "right to discriminate." Moreover, he points out that while such assertions of colorblindness rest on a rejection of the "reality" of race, the imperative of racial "nonrecognition" actually turns on an inherent paradox—one must know what race is (and recognize it as such) before ignoring it—thus reifying race as a stable, fixed category of human existence.[12]

Legal theorist Kimberle Crenshaw similarly explains that this vision of race relations is analogous to (and extends from) a model of laissez-faire economic relations and the privatization of inequality within the marketplace, the same principles that animated the U.S. Supreme Court's 1896 *Plessy v. Ferguson* decision upholding the "separate but equal" doctrine of Jim Crow segregation.[13] Indeed, the assertion of a private right to discriminate fueled both the effort to defeat the 1946 fair employment initiative and the 1964 anti–fair housing measure sponsored by the Realtors, and also formed the basis for much of the opposition in the South to the Civil Rights Act of 1964. In this sense, the RPI drew upon long-standing ideas about the naturalized functioning of white supremacy within the "free" market and the folly of state interference in this arena. It was no coincidence that after the provision exempting the Department of Fair Housing and Employment from the RPI's mandates expired in 2015, the measure would essentially accomplish the original objective of Proposition 14 in 1964: preventing the state from enforcing antidiscrimination laws in the housing market.

These facets of the RPI made the measure particularly attractive to antistatist and free-market conservatives, who eagerly echoed Connerly's charge that the government itself was the chief perpetrator of racial divisions and race consciousness. Not only did the measure disparage the "bean-counting bureaucrats" Connerly insisted were responsible for sustaining racial boundaries, it also took square aim at the civil rights advocacy groups that relied on government-collected data to press antidiscrimination claims in the courts and legislature. Connerly's supporters were delighted that the RPI would hamstring such organizations and limit their ability to demand greater state oversight and monitoring in the name of civil rights enforcement. Conservative funders and donors would eventually direct millions of dollars to help qualify the measure for the ballot. As soon as Connerly announced the measure, conservative columnists, including Shelby Steele, George Will, Thomas Sowell, and David Horowitz, all editorialized in favor of the initiative, as did the *Wall Street Journal* and the *Orange County Register*.[14]

Connerly also selectively drew upon and incorporated themes and arguments offered by left-oriented antiracist scholars and activists about the instability of racial meanings and categories. He frequently invoked a long legacy of using racial categories to sustain racial domination: "Dare we forget the lessons of history? Classification systems were invented to keep certain groups 'in their place' and to deny them full rights. . . . The slave owners and segregationists of the American past knew it; the Nazis knew it when they labeled European Jews a separate and inferior 'race'; . . . Now, the advocates of racial categorization tell us that government-imposed racial categories will somehow yield the very opposite of what they were originally intended to do!"[15]

The equation of chattel slavery and the Holocaust with contemporary efforts to collect racial and ethnic data was certainly spurious on many grounds; the comparison implied that racial taxonomies were a cause, rather than an effect, of these atrocities and divorced the events from any historical context. But it is important to note that in criticizing the basis and legitimacy of racial distinctions, Connerly was attempting to summon an antiessentialist concept of race that was widely influential among many racial justice advocates and scholars.

In an essay Connerly penned for the Web site Interracial Voice, he quoted extensively from critical race theorist Ian Haney Lopez's scholarship on the legal construction of race, which examined a series of early twentieth-century immigration cases centering on the legal definition of whiteness. He suggested that Haney Lopez's work could be understood as "a case against the reliability of science and common understanding in deciding what constitutes race."[16] Consistent with most critical race scholarship, he pointed to the sociohistorical dimensions of racial categories and their inextricable links to the exercise of political power. Indeed, many of Connerly's claims about the meaning of race would comport with sociologists Michael Omi and Howard Winant's influential definition of race as "an unstable, 'decentered' complex of social meanings constantly being transformed by political struggle."[17]

But whereas Haney Lopez, Omi, and Winant argued that such insights demanded greater attention to the effects of racial power, Connerly used such claims to reinforce his contention that a race-based analysis could not address the root causes of social problems because it dealt only with the "superficial" manifestations of those problems: "Race classifications focus our attention on what divides us, rather than what unites us. . . . A person's skin color does not determine how well he can read, how much money he has, or how hard he works. Asking about a person's race simply diverts precious time and effort away from the real solutions."[18]

Connerly insisted that race itself had become increasingly irrelevant to contemporary American life, an anachronistic sign of an earlier, more divisive period. This critique echoed a perspective among commentators from across the political spectrum who believed that a focus on the shallow forces of race masked more fundamental explanations involving class, geography, "culture," or individual initiative.[19] Connery often pointed to the dramatic rise in the self-identified multiracial population as evidence that the polity was already abandoning antiquated definitions of racial identity and that only self-interested bureaucrats and the professional "race industry" were interested in sustaining outdated racial labels.[20] He wrote in the *Sacramento Bee*, "When I stroll through Sacramento's parks, I routinely see couples whose devotion to each other far outweighs the social taboos against interracial dating and marriage. In such a world, for the state to embrace the traditional notions of black and white is anachronistic, at best. At worst . . . it perpetuates the divisions our nation wants to overcome."[21]

In addition, the frequent allusions Connerly had made during the Proposition 209 campaign to white victimhood and the cost of unearned racial preferences were largely absent from the racial privacy campaign, and Connerly did not argue that the ban on race and ethnicity data was intended to bolster curbs against race preferences. Though he suggested systemic racial hierarchies had been overcome, he conceded that individual prejudice endured in some forms. He contended during a National Public Radio debate with civil rights attorney Eva Patterson in early 2003 that "there is racism, don't think for one moment that I'm not saying there isn't racism . . . but we recognize that largely prejudice and racism flow from ignorance and fear . . . that it resides in the heart and we have to work with people at almost a one-on-one level to move to the next level."[22]

Such representations of racism as an individual rather than a social or structural phenomenon were a stable part of postwar liberal ideology. But Connerly invoked these claims to assert that most Californians were already living in an idealized colorblind society—happily accepting one another as individual citizens. He regularly cited the state's "rich heritage of cultural traditions [that] represent the future of the entire country" and insisted that Californians were "proud" of being "the most racially and ethnically diverse people in the world."[23] Whereas most conservatives had sounded ominous warnings about the declining white share of the populace in states like California, and had ridiculed affirmations of diversity and multiculturalism, Connerly took a different tact; he celebrated such developments in order to justify an attack on the antidiscrimination protections of the state.

Finally, Connerly sought to exploit a larger public ambivalence regarding the rationale for collecting racial data in the first place. His Zogby Poll suggested that less than one in ten respondents believed that such data were collected in order to protect against discrimination. Why then, Connerly demanded, did the government insist on continuing to use those "silly little race boxes"?[24] This was a question that had even divided civil rights groups at one point. Several of the first bills advocated by California civil rights advocates in the 1940s and 1950s sought to ban state agencies, officers, or employees from asking about a person's race or religion. In the early 1960s, the national ACLU had an extended internal debate over whether to press the federal government to stop asking individuals to disclose racial information on the decennial census.[25] The ACLU's national Equality Committee specifically suggested that "the right of privacy is so important, misuse of racial data so frequent, and governmental use of such information so limited, that the Union should not approve of governments' *requiring* individuals to give information about their race under any circumstances."[26] In 1962, the longtime research director of the National Urban League similarly asserted at a public hearing, "I fail, at this date, to see the contribution that any public agency makes to the general welfare by gathering 'racial' statistics which set apart one group, 'Negroes,' from the body politic."[27]

THE COALITION FOR AN INFORMED CALIFORNIA

By the time Connerly filed his initiative with the secretary of state in February 2001, a coalition made up of representatives from the ACLU, Californians for Justice (CFJ), the Mexican American Legal Defense and Education Fund (MALDEF), the Lawyers Committee for Civil Rights (LCCR), and several other organizations had already begun meeting and tracking the legal review of the initiative's language by the attorney general's office. They were profoundly alarmed. An early internal poll commissioned by the group suggested that the measure started out with 56 percent of voters in favor and only 26 percent against. In every major demographic group polled, the measure enjoyed an advantage of at least twenty points. And 68 percent of respondents agreed with Connerly's core contention that the initiative was a "long overdue step toward achieving a color-blind society that treats all people equally."[28] The ideological investments seemed clearly to be on Connerly's side. And with well-heeled donors, a seductive title, and a commanding lead in the polls, the measure seemed destined for a victory.

Many coalition members, including Eva Patterson of the LCCR, Abdi

Soltani of CFJ, Maria Blanco of MALDEF, and Dorothy Ehrlich of the ACLU, had played central roles in the campaigns to defeat various ballot measures during the last ten years. As a result of these losses, however, they were no longer direct-democracy neophytes.[29] Confronted with the RPI, opponents would be better prepared. The campaigns against Propositions 187 and 227 had been late to organize, ceding much of the initial public debate to their opponents. By contrast, the anti-RPI coalition had struck back as soon as Connerly announced the measure, attacking the proposal as "extremely harmful and far-reaching" and depicting Connerly as a divisive and self-interested figure.[30] Before the measure even qualified for the ballot, the coalition had conducted initial polling, established a well-organized statewide executive committee, developed a fund-raising and media strategy, and compiled a five-page list of organizations and prominent individuals endorsing their campaign. Having learned a key lesson from the review of the ballot title and summary during the Proposition 209 campaign, MALDEF attorneys successfully convinced the state attorney general's office (now headed by Democrat Bill Lockyer) to reject Connerly's chosen "Racial Privacy Initiative" moniker for Proposition 54; instead, they won the more cumbersome title "Classification by Race, Ethnicity, Color or National Origin," or CRECNO. They also quickly met with many Democratic and Republican lawmakers to dissuade them from embracing the measure, in order to ensure that Connerly would not benefit from unqualified partisan support and funding during the election. Finally, the steering committee made an internal commitment not to succumb to the internal feuding that torpedoed the campaigns against Propositions 187, 209, and 227. Patterson explained that the core group decided early on "that there was no way we were going to let the campaign split. There were several times when it could have fractured and we just said—this isn't happening."[31]

Even with the benefit of this experience and these lessons, the anti-Connerly effort, which soon named itself the Coalition for an Informed California (CIC), still had to wrestle with the dilemma of how to frame its public campaign. On the one hand, civil rights groups knew full well that if the RPI were to pass their efforts to address racial justice issues in the state would be severely undermined. As an attorney with the Asian Law Caucus in San Francisco explained, the RPI was "much more dangerous than 187 or 209 because it wipe[d] out civil rights enforcement in all arenas."[32] Groups such as the ACLU were in the midst of a campaign against racial profiling, or "driving while black," which involved promoting state legislation to require local law enforcement agencies to collect data about the race of motorists they stopped; the RPI explicitly outlawed such mandates. The ACLU and several other groups were also preparing to file a major educational adequacy lawsuit against the state for the decrepit conditions endemic to many of the schools attended by students of color; much of the data revealing racial inequities in rates of student suspension, dropouts, college attendance, and teacher certification could be eliminated.[33]

At the same time, opponents concluded that Connerly's cleverly framed proposition could not be defeated by simply attacking it as racist or arguing that it abetted discrimination. White voters still made up nearly 75 percent of the California electorate, and the experiences of the last seven years suggested that when strident antiracist claims entered the debate, opponents lost ground; the currents of political whiteness were too powerful to overcome in a single election cycle.

As Eva Patterson explained, the "discrimination argument works with the base [of liberal voters and voters of color] but not with the electorate [as a whole], and if we just stick with that argument, we will lose."[34] In addition, the CIC's internal polls suggested that civil rights groups like the ACLU, MALDEF, and the NAACP had limited credibility with many voters, in part a result of Connerly's frequent attacks on what he called the "the grievance industry."[35] That is, opposition to the measure could not be singularly identified as coming from the civil rights community. While the opponents of the Connerly initiative were clearly aware of the devastating impact the measure could have on their racial justice advocacy efforts, they were certain that this claim alone would not decisively influence the statewide electorate. Yet this conclusion seemed to put the RPI's opponents in a difficult bind: how could a measure that was a clear attack on civil rights protections be opposed without prominently emphasizing race?

The preliminary poll commissioned by the anti-Connerly group in 2002 suggested that there was no silver bullet message to defeat the measure.[36] But one area did seem promising. Public health advocacy and research groups were deeply concerned that while the measure included a vaguely defined exemption for the "lawful classification of medical research subjects and patients," the ban on data collection and analysis would still effectively "exclude most environmental, epidemiological, and other population-based research, as well as research that links data from patient records to survey data."[37] The state compiled dozens of databases collecting health statistics and other demographic data, many with information related to race, and it was not certain that the measure's medical-research exemptions would protect them. For example, data related to hospital discharges and use, access to health coverage, and health-behavior surveys could be determined to be outside the scope of direct medical research and thus subject to the ban. Connerly clearly had little interest in attacking such programs or studies and believed that the medical-research exception he included had rendered them permissible. But public health groups who joined the CIC effort, including the nonprofit Public Health Institute and representatives from the health insurance giant Kaiser Permanente, knew the intricacies of this data well. In addition, unlike defenders of affirmative action in 1996, they had no difficulty in making clear the real-world consequences the initiative could have.

Concluding that this might indeed represent the measure's Achilles heel, the CIC's early materials prominently emphasized the initiative's threat to public health research as part of a multipart messaging strategy. The materials also emphasized dangers to accountability in public education, civil rights enforcement and antidiscrimination protections, and law enforcement.[38]

ENTER THE RECALL

In early 2003, the prospects for the Racial Privacy Initiative still seemed bright. The national mood in the wake of the September 11, 2001, attacks was certainly sympathetic to Connerly's emphasis on overcoming internal divisions and uniting as a singular, colorblind nation. Field Polls conducted throughout 2002 suggested that the measure enjoyed a twenty to thirty percentage point advantage among likely voters. Connerly also successfully overcame an initial shortfall in fund-raising, which had delayed the signature-gathering phase; by June 2002, the campaign reported donations of $1.8 million, including $250,000 from the conservative magnate Joseph Coors and $300,000 from media titan Rupert Murdoch. State records ultimately documented that 95 percent of the contributions to Proposition 54 came from just seven individual donors, all with extensive conservative affiliations.[39] The funding permitted the signature gathering to move ahead, and by the summer of 2002 the secretary of state confirmed that the measure would appear on the next statewide general election ballot in March 2004.[40]

Connerly was also able to surmount some initial opposition he faced among fellow Republicans, who were concerned about the legacy of earlier criticism that the GOP had exploited racialized fears during the campaigns for Propositions 187 and 209.[41] In addition, Thomas Wood, the coauthor of Proposition 209, urged Republicans to oppose the RPI because he felt the ban on race data collection would make it impossible to tell whether the

University of California system was enforcing the anti–affirmative action measure. "The racial check boxes are in our interest," Wood contended, saying of the RPI, "This is the anti-209." At the February 2003 GOP convention, however, the party's leadership decided to back Connerly and voted unanimously to endorse the measure.[42]

Another burgeoning political controversy at the same convention, however, overshadowed the debate about the Connerly measure. For weeks an insurgent campaign, fueled by a bevy of conservative radio talk-show hosts and activists, had been mobilizing to recall Governor Gray Davis from office. A budget shortfall approaching $35 billion, an energy crisis the previous summer, and accusations of tax hikes fueled the effort to recall the Democratic governor, who had just won reelection in November.[43] After backers gathered more than 1.6 million signatures in two months, the secretary of state qualified the recall for the ballot and announced a special election on October 7, 2003. As this became the next statewide election, Connerly's initiative was placed on the same ballot and given the designation Proposition 54.[44]

At first, the shift of the measure to the October 2003 special election seemed as if it would benefit Connerly. Though the CIC had already retained a team of veteran Democratic consultants, raised nearly a million dollars, launched a Web site, and set up several affinity groups to organize locally, the accelerated election timeline was generally regarded as bad news by the CIC leadership. Pundits predicted that the off-cycle election, triggered by a conservative-sponsored effort to remove an unpopular Democratic governor, would bring more Republicans to the polls than for the March 2004 ballot, when a hotly contested Democratic presidential primary (and no Republican primary) could attract a more liberal electorate.[45] In addition, according to a mid-July Field Poll, the initiative still enjoyed a twenty-one-point advantage among likely voters—enormous ground to make up in less than twelve weeks. Attorneys with MALDEF filed an unsuccessful legal motion to have Proposition 54 delayed until 2004 on the grounds that an October election would violate the rights of Latino voters in several Central Valley counties.[46]

Ultimately, however, the timing of the gubernatorial recall proved disastrous for Connerly and a blessing for his opponents. With the attention of Republican activists and donors fixated on the dueling campaigns of Arnold Schwarzenegger, state senator Tom McClintock, and several other high-profile candidates to replace Davis, Connerly received neither funding nor organizing support from the state GOP. Suddenly starved for contributions, Connerly could only afford a handful of talk-radio advertisements in

Los Angeles and Sacramento for a few days in early September. By the end of the election, Connerly estimated that his campaign had been outspent fifty-seven to one.[47]

Democrats and labor unions, by contrast, which were frantically attempting to defeat the recall, hoped that Proposition 54 would draw more Black, Asian, and Latino voters to the polls; they gave generously to the anti-54 effort. Unions and Democratic leaders around the state included messages against Proposition 54 in their extensive voter mobilization and education efforts, in sharp contrast to the anemic opposition they offered to earlier ballot measures. Lieutenant Governor Cruz Bustamante alone spent $4.5 million on television advertising against the measure, most of it channeled from tribal contributions originally made to his gubernatorial campaign.[48]

The successful fund-raising not only allowed the CIC to purchase nearly $3 million in television and radio advertising, it also permitted the group to retain a coterie of experienced Democratic consultants to help develop the campaign messaging and strategy. The consulting team included Larry Grisolano, a veteran strategist who would later oversee the direct-mail efforts of the Obama presidential campaign; David Axelrod, the Chicago-based media consultant who would soon become one of Obama's closest advisors; the corporate public relations giant Buron-Marsteller, which maintained offices in more than thirty countries and represented many Fortune 500 companies and national governments; and the Feldman Group, a Washington, D.C.–based polling and research firm that had worked on several presidential elections and with many members of Congress. Not only could the CIC Executive Committee draw on some of the most experienced political minds in the nation, the well-connected consultants helped give them access to the Democratic Party and labor leaders who could help fund the campaign.

BAD MEDICINE

During the first polling and focus groups conducted on the Connerly initiative in 2002, the pollsters concluded that while racial discrimination should not be the focal point of the anti-RPI campaign, it could still be addressed because "white Anglo voters are almost as strong as Latinos in their belief that racial discrimination is widespread in California." The polling acknowledged that "white voters express a certain weariness with the whole topic of race and would prefer not to have to think about it" but did suggest that an emphasis on combating discrimination, in conjunction with the threats to public health and medical research, could prove persuasive to voters.[49]

But a series of subsequent polls and focus groups convinced the CIC's leadership to heed the recommendation of its main pollster "to make health and not race the topic of the initiative." This meant that the health care message had to emphasize the harm posed to "all Californians," not just people of color. That is, white Californians had to be specifically reminded of their own investment in health data about race.[50] The focus groups in particular seemed to confirm the notion that an antidiscrimination message would have little resonance with most white voters. Only voters in "the base"—liberal Democrats and African Americans and Latinos—could be targeted with a message relating to discrimination. The health care arguments, by contrast, seemed persuasive to a much wider group of moderate voters and did not trade in the kind of stigmatizing language that tarnished the mainstream campaign against Proposition 187. As Eva Patterson later commented, "If you can work for something and your arguments do no harm, you have got to try and win."[51]

The CIC framed its mainstream campaign around a simple message: "Proposition 54 is bad medicine." The only English-language television commercial that ran the week before the election featured former surgeon general C. Everett Koop and focused exclusively on the health effects of the initiative. Sitting behind a desk, Koop warned sternly that "Proposition 54 would block information that can help save lives. It would end prevention efforts directed to those most at-risk from cancer, diabetes and other diseases." The ad made no reference to race or racial discrimination and emphasized the health advocacy organizations that opposed the measure.[52]

The final ballot argument written by the CIC similarly focused primarily on the health research argument, emphasizing that the measure would "endanger the health of every Californian." Voters were warned that racial data was needed "to identify groups at risk for infectious disease" because "if there is an outbreak of disease in one group, we have to be able to identify and contain it before it spreads to the general population." The ballot argument also referenced the higher rates of breast cancer diagnoses among white women and other conditions and diseases that had race-specific risk factors. All but one of the official signers of the ballot argument were medical or health professionals; none were civil rights advocates or elected officials of color. Nor did the terms "civil rights" or "discrimination" appear in the argument, though one sentence did mention hate crimes in a section on law enforcement. And both the official ballot argument and many of CIC's statements to the press began with an endorsement of Connerly's main racial proposition—"We all want to live in a colorblind society"—before explaining how the initiative would not help realize this lofty goal.[53]

Figure 14. "No on Prop. 54" Coalition for an Informed California bumper sticker, 2003. The message stressed the negative impact the measure would have on health care. From author's personal file.

The campaign's careful avoidance of antidiscrimination issues was so pronounced that Proposition 209 coauthor Thomas Wood felt comfortable joining the No on 54 effort. Although he was always opposed to the RPI because he thought the data was necessary to ensure that the affirmative action ban was being enforced, he was initially hesitant to come out publicly against Connerly. But he became increasingly concerned that Proposition 209 supporters would vote for the new Connerly measure and decided he could no longer remain on the sidelines. "My concern when I reached out to the No on 54 people was that they would use this as a way of striking back at 209," Wood said. But he was encouraged by the campaign's disciplined commitment not to link the two issues or to mention race more generally. Wood happily offered his endorsement.[54] And among the Republican candidates to replace Gray Davis, only conservative state senator Bill Simon endorsed Proposition 54, and he did little to campaign on behalf of the measure. Schwarzenegger, the election's biggest presence, quietly came out against the measure, and unlike the Proposition 209 and 187 campaigns, the state GOP ignored Connerly's requests for assistance.

While the statewide media campaign and ballot arguments were sanitized of any mention of racial discrimination or civil rights, such issues were stressed prominently in a more targeted campaign focusing on Black and Latino voters. A series of radio ads targeting urban Black voters featured Rev. Jesse Jackson and Danny Glover. In Jackson's sixty-second spot, he declared, "We are at a critical crossroads in the fight against racial discrimination in this country. . . . We see it every day. Yet our opponents are engaged in a systematic effort to roll back our progress. If 54 passes, it will give a green light to law enforcement agencies to engage in racial profiling that could never be detected. . . . And Proposition 54 will provide a license to discriminate, erecting new barriers to opportunity and progress."[55]

Similarly, a spot produced for Spanish-language television markets in Los Angeles and the Bay Area featured Los Angeles City Council member Tony Cardenas explaining that Proposition 54's proponent was an appointee of former governor Pete Wilson, reminding viewers of Wilson's connection to Proposition 187.[56] Printed outreach materials to Black and Latino voters also devoted prominent attention to issues of discrimination. Before these audiences, the CIC directly challenged Connerly's fundamental racial propositions.

While most of the CIC's attention focused on sustaining the mainstream media-based campaign against Proposition 54, some anti-54 organizations also launched grassroots efforts to reach voters directly. While not approaching the scale of the field effort against Proposition 209, a broad base of organizations and constituencies were involved. Campaign kickoff events in Los Angeles and San Francisco in early August attracted some press coverage. Californians for Justice targeted several dozen neighborhoods in Long Beach, San Jose, San Diego, and Oakland with bilingual materials. A coalition of unions and community organizations in South Los Angeles conducted a three-week voter-education program focused on the recall and Proposition 54. Other affinity groups, such as Asian Pacific Americans for an Informed California, conducted multilingual phone banks, distributed multilingual campaign materials, and held press conferences targeting ethnic media outlets. Unlike the mainstream campaign against Proposition 187, when consultants advised the campaign to shut down or silence their activist base, the CIC leadership encouraged these grassroots efforts.[57]

THE PROPOSITION 54 ELECTION AND ITS AFTERMATH

Ultimately, the attention consumed by the gubernatorial recall election almost guaranteed the demise of Proposition 54. From April 2002 to July 2003, polls consistently gave the measure a fifteen-to-twenty-five percentage point advantage among likely voters and suggested widespread support for Connerly's colorblind ideal. But as soon as the date for the recall election was announced in late July by the secretary of state, support for the measure plummeted. By mid-August, before the Coalition for an Informed California or any other anti-54 group had even begun its public campaigning, the measure's lead dropped in half. By September 17, before any television or radio ads against Proposition 54 began to air, a statewide poll found the measure trailing by seven points.[58]

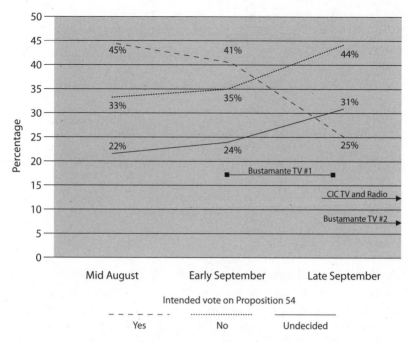

Figure 15.   Polling trends for Proposition 54, August–September 2003. Once the gubernatorial recall qualified for the ballot and the October special election was announced, support for Proposition 54 began to plummet. "CIC TV and Radio" represents the run time of television and radio ads against the measure sponsored by the Coalition for an Informed California. "Bustamante TV #1" and "TV #2" represent the run times of the lieutenant governor's television ads against the measure. By the time all of the ads began to run, the measure was well on its way to defeat. From California Field Poll Release nos. 2084, 2079, 2071, and 2040.

On Election Day, as Californians voted to recall Gray Davis and install Arnold Schwarzenegger in the state's highest office, they sent Proposition 54 to a resounding twenty-eight -point defeat. White voters, who made up 73 percent of the electorate, rejected the measure by a twenty-four-point margin, and it was defeated in every major subgroup except for conservative Republicans (see table 8). After nearly a decade of heartbreaking defeats, civil rights groups were finally the ones celebrating on election night.[59]

Not surprisingly, some political figures interpreted the defeat of Proposition 54 as the harbinger of a new era of racial politics in California. Lieutenant Governor Cruz Bustamante, a Proposition 54 opponent who lost his bid to replace Governor Davis, summed up the perspective of many

TABLE 8 Proposition 54 Exit Poll Data by Race/
Ethnicity, 2003

Group (% of electorate)	Yes (%)	No (%)
All (100%)	36	64
White (73%)	38	62
Black (5%)	13	87
Latino (11%)	25	75
Asian (6%)	28	72

SOURCE: *LAT* exit poll, Study no. 490, California Special Recall
Election, October 7, 2003.

people who worked against the initiative: "This is dramatic victory; it marks a dramatic turnaround for this state. Finally, voters are saying no more wedge politics. . . . Californians rejected 54 because they believe discrimination is wrong in California."[60] Wade Henderson, executive director of the national umbrella group the Leadership Conference on Civil Rights, issued this statement: "The voters of California have spoken clearly and forcefully that the collection of data is a critical tool in the process by which the state attempts to protect individuals from discrimination in areas including law enforcement, monitors and prevents disease, and ensures that all children have an equal opportunity to education."[61]

Considerable evidence, however, suggests that a commitment to antidiscrimination was not the underlying conviction ratified by the defeat of Proposition 54. According to a Field Poll taken close to the election, only 12 percent of those intending to vote against the measure cited concerns over Proposition 54's effects on health care or the medical community. Only 3 percent cited the need to collect data for education and 1 percent cited the prosecution of hate crimes. Ten percent said, "There's no need to classify people by race," suggesting the formal title of the initiative may have confused voters to the advantage of opponents. As an example of the diverse interpretations to which the initiative may have been subject, one caller to conservative Bill Handel's Los Angeles talk-radio show after the election said she voted against Proposition 54 because the racial data "allowed her to evaluate schools by the level of white academic achievement—'kids whose parents really care.'"[62]

While CIC members acknowledged that they benefited from the circumstances of the recall election, they also insisted that the their media and messaging strategy, and the decision to frame the Connerly measure as an attack on health care, played a large role in ensuring the measure's overwhelming defeat. But the timing of the polling shifts suggests that it was the recall that sabotaged any prospect that Proposition 54 would garner significant public attention. The *Los Angeles Times* exit poll found that only 2 percent of voters cited Proposition 54 as the main reason they came to the polls.[63]

Indeed, the only other initiative on the ballot, Proposition 53, which sought to boost spending on infrastructure projects, mirrored Proposition 54's decline in the polls. That measure, which enjoyed bipartisan support and only minimal organized opposition, also had double-digit leads in the polls before the recall was announced. Once the recall qualified for the ballot, public interest and approval in the measure plummeted, and it was ultimately defeated by the exact same margin as Proposition 54.[64]

This evidence invites greater scrutiny of the assumption that the CIC's campaign was the decisive factor in defeating Proposition 54. To be sure, the CIC implemented its strategy nearly flawlessly. Connerly himself declared, "It cannot be overstressed how disciplined the opponents of Proposition 54 were."[65] Learning from the mistakes of previous campaigns, the committee began organizing early, developed a broad-based coalition, raised sufficient funds to have a significant television and radio campaign, secured the endorsements of a wide range of elected officials, and managed to sustain both a grassroots organizing effort and a major statewide media campaign with little tension or friction. Unlike the campaigns against Propositions 187 or 209, the opponents of the RPI refused to partake in attacks against the constituencies they sought to defend in order to gain influence with moderate voters. Indeed, in comparison to every other campaign led by civil rights proponents examined in this book, the CIC's effort was by far the most efficient, competent, and well executed.

But it is also important to remember that while the CIC campaign was effectively executed, it did not represent a fundamental departure from the previous (failed) campaign strategies to defeat racialized ballot measures. As in these earlier efforts, the CIC concluded that for Proposition 54 it would also be nearly impossible to directly challenge the core racial propositions implicit in the initiative. Nor did the measure's opponents feel they could prominently defend antidiscrimination or civil rights principles to the white electorate. In choosing to emphasize the dangers posed to health care in general and in highlighting the investments of white voters in maintaining the collection of racial data in particular, the CIC concluded that it had little choice but to defer to the norms of political whiteness. As Maria Blanco later explained, "To think that once an initiative is on the ballot . . . that you're going to educate people about racism" is simply not realistic. Eva Patterson agreed: "For us it was axiomatic that it was not an education campaign, it was an election."[66]

Few experienced political operatives in California would disagree with Patterson's and Blanco's assessments. What remains important about the CIC's campaign is not the tactical judgment on which it was based but what it reveals about the political impact of the racialized initiative campaigns of the 1990s, and indeed, across the entire post–World War II era. It was the experiences in Propositions 187, 209, and 227 that helped shaped the consensus that there were no effective arguments to convince most white voters about the need for an ongoing systematic commitment to fight racial discrimination in the midst of an initiative campaign. And it is the longer inheritance of the postwar struggles over fair employment, fair housing, school desegregation, English Only, and other issues that explains why such ideas and arguments were not available. In those debates, nearly all of the ideological investments and emphasis were placed on the dominant liberal notions of antiracism: the importance of individual tolerance, the role of extremists as the main purveyors of racial discrimination, and a representation of California as an exceptional site of progress, inclusion, and diversity. When the initiative struggles of the 1990s erupted, civil rights advocates learned as their predecessors had before that these ideas alone could not counter appeals to political whiteness that still operated powerfully within the state's political culture. Moreover, they came to understand that they held no exclusive claim on the signifiers of racial liberalism. Political actors like Ward Connerly and Ron Unz demonstrated that claims to fairness, empowerment, and inclusion that once justified support for programs like affirmative action and bilingual education could also be used to discredit them.

Facing these conditions, the CIC had limited choices. They could either reach again into the same limited cache of arguments and claims about the importance of tolerance, diversity, extremism, and forbearance that had proved so anemic in the past, or they could accept that political whiteness still asserted a powerful influence on the electorate and craft a reasonable set of arguments that recognized this reality. The CIC's decision to embrace the latter strategy, then, speaks not to the group's political commitments or judgments but to the long legacy of these other struggles. When civil rights organizations themselves concluded that any robust defense of racial justice principles before the California electorate is a reckless and self-defeating strategy, it demonstrated how restrictive the prevailing political discourse on race had become, even in such a definitively blue state.

Once Connerly framed Proposition 54 as an idealized quest for color-blindness, and opponents determined that little could be done to challenge Connerly's fundamental racial propositions, the pro and anti arguments converged in several ways. The CIC's assertion that racial data was necessary to track illnesses and health outcomes within certain racial or cultural groups drew upon a conception of race as a marker of cultural or biological difference rather than as a signifier of social privilege and status. These arguments conjured a political vision in which race marked only difference, not hierarchy, grounded in either disparate cultural histories or distinctions in body types. Fundamentally, this comported with Connerly's assertion that the state had little authority to guard against racial discrimination or ensure racial equity; it was only because of (private) natural and cultural differences that the collection of race data became defensible. Society may be nearly colorblind, but nature was not. Connerly forced his opponents, at least during the campaign, to abandon nearly all explicit commitments to race consciousness linked to a more emancipatory and democratic vision. All of the prevailing conditions that motivated the day-to-day work of most CIC members—deep-seated patterns of segregation and inequality in schools, housing, law enforcement, health, and employment—became inadmissible in this statewide initiative debate about the role of race in California life.

If CIC leaders concluded that ballot initiative campaigns were not the appropriate venues for educating or influencing voters or for contesting broader ideological currents, Connerly's approach was quite different. He conceded after the election that the medical research exemption was indeed poorly written and that he had been outorganized by his opponents. But he was not altogether discouraged. In an interview with the *San Francisco Chronicle*, he suggested that Proposition 54's outcome was not a complete loss: "You don't have to win (in order) to win. . . . If you frame the issue the right way, you put out the issues for discussion. We are waging a campaign of ideas and the proof of the pudding is not what happens on one day in October but what comes after that. People are thinking about it."[67] While Connerly was undoubtedly disappointed that Proposition 54 was so soundly rejected, he could take some comfort in the knowledge that the underlying racial proposition of his initiative, racial colorblindness, would continue to dominate public debates about race and racism in California.

Conclusion

Blue State Racism

The norms of racial liberalism—expressed through commitments to "rights," "opportunity," "tolerance," "freedom," and related signifiers—now constitute the dominant framework through which racial issues are publicly deliberated in California. The price of admission to credibly enter such debates is a recognition and acceptance of such ideals.

How then can one account for the fate of the ballot measures chronicled in this book? As a growing number of Californians seemed to steadily embrace the norms of racial liberalism, the state's electorate passed ballot measures that civil rights advocates warned would strengthen the boundaries of segregation and heighten levels of racial inequality. These measures, I have argued, were implicitly premised on the political logics of apartheid—a natural and inevitable stratification of society on the basis of race that the state had minimal authority to address. Ballot measures that preserved employment and union discrimination in the 1940s, housing discrimination in the 1960s, or school segregation in the 1970s clearly expressed these dynamics. Initiatives in the 1980s and 1990s to discredit public multilingualism, to exclude a vast class of immigrants and criminal offenders from any civic recognition, and to end programs like affirmative action and bilingual education were naturalized and justified in similar ways. Taken together, these measures reveal the contingent process through which some ideas about race came to win out over others, marking certain claims and demands as natural and credible while deeming others as unfounded and specious.

Most of the accounts offered by scholars and even many of the political actors involved in these contests have insisted that the outcomes of these elections ultimately expressed a rejection of liberal ideals regarding race. After voters pulled the curtain safely behind them in their polling places, they demonstrated their decidedly illiberal commitments. From this perspective, the ballot measures "enable[d] voters' racial beliefs and fears to be recorded and tabulated in their pure form."[1] Whether driven by anxiety over demographic changes, uncertainty in the economy, or appeals made by ambitious political figures, such voters used ballot measures to express their latent racial hostilities. While particular initiative proponents such as Senator Alan Robbins might have cloaked their campaigns in the polite rhetoric of tolerance and inclusion, these overtures masked an underlying antipathy toward liberal ideals.

Voting patterns and exit polls certainly confirm some of this story. Republicans and self-identified conservatives tended much more often to support ballot measures that sought to undo civil rights protections; Democrats and self-identified liberals more often opposed them. But these initiatives were not transparent plebiscites that merely revealed the strength of particular parties or particular ideological blocs of voters. They instead require a different analysis of the relationship between a liberal political culture and the endurance of racial hierarchy and power.

Though these ballot measures were never racially neutral, and often preserved race as a defensible basis for the unequal distribution of resources and power, the electorate that embraced them also largely professed its fealty to the norms of racial liberalism. Over time, these initiatives helped elaborate the dominant racial proposition of the early twenty-first century: racial colorblindness. Colorblindness limits political criticism of racism almost entirely to individual actions and beliefs; wider structures of power and history become exonerated. Charges of racial subordination are largely inadmissible in the dominant political discourse unless accompanied by some evidence of deliberate and malicious intent. Colorblindness's command of the political discourse is so dominant that liberal political actors, even some civil rights groups, feel compelled to obey its norms in many settings. While many other political and cultural forces played a role in the rise of the racial colorblindness, ballot measures offer a particularly generative location to understand the political and ideological labor and conflict that has been necessary to transform colorblindness from a conditional proposition into a widely accepted political truth.

THE DURABILITY OF POLITICAL WHITENESS

For the political figures and organizations originally committed to the expansion of racial liberalism in the immediate postwar era, the capacity of liberal ideas to transform the prevailing racial order resided precisely in their universality. The abstractions that constitute the basic grammar of political liberalism—appeals to the "common good," invocations of "the people," assertions about "fairness" and "individual merit"—secure their power by disavowing any attachment to particular social identities, locations, or perspectives. Proponents of racial liberalism reasoned that once political judgments became guided by a universal and disinterested standard, hierarchies based on ascribed characteristics such as race, religion, or national origin would inevitably wither.

The neutral and disembodied gaze on politics that liberalism prized, however, could never fully divorce itself from a broad economy of racialized signifiers, meaning, and power. To explore how this process operated within racialized ballot measures, I have used the concept of "political whiteness"—a formulation of political subjectivity, identity, and community in which whiteness functions as an absent referent within the putatively neutral and abstract terms of liberalism. Thus, when Proposition 14 proponents exhorted voters to "Get Back Your Rights" (and were referring to a right to discriminate), they demonstrated that abstract appeals to rights could be fully invested with racial meaning; the neutral gaze on politics was already racialized. The abstract grammars of liberalism permitted this measure's proponents to simultaneously transmit and disavow racialized appeals. The harms and injuries summoned in other ballot measures as threats to "our jobs," "our homes," "our schools," "our language," and "our state" performed similar political labor. They were race-neutral appeals to political whiteness, made recognizable through a discourse of racial liberalism. At the same time, this discourse rendered other types of harms and injuries—the denial of employment, shelter, education, or public services that these initiatives also legitimized—beyond public recognition or action. These processes were not particular to postwar California ballot measures; they could be found in a wide range of times, places, and institutional locations. But direct-democracy discourse, which requires proponents to frame their claims through populist, abstract signifiers—advocating for the people rather than any invested or particular group—brings this dynamic into particularly sharp focus.[2]

This analysis recalls the influential mid-twentieth-century work of Louis Hartz and his argument that the ascendance of liberal norms shaped a collective political consciousness that was both insular and "conformitarian," that often identified "the alien with the unintelligible." Implicit in Hartz's formulation is the construction of a political subjectivity within American liberalism incapable of recognizing its own partiality—a commitment to universality that renders some types of harms and claims unrecognizable. It is a political optic premised on a capacity to see the full spectrum of political possibility that in practice can detect only a limited range of alternatives. These are precisely the characteristics of political whiteness that I have traced in this book.[3]

Indeed, it has been the conformitarian dynamics and characteristics of a liberally conditioned gaze on politics that served to sustain whiteness as a normative standard of political judgment within these ballot measure campaigns. Initiative campaigns, premised on swaying the median voter, continually recentered whiteness within these debates. This dynamic proved vexing to civil rights groups and their allies, as it forced them to navigate a tension between remaining politically credible (by addressing the perceived expectations of political whiteness) while seeking to legitimize policy goals that might challenge this political subjectivity. Ultimately, these groups concluded that an emphasis on the problems and conditions that made these civil rights protections necessary—the deep-seated discrimination in housing and employment, the vast inequalities within the public school system, the long history of state-sponsored language discrimination—would be unintelligible within the framework of political whiteness. Refusing, for the most part, to emphasize these harms and conditions, they appealed instead to the abstract principles of fairness and tolerance while branding their opponents as unreconstructed bigots and extremists. In every instance, this approach failed at the ballot box and implicitly affirmed the underlying racial proposition that once an individual had renounced bigotry and prejudice in her or his own mind, the work of antiracism was complete.

These dynamics help to explain why the triumph of racial liberalism in postwar California has not brought about a more fundamental realization of racial justice and why race remains a potent ideological heuristic to explain expansive forms of social inequality. As a political framework, racial liberalism's emphasis on universal, abstract, and atomized conceptualizations of political affinity and action offers limited purchase in deciphering and critiquing the forms of racial subordination that developed in postwar California. Liberal commitments to equal treatment, individual enlightenment, and some state intervention certainly have provided the ideological warrants to critique and delegitimize some types of racial domination: explicit acts of racist violence, formal policies of segregation, and some types of individual discrimination. And though some portion of the California populace has refused even these liberal norms, these more extreme forces were not capable of singularly shaping the state's political culture. In 1964, had the John Birch Society been charged with running the Proposition 14 campaign to undo fair housing laws, the measure would have failed miserably. The political movement to oppose school desegregation in the early 1970s largely faltered under the leadership of conservative Floyd Wakefield; it succeeded under the guidance of a self-proclaimed liberal Democrat, Alan Robbins. Ward Connerly wanted nothing to do with Pat Buchanan in the effort to defeat affirmative action, just as bilingual education foe Ron Unz rebuffed Governor Pete Wilson.

Figures like Robbins, Connerly, and Unz recognized that the key ideas and signifiers of racial liberalism could serve as a resource for their efforts to attack civil rights and racial justice policies rather than as a restraint. Within the liberal repertoire of individual rights, tolerance, and a renouncement of bigotry, they saw the ideological grounds for their own political purposes. Especially after the late 1950s, when racial liberalism became almost entirely associated with the transformation of individual attitudes rather than the transformation of broader structures of economic and political power, liberal political narratives became ideologically polyvalent. The California Real Estate Association used them to attack fair housing laws. Alan Robbins used them to resegregate California public schools. U.S. English used them to advance English Only policies. Immigration restrictionists used them to demand the civic exclusion of many immigrants. Thus, by the time Connerly's California Civil Rights Initiative and Unz's English for the Children measure emerged in the late 1990s, there was no need to steal the language of racial liberalism. Not only could particular signifiers such as "equal opportunity" and "nondiscrimination" be used to buttress claims of white political injury, but the broader ideological valence of racial liberalism had been transformed; one could embrace civil rights and antidiscrimination ideals while voting to eliminate affirmative action.[4]

At the same time, as the formal vestiges of state-sponsored discrimination were being eradicated, civil rights groups and their allies found it increasingly difficult to employ the language of racial liberalism to critique enduring forms of racial subordination. These challenges were noted relatively early in the postwar era. The attorney Loren Miller observed in a 1961 speech after the passage of California's fair employment practices legislation that "simple minded discrimination has given way to sophisticated discrimination," as employers developed new methods to maintain racial barriers while upholding their claims of racial innocence.[5] The conceptual grammar of racial liberalism, with its emphasis on individual behavior and state-enforced protections against individual acts of discrimination, could not account for the interconnected structures, norms, and policies that combined to secure racist outcomes. Civil rights advocates like Miller and the NAACP's Virna Canson and Marnesba Tackett labored vigorously to explain how these systems operated to maintain rigid boundaries of segregation and hierarchy within education, housing, and employment. But their opponents—Realtors, school board members, "neighborhood school" supporters, and so on—simply invoked their commitments to individual rights and colorblind innocence. By the 1990s, many established civil rights groups had altogether given up on trying to demonstrate or account for the systematic presence of racism in California society, retreating once again to pleas for tolerance over hatred.

POLITICAL WHITENESS AND THE HISTORICAL CRITIQUE OF RACIAL LIBERALISM

During the rise of the postwar civil rights movement, the limitations of racial liberalism (and white liberals) were subject to intense debate. Loren Miller's 1962 essay in *The Nation*, "Farewell to Liberals," characterized the "liberal outlook on the race question" as demanding "accommodation" and "acquiescence" on the part of Black people while abetting a white "resistance" rooted in "the existence of customs, sometimes jelled into law," that insisted upon a "gradualist approach." Similar critiques of liberal claims to neutrality and orderly progress erupted across the civil rights movement at this time, evident in Martin Luther King's 1963 "Letter from a Birmingham Jail," Fannie Lou Hammer's confrontation with the Democratic establishment at the 1964 national convention, women of color critiques of white feminism, and nationalist efforts that altogether rejected white participation and leadership.[6]

Among the most penetrating and forceful analysts of racial liberalism was author James Baldwin. In 1963, Baldwin controversially insisted that in the movement for social change and racial justice, "there is no role for the white liberal, he is our affliction." Baldwin was not a "racial separatist" in the terms of the day. His essays and books found diverse audiences, and as a gay Black man from a working-class background he understood the complex terms on which racial subordination took place. Baldwin was instead critiquing a liberal subjectivity predicated on what he described as a "missionary complex" that refused to imagine Black people as capable, autonomous political beings.[7] In later writings, he focused more particularly on white political identity itself. Presaging a sizable scholarly literature on the "invention" of whiteness, Baldwin insisted that "there is in fact, no white community."[8]

Whiteness was for Baldwin "absolutely, a moral choice," an identity derived from and constructed through a set of political convictions. It was by inhabiting a particular political subjectivity—one that rested upon a series of destructive assumptions—that one became white. To embrace the myth of whiteness, he argued, was to "believe, as no child believes, in the dream of safety"; that one could insist on an inalienable and permanent protection from vulnerability. Across several essays, he stressed the centrality of a particular historical amnesia—a national imagination that disavowed a bloody past and the inheritances such a past bequeathed—which left many "trapped in a history which they do not understand."[9] And he repeatedly criticized the familiar proclamations of innocence—a denial of culpability that precluded a broader perception of one's place in the world. "It is the innocence that constitutes the crime," he explained.[10] He recognized the powerful hold these characteristics had on those who embraced whiteness and the psychic "danger" that would accompany a commitment to an alternative course of action.[11]

For Baldwin, however, it was inconceivable to abet, assuage, or nurture the fantasies of this political subjectivity, as it produced a people that "cannot allow themselves to be tormented by the suspicion that all men are brothers."[12] Baldwin believed this subjectivity could not be appeased because to do so would be to foreclose any wider possibility for human liberation and transformation. This was not merely a preference for militant over conciliatory strategies; it was simply impossible to build any robust movement for justice (racial or otherwise) on the impoverished notions of political community nurtured by the fantasy of whiteness.

In Baldwin's formulation, we might recognize a new story about the relationship between racial liberalism and the disorganization of progressive politics and the so-called New Deal Order after the 1960s. Instead of characterizing racial liberalism as having gone too far and provoking its own demise by fanning the flames of backlash, we might contend that the New Deal Order collapsed because racial liberalism did not go far enough. By ultimately affirming rather than displacing political whiteness, racial liberalism failed to dislodge a normative standard of political judgment that proved quite accommodating to subsequent conservative efforts that opposed an equitable distribution of rights, resources, and recognition.[13] The core commitments of political whiteness simply could not sustain any robustly egalitarian and democratic politics.

Indeed, a central tenet in the common sense of many contemporary progressive political activists and leaders holds that a deliberate focus on racial identity and race-based oppression undermines the formation of a broad-based popular alignment necessary to win political power. We might also consider the opposing argument: without a sustained and intentional effort to address the role that race plays in naturalizing and animating expansive structures of inequality, the growing disparities in resources, rights, and power can only continue. The ascension and authority of the colorblind discourse that so effectively organizes and structures debates about race and racism in California today has consequences for wide segments of the populace, including those who identify as white.[14] The state simply cannot solve the myriad crises it chronically faces—related to prisons, budgeting, resource management, health, education, transportation, and the like—without coming to terms with the racial propositions that underlie all of these issues. A 2008 study ranked the 436 congressional districts in the United States based on a broad "human development index," which considered education, employment, health, housing, and other basic outcomes. The bottom 10 percent of the list—those areas of the country most ravished by poverty, vulnerability, and premature death—was primarily populated by districts in the South. But of the eight districts in this group from outside the South, five were in California, including the lowest-ranked district in the nation.[15]

The South has a story to tell about its ignominious representation on this list. What is California's story? Can it be told through the language of racial colorblindness? And can it be understood by a populace that, according to Joan Didion, "did not believe history could bloody the land, or even touch it?"[16]

BEYOND POLITICAL WHITENESS?

The most enduring political lessons, insights, and legacies that came out of the ballot struggles of the 1990s largely embraced Baldwin's assertions that political whiteness could and should not remain at the center of California political life. While the marches and walkouts against Proposition 187 in October and November of 1994 were opposed by many of the initiative's opponents, who feared that unapologetic assertions of immigrant rights would only strengthen the hand of immigration restrictionists, over time the opposite effect occurred. These actions' resolute demand for political recognition and respect shaped the terrain for the single-largest political transformation in state politics in the last generation.

In the fifteen years after Proposition 187's passage, more than one million Latinos have registered to vote in the state, the vast majority of them as Democrats who strongly support immigrant rights and civil rights as well as investments in public education, health care, and transportation. (In the 1980s, it should be remembered, Republican candidates captured up to 40 percent of the Latino electorate, which was often divided on the subject of immigration policy.)[17] By 2008, 21 percent of the state's registered voters would be Latino, as would 27 percent of registered Democrats. Such voters proved crucial to Democratic victories in a series of statewide elections since 1998.[18] This transformation was fueled both by the political spirit of Proposition 187 marches—and their complete rejection of the claim that immigrants should hide from political view to avoid upsetting those who opposed their presence—as well as a rapidly expanding network of community- and labor-organizing groups committed to building the electoral power of the state's "emerging majority."[19]

These political developments also shaped the fortunes of California Republicans. Former governor Pete Wilson, who loudly supported all the racialized ballot measures of the 1990s, increasingly came to be blamed for the Republican Party's string of electoral failures in the state; grassroots efforts to stigmatize Wilson as a divisive and unprincipled political figure were largely successful. They have also prevented the state GOP leadership from embracing the many subsequent attempts to qualify various so-called Son of 187 measures since 1994, all of which have failed to reach the ballot.[20] Both Ward Connerly and Ron Unz have mostly disappeared from California politics since their forays onto the statewide ballot. While championing successful ballot measures, both failed in their long-term efforts to realign California voters around a multiracial and antistatist conservatism. In the end, what stymied Wilson, Connerly, and Unz was not the mainstream strategy proffered by Democratic strategists and consultants to affirm the racial propositions underlying these ballot measures in order to prevent their passage, but the more confrontational and insistent political claims made by the anti-187 protesters and the grassroots organizing efforts against Propositions 209 and 227.

The ongoing transformation of the California electorate and the lessons gleaned from the declining fortunes of Connerly, Unz, and Wilson suggest that if another racial proposition akin to Propositions 187 or 209 were to qualify for the ballot in the second decade of the twenty-first century, it would face a much different fate. Vote-counting Republican Party leaders would likely keep their checkbooks closed, while Democratic leaders would be much more likely to mobilize on behalf of a key part of their electoral base. Grassroots community organizations, some now with more than a decade's worth of experience in organizing voters, would not watch idly from the sidelines. And with white voters comprising only 65 percent of the electorate in 2009, proponents could not count on a plurality of the white electorate alone to carry a measure to victory, as was true in the 1990s.[21]

But a primary lesson of this book has been that racial propositions never remain static for very long and that political whiteness can endure in complex ways. Key to any such transformations will be the ability of future initiative campaigns to mobilize and incorporate a significant number of voters of color, essentially fashioning a multiracial political whiteness.

One 2004 ballot measure suggests how such a seemingly paradoxical transformation might take place. Ten years after the passage California's Three Strikes law, critics successfully qualified a ballot measure to modify the particularly cruel punishments that the legislation meted out to nonviolent offenders, the large majority of whom were Black or Latino.[22] Imprisonment rates for those convicted of a third-strike offense were thirteen times higher for African Americans than white Californians.[23] With California's corrections budget already spiraling out of control, and with media accounts of shoplifters facing life sentences in prison, polls gave the measure—Proposition 66—a three-to-one advantage as the November election approached. But an eleventh-hour opposition campaign led by Pete Wilson and Governor Arnold Schwarzenegger, which included the prominent endorsements of former Democratic governors Jerry Brown and Gray Davis, warned voters that the measure would "flood our streets with thousands of dangerous felons, including rapists, child molesters, and murderers."[24] While their campaign did not employ explicitly racialized representations of offenders akin to George Bush's "Willie Horton" effort in 1988, it did address a sense of victimhood, violation, and vulnerability that had been constructed over time in deeply racialized terms.[25] The victims' rights advocates who publicly spoke out against the measure were almost always white, and the language they employed resonated with a long history of appeals to political whiteness.[26]

The campaign to pass Proposition 66 and revise the harsh sentencing mandates made no mention of the racial impact of the Three Strikes policy and affirmed many of the original claims made by Three Strikes proponents about incapacitating a vast class of criminal offenders. Sentencing reformers believed that linking their campaign in any way to race, by pointing out, for example, that five times as many Black men in California were in prison as were enrolled in public higher education in California at the time, would jeopardize its fate before the voters.[27] The measure lost anyway. In a state notorious for rancorous partisan divides, a bipartisan coalition emerged to defend a profoundly racist system of mass incarceration that would soon send the state to the brink of insolvency. Following the contradictory logics of colorblindness, no explicit mention of race was made by either side during the campaign, even though debates about crime in California are always debates about race.[28] Race can perform diverse political and ideological labor. A demographic transformation in the electorate alone will not necessarily abolish the constitutive role of political whiteness. Racial demography is not always political destiny.

THE FUTURE OF RACIALIZED DIRECT DEMOCRACY

It is likely, then, that ballot measures will continue to pose a conundrum for civil rights and racial justice advocates. On the one hand, such groups would undoubtedly be cheered if the provisions for direct democracy were ever removed from the California Constitution, as some initiative critics have advocated.[29] It is generally easier to make arguments about racial impact and equity in the courts and legislature than during a ballot measure campaign, even as the demographic transformation of the electorate continues.

On the other hand, there are few indications that California voters are prepared to disavow the instruments of direct democracy, even in the face of widespread criticism of its misuse.[30] And proponents are likely to continue to view the initiative process as a relatively inexpensive way to garner public attention for their particular issues, regardless of the outcome of the election. Thus, the era of racial propositions in California is likely to continue, though the range of issues that will be engaged is uncertain.[31]

What does this mean for the fate of racial colorblindness? Like all racial propositions, colorblindness has ascended through a process of political and ideological struggle; there is nothing natural or inevitable about it. As Raymond Williams has explained, the features of what are regarded as politically "dominant have always to be stressed, but not in ways which suggest any a priori totality." Williams argues for the development of "modes of analysis which . . . are capable of discerning, in good faith, the finite but significant openness" of dominant political ideas and projects.[32]

In many ways, the opponents of specific civil rights policies—the Los Angeles Chamber of Commerce, the California Real Estate Association, Alan Robbins, U.S. English, Ward Connerly, and Ron Unz—have understood the "openness" described by Williams far better than their adversaries. While their claims and politics should be subjected to vigorous critique, their efforts hold critical lessons for antiracist political projects today. They remind us of the importance of forging proactive struggles that seek to redeploy ideological symbols and narratives toward new ends—crafting racial propositions built on alternative ethics and commitments. They demonstrate how we must aggressively and creatively constitute new audiences for these efforts. Such initiatives, and the contradictions they engage, can help us to imagine new forms of political community and the new worlds we might make together.

Acknowledgments

I have accumulated countless debts, both personal and professional, in writing this book. I first wish to thank the many colleagues, mentors, and friends with the Center for Third World Organizing, the Applied Research Center, People United for a Better Oakland, and Oakland Kids First that made the twelve years I spent working as an organizer in the San Francisco Bay Area so deeply rewarding.

I moved to Los Angeles with only the vaguest sense of how my experiences as a community organizer might relate to a career of academic labor. But in the American Studies and Ethnicity PhD program at the University of Southern California (USC), I was welcomed into a remarkable community of scholars who helped me understand that all intellectual projects remain shaped by personal and political investments. My cherished mentor, Laura Pulido, advised the dissertation on which this book is based and was always ready with candid and engaged feedback. Ruthie Gilmore has been a singular influence on my intellectual and political development, providing me a framework within which to pose and answer questions and reminding me that humor and kindness matter enormously. George Sanchez modeled the habits of generosity, mentorship, and commitment that I will always aspire to replicate. Bill Deverell and Janelle Wong shared rich insights from their respective scholarship and fields while encouraging my interdisciplinary interests. My dissertation writing group at USC, which included Michan Connor, Jerry Gonzalez, Hilary Jenks, and Phuong Nguyen, patiently read several chapters and offered skilled advice, as did Laura Barraclough and Wendy Cheng. I also thank the department's talented staff, including Sonia Rodriguez, Kitty Lai, and especially Sandra Hopwood. Across a series of presentations, workshops, and individual meetings during my time at USC, I also received helpful feedback from

Evelyn Nakano-Glenn, Robert Self, Mark Brilliant, Michelle Nickerson, Daria Roithmayr, Ariela Gross, Ricardo Ramirez, Eduardo Bonilla-Silva, Neil Gotanda, and Marta Lopez-Garza.

At the University of Oregon, my extraordinary colleagues in the Department of Ethnic Studies and the Department of Political Science helped me move the book to completion. In Ethnic Studies, I thank Michael Hames-García, Lynn Fujiwara, Irmary Reyes-Santos, Charise Cheney, Lynn Stephen, and Peggy Pascoe for constructive comments on various parts of the manuscript. Along with other faculty, including Brian Klopotek, Jeff Ostler, Ernesto Martinez, David Vasquez, Shari Huhndorf, Priscilla Ovalle, Loren Kajikawa, and Michelle McKinley, these colleagues have built a flourishing intellectual community for the interdisciplinary study of race and ethnicity at the University of Oregon. Peggy Pascoe was a cornerstone of this community; in her passing we have lost a groundbreaking scholar and an irreplaceable mentor and friend.

In Political Science, Dan Tichenor generously organized a roundtable discussion on a preliminary version of the entire manuscript, which provided me with extremely helpful feedback from Matthew Lassiter, Naomi Murakawa, and Richard Ellis. Tichenor also read an unwieldy version of the chapter on Proposition 187 and shared insights from his own work on immigration history. Bob Bussel and Gerry Berk honored last-minute requests to read different chapters. Joe Lowndes has been an invaluable interlocutor since my arrival in Eugene and his insights and writing on the relationship between discourse and political transformation have strengthened my own analysis immensely. I am also grateful to Priscilla Yamin for thoughtful criticism about the relationship between political history, culture, and institutions and for her steady encouragement in the face of a looming deadline. Finally, I thank numerous undergraduate students in Political Science and Ethnic Studies who shared my interest in the political and ideological labor of ballot measures and who offered useful questions and ideas across several courses.

I am indebted to the Department of Political Science for providing superb graduate research fellows, including Dan Anderson, Abdurrahman Pasha, Forrest Nabors, Robin Barklis, and especially Brian Guy and Sarah Cate, who provided heroic assistance in preparing the final manuscript. The department's gifted staff, including Kristina Mollman, Tish Ramey, Mark Turner, Jeannine Anderson, and Chung-Fei Tsai, make me look forward to coming to work, as does Donella-Elizabeth Alston in Ethnic Studies.

In the last stages of research and writing, I received critical support from the Huntington Library, the Department of Special Collections at UCLA

(Thayer Fellowship), a University of Oregon Junior Faculty Professorship award, and a Resident Scholar Fellowship at the Wayne Morse Center for Law and Policy at the University of Oregon. I thank Margaret Hallock and Elizabeth Webber for the rich and rewarding year at the Morse Center.

I relied on the kindness and expertise of dozens of archivists and manuscript specialists to complete this research. I especially thank Gabriela Gray at UCLA's Young Research Library, Alan Jutzi and Bill Frank at the Huntington Library, David Sigler and Robert Marshall at California State University, Northridge, and all of the dedicated staff at the Southern California Library for Social Studies and Research for their assistance.

Ed Lee and Californians for Justice allowed me access to their organizational archives; the story of that group's remarkable work around Proposition 209 in particular has yet to be fully written. Jan Adams kindly shared various personal papers from her work on Propositions 187 and 209. I thank her and the other people who allowed me to interview them: Tom Bartman, Ignatius Bau, Maria Blanco, Rona Fernandez, Emily Goldfarb, Eva Patterson, Gary Orfield, Julie Quiroz-Martinez, Rigo Rodriguez, Dan Schnur, Arnold Steinberg, and Frank Wu. I also thank Scott Braley for allowing me to reprint his photographs from the Proposition 209 campaign.

Different versions of this project were presented at the University of Washington; the University of California, Santa Barbara; New York University; the Politics of Race, Ethnicity, and Immigration Consortium; Sunbelt Rising conferences at the Huntington Library and Clements Center for Southwest Studies at Southern Methodist University; the Western Political Science Association; the American Studies Association; and an invaluable seminar on racial colorblindness convened by Kim Crenshaw, Luke Harris, and George Lipsitz at the Center for Advanced Studies in the Behavioral Sciences at Stanford University. I was also privileged to present portions of this work at meetings of the Western States Center, Basic Rights Oregon, and the Rural Organizing Project.

I also thank friends and colleagues with the Edward W. Hazen Foundation, the Northwest Federation of Community Organizations, Asian Communities for Reproductive Justice, and the Western States Center for helping me to stay connected to innovative organizing work after my transition to Oregon. From afar, I turn regularly to the work of Lisa Duggan, Howard Winant, and Michael Omi, and I thank each of them for their generative scholarship and personal encouragement.

At the University of California Press, I thank Niels Hooper for his early and enduring enthusiasm for the project and Eric Schmidt and Emily Park for critical support during production. I was incredibly fortunate to draw on Julie Van Pelt's immense talents as copy editor. George Lipsitz and Nikhil Singh have been generous mentors for several years, and both provided astute feedback and advice on the entire manuscript, as did an anonymous reader for the press.

Throughout this process, I have been supported by loving family and friends, including Alex Li; Oneka LaBennett; Nicole Davis; Niru Somasundaram; Silvia Ibarra; Anita Gutierrez; Larry Salomon; David Isenman; Laura Dansky; Yvonne Paul; Carolina Martinez; Silvia, Mike, Zulema, and Ethan Solis; Silvia Martinez; Elizabeth, Mateo and Diego Martinez; and Carolina Leyva. My family in New York and Kingston, including Martha HoSang, Dennis HoSang, Marjorie Brown-HoSang, Robert HoSang, and Judith HoSang, always sustain me no matter far away they are.

Finally, I am blessed to share each day with Umai Norris, Isaac Martinez-HoSang, and Norma Martinez-HoSang. Norma is an enormously talented organizer who understood the aspirations of this project from the beginning. It has been through countless conversations with her that this book has come to life. Her thoughtful advice, ceaseless support, and unreserved love made this project possible. Norma, Umai, and Isaac make my life rich in ways I continue to discover. I dedicate this book to them with gratitude and love.

Notes

Epigraph: Didion, *Where I Was From,* 71.

1. In November 2000, 45.4 percent of California voters registered as Democrats and 34.9 percent registered as Republicans. See "Report of Registration as of October 10, 2000," California Secretary of State, www.sos.ca.gov/elections/ror/ror-pages/29day-presgen-oo/county.pdf (accessed April 25, 2007). The voucher initiatives, Propositions 174 (in 1993) and 38 (in 2000), were both defeated by margins of nearly forty points. The medical marijuana initiative, Proposition 215, passed by a margin of 55.6 to 44.4 percent in 1996. The antiunion measure, Proposition 226, lost by a margin of 53.4 to 46.6 percent in 1998. See "A History of California Initiatives," 2002, California Secretary of State, www.sos.ca.gov/elections/init_history.pdf (accessed March 5, 2007).

2. On this framing, see Schrag, *Paradise Lost;* and Gibbs and Bankhead, *Preserving Privilege.*

3. This approach is heavily influenced by Michael Omi and Howard Winant's theory of "racial formation," which they define as "the sociohistoric process by which racial categories are created, inhabited, transformed and destroyed." Omi and Winant, *Racial Formation in the United States,* 55.

4. The emphasis on the contingency and transformation of political meaning draws broadly from the work of the Italian theorist Antonio Gramsci. See Gramsci, *Selections from the Prison Notebooks.* See also Hall, *Hard Road to Renewal.*

5. Saxton, "Genteel Apartheid," *Frontier Magazine,* August 1961. Saxton later explored the roots of white working-class support of racial exclusions in several important works. See Saxton, *Rise and Fall of the White Republic;* and Saxton, *Indispensable Enemy.*

6. "Jim Crow Is Dying," *Los Angeles Sentinel,* October 7, 1948.

7. "Courier Salutes San Diego," *Pittsburgh Courier,* June 18, 1949.

8. Gerstle, *American Crucible,* 4.

9. On eugenics research, see Stern, *Eugenic Nation.* On lynching, see

279

Gonzales-Day, *Lynching in the West*. See also Akers Chacón, Davis, and Cardona, *No One Is Illegal*.

10. Winant, *World Is a Ghetto*, 2.

11. Gerstle, *American Crucible*, 1–13.

12. Patt Morrison, "Land of Reinvention," *Los Angeles Times* (hereafter *LAT*), December 3, 2006, S2.

13. It is important to note, however, that key California-based figures in the early twentieth century were engaged with leaders of South Africa's white supremacist regime. See Brechin, *Imperial San Francisco*. During much of the postwar era, with some notable exceptions, residential segregation by race in California has remained stark. See, for example, Ethington, Frey, and Myers, *Racial Resegregation of Los Angeles County, 1940–2000*. The state also had numerous "Sundown Towns," which threatened violence toward African Americans within town limits after dark. See Loewen, *Sundown Towns*. Many schools, particularly in urban coastal areas, were more segregated in 2008 than during the time of the *Brown v. Board of Education* decision. See Oakes et al., *Separate and Unequal 50 Years after "Brown"*; and Orfield and Lee, *"Brown" at 50*.

14. As Aletta Norval notes, there is extensive academic and popular debate over the meaning and history of the term "apartheid," and there are critical distinctions between the post-1948 apartheid regime and earlier systems of segregation. See Norval, *Deconstructing Apartheid Discourse*.

15. My use of political culture is drawn from K. Baker, *Inventing the French Revolution*, 5.

16. For example, in 2006, African American men in California were incarcerated at a rate of 5,125 per 100,000 in the population, compared to 1,142 for Latino men, 770 for white men, and 616 for the population as a whole. A 1996 study found five times as many African American men in prison as were enrolled in public higher education in the state. See Connolly et al., *From Classrooms to Cell Blocks*; and Mauer and King, *Uneven Justice*. For a report summarizing a range of racial disparities in the state, see Johnson and Krajcer, *Facing Race*. For a comprehensive analysis across many areas of social well-being by race, see California Legislative Black Caucus, *State of Black California 2007*. While these patterns can be found across the United States, my argument here is that, in California, racial liberalism triumphed even as the possibilities for racial justice declined.

17. On the "disappearance rates" of California students, see HoSang, "Beyond Policy"; Oakes et al., *Separate and Unequal 50 Years after "Brown"*; and InnerCity Struggle, *Student and Parent Vision for Educational Justice in the Eastside*.

18. Among many discussions of these complicated relationships, see Omi and Winant, *Racial Formation in the United States*; Fields, "Slavery, Race, and Ideology in the United States of America"; and Cox, *Caste, Class, and Race*.

19. A. Davis, "Color of Violence against Women." See also Crenshaw,

"Mapping the Margins"; Collins, *Black Feminist Thought;* and Glenn, *Unequal Freedom.*

20. Hall, "Race Articulation and Societies Structured in Dominance."

21. I thank Nikhil Singh for this point. See also Robinson, *Black Marxism;* Fields, "Slavery, Race, and Ideology in the United States of America"; and Cox, *Caste, Class, and Race.*

22. Hall, "Race Articulation and Societies Structured in Dominance."

23. Gilmore, "Fatal Couplings of Power and Difference."

24. Didion, *Where I Was From,* 48.

25. Center for Governmental Studies, *Democracy by Initiative,* 1–16; "History of California Initiatives," 2002, California Secretary of State, www .sos.ca.gov/elections/init_history.pdf (accessed March 5, 2007).

26. Schattschneider, *Semisovereign People,* 1–2.

27. "California's Expanding Latino Electorate," in *California Opinion Index,* vol. 1 (San Francisco: Field Institute, 2000), 1.

28. Among many examples, see Allswang, *Initiative and Referendum in California, 1898–1998.*

29. Bell, *"The Referendum,"* 14–15.

30. Hajnal and Louch, *Are There Winners and Losers?;* Gamble, "Putting Civil Rights to a Popular Vote." For a competing view, see Donovan and Bowler, "Direct Democracy and Minority Rights."

31. Key and Crouch, *Initiative and the Referendum in California,* 506.

32. See Bell, "Referendum," 15–16. See also Haskell, *Direct Democracy or Representative Government?*

33. Laclau, "Politics and Ideology in Marxist Theory."

34. On currents of populism in U.S. political history more broadly, see Kazin, *Populist Persuasion.*

35. Marx and Engels, "German Ideology: Part I."

36. Hall, *Hard Road to Renewal,* 169.

37. Edelman, *Constructing the Political Spectacle,* 10. The literature on the social construction of public policy is also relevant here, especially Stone, *Policy Paradox;* and Schneider and Ingram, *Deserving and Entitled.*

38. Edelman, *Constructing the Political Spectacle,* 2.

39. These arguments are also made in some of the scholarly literature on direct democracy. See Smith and Tolbert, *Educated by Initiative;* and Bowler and Donovan, "Information and Opinion Change on Ballot Propositions."

CHAPTER 1

1. The quotes are from L.A. Council for Civic Unity, "Statement of Policy," box 5, folder 3, Loren Miller Papers, Huntington Library, San Marino, Calif. (hereafter LM). See also "Home Front Unity Group Created Here," *LAT,* January 11, 1944, A1. As historian Scott Kurashige and others have argued, the committee's formation and Bowron's commitments are best understood as a "crisis management" strategy aimed at curbing domestic conflict during a

time of war rather than a call for political empowerment. Kurashige, *Shifting Grounds of Race,* 154. See also Sitton, *Los Angeles Transformed,* 66–72.

2. The figure is from "Report on Interracial Committees in Los Angeles," April 17, 1944, box 72/b IV 5 a dd(3), folder "1944," John Anson Ford Papers, Huntington Library, San Marino, Calif. (hereafter JAF).

3. Myrdal, *American Dilemma,* 48. On Myrdal, see R. King, *Race, Culture, and the Intellectuals,* 3–6.

4. Gramsci, *Selections from the Prison Notebooks,* 324.

5. Quoted in Hall, "Variants of Liberalism," 34.

6. See Singh, "Liberalism"; Horton, *Race and the Making of American Liberalism;* and Duggan, *Twilight of Equality?*

7. The emphasis on state enforcement of nondiscrimination laws serves as the central definition of racial liberalism in Chen, *Fifth Freedom,* 8.

8. The quote is from the letterhead of the group called Society for the Prevention of Un-American Activities. Letter dated March 27, 1939, box 5, folder 1 "Miller Correspondence, 1937 to 1946," LM.

9. "July 4 Observance Tempered by War," *LAT,* July 5, 1945, A1; Murphy's speech, box 76/b IV 5 j(2) (1945), JAF.

10. See, generally, Elinson and Yogi, *Wherever There's a Fight.*

11. An NAACP attorney documented as many as fifteen advertisements for minstrel shows in Northern and Southern California in the early 1950s. See "Another View of Amos and Andy," by Frank Williams, and other examples in box 105, folder 25 "Minstrel Shows," National Association for the Advancement of Colored People Records, Region I, 1942–86, Bancroft Library, University of California, Berkeley (hereafter NAACP-UCB).

12. Stern, *Eugenic Nation,* 82–84.

13. CFCU blueprint for action, "Exclusion in Public Places," September 20, 1949, folder "Race Relations," California Federation for Civic Unity Records, 1946–52 Bancroft Library, University of California, Berkeley (hereafter CFCU).

14. "Brief Historical Report of the Pacific Coast Committee of American Principles and Fair Play," box 4, folder 8, Clarence Gillett Papers, Young Research Library, University of California, Los Angeles (hereafter CG).

15. Stears, "The Liberal Tradition and the Politics of Exclusion," 94.

16. Statement of Augustus F. Hawkins at California Hearings of the U.S. Commission on Civil Rights, Los Angeles, January 25, 1960, p. 4, box 99, folder "Civil Rights in California 1960," Augustus Hawkins Papers, Young Research Library, University of California, Los Angeles (hereafter AH).

17. See especially Gerstle and Fraser, *Rise and Fall of the New Deal Order, 1930–1980.*

18. Edsall and Edsall, *Chain Reaction,* 5.

19. On the backlash narrative used in the housing initiative, see Nicolaides, *My Blue Heaven;* McGirr, *Suburban Warriors;* and Boyarsky, *Big Daddy.* On affirmative action and immigrant rights, see Gibbs and Bankhead, *Preserving Privilege.*

20. See, among many examples, Micklethwait and Woolridge, *Right Nation,* chapter 3; and Thernstrom and Thernstrom, *America in Black and White.*

21. Centrist versions of this argument can be found in Schlesinger, *Disuniting of America.* The critique from the left has been sounded in Gitlin, *Twilight of Common Dreams.* For an astute analysis of these broader dynamics, see Duggan, *Twilight of Equality?*

22. Theoharis, "'We Saved the City,'" 63.

23. Lowndes, *From the New Deal to the New Right,* 4.

24. Saxton, *Rise and Fall of the White Republic,* 4.

25. Fields, "Slavery, Race, and Ideology in the United States of America," 101.

26. Carmichael and Hamilton, *Black Power,* 56.

27. Ibid., 81–82.

28. Baldwin, *Price of the Ticket;* Morrison, *Playing in the Dark;* DuBois, *Black Reconstruction in America.*

29. Sitton, *Los Angeles Transformed,* 70. Sitton describes Bowron's racial politics as contradictory and conflicted during this period.

30. Bowron's comments are quoted in a letter from Clore Warne to Loren Miller, May 25, 1943, box 5, folder 1 "Miller Correspondence, 1937 to 1946," LM. Scott Kurashige's discussion of Bowron's role in attacking Japanese Americans during this time suggests that the mayor's comments cannot be dismissed as a function of the prevailing wartime zeitgeist alone; he played a leadership role in elaborating the case for the racial inferiority of those he attacked. Kurashige, *Shifting Grounds of Race,* 118–22.

31. Loren Miller to Clore Warne, attorney, May 28 1943, box 5, folder 1 "Miller Correspondence, 1937 to 1946," LM.

32. Lipsitz, *Possessive Investment in Whiteness,* chapter 1; DuBois, *Black Reconstruction in America,* 700. See also Roediger, *Wages of Whiteness.*

33. Harris, "Whiteness as Property," 1713, 1761.

34. "An Open Letter to My Sister, Angela Davis," *New York Review of Books,* January 7, 1971.

35. Williams, *Marxism and Literature,* 113.

36. Ibid., 114.

37. In political science, the most influential expression of this thesis can be found in King and Smith, "Racial Orders in American Political Development." For an alternative interpretation, see Skowronek, "Reassociation of Ideas and Purposes."

CHAPTER 2

1. "Proposition 11 Called Unfair," *LAT,* October 7, 1946.

2. On the transformation of racial politics in Los Angeles and California during World War II, see K. Leonard, *Battle for Los Angeles,* 88; Kurashige, *Shifting Grounds of Race;* and Sides, *L.A. City Limits.*

3. "Proposition 11 Called Unfair," *LAT,* October 7, 1946.

4. The two important exceptions are Chen, *Fifth Freedom;* and K. Leonard, *Battle for Los Angeles.*

5. Allswang, *Initiative and Referendum in California, 1898–1998,* 73.

6. Quoted in Regina Freer, "Charlotta Bass," 56. See also Bass, *Forty Years Memoirs from the Pages of a Newspaper.*

7. On Mexican Americans and the FEPC, see Vargas, *Labor Rights Are Civil Rights.* On the FEPC more generally, see Chen, *Fifth Freedom;* and Self, *American Babylon.*

8. The Allied Organizations against Discrimination in National Defense to Governor Culbert Olsen, November 21, 1941, box 76/b IV 5 I ee(5), folder "1941," JAF.

9. Quoted in Self, *American Babylon,* 82. On the California FEPC hearings, see Sides, *L.A. City Limits;* Johnson, Korstad, and Lichtenstein, "Opportunities Found and Lost," 786–811; and Vargas, *Labor Rights Are Civil Rights.*

10. Self, *American Babylon,* 82.

11. On Hawkins's ascension to the assembly in 1934, see Flamming, *Bound for Freedom,* 314–17.

12. "Where Do You Stand Gentlemen?" *Los Angeles Sentinel,* March 21, 1946.

13. "People Want FEPC, Says Rep. Hawkins," *Los Angeles Sentinel,* February 21, 1946.

14. "Another Chance for California," *Los Angeles Sentinel,* January 3, 1946.

15. "People Want FEPC, Says Rep. Hawkins," *Los Angeles Sentinel,* February 21, 1946.

16. On the Mexican American and Japanese American strikes in Oxnard in 1903, see Almaguer, *Racial Fault Lines.* On the struggle against restrictive covenants, see Flamming, *Bound for Freedom.*

17. Flamming, *Bound for Freedom,* 231.

18. See Self, *American Babylon,* 82–84.

19. Chen, "'The Hitlerian Rule of Quotas.'"

20. See Hall, "Problem of Ideology."

21. Selig, *Americans All.*

22. American Council on Race Relations, "Formation of the San Francisco Civic Unity Council," February 23, 1945, Clearinghouse release number 1, box 1, folder 20, CFCU.

23. See "Report on Conference of California's Councils of Civic Unity and Similar Community Organizations," July 6, 1945, box 1, folder "XI," CFCU.

24. Ibid. See also Bernstein, "Building Bridges at Home in a Time of Global Conflict."

25. Kennedy, *Freedom from Fear.*

26. R. King, *Race, Culture, and the Intellectuals,* 29.

27. Gilroy, *Ain't No Black in the Union Jack,* 26.

28. "Minutes from 3rd annual meeting, 1949, Edward Howden," folder "XI," CFCU.

29. Quoted in Self, *American Babylon*, 86.

30. See M. Johnson, *Second Gold Rush*.

31. On this period, see Igler, *Industrial Cowboys*; and Almaguer, *Racial Fault Lines*.

32. Burt, *Search for a Civic Voice*; Ruiz, *Cannery Women, Cannery Lives*.

33. Matt Garcia, *World of Its Own*, 158–60.

34. Nelson, *Divided We Stand*.

35. Burt, "The Fight for Fair Employment and the Shifting Alliances among Latinos and Labor in Cold War Los Angeles."

36. On the debate surrounding the New York act, see Chen, "'The Hitlerian Rule of Quotas.'"

37. Pro-FEPC flyer, box 1, folder 20, Charles Bratt Papers, Southern California Library for Social Studies and Research, Los Angeles (hereafter CB).

38. *Associated Farmer* 5, no. 12, folder "Legislature 1945," carton 15, Ellen Leary Legislative Papers, University of California, Berkeley (hereafter EL).

39. *Among These Rights . . .* , newsletter of the Council for Civic Unity of San Francisco, vol. 1, no. 6, October 26, 1946, box 18, folder 6, Civil Rights Congress of Los Angeles Papers, Southern California Library for Social Studies and Research, Los Angeles (hereafter CRC).

40. A recent study drawing on Warren's personal correspondence on the issue argues that the governor was a strong supporter of the legislation but that Republican voters and representatives vehemently opposed it. Chen, *Fifth Freedom*.

41. Chen, "From Fair Employment to Equal Employment Opportunity and Beyond," 185.

42. *Proposed Amendments to Constitution: Propositions and Proposed Laws, Together with Arguments; General Election, November 5, 1946* (Sacramento: California Secretary of State, 1946). The legislation did include provisions for judicial review of the commission's findings on appeal. It also provided for an annual budget allocation of $250,000.

43. *Among These Rights . . .* , newsletter of the Council for Civic Unity of San Francisco, vol. 1, no. 6, October 26, 1946, box 18, folder 6, CRC.

44. "Solicitation letter from Statewide Committee," July 25, 1945, box 22, folder 43, Jacob Zeitlan Papers, University of California, Los Angeles (hereafter JZ).

45. D. Leonard, "'No Jews and No Coloreds Are Welcome in This Town,'" 311–20; *California Eagle*, February 14, 1946.

46. "FEPC Drive Has 220,000 Names to Date," *Los Angeles Sentinel*, April 4, 1946. See also "California Cities Gear for FEPC Petition Drive," *Los Angeles Sentinel*, January 31, 1946; and "Watts Acts to Push State FEPC," *Los Angeles Sentinel*, February 7, 1946.

47. All quotes in paragraph are from "Lets Gird for Battle," *Los Angeles Sentinel*, June 27, 1946.

48. Rosenbaum, "Legislative Participation in California Direct Legislation, 1940–1960," 116.

49. *Proposed Amendments to Constitution: Propositions and Proposed Laws, Together with Arguments; General Election, November 5, 1946* (Sacramento: California Secretary of State, 1946).

50. "Committee for a State FEPC, Yes on Proposition #11" flyer, folder "1946 General Election," Campaign Literature Archive, Young Research Library, University of California, Los Angeles (hereafter CL).

51. *Proposed Amendments to Constitution: Propositions and Proposed Laws, Together with Arguments; General Election, November 5, 1946* (Sacramento: California Secretary of State, 1946).

52. Congress of Industrial Organizations election brochure, November 1946 (emphasis in original), California State Archives, Sacramento.

53. Burt, "The Fight for Fair Employment and the Shifting Alliances among Latinos and Labor in Cold War Los Angeles," 84–85.

54. All quotes in paragraph are from "Jewish Labor Maps Campaign against Bigotry," *LAT*, July 17, 1946.

55. "International President of the Brotherhood of Sleeping Car Porters and Civil Rights Leader: Oral History Transcript/Cottrell Laurence Dellums," p. 116, oral history interview, conducted 1973 by Joyce Henderson for the Earl Warren Oral History Project, Regional Oral History Office, Bancroft Library, Berkeley.

56. *Amendments to Constitution and Proposed Statutes, November 2, 1920* (Sacramento: California Secretary of State, 1920), 5–6.

57. See Sanchez, *Becoming Mexican American;* and Kurashige, *Shifting Grounds of Race.*

58. Quoted in D. Leonard, "'No Jews and No Coloreds Are Welcome in This Town,'"132.

59. "Broadcast by Mayor Fletcher Bowron, Radio Station KMPC, September 15, 1946," box 20, folder 1, CB.

60. D. Leonard, "'No Jews and No Coloreds Are Welcome in This Town.'"

61. Governor Earl Warren, quoted in the Council for Civic Unity (Los Angeles), "UNI-FACTS: The Ku Klux Klan in California," June 1946, box 1, folder 20, CB.

62. Proposition 11 campaign filing statements, 1946, Campaign Filing Statements, California State Archives, Sacramento (hereafter CFS).

63. Chen, *Fifth Freedom,* 128.

64. Herbert M. Baus, oral history interview, p. 178, conducted 1990 by Enid H. Douglass for the Claremont Graduate School Oral History Program, part of the State Government Oral History Program, California State Archives, Sacramento.

65. "Recommendations of Los Angles Chamber of Commerce on State Ballot Measures, November 5, General Election 1946," box 8, folder 6, Clarence Gillett Papers, University of California, Los Angeles (hereafter CG).

66. "Don't Be Misled" pamphlet (emphasis in original), box 8, folder 6, CG.

67. "Farm Bureaus in State Oppose Proposition 11," *LAT,* October 29, 1946.

68. "An Unsatisfactory Remedy," *San Francisco Chronicle,* October 10, 1946; "Promotion of Race Prejudice," *LAT,* October 27, 1946.

69. Allport, *Nature of Prejudice,* 468–71; Gossett, *Race, the History of an Idea in America.* See also Foner, *Reconstruction;* and DuBois, *Black Reconstruction in America.*

70. Chen, *Fifth Freedom.*

71. Brown, *Regulating Aversion,* 15.

72. *Proposed Amendments to Constitution: Propositions and Proposed Laws, Together with Arguments; General Election, November 5, 1946* (Sacramento: California Secretary of State, 1946).

73. "Don't Be Misled" pamphlet, box 8, folder 6, CG.

74. "Chamber Opposes FEPC Act," *Southern California Business,* October 16, 1946.

75. "Workers Told of Danger in Proposition 11," *LAT,* October 20, 1946.

76. "Proposition 11 Called Unfair," *LAT,* October 7, 1946.

77. "Fair Practices Act Assailed as Public Menace," *LAT,* October 27, 1946. The CIO-PAC was formed in 1944 to coordinate the federation's political activities nationally.

78. See especially Kazin, "Reform, Utopia, and Racism." See also Kazin, *Barons of Labor;* and Saxton, *Indispensable Enemy.*

79. Quoted in K. Leonard, *Battle for Los Angeles,* 288.

80. Voting returns, box 12, folder "FEPC," Edward Roybal Papers, University of California, Los Angeles (hereafter ER).

81. One study examining local returns for Proposition 11 estimates that the vote correlated strongly with partisan preferences. The authors estimated that in precincts composed of at least 80 percent Democratic voters, between 61 and 76 percent cast ballots in favor of the measure; while in precincts composed of at least 80 percent Republican voters, not more than 16 percent voted for Proposition 11. Chen, Mickey, and Van Houweling, "Explaining the Contemporary Alignment of Race and Party."

82. "Recommendations of Los Angles Chamber of Commerce on State Ballot Measures, November 5, General Election 1946," CG. On Proposition 15 generally, see K. Leonard, *Battle for Los Angeles.*

83. Pamphlet against Proposition 15 in box 8, folder 6 "Election Materials," CG.

84. Kurashige, *Shifting Grounds of Race,* 120.

85. *Perez v. Sharp,* 32 Cal. 2d 711 (1948). See also Pascoe, *What Comes Naturally.*

86. Brown is quoted in *The Open Forum* (ACLU of Southern California newsletter), vol. 29, no. 12, June 7, 1952, box 5, folder 13, Register of the California CIO Council Union Research and Information Services Records, 1935–56, Southern California Library for Social Studies and Research, Los Angeles (hereafter CIO). The State Supreme Court had already essentially eviscerated the Alien Land Laws in its 1948 *Oyama* decision.

87. Summarized in "Civil Rights in California," box 99, folder "1960 Civil Rights," AH.

88. "Tenney Bill Sponsors Fade Out," *People's Weekly World*, March 10, 1953; "Tenney Proposal Backer Withdraws His Support," *San Francisco Chronicle*, March 8, 1953.

89. "Poll Discloses State Support for FEPC Law," *LAT*, September 4, 1952. The California Poll found that 61 percent of voters favored either federal or state FEPC legislation, with only 32 percent opposed.

90. Max Mont to Edward Roybal (emphasis in original), December 12, 1957, box 12, folder "FEPC," ER.

91. NAACP Policy Committee statement, May 13, 1957, box 12, folder "FEPC," ER.

92. California Legislature, Joint Fact-Finding Committee on Un-American Activities, *Third Report of Un-American Activities in California* (Sacramento, 1947), 45–47.

93. "Some Questions and Answers" flyer, n.d. (probably 1945–46), box 12, folder "FEPC," ER.

94. See "Final Report on the Campaign for a Los Angeles Equal Employment Opportunity Ordinance," 1949, p. 6, box 31/b III 6c(7), JAF.

95. NAACP press release for mobilization, February 19, 1953, box 2206, folder 5, Terea Pittman Papers, California State Archives, Sacramento (hereafter TP).

96. Frank Williams comments, box 3, folder 19, NAACP-UCB.

97. "For FEP in '53!" *People's World*, n.d. (probably May 1953), box 15, folder 11, NAACP-UCB.

98. Bernstein, "Building Bridges at Home in a Time of Global Conflict."

99. Lichtenstein, "From Corporatism to Collective Bargaining: Organized Labor and the Eclipse of Social Democracy in the Postwar Era," in *Rise and Fall of the New Deal Order, 1930–1980*, ed. Gerstle and Fraser.

100. Frank Williams to Los Angeles County Conference on Human Relations, speech, October 11, 1952, p. 5, box 3, folder 50, NAACP-UCB.

101. California Federation for Civic Unity press release on voter registration drive, March 20, 1950, box 1, CFCU. Unable to reach a consensus on such strategies, the CFCU folded in 1956, though many of its functions were continued by local affiliates.

102. "The Case for Fair Employment Practices Legislation in California in 1953," California Committee for Fair Employment Practices, box 12, folder "FEPC," ER.

103. "Council for Equality in Employment Answers the Critics of the Proposed Ordinance for Los Angeles Creating a Commission for Equal Employment Opportunity," n.d. (probably 1956), box 31/b III 6c(7), JAF.

104. "Let's Have a Showdown," *California Eagle*, March 3, 1959.

105. "Civil Rights: Today and Tomorrow," UAW Lake Arrowhead conference, January 21, 1964, pp. 7–8, box 44, folder 2, LM.

CHAPTER 3

1. *Time*, September 25, 1964, 23. Also cited in Casstevens, *Politics, Housing and Race Relations*, chapter 5.

2. Edward Howden, executive director of the state Fair Employment Practices Commission, to the McCone Commission, *Fair Practice News*, no. 22 (1965). See also Horne, *Fire This Time*. The U.S. Supreme Court decision overturning the proposition was *Reitman v. Mulkey*, 387 U.S. 369 (1967).

3. See for example McGirr, *Suburban Warriors*, 133; Nicolaides, *My Blue Heaven*, 308; Boyarsky, *Big Daddy*. Robert Self specifically critiques the label "backlash" because it "distracts attention from the central fact of that resistance: it took the form of race-based counter claims." Self, *American Babylon*, 268.

4. Brilliant, "Color Lines," chapter 5.

5. Fogelson, *Fragmented Metropolis;* Pulido, "Rethinking Environmental Racism."

6. Quoted in Moore, *To Place Our Deeds*, 23.

7. Flamming, *Bound for Freedom*, 66.

8. Deverell and Flamming, "Race, Rhetoric, and Regional Identity," 140.

9. Lipsitz, *Possessive Investment in Whiteness*, 26.

10. Self, *American Babylon*, 261

11. Southwest Realty Board's Race Restrictions Committee update in *California Real Estate Magazine*, December 1940. The CREA's activities in the early 1950s are described in "No One 14 [Fair Housing Revocation]," press release of CAP 14, September 29, n.d., box 29, folder 1, California Democratic Council Records, Southern California Library for Social Studies and Research, Los Angeles (hereafter CDC-SCL).

12. *California Real Estate Magazine*, June 1949, 68.

13. Sanchez, "Reading Reginald Denny."

14. Nicolaides, *My Blue Heaven*, 42.

15. Ibid., 19.

16. Ibid., 180.

17. Cited in Loewen, *Sundown Towns*, 128.

18. Freund, "Marketing the Free Market."

19. *California Real Estate Magazine*, September 1948; *Shelley v. Kraemer*, 334 U.S. 1 (1948).

20. Self, *American Babylon*, 105, 261.

21. "Racial Restrictions—Brokers' Rights Under Supreme Court Decisions," *California Real Estate Magazine*, August 1948, 10.

22. U.S. Commission on Civil Rights, *Hearings before the United States Commission on Civil Rights*, 640.

23. "Democracy's Key Fits Any Door," prepared for Ninth Annual Meeting of the Los Angeles County Conference on Community Relations, October 22, 1955, box 32, folder 6, LM.

24. *Human Relations* 1, no. 1 (1964), box 169, folder 2, Alexander Pope Collection, Huntington Library, San Marino, Calif. (hereafter AP).

25. Jack Lagguth, "Figures Tell of Segregation," *Valley Times*, February 28–March 6, 1963.

26. U.S. Commission on Civil Rights, *Hearings before the United States Commission on Civil Rights*, 275.

27. Self, *American Babylon*, 265.

28. Ibid., 265.

29. Sanchez, "'What's Good for Boyle Heights Is Good for the Jews.'"

30. Self, *American Babylon*, 104.

31. Ibid., 160.

32. "Population and Housing in Los Angeles County: A Study in the Growth of Residential Segregation," Los Angeles Commission on Human Relations, March 1963, box 2, folder 1, Deborah Louis Collection, University of California, Los Angeles (hereafter DLC).

33. Flamming, *Bound for Freedom*, 353.

34. See, for example, folder 38 "Program Files, Herlong, Calif.," NAACP-UCB.

35. "Negroes Raise Civil Rights War Chant in Westside Mass Meeting," *Westwood Hills Citizen*, July 11, 1963, box 111, folder 7, American Civil Liberties Union of Southern California Records, University of California, Los Angeles (hereafter ACLU).

36. "Owner Agrees to Integrate Torrance Tract," *LAT*, July 13, 1963.

37. See, for example, various news articles about vigilante violence in box 15, folder 5, CRC.

38. On Chicago and Detroit, see Hirsch, "Massive Resistance in the Urban North"; and Sugrue, *Origins of the Urban Crisis*. Outbreaks of violence certainly did occur; vigilantes set fire to a Fontana home in 1945, killing Los Angles civil rights activist O'Day Short and his family. But such episodes occurred less and less frequently in the aftermath of the war. See M. Davis, *City of Quartz*, 399–400.

39. "A Study of Racial Attitudes in Neighborhoods In-filtrated by Nonwhites," Bay Area Real Estate Report, second quarter, 1955, p. 127, folder "Proposition 14," Institute for Governmental Studies, University of California, Berkeley (hereafter IGS).

40. "Population and Housing in Los Angeles County: A Study in the Growth of Residential Segregation," Los Angeles Commission on Human Relations, March 1963, box 2, folder 1, DLC.

41. California Civil Code, section 51 (1960).

42. Casstevens, *Politics, Housing and Race Relations*, 10.

43. Twelve cities nationally also had local open housing ordinances on the books. *LAT*, September 20, 1964.

44. Kennedy's executive order of November 20, 1962, covered all FHA- and VA-financed mortgages made after that date as well as all public housing and urban-renewal projects. Denton, *Apartheid American Style*, 9.

45. Lewis, *Analysis of Proposition 14*, 22. Lewis was a CREA member opposed to Proposition 14, and he self-published a lucid analysis of the ballot measure's contradictions.

46. Hayward, "Ronald Reagan and the Transformation of Modern California," 240.

47. Casstevens, *Politics, Housing and Race Relations*. Rumford's original bill would have applied to all individual homeowners and included modest criminal penalties for violators, but those provisions were removed during negotiations.

48. See Edward Rutledge memorandum, p. 12, box 168, folder "Housing: Prop 14," ACLU. Local referendums or initiatives opposing antidiscrimination measures were also being supported by the NAREB in Berkeley in 1963 and in Detroit and Seattle in 1964, but all observers agreed that California would be a singularly important arena for this debate. Denton, *Apartheid American Style*.

49. Cited in Casstevens, *Politics, Housing and Race Relations*, 58.

50. "Brown Calls on Aides to Save Housing Act," *LAT*, October 29, 1963.

51. Casstevens, *Politics, Housing and Race Relations*, 41.

52. The organizing committee was originally to be called Americans against Forced Housing before it adopted the moniker Committee for Home Protection (CHP), again revealing how cautious the Realtors were of associating their effort too explicitly with rhetoric that could be identified as openly racist. See *California Real Estate Magazine*, November 1963.

53. *California Real Estate Magazine*, May 1963, 19. A 1965 assessment of the Proposition 14 debate written by the National Committee against Discrimination in Housing suggested that the CREA had been planning the strategy for an initiative amendment for several years.

54. *Proposed Amendments to Constitution: General Election, November 3, 1964* (Sacramento: California Secretary of State, 1964), 13.

55. The legal analysis is cited from "A Legal Opinion on Prop 14 and a Description of Its Effects on the Constitution and the Laws of the State of California," n.d., box 29, folder 1, CDC-SCL.

56. One of the main campaign spokespersons for the CHP, William Shearers, was a regular contributor to the White Citizens Council of America. See NAACP flyer in box 105, folder 61, NAACP-UCB. Reference to the assessment of Realtors is from a memorandum from William Becker to Governor Brown, November 6, 1963, carton 1, CFCU.

57. Cited in Casstevens, *Politics, Housing and Race Relations*, 49.

58. *Realtor's News*, n.d., box 17, folder "Rumford," Marie Koenig Papers, Huntington Library, San Marino, Calif. (hereafter MKP).

59. See, for example, closed minutes, Southwest Realty Board, January 20, 1964, box 26, folder 12, LM.

60. "Apartment Association Kickoff Rally Memo," December 3, 1964, box 26, folder 12, LM.

61. The CREA estimated that it collected nearly one million signatures in total, including those gathered for a supplemental filing. See *California Real Estate Magazine*, March 1964, 5.

62. At one point, Dr. Nolan Frizzle, president of the California Republican

Assembly, was quoted as saying that "the essence of freedom is the right to discriminate." Such candid expressions, however, rarely appeared in official campaign literature of statements of the CHP, and Frizzle was quickly condemned by other Proposition 14 supporters. See Schuparra, *Triumph of the Right,* 105.

63. "Statement of Policy," adopted June 4, 1963, by the NAREB, and June 22, 1963, by the CREA, box 26, folder 12, LM.

64. "Director's Minutes," *California Real Estate Magazine,* August 1963, 16, 18.

65. L. H. Wilson speech at the "Changing Peninsula Forum, Part III," February 20, 1964, folder "Proposition 14 Campaign Materials," IGS.

66. Charles Shattuck, "Address before the Sacramento Real Estate Board, Feb. 20, 1964," pp. 2, 6, box 6, folder 3, Max Mont Papers, California State University, Urban Archives Center, Oviatt Library, Northridge (hereafter MM).

67. "Decision on Housing Initiative," *LAT,* February 2, 1964. The majority of major daily newspapers in Northern California came out against the initiative. See Casstevens, *Politics, Housing and Race Relations.*

68. "Property Owners Bill of Rights" pamphlet, published by CREA, box 17, folder "Rumford," MKP.

69. CHP pamphlet, box 17, folder "Rumford," MKP.

70. "Yes on 14" pamphlet, box 17, folder "Rumford," MKP.

71. *Proposed Amendments to Constitution: General Election, November 3, 1964* (Sacramento: California Secretary of State, 1964), 18–19.

72. Pamphlet, produced by "CHP, San Gabriel, CA," box 17, folder "Rumford," MKP.

73. *Realtor News,* n.d., box 17, folder "Rumford," MKP.

74. "Proposition 14: The Cases for and Against," *LAT,* September 20, 1964.

75. Ibid.

76. Harris, "Whiteness as Property," 1714.

77. *Proposed Amendments to Constitution: General Election, November 3, 1964* (Sacramento: California Secretary of State, 1964), 18.

78. CREA pamphlet, box 17, folder "Rumford," MKP.

79. *Realtor News,* n.d., box 17, folder "Rumford," MKP.

80. L. H. Wilson speech at the "Changing Peninsula Forum, Part III," February 20, 1964, "Proposition 14 Campaign Materials," IGS.

81. Cited in "No on Prop 14 Alameda County," press release, October 12, 1964, "Proposition 14 Campaign Materials," IGS.

82. "Rockefeller Backs Housing Law," *Bay Area Independent,* February 1, 1964, box 104, folder 1, NAACP-UCB.

83. On church-based activism on behalf of Proposition 14, see Dochuk, *From Bible Belt to Sunbelt;* Dallek, *Right Moment;* and Cannon, *Governor Reagan.*

84. Casstevens, *Politics, Housing and Race Relations,* 57; Ronald Reagan's "A Time for Choosing" address, October 27, 1964, available from the Ron-

ald Reagan Presidential Library, www.reagan.utexas.edu/archives/reference/ timechoosing.html (accessed October 1, 2009).

85. "Stenographers Reports," May 7 and 28, 1964, box 16, Los Angeles County Chamber of Commerce Papers, University of Southern California, Los Angeles (hereafter LAACP). See also minutes of board meetings, January 19, 1964–December 17, 1964, box 35, LAACP.

86. "Fight on Housing Law Hit," *Palo Alto Times,* November 19, 1963; "News from CAP 14," newsletter no. 10, October 2, 1964, "Proposition 14 Campaign Materials," ISG.

87. Earle Vaughan, "Facing the Inevitable Changes," *The Apartment Journal,* October 1963, carton 1, CFCU.

88. Cited in Edward Rutledge memorandum, p. 8, box 198, folder "Housing: Prop 14," ACLU.

89. Belford Gardens letter, November 26, 1963, box 26, folder 12, LM.

90. Minutes, CDC statewide convention in Long Beach, Calif., December 1963, box 29, folder 1, CDC-SCL.

91. Casstevens, *Politics, Housing and Race Relations,* 62.

92. On "responsible liberalism," see Schiesl, *Responsible Liberalism.*

93. Lucien Haas, oral history interview, p. 135, conducted 1989 by Carlos Vasquez for the UCLA Oral History Program, part of the State Government Oral History Program, California State Archives, Sacramento.

94. CDC memorandums, box 29, folder 1, CDC-SCL.

95. Brown speech to the Jewish women's group on August 20, 1964, box 29, folder 1, CDC-SCL; Brown speech to National Women's League at University of Judaism, October 12, 1964, box 29, folder 1, CDC-SCL. Brown spent much of the fall condemning Goldwater as an extremist as well, declaring that there was "the stench of fascism in the air." Cited in Rarick, *California Rising,* 288.

96. *Proposed Amendments to Constitution: General Election, November 3, 1964* (Sacramento: California Secretary of State, 1964), 18 (emphasis in original).

97. Glenn Anderson's speech, excerpted in an October 9, 1964, CAP 14 press release, box 29, folder 1, CDC-SCL.

98. Martin Luther King's speech, cited in an October 27, 1964, CAP 14 press release, box 29, folder 1, CDC-SCL.

99. The largest of the Protestant denominations were the United Church of Christ, the Methodist Church, and the Presbyterian Church. The Mexican American Chamber of Commerce of Los Angeles endorsed Proposition 14, though dissenting members charged procedural irregularities in the vote. *LAT,* August 13, 1964; J. Gonzalez, "A Place in the Sun."

100. Various materials related to Hollywood involvement in CAP 14, box 29, folder 1, CDC-SCL. CAP 14 leaders described the effort as "perhaps the largest group of artists and craftsmen who have ever met together for a single, political purpose." See also, "Statement of Executive Committee of the Arts Division of CAP 14," September 10, 1964, box 29, folder 1, CDC-SCL.

101. Robert Coate to William Becker, March 2, 1964, in William Becker,

oral history interview, p. 63, conducted 1980 by Gabrielle Morris, for the State Government Oral History Program, California State Archives, Sacramento.

102. Campaign fund-raising estimates compiled from Proposition 14 campaign filing statements, 1964, CFS.

103. See "Press Release: United Civil Rights Committee," n.d., box 116, folder "1964 United Civil Rights Committee," ACLU. For an example of MAPA flyers, see box 9, folder 20, Eduardo Quevedo Papers, Stanford University, Department of Special Collections, Palo Alto, Calif. (hereafter EQ).

104. "Eliminating Housing Discrimination in California" flyer, box 27, folder 14, CDC-SCL. Civil rights groups also made the connection between Proposition 14 and Jim Crow segregation but more often spoke to the conditions facing Black people in California than the abstract ideals of integration. CORE continued small demonstrations against some Realtors. "Outside the Law," *Daily Review Hayward*, June 8, 1964.

105. CORE leaflet, box 5, folder 7, MM.

106. Brilliant, "Color Lines."

107. Sal Montenegro, "Effects of the Initiative and Fair Housing Law on the Mexican-American Community," March 19, 1964, box 57, folder 5, Ernesto Galaraza Papers, Stanford University, Department of Special Collections, Palo Alto, Calif. (hereafter EG).

108. For examples of such reports, see box 5, folder 20, MM.

109. "Report on Operation of NAACP Headquarters for No on Proposition 14," November 16, 1964, box 5, folder 21, MM.

110. Editorial, *Carta* 2, no. 6 (August 20, 1964), p. 3, MO224, box 54, folder 8, EG. I thank Jerry Gonzalez for sharing these findings with me. Gonzalez's own work points to the contradictory impulses shaping Mexican Americans who moved to suburban communities in the 1950s and 1960s as they reconciled their desire to become homeowners with the discrimination they faced in many neighborhoods. J. Gonzalez, "Place in the Sun."

111. Editorial, *Carta* 2, no. 10 (October 29, 1964), box 9, folder 20, EQ.

112. "A Manual for the 'Constitutional Amendment-No!' Campaign," February 5, 1964, p. 2, California Committee for Fair Practices, box 4, folder 20, "Campaign Manual and Organization," MM.

113. William Becker to Max Mont et al., April 10, 1964, box 5, folder 1, MM.

114. Excerpted from the press release "Clergy and Christian Social Relations Chairman of the Episcopal Diocese of Los Angeles: Fact Sheet on Proposed Initiative to Cancel the Rumford Fair Housing Act," box 16, folder "Housing," MKP.

115. "The Church Says No on Proposition 14," Council of Churches in Northern and Southern California, box 16, folder "Housing," MKP.

116. "An Open Letter to an American Community," Los Angeles County Commission on Human Relations, box 16, folder "Housing," MKP.

117. Brown's comments, widely quoted in the press, were seized upon by

the CHP, who charged that the governor was resorting to desperate scare tactics. See CHP pamphlets, box 17, folder "Rumford," MKP.

118. From ACLU fundraising letter to supporters, February 1, 1964, box 16, folder "Housing," MKP.

119. See daily news releases from CAP 14, October 1964, box 29, folder 1, CDC-SCL.

120. For an excellent case study of such activity, see Nicolaides, *My Blue Heaven*.

121. Gathered from data cited in Casstevens, *Politics, Housing and Race Relations*, 56, 68.

122. Ibid., 68–74.

123. Los Angeles County election returns, California Democratic Council report, box 29, folder 1, CDC-SCL.

124. Richard Kline, oral history interview, pp. 18–19, conducted 1977 by Eleanor Glaser for the State Government Oral History Program, California State Archives, Sacramento.

125. Lucien Haas, oral history interview, pp. 134–35, conducted 1989 by Carlos Vasquez for the UCLA Oral History Program, part of the State Government Oral History Program, California State Archives, Sacramento.

126. African Americans constituted 1.06 percent of the total population of West Los Angeles in 1950 and 1.75 percent in 1960. "A Comparative Statistical Analysis of Population by Race for Incorporated Cities of Los Angeles County, 1950–1956–1960," box 169, folder 3, AP.

127. See Edward Rutledge memorandum, p. 12, box 198, folder "Housing: Prop 14," ACLU.

128. Ibid., 12.

129. Ibid., 14.

130. Ibid., 10.

131. *California Real Estate Magazine,* May 1964, 11.

132. See Lipsitz, *Possessive Investment in Whiteness.*

133. Loren Miller, "Relationship of Racial Residential Segregation to Los Angeles Riots," prepared for the governor's commission, October 7, 1965, box 33, folder 16, LM.

134. *Mulkey v. Reitman,* 64 Cal. 2d 877 (1966).

135. Petition for a Writ of Certiorari to the Supreme Court of the State of California, William French Smith, counsel for petitioners, *Mulkey v. Reitman,* 64 Cal. 2d 877 (1966). (Smith was retained to represent apartment owners who had evicted tenants after the passage of Proposition 14.)

136. *Reitman v. Mulkey,* 387 U.S. 369 (1967). See also Karst and Horowitz, "*Reitman v Mulkey*"; and Fred Graham, "High Court Voids Fair Housing Ban in California," *New York Times* (hereafter *NYT*), May 30, 1967.

137. "Reasons Given for Size of Reagan and Yorty Votes," *LAT*, June 12, 1966.

138. Boyarsky, *Rise of Ronald Reagan,* 205.

139. Cited in Edwards, *Reagan,* 156; See also "Reagan Assails Rumford Act Study in Hard Attack on Brown," *LAT,* October 13, 1966.

140. Boyarsky, *Rise of Ronald Reagan,* 205.

141. Ibid., 203; Cannon, *Governor Reagan,* 201–4.

142. M. Davis, *City of Quartz,* 153.

143. William Becker memorandum, November 12, 1964 (emphasis in original), box 4, folder 14, MM. A collection of anti-14 activists met for a statewide meeting in Fresno in December 1964 but could not come to agreement after one faction insisted that housing be addressed together with other issues of racial discrimination, while another wanted to keep an exclusive focus on housing. "Fair Practices Group Splits Over Goals," *Fresno Bee,* December 13, 1964.

144. For a description of fair housing activities in Los Angeles County, including West Los Angeles, see series 1, box 1, folder 22, Catholic Human Relations Series Records, Loyola Marymount University, Center for the Study of Los Angeles Research Collection, Los Angeles (hereafter CHRS).

145. California Housing Coalition: Legislative Program, January–March 1972, box 6, folder 5, MM. The coalition, which formed in 1970, had some two hundred members at the time.

146. A 1971 report, "An Outsider's View," by a UCLA graduate student working for the umbrella group the Housing Opportunities Center, leveled this charge at some local fair housing groups. See series 1, box 1, folder 15, CHRS.

CHAPTER 4

1. *Crawford v. Los Angeles Board of Education,* 458 U.S. 527 (1982).

2. In addition, the vast majority of the hundreds of desegregation plans approved by the U.S. Department of Health, Education, and Welfare for southern school districts actually decreased total busing. Under segregated (dual) systems, students were often transported beyond their nearest school. See Durham, "Sense and Nonsense about Busing"; and "School Busing a U.S. Tradition," *NYT,* May 24, 1970. The California busing figure is from Wollenberg, *All Deliberate Speed,* 159.

3. Fischel, *Homevoter Hypothesis.*

4. Democratic assemblyman Bruce Young of Cerritos made the comment at a state assembly hearing. "Assembly Approves Antibusing Measure," *LAT,* March 23, 1979.

5. *Santa Barbara School District v. Superior Court,* 13 Cal. 3d 315, 324 (1975).

6. Nicolaides, *My Blue Heaven,* 273.

7. Ibid.

8. Ibid., 288.

9. *Wysinger v. Crookshank,* 82 Cal. 588, 720 (1890).

10. *Mendez v. Westminster School Dist. of Orange County,* 64 F. Supp. 544 (D. Cal. 1946). On this case, see Ruiz, "South by Southwest"; G. Gonzalez, "Segregation of Mexican Children in a Southern California City." On

an earlier antisegregation case near San Diego, see Alvarez, "Lemon Grove Incident."

11. "Who Is Becoming Color Blind?" *LAT,* September 13, 1962.

12. "'Gerrymandering in the Los Angeles City School Districts' Presented by NAACP and UCRC, June 27, 1963, by Marnesba Tackett," box 5, folder 3, Dorothy Doyle Papers, Southern California Library for Social Studies and Research, Los Angeles (hereafter DD).

13. On this argument more broadly, see Lassiter, "De Jure/De Facto Segregation."

14. "For Free Men: Freedom" speech, box 44, folder 2, LM.

15. On the history of African American segregation in California schools, see Wollenberg, *All Deliberate Speed;* Hendrick, *Education of Non-Whites in California, 1849–1970;* and Caughey and Caughey, *School Segregation on Our Doorstep,* 4.

16. On the early protests before the LAUSD, see Caughey and Caughey, *School Segregation on Our Doorstep.*

17. Nicolaides, *My Blue Heaven,* 294.

18. Ibid., 295.

19. *1964 General Election Statement of Vote* (Sacramento: California Secretary of State, 1964).

20. *Reitman v. Mulkey,* 387 U.S. 369 (1967).

21. A 1970 UCLA poll found that 75 percent of Los Angeles County residents favored desegregation, yet 69 percent opposed busing as a means of achieving this goal. Wollenberg, *All Deliberate Speed,* 159.

22. *Jackson v. Pasadena City School District,* 59 Cal. 2d 876 (1963).

23. Hendrick, *Education of Non-Whites in California, 1849–1970,* 110.

24. "Ms. Hardy Delivers Blast at Suburbia," *LAT,* May 29, 1968.

25. Case studies of desegregation and busing struggles in these cities include Fine, *When Leadership Fails;* and Rubin, *Busing and Backlash.*

26. On the contradictory attitudes toward desegregation and busing, see Orfield, "Lessons of the Los Angeles Desegregation Case"; Orfield, "Public Opinion and School Desegregation"; and Sears, "Whites' Opposition to Busing."

27. One survey suggested that private school enrollment within LAUSD boundaries rose from 87,569 to 91,589 between July 1, 1977, and April 7, 1978, the first year of the district's mandatory desegregation program. "White Flight: The Unknown Factor," *LAT,* June 18, 1978.

28. University of Chicago sociologist James Coleman became the leading advocate for the theory that mandatory desegregation programs resulted in increased segregation, because such plans drove white students out of large districts. Coleman's 1975 report was answered by critics such as Gary Orfield and Thomas Pettigrew, who challenged several methodological issues in his study. They generally contended that, at most, mandatory desegregation only accelerated white flight in the first year or two of the programs, and generally not by large proportions. For a summary of this debate, see Ravitch, "'White Flight' Controversy."

29. Lopez, *Racism on Trial.*

30. After a two-year trial, Gitelson found that the Los Angeles school board "knowingly, affirmatively and in bad faith . . . segregated, de jure, its students" through its attendance boundary and school location decisions. Gitelson ordered the district to develop a desegregation plan immediately, an order the school board promptly appealed. Gitelson lost his reelection bid in 1970, largely on the desegregation issue. Wollenberg, *All Deliberate Speed*, 157.

31. "Wakefield Requests Veto on Racial Bill," *LAT,* December 12, 1971.

32. "Dear Fellow Californian" letter, October 26, 1972, and storyboard, folder "Proposition 21 (1972)," CL. Campaign filing reports suggest the campaign never purchased any television advertising time.

33. "2 Groups Promise Court Challenge to Busing Proposition," *LAT,* November 9, 1972.

34. For an example of how the freedom of association defense was deployed in Atlanta school desegregation debates, see Kruse, *White Flight.*

35. Florida voters also adopted by a greater percentage—79 percent—a resolution to guarantee "quality education" and "equal opportunity" for all children and to prohibit a return to dual-school systems. "Retreat from Integration," *Time,* March 27, 1972. The Nixon and congressional measures were largely symbolic, as they did not delay the implementation of any local desegregation actions.

36. "Proposition 21: Is It Anti-Busing or Anti-Integration?" *LAT,* September 26, 1972; "County Board Supports Bible Version for Texts," *LAT,* October 26, 1972.

37. "Proposition 21: Is It Anti-Busing or Anti-Integration?" *LAT,* September 26, 1972. Proposition 21 campaign filing statements, folder "1972, Proposition 21," CFS.

38. "Proposition 21: Is It Anti-Busing or Anti-Integration?" *LAT,* September 26, 1972.

39. "Most Voters Undecided on Prop. 19, Poll Finds," *LAT,* October 25, 1972.

40. "Proposition 21: Is it Anti-Busing or Anti-Integration?" *LAT,* September 26, 1972; Proposition 21 campaign filing statements, folder "1972, Proposition 21" CFS. See various CAUSE leaflets in folder "1972, Proposition 21," CL.

41. *Proposed Amendments to Constitution: Propositions and Proposed Laws, November 7, 1972* (Sacramento: California Secretary of State, 1972), 57.

42. The figures are from the 1972 LAUSD racial and ethnic student census as reported in Caughey and Caughey, *To Kill a Child's Spirit.*

43. African American assemblywoman Yvonne Braithwaite Burke from Los Angeles served as a spokesperson for CAUSE, and several African Methodist Episcopal bishops spoke out against the measure, but CAUSE made few other attempts to address or organize Black or Mexican American voters. CAUSE press releases in box 5, folder 8, DD.

44. "Death Penalty Initiative Favored 2 to 1 in Poll," *LAT,* November 3, 1972.

45. *Statement of Vote: 1972 General Election* (Sacramento: California Secretary of State, 1972).

46. "S.F. School Busing: No Miracles, No Disasters," *LAT*, November 27, 1972.

47. These were local cases brought about by the NAACP to seek desegregation orders. The courts used the cases to determine the constitutionality of Proposition 21. See *National Assn. for Advancement of Colored People v. San Bernardino City Unified Sch. Dist.*, 17 Cal. 3d 311 (1976).

48. *Santa Barbara School District v. Superior Court*, 13 Cal. 3d 315, 324 (1975); "State High Court Rules Ban on School Busing Unconstitutional," *LAT*, January 16, 1975. In *Swann v. Charlotte-Mecklenburg Board of Education*, 402 U.S. 1 (1971), the U.S. Supreme Court upheld a districtwide busing plan that was enacted primarily in response to racially segregated housing patterns, rather than explicit race-based assignments, in order to achieve compliance with the *Brown* mandate. See Lassiter, *Silent Majority*.

49. "School Integration: Light and Shadow," *LAT*, January 27, 1974.

50. "After the Election, What Happens to Those Who Lose?" *LAT*, July 13, 1975.

51. "Wakefield Action Disturbs Women," *LAT*, March 10, 1974; "Welch Assails Nixon at Birch Society Dinner," *LAT*, March 11, 1974.

52. Tom Bane, oral history interview, p. 96, conducted 1994 and 1995 by Steven Isoardi for the UCLA Oral History Program, part of the State Government Oral History Program, California State Archives, Sacramento; Alan Robbins open letter, August 31, 1978, series 1, box 2, folder "Busing Press Releases," Alan Robbins Collection, California State University, Urban Archives Center, Oviatt Library, Northridge (hereafter AR).

53. *LAT*, May 26, 1976.

54. *LAT*, December 11, 1976.

55. John Gorham, "Weintraub and Fiedler and the Rise of Middle Class Populism," *LA Weekly*, June 6, 1980, 8; Arnold Steinberg, interview with author, August 11, 2008, Calabasas, Calif.

56. On Fiedler, see Bobbi Fiedler, interviewed November 17, 1988, by Richard McMillian, transcribed by Farah Ortega, California State University, Department of History and Urban Archives Library, Northridge. This shift in strategies used to discredit school desegregation was occurring in other cities as well. See, for example, Lassiter, *Silent Majority*.

57. "Robbins Says He Won't Make Issue of School Busing," *LAT*, January 11, 1977.

58. On Bradley's defeat of Robbins in the 1977 mayoral contest, see Sonenshein, *Politics in Black and White*. Robbins did turn to the busing issue in the final week of his campaign, even though he had told BUSTOP earlier in the campaign that he would not make busing an issue in the election. "Busing to Dominate Robbins' Campaign," *LAT*, March 31, 1977.

59. *Jackson v. Pasadena City School District*, 59 Cal. 2d 876 (1963).

60. It is important to note that the initial state superior court rulings in both the Pasadena and Los Angeles cases had determined that the school districts did practice intentional segregation, rulings the U.S. Supreme Court

ultimately chose to ignore. See Landis, "Crawford Desegregation Suit in Los Angeles, 1977–1981."

61. *California Ballot Pamphlet: Special Statewide Election, November 6, 1979* (Sacramento: California Secretary of State, 1979).

62. *Milliken v. Bradley*, 418 U.S. 717 (1974), overturned a metropolitan desegregation order in the Detroit area.

63. Virna Canson to Alan Robbins, February 18, 1979, box 36, folder 34, NAACP-UCB.

64. Alex Garcia letter, November 30, 1977, series 1, box 2, folder "Busing," AR.

65. *Serrano v. Priest*, 5 Cal. 3d 584 (1971) *(Serrano I); Serrano v. Priest*, 18 Cal. 3d 728 (1976) *(Serrano II); Serrano v. Priest*, 20 Cal. 3d 25 (1977) *(Serrano III); Ballot Arguments for 1977 Special Election* (Sacramento: California Secretary of State, 1977).

66. For a discussion of the "conflicting avenues of redress" pursued by advocates of desegregation and bilingual education, see Brilliant, "Color Lines," chapter 9. The court ruling affirming the right to bilingual education was *Lau v. Nichols*, 414 U.S. 563 (1974).

67. Haro, *Mexicano/Chicano Concerns and School Desegregation in Los Angeles*.

68. *Sin Fronteras*, June 1977, 8.

69. Chicano Integration Coalition policy statement, box 3b, folder 23 "Chicano Integration Coalition," Chicano Desegregation Collection (Carlos Haro Papers), University of California, Los Angeles (hereafter CD).

70. "Latins Hit School Integration Planning," *LAT*, February 10, 1977.

71. *Diaz v. San Jose Unified School District*, 412. F. Supp. 310 (N.D. Cal. 1976); *Soria v. Oxnard School District* 328 F. Supp. 155 (C.D. Cal. 1971).

72. The quote is from the statement by Peter Roos in opposition to Senate Constitutional Amendment 48, January 19, 1978, series 1, box 5, folder "Committee Testimony," AR. See also "A Summary of the Position and Policy statement of the Chicano Subcommittee of the Citizens' Advisory Committee on Student Integration," box 5, folder 10, DD.

73. Quoted in Haro, *Mexicano/Chicano Concerns and School Desegregation in Los Angeles*, 38.

74. Press release, January 4, 1978, series 1, box 2, folder "Busing Press Releases," AR.

75. "Assembly Unit Kills Robbins Antibusing Bill," *LAT*, January 20, 1978.

76. Stanfield, "Urban Public School Desegregation."

77. "Anti-Busing—List Order," July 5, 1978, series 1, box 3, folder "Support SCA 46, 1975," AR.

78. Bobbi Fiedler, interviewed November 17, 1988, by Richard McMillian, transcribed by Farah Ortega, California State University, Department of History and Urban Archives Library, Northridge.

79. Testimony before the assembly judiciary committee in opposition to anti-integration measures, March 14, 1979, box 37, folder 49, NAACP-UCB.

80. "Quarrels with the Courts," *Los Angeles Herald Examiner*, January 12, 1979.

81. Alan Robbins, "Guest Editorial," *LAT*, October 28, 1977.

82. The program was known as Permits with Transportation, or PWT. Lynn Pineda, memorandum, voluntary busing program, December 6, 1979, box 7B, folder "Black-Chicano School Education Task Force," CD; "Bused Pupils Up 36%, Most to Valley," *LAT*, September 21, 1975.

83. Ettinger, "Quest to Desegregate Los Angeles Schools."

84. Lo, *Small Property versus Big Government.*

85. "Antibusing Initiative Misses 1st Deadline," *LAT*, May 6, 1978.

86. "Antibusing Initiative Can't Meet Deadline," *LAT*, June 6, 1978; "Sentencing Set in Petition Bilking," *LAT*, November 8, 1978. The following year, Weintraub was also accused of participating in an effort to forge signatures in the campaign to recall Los Angeles school board member Howard Miller. She invoked the protections of the Fifth Amendment in the investigation, which some say soured her prospects for running for higher office. "Activists of Busing Era: Where They Are Now," *LAT*, October 14, 1984.

87. Frye, "Quarrels with the Courts," 66; "3 Antibusing Groups Launch Fund Drives," *LAT*, June 16, 1979.

88. "Bustop's Future, Number of Members Still Mystery," *LAT*, October 27, 1977; "Shaky Coalition Almost Collapsed," *LAT*, October 3, 1977.

89. Arnold Steinberg, interview with author, August 11, 2008, Calabasas, Calif.

90. Bobbi Fiedler fundraising letter, 1977, box 1, folder 17, DD.

91. "Bustop Expands Mail Campaign to Get Funds to Continue Antibusing Court Fight," *LAT*, January 21, 1979.

92. Arnold Steinberg, interview with author, August 11, 2008, Calabasas, Calif.

93. "Donations to Bustop Top $550,000 in 3 Years," *LAT*, August 10, 1979. On Butcher-Forde and the rise of the initiative industry in the late 1970s, see Schrag, *Paradise Lost;* and Magelby, *Direct Legislation.*

94. Butcher-Forde collected at least $100,000 in fees from Californians against Forced Busing (the legal name of Robbins's direct-mail campaign) and was permitted to keep the names and addresses of all donors as well as all the materials they created. "Agreement between Butcher-Forde Consulting and Californians against Forced Busing," series 1, box 6, folder "Californians against Forced Busing," AR.

95. Orfield, "Lessons of the Los Angeles Desegregation Case." This was essentially the conclusion of a study of attitudes toward busing among West Los Angeles parents during this debate. See Sears and Allen, "Trajectory of Local Desegregation Controversies and Whites' Opposition to Busing." This work was part of a lively scholarly debate concerning whether opposition to mandatory busing was motivated by parents' self-interest or a more ideologically driven commitment to racial segregation. See also Green and Cowden, "Who Protests."

96. "Assembly Unit Kills Robbins Antibusing Bill," *LAT*, January 20, 1978.

97. Creighton, "Proposition 1 and Federal Protection of State Constitutional Rights," 690.

98. "Simi-Conejo Busing Rally Attracts Few," *LAT*, December 1, 1978.

99. On school climate in the wake of desegregation, see "I Love It," *LAT*, October 2, 1978; "2 Sides Gear Up for Start of L.A. Busing," *LAT*, September 10, 1978; "Busing Becomes a One-Issue Dispute," *LAT*, September 24, 1978; and "Rumors Threaten Racial Calm at School," *Los Angeles Herald Examiner*, May 21, 1978.

100. Linda Litwan, "Letters to the *Times*," *LAT*, October 4, 1978; "Letters to the *Times*," *LAT*, September 18, 1978.

101. "Desegregation Turbulence Easing," *LAT*, August 26, 1979. See also *Community Networker* newsletters of the LAUSD documenting implementation of the plan, box 4d, folder 66, CD.

102. See "Community Networker" newsletters of the LAUSD, 1978–79, documenting implementation of the plan, box 4d, folder 66, CD.

103. Orfield, "Lessons of the Los Angeles Desegregation Case."

104. "Busing Election Bill OKd, Sent to Brown," *LAT*, June 21, 1979.

105. "Switch by Assembly Power Berman Adds Clout to Robbins' Antibusing Bill," *LAT*, March 11, 1979.

106. "Assembly Approves Antibusing Measure," *LAT*, March 23, 1979.

107. "The Defeat of SCA-2," *Los Angeles Sentinel*, March 22, 1979.

108. "The Reluctant 'Yes' Vote," *Sacramento Bee*, March 29, 1979.

109. "Busing Election Bill OKd, Sent to Brown," *LAT*, June 21, 1979.

110. The poll also found that less than one-third of the respondents were aware that Proposition 1 was going to be on the ballot. California Poll, Study no. 7903, August 20–27, 1979, http://ucdata.berkeley.edu/data_record.php?recid=3 (accessed January 25, 2007).

111. "Prop 1, 4 Backers May Form Alliance," *LAT*, October 14, 1979. On Proposition 13 and the antitax movement in California in general, see Schrag, *Paradise Lost;* and D. Smith, *Tax Crusaders and the Politics of Direct Democracy*.

112. Alan Robbins, "Dear Opponent of Forced Busing" letter, n.d. (probably 1979), box 38, folder 9, NAACP-UCB.

113. "Students Boycott Sunland-Tujunga Area Schools to Protest Forced Busing Plan," *LAT*, January 22, 1977.

114. "L.A. Antibus Groups Changing Strategy," *LAT*, December 10, 1978.

115. No on Proposition 1 endorsement list, box 5, folder 17, DD.

116. "Vote No on Prop. 1," *Los Angeles Sentinel*, November 1, 1979. The desegregation issue bitterly divided the city's Jewish community, reflecting both ideological disagreements as well as geographic divisions between those in the Valley and those in West Los Angeles. Arnold Steinberg, interview with author, August 11, 2008, Calabasas, Calif. See also John Gorham, "Weintraub and Fiedler and the Rise of Middle Class Populism," *LA Weekly*, June 6, 1980, 8.

117. Virna Canson memorandum to all NAACP branches, July 25, 1979, box 37, folder 50, NAACP-UCB.

118. Virna Canson to Diane Watson memorandum, August 19, 1979, box 37, folder 50, NAACP-UCB.

119. "Anti-Prop 1, 4 Rally Attracts Only 100 Blacks," *LAT*, October 22, 1979.

120. CAP 1 press release, August 3, 1978, box 38, folder 9, NAACP-UCB.

121. "No on One" rally (November 4, 1979) poster, Californians against Proposition 1, box 5, folder 8, DD.

122. Jackie Goldberg, "Arguments against Proposition One," the Integration Project, September 7, 1979, box 5, folder 17, DD.

123. *Proposition 1 Ballot Arguments: November 1979* (Sacramento: California Secretary of State, 1979).

124. The Integration Project set out to build the case among white voters in particular that a fully integrated school district, bolstered by reductions in class size, building improvements, and adequate training, could provide quality education for all students. "An Integration Plan," box 5, folder 3, DD.

125. *Proposition 1 Ballot Arguments: November 1979* (Sacramento: California Secretary of State, 1979).

126. "Most of L.A. Voted Heavily for Prop. 1," *LAT*, November 9, 1979; "Prop 1 May Face Early Court Test," *LAT*, November 8, 1979.

127. "Prop 1 Called Biased against Minorities," *LAT*, December 9, 1980.

128. "Prop 1, Upheld: Bars L.A. Busing," *LAT*, December 20, 1980. See also *Crawford v. Los Angeles Board of Education*, 170 Cal. Rptr. 495 (1981); "Foes of Busing Hail Los Angeles Victory," *NYT*, March 13, 1981; and Ettinger, "Quest to Desegregate Los Angeles Schools."

129. "Prop 1 Upheld," *LAT*, December 20, 1980.

130. Respondent's brief, Board of Education of City of Los Angeles, G. William Shea, counselor of record, p. 42, box 342, folder 7, ACLU.

131. "Administration Asks Court to Back Prop. 1," *LAT*, February 2, 1982.

132. Brief for the United States as Amicus Curiae, Rex Lee, solicitor general, William Bradford Reynolds, assistant attorney general, *Crawford v. Los Angeles Board of Education*, 458 U.S. 527 (1982) (No. 81–38).

133. Brief as Amicus Curiae, Alan Robbins, *Crawford v. Los Angeles Board of Education*, 458 U.S. 527 (1982) (No. 81–38), pp. 2–3.

134. "Brief of Amici Curiae Margaret Tinsley et al. in Support of Petitioners," pp. 2, 11, 18, box 342, folder 10 "Tinsley AC," ACLU.

135. *Crawford v. Los Angeles Board of Education*, 458 U.S. 527 (1982).

136. "Pasadena Free of All Integration Rules in Schools," *LAT*, October 1, 1981; "20-Year School Struggle," *LAT*, February 16, 1983; "Waiting for Integration," *LAT* November 21, 1982; "Prop. 1 Cited in Schools Suit Dismissal," *LAT*, July 11, 1980.

137. "For L.A. Schools, Double Jeopardy: Segregation, Overcrowding," *LAT*, October 27, 1985.

138. "School Busing Furor Erupts in South Gate," *LAT*, June 28, 1981.

139. "School Busing Takes a U-Turn," *LAT,* December 13, 1981.

140. Orfield, *Public School Desegregation in the United States, 1968–1980,* 8.

141. Orfield and Lee, *"Brown" at 50.*

142. Gary and Jody Washburn to Senator Ed Davis, n.d. (probably 1981), series 1, box 6, folder "Constituent Correspondence," AR.

143. "More Schools Shut but 3 Will Stay Open," *LAT,* May 30, 1982.

144. Schrag, *Paradise Lost,* 60.

CHAPTER 5

1. Correspondence between U.S. English and Paul Gann, box 140, folder "U.S. English Correspondence," Paul Gann Papers, California State Library, Sacramento (hereafter PG).

2. John Tanton's memo, titled "Quo Vadis" (July 11, 1986), was a survey of FAIR's growth over the eight years since its founding and offered ideas for future directions. Series 5, box 176, folder 7, National Council of La Raza Collection, Stanford University, Department of Special Collections, Palo Alto, Calif. (hereafter NCLR).

3. "U.S. English's Links to Anti-Immigration Groups," *Asian Week,* August 15, 1986.

4. Among many works about the role of nativism in California political history and culture are Pagan, *Murder at the Sleepy Lagoon;* Saxton, *Indispensable Enemy;* Gaines and Cho, "On California's 1920 Alien Land Law"; and Ngai, *Impossible Subjects.*

5. See, for example, Citrin, Reingold et al., "The 'Official English' Movement and the Symbolic Politics of Language in the United States"; Tatalovich, *Nativism Reborn?;* and Schildkraut, *Press One for English.*

6. Bennett, *Party of Fear;* Higham, *Strangers in the Land;* Gerstle, *American Crucible;* R. Smith, *Civic Ideals.*

7. Ruth Wilson Gilmore, "Profiling Alienated Labor: Racialization, Externalities, and Re-Partitioned Geographies" (unpublished paper, 2004; in author's possession).

8. "Hayakawa Puts Sour Senate Experience Behind, Pursues New Interests," *LAT,* February 1, 1984.

9. *Congressional Record,* 97th Cong., 2nd sess., June 17, 1982, vol. 128, no. 77.

10. "Communication Assessment and Action Plan (February 19, 1982), English Language Amendment 1982" (emphasis in original), box 25, folder "SJ Res 72," Samuel I. Hayakawa Papers, Stanford University, Hoover Institution, Palo Alto, Calif. (hereafter SH). Butcher-Forde's role in the subsequent 1982 campaign is unclear.

11. In 1984, Los Angeles County spent $120,000 out of an election budget of $7 million to print and distribute thirty-nine thousand multilingual ballots. San Diego County spent $14,000 out of a budget of $1 million the same year. "Bilingual Ballots Gone for Many," *LAT,* October 7, 1984.

12. Citrin, Reingold et al., "The 'Official English' Movement and the Symbolic Politics of Language in the United States," 536.

13. The language minority provisions of the Voting Rights Act were first adopted in 1975, for a period of ten years, and then were extended in 1982 for ten years and in 1992 for fifteen years. On the VRA's renewal, see Valelly, *Voting Rights Act.*

14. Magelby, *Direct Legislation.*

15. Census figures released in 1976 required San Francisco to provide election materials in both Chinese and Spanish.

16. Kopp had seized on the issue as early as 1980 when he charged that bilingual ballots represented a "mandate from Big Brother" that would lead to "segregation of people." "A Ballot Box Albatross," *San Francisco Chronicle,* January 27, 1981. In addition, San Francisco had a long tradition of using local referenda to debate a wide range of issues, and the threshold to qualify a measure for the ballot was not high; Kopp needed only to submit 9,679 valid signatures to the Registrar of Voters.

17. Woolard, "Voting Rights, Liberal Voters and the Official English Movement."

18. *Congressional Record,* 97th Cong., 1st sess., April 27, 1981, vol. 127, no. 61.

19. Woolard, "Voting Rights, Liberal Voters and the Official English Movement," 135–36.

20. Ibid., 128.

21. Ibid.

22. Diamond, "English—The Official Language of California, 1983–1988," 112.

23. Campaign expenditures filings for Proposition 36, CFS.

24. *Asian Week,* June 29, 1984.

25. *California General Election Ballot Pamphlet, November 6, 1984* (Sacramento: California Secretary of State, 1984).

26. "Charting Wilson's Transformation on Immigration," *LAT,* November 2, 1994.

27. Unz, "California and the End of White America." The Simpson-Mazzoli Act was eventually passed in 1986.

28. The quote is from a form letter Koenig sent to associates in early 1982. See also letters between Koenig and Tanton from this period, box 13, folder "Immigration: Federation for Immigration Reform," MKP. On Koenig, see Nickerson, "Women, Domesticity, and Postwar Conservatism."

29. Ngai, *Impossible Subjects.*

30. "The New Ellis Island," *Time,* June 13, 1983.

31. Laham, *Ronald Reagan and the Politics of Immigration Reform;* Tichenor, *Dividing Lines.*

32. "U.S. English's Links to Anti-Immigration Groups," *Asian Week,* August 15, 1986.

33. Crawford, *Hold Your Tongue,* 153.

34. E. Gutiérrez, *Fertile Matters.*

35. Reimers, *Unwelcome Strangers,* 46.

36. Crawford, *Hold Your Tongue,* 152–53.

37. Ibid., 153.

38. *California General Election Ballot Pamphlet, November 6, 1984* (Sacramento: California Secretary of State, 1984), 52–53. On the Workingman's Party, which championed the exclusion of Chinese workers in the late nineteenth century, see Saxton, *Indispensable Enemy.*

39. Crawford, *Hold Your Tongue,* 153.

40. *California General Election Ballot Pamphlet, November 6, 1984* (Sacramento: California Secretary of State, 1984), 52–53.

41. I turn to Honig following political scientist Ron Schmidt. Schmidt makes productive use of Honig to understand the ideological commitments of the national English Only movement. See Schmidt, "Defending English in an English-Dominant World."

42. Honig, *Democracy and the Foreigner,* 76.

43. *California General Election Ballot Pamphlet, November 6, 1984* (Sacramento: California Secretary of State, 1984), 52–53.

44. California's 1879 constitution did include an English-language provision that was later deleted as surplusage in 1966, when the legislature streamlined the constitution. Dyste, "Proposition 63," 314.

45. Honig, *Democracy and the Foreigner,* 76.

46. "English Ballots Only: No on 38," *LAT,* October 12, 1984; *California General Election Ballot Pamphlet, November 6, 1984* (Sacramento: California Secretary of State, 1984), 52–53; Honig, *Democracy and the Foreigner,* 99.

47. The quote is from Cesar Chavez's "Dear Friend" letter against Propositions 36, 38, 39, and 41, folder "1984 General Election Ballot Initiatives," CL. See also "Chavez Mobilizing to Defeat 4 Ballot Issues," *LAT,* October 6, 1984.

48. The ballot argument against Proposition 38 did mention the Voting Rights Act several times, but the 1965 legislation received little attention in media coverage of the issue.

49. Bill Press, "Proposition 38, an Exercise in Degrading Democracy," *LAT,* October 28, 1984.

50. *Supplement to the Statement of the Vote, November 6, 1984* (Sacramento: California Secretary of State, 1984).

51. "$32 Million Spent on '84 Initiatives," *LAT,* May 9, 1985.

52. "Prop 38. Seeks End to Bilingual Ballot Data," *LAT,* September 20, 1984. In fact, a revision to the Voting Rights Act in 1982 lowered the obligation of political jurisdictions to send out bilingual voting materials; in California, only ten counties in the Central Valley had large enough percentages of Spanish-speaking voters to invoke the law's requirements for bilingual election materials. "Minorities in County See Disenfranchisement," *LAT,* August 9, 1984.

53. *Asian Week,* January 11, 1985.

54. "Bill Introduced to Make English California's Official Language," *LAT,* January 9, 1985.

55. "The State," *LAT,* May 22, 1985. See also Diamond, "English—The Official Language of California, 1983–1988."

56. "Dear Friend" letter from Samuel Hayakawa to U.S. English supporters, n.d. (probably 1985), box 161, folder 8 "U.S. English Materials," NCLR.

57. Letters from Samuel Hayakawa, box 161, folder 8 "U.S. English Materials," NCLR.

58. In 1982, an antinuclear weapons advisory measure was approved by voters (Proposition 12); and in 1986, voters passed Proposition 65, a toxic-discharge warning and disclosure initiative sponsored by environmental groups.

59. "Republicans Take the Initiative," *LAT,* October 28, 1984.

60. Paul Gann, oral history interview, pp. 28–37, conducted 1987 by Gabrielle Morris for the State Government Oral History Program, Regional Oral History Office, Bancroft Library, University of California, Berkeley, and California State Archives, Sacramento; "Political Thunder Coming from the Right," *San Jose Mercury News,* September 2, 1986.

61. On a handful of occasions, Diamond and Hayakawa did intervene in local disputes related to language policy. In the Ventura County town of Fillmore, they advised a group of residents upset over the expansion of bilingual education programs in a local school. To enormous controversy, the town council of the small citrus community approved a nonbinding Official English resolution, making it the first municipality in the state to do so. Diamond and Hayakawa became similarly involved in a controversy in the Los Angeles suburb of Monterey Park, counseling residents there to circulate a petition to put an Official English measure on the ballot. The petition effort stalled but, as in Fillmore, the controversy attracted considerable public attention and fulfilled U.S. English's objective of starting a public conversation over immigration and language policy. See Crawford, *Hold Your Tongue,* 13–15. On Monterey Park, see Saito, *Race and Politics.*

62. Proposition 63 campaign filing statements, CFS.

63. "Ideas and Trends; Is English the Only Language for Government?" *NYT,* October 26, 1986.

64. "California Elections Prop. 63 Roots Traced to Small Michigan City Measure to Make English Official Language of State Sprang from Concern over Immigration, Population," *LAT,* October 20, 1986.

65. Crawford, *Hold Your Tongue.*

66. "Prop. 63 Deserves Approval," *San Francisco Examiner,* October 24, 1986, reprinted in Crawford, *Language Loyalties.*

67. U.S. English brochure, folder "General Election, 1986," CL.

68. Box 161, folder 8 "U.S. English Materials," NCLR.

69. "Ideas and Trends; Is English the Only Language for Government?" *NYT,* October 26, 1986.

70. Felix Gutierrez, "A New Language of California Commerce—Spanish," *Los Angeles Herald Examiner,* October 3, 1986.

71. "California Elections Many Supporters Also Favor Bilingual Education, Ballots Latino Backing of 'English-Only' a Puzzle," *LAT*, October 25, 1986. See also "Prop. 63—A New Battle in Historical War of Words," *LAT*, October 21, 1986.

72. For an example of the way this question has been explored in relation to immigration and public health, see Molina, *Fit to Be Citizens?*

73. "U.S. English's Links to Anti-Immigration Groups," *Asian Week*, August 15, 1986.

74. "English Only Foes Get Some Legislative Help," *LAT*, August 14, 1986.

75. "Minorities Fight English-Only Movement," *San Francisco Chronicle*, August 21, 1986.

76. Campaign filing statements, Proposition 63, CFS.

77. "Norman Cousins Drops His Support of Prop. 63," *LAT*, October 16, 1986.

78. Memo from Governor Deukmejian in opposition to Proposition 63, September 2, 1986, box 161, folder 4 "Prop 63 (1 of 3)," NCLR.

79. Tatalovich, *Nativism Reborn?* 116.

80. *Sacramento Bee*, September 10, 1986.

81. "Prop 63 Backer Will Try to Defeat Opposing Candidates," *LAT*, October 1, 1986. See also "California Elections English-Only Proposition Kindles Minorities' Fears," *LAT*, October 12, 1986.

82. *California General Election Ballot Pamphlet, November 4, 1986* (Sacramento: California Secretary of State, 1986), 47.

83. In 1986, the Los Angeles Unified School District turned away forty thousand people from its ESL programs. "Immigrants a Rush to the Classrooms," *LAT*, September 24, 1986.

84. *California General Election Ballot Pamphlet, November 4, 1986* (Sacramento: California Secretary of State, 1986), 47.

85. Mailer, box 161, folder 5, NCLR

86. "English-Only Foes Get Some Legislative Help," *LAT*, August 14, 1986.

87. "Winners to Take Initiatives on Road," *San Jose Mercury News*, November 5, 1986.

88. "Prop. 63 Pot Begins to Boil," *San Jose Mercury News*, August 14, 1986.

89. "Voters Back 'English-Only' Proposition," *San Francisco Examiner*, September 12, 1986.

90. *Supplement to the Statement of the Vote, November 4, 1986* (Sacramento: California Secretary of State, 1986).

91. Dyste, "Proposition 63," 327; California Poll, November 1986 (N = 1034), reprinted in Citrin, Reingold et al., "The 'Official English' Movement and the Symbolic Politics of Language in the United States," 549, 550.

92. *Oakland Tribune*, November 7, 1986.

93. *San Francisco Chronicle*, November 6, 1986.

94. Quoted in Crawford, *Hold Your Tongue*, 20.

95. *Update* 5, no. 1 (January–February 1987), box 161, folder 3, NCLR.

96. " Assemblyman Vows to Carry the Ball for English-Only Action," *LAT*, November 6, 1986.

97. Gerber et al., *Stealing the Initiative*, 35–37.

98. Quoted in Crawford, *Hold Your Tongue*, 21.

99. "Proposition 63: Much Talk, Few Effects," *Education Week*, June 17, 1987.

100. "Assemblyman Vows to Carry the Ball for English-Only Action," *LAT*, November 6, 1986.

101. "Fighting Words: California's Official-Language Law Promises to Preserve and Protect English; The Question Is, Can the State Preserve and Protect Its Citizens' Civil Rights at the Same Time?" *LAT*, June 10, 1990.

102. Hayakawa always seemed less intent on eviscerating specific programs than Diamond, Hill, and others. He commented before the election: "My colleagues in U.S. English and the California English campaign are much more doctrinaire than I am. . . . They are asking for much more in the way of results." "California Elections English-Only Proposition Kindles Minorities' Fears," *LAT*, October 12, 1986.

103. Mandates to hire multilingual state employees stemmed from a 1973 law stipulating that when 5 percent or more of the clientele seeking state services did not speak English, the state was required to hire appropriate bilingual staff. "California Braces for Change with English as Official Language," *NYT*, November 26, 1986.

104. Dyste, "Proposition 63," 325.

105. Cited in Citrin, Reingold et al., "The 'Official English' Movement and the Symbolic Politics of Language in the United States," 549.

106. Dyste, "Proposition 63," 323, 325.

107. Citrin, Reingold et al., "The 'Official English' Movement and the Symbolic Politics of Language in the United States," 549, 550.

108. "Voters Back 'English-Only' Proposition," *San Francisco Examiner*, September 12, 1986.

109. "Assemblyman Vows to Carry the Ball for English-Only Action," *LAT*, November 6, 1986.

110. Quoted in Crawford, "What's Behind Official English?" 172.

111. Memo to WITAN IV attendees from John Tanton, October 10, 1986. ("Witan" is an Old English term for a meeting or council summoned by Anglo-Saxon kings.) In the memo, Tanton recites a number of crude assertions and rhetorical questions: "What are the differences in educability between Hispanics (with their 50% dropout rate) and Asiatics (with their excellent school records and long tradition of scholarship)?" Yet he concludes the memo with a surprising and revealing self-identification. Just as only Nixon could go to China, "the issues we're touching on here must be broached by liberals. The conservatives simply cannot do it without tainting the whole subject." Tanton fully identified as a liberal. A copy of the memo is available at the Southern Poverty Law Center's Intelligence Report, Summer 2002, www.splcenter.org/intel/intelreport/article.jsp?sid=125 (accessed February 1, 2007).

112. Crawford, *Hold Your Tongue*, 162. Tanton continued to be centrally involved in debates over immigration and language after resigning from U.S. English. See the Southern Poverty Law Center's *The Puppeteer*, no. 106 (Summer 2002), www.splcenter.org/intel/intelreport/intrep.jsp?iid=7 (accessed February 23, 2007).

113. Though it is important to note that, as of 2005, twenty-three of the twenty-eight states that have Official English policies on their books have adopted the legislation since 1980, and efforts to aggressively enforce the legislation, while rare in California, continue to occur in other states. Schildkraut, *Press One for English*, 1–3, 15.

CHAPTER 6

1. "Economy Slows Voters' Ballot Measures to a Crawl," *LAT,* January 5, 1994.

2. "Voters Approve 'Three Strikes' Law, Reject Smoking Measure Proposal for Government-Run Health Care System, Gasoline Tax to Fund Rail Projects are Also Defeated," *LAT*, November 9, 1994.

3. *Second and Third Strikers in the Adult Institutional Population* (Sacramento: Department of Corrections and Rehabilitation, Offender Information Services Branch, Estimates and Statistical Analysis Section, Data Analysis Unit, September 30, 2007), 46–51; Ehlers, Schiraldi, and Lotke, *Racial Divide.*

4. Lustig and Walker, *No Way Out.*

5. Haefele, "California Shipwreck."

6. Hood and Morris, "Brother, Can You Spare a Dime?" 194; Citrin, Green et al., "Public Opinion toward Immigration Reform," 858–81; K. Johnson, "An Essay on Immigration Politics, Popular Democracy, and California's Proposition 187," 629–73; Alvarez and Butterfield, "The Politics—The Resurgence of Nativism in California?" 167–80; Hero and Tolbert, "Race/Ethnicity and Direct Democracy," 806–18.

7. "Governor's Remarks in News Conference," November 9, 1994, box 319, folder 14, Anthony Beilenson Papers, University of California, Los Angeles (hereafter AB).

8. Wroe, *Republican Party and Immigration Politics*, 58–59.

9. "Prop. 187 Creators Come Under Closer Scrutiny," *LAT*, September 4, 1994.

10. Quoted in Wroe, *Republican Party and Immigration Politics*, 59.

11. " Figures behind Prop. 187 Look at Its Creation," *LAT*, December 14, 1994.

12. *California Ballot Pamphlet, General Election, November 8, 1994* (Sacramento: California Secretary of State, 1994), 51–53.

13. Ibid., 91.

14. Wroe, *Republican Party and Immigration Politics*, 78.

15. Gaines and Cho, "On California's 1920 Alien Land Law."

16. Wroe, *Republican Party and Immigration Politics*, 33; Simon and Alexander, *Ambivalent Welcome*.

17. "O.C. Reaction: Strong Praise, Condemnation," *LAT*, August 10, 1993.

18. Tichenor, *Dividing Lines*, 241.

19. "Immigration Bill Signed by Reagan," *San Diego Union-Tribune*, November 7, 1986.

20. Laham, *Ronald Reagan and the Politics of Immigration Reform*.

21. "Lobbyists Back Border Ditch Plan," *San Diego Union-Tribune*, March 16, 1989; "Border Protests Growing with Illegal Immigration," *Daily News of Los Angeles*, June 23, 1990; "Poway Control over Migrants, Limited," *San Diego Union-Tribune*, May 7, 1988.

22. Quoted in Wroe, *Republican Party and Immigration Politics*, 58. See also "O.C. Group Helps Fuel Anti-Immigrant Furor Viewpoint," *LAT*, August 30, 1993; and "Prop. 187 Creators Come Under Closer Scrutiny Initiative," *LAT*, September 4, 1994.

23. "Striking a Balance," *Orange County Register*, July 17, 1992.

24. In California, groups such as Zero Population Growth in Los Angeles demanded tough immigration restrictions. E. Gutiérrez, *Fertile Matters*, chapter 7.

25. Dianne Klein, "State Puts New Edge on Immigration Debate Border," *LAT*, September 6, 1993.

26. Cacho, "'People of California are Suffering'"; Santa Ana, *Brown Tide Rising*; Leo Chavez, *Covering Immigration*; Ono and Sloop, *Shifting Borders*.

27. See, for example, Almaguer, *Racial Fault Lines*; Sanchez, *Becoming Mexican American*; Deverell, *Whitewashed Adobe*; and E. Gutiérrez, *Fertile Matters*.

28. H. Johnson, *Undocumented Immigration to California, 1980–1993*.

29. See M. Davis, "Social Origins of the Referendum." For other accounts, see Mehan, "Discourse of the Illegal Immigration Debate," 249–70; and Calavita, "New Politics of Immigration."

30. For a critique of the ambivalent stance of Republicans in general during the preceding decade, see Laham, *Ronald Reagan and the Politics of Immigration Reform*.

31. Brimelow, "Time to Rethink Immigration?"

32. "Migrants Hear Buchanan Pitch a Tighter Border Speech," *LAT*, May 13, 1992; "Buchanan Sees California as Battle after War's End," *LAT*, April 4, 1992.

33. "State Puts New Edge on Immigration Debate Border," *LAT*, September 6, 1993.

34. "Immigration Ballot Initiative Possible," *San Diego Union-Tribune*, May 27, 1992.

35. John Tanton, "Immigration on the News Stands," *Social Contract* (Fall 1992): 1–2.

36. "Charting Wilson's Transformation on Immigration," *LAT*, November 2, 1994; "Wilson Urges INS to Ease Up Enforcement to Aid Growers," *LAT*, June 19, 1987.

37. Pete Wilson, "Pass More Laws, Set More Limits?" *LAT*, October 16, 1990.

38. "Wilson Backs Initiative for English-Only Law in State," *LAT*, August 21, 1986. See also Tichenor, *Dividing Lines*.

39. FAIR did praise Wilson at the time for pointing out that "illegal immigration" was a "prime contributor to California's and the nation's budget woes." "Cut Off Aid to Immigrants, Group Urges," *LAT*, November 21, 1991.

40. "Wilson to Seek Funds for Immigrant Services," *LAT*, November 22, 1991. In the same article, Democratic state senator Art Torres of Los Angeles said he was "disappointed" by Wilson's "anti-immigrant sentiment" but supported the governor's lobbying mission.

41. "Wilson's Huge Bill to U.S. Uses Sleight of Hand Budget," *LAT*, February 8, 1993.

42. "Why Governor Wants U.S. Immigrant Aid," *San Francisco Chronicle*, January 11, 1993.

43. "Welfare Rolls Reach Record Level," *LAT*, March 3, 1992. Wilson had begun attacking the state's assistance programs as "welfare magnets" in 1991, in the wake of criticism he received from Republicans for raising taxes earlier in the year, failing to cut state spending more, and supporting abortion rights. Wilson had difficulty with conservative voters and the Republican base throughout his first term in office. See George Skelton, "Wilson Backed in Welfare Cuts for Newcomers," *LAT*, December 12, 1991.

44. "Democrats and Unions Lead Prop. 165 Fight," *LAT*, October 7, 1992. See ballot arguments in *California Ballot Pamphlet, General Election, November 3, 1992* (Sacramento: California Secretary of State, 1992).

45. George Skelton, "Beleaguered Wilson Needs a Winner on Election Day," *LAT*, November 2, 1992; "Welfare Measure That Boosts Governor's Power Sparks Costly War," *LAT*, October 25, 1992.

46. "Anti-Immigration Bills Flood Legislature," *LAT*, May 3, 1993; Eric Bailey, "Bill Would Bar Illegal Migrants at State Schools," *LAT*, January 5, 1994.

47. George Skelton, "Rational Talk on Immigrants for a Change," *LAT*, May 27, 1993.

48. Diane Feinstein, "Perspective on Illegal Immigration," *LAT*, June 16, 1993; Stein quoted in Glenn F. Bunting and Alan C. Miller, "Feinstein Raises Immigration Profile Politics," *LAT*, July 18, 1993. See also George Skelton, "Feinstein Takes Immigration Out of Closet," *LAT*, July 12, 1993; and "Immigration Foe Supporting Feinstein's Bill," *San Francisco Chronicle*, July 16, 1993.

49. John M. Broder, "Immigration Delicate Issue for Clinton," *LAT*, September 7, 1993; "Brown Endorses Proposal to Issue Tamper-Proof ID Cards," *LAT*, September 2, 1993; "State Puts New Edge on Immigration Debate Border," *LAT*, September 6, 1993.

50. Alan C. Miller, "Beilenson, Gallegly Ideas in U.S. Spotlight Politics," *LAT*, August 29, 1993.

51. Ronald Brownstein, "Polarization Marks Debate on Immigration Policy Politics," *LAT*, November 30, 1993.

52. The newspaper ads are quoted in Wroe, *Republican Party and Immigration Politics*, 44. See also "Many Obstacles to Wilson Plan on Immigration," *LAT*, August 11, 1993.

53. "O.C. Reaction: Strong Praise, Condemnation," *LAT*, August 10, 1993.

54. "Residents Call Migrants a Burden Immigration," *LAT*, August 22, 1993; "Immigration Stance Helps Wilson's Rating," *LAT*, August 21, 1993. Wilson's August approval rating grew to 22 percent, up from 15 percent in May, while his negative rating fell to 33 percent, the lowest it had been during the preceding year.

55. "Democrats' Ad Attacks Wilson on Immigration Politics," *LAT*, August 18, 1993.

56. Quoted in Chin, "Civil Rights Revolution Comes to Immigration Law," 343. See also Tichenor, *Dividing Lines*, 191.

57. Nevins, *Operation Gatekeeper*, 1.

58. Richard G. Polanco, "Cut the Rhetoric and Work on Solutions Immigration," *LAT*, August 13, 1993; George Skelton, "Straddling the Line on Illegal Immigration," *LAT*, August 26, 1993.

59. "Polarization Marks Debate on Immigration Policy Politics," *LAT*, November 30, 1993.

60. "Scope of Immigrant-Control Initiative in Dispute," *San Diego Union-Tribune*, November 21, 1993.

61. Wroe, *Republican Party and Immigration Politics*, 61–62, 67; "Immigration Opponents May Link Up with Perot," *Orange County Register*, August 20, 1993; "Backers of Anti-Illegal Immigrant Petition Deliver Signatures Initiative," *LAT*, May 17, 1994.

62. "Backers of Anti-Illegal Immigrant Petition Deliver Signatures Initiative," *LAT*, May 17, 1994.

63. Wroe, *Republican Party and Immigration Politics*, 68; Dan Schnur, telephone interview with author, October 15, 2008.

64. "Wilson Ad Sparks Charges of Immigrant-Bashing Politics," *LAT*, May 14, 1994. The ad ran for about two weeks at a cost of approximately $1 million.

65. On the role of racialized political advertisements, see Mendelberg, *Race Card*.

66. Domanick, *Cruel Justice*, 65. On the complex roots of California prison expansion, see especially Gilmore, *Golden Gulag*.

67. Based on an analysis using the keyword search term "crime" in the California Ballot Propositions Database, Hastings Law Library, http://holmes.uchastings.edu/library/california-research/ca-ballot-measures.html (accessed December 8, 2008).

68. Zimring, Hawkins, and Kamin, *Punishment and Democracy*, 17.

69. *California Ballot Pamphlet, General Election, November 8, 1994* (Sacramento: California Secretary of State, 1994), 36.

70. This was the tagline of several of Governor Wilson's campaign commercials, including one on immigration, www.youtube.com/watch?v=oof1 PE8Kzng (accessed January 31, 2009).

71. "Grass-Roots Movement Pushes 'SOS' Initiative," *San Francisco Chronicle*, June 15, 1994; Wroe, *Republican Party and Immigration Politics*.

72. "Initiative to Deny Aid and Education to Illegal Immigrants Qualifies for Ballot," *LAT*, June 24, 1994.

73. "Firm Targets Illegal-Alien Proposition," *Daily News of Los Angeles*, August 15, 1994; Wroe, *Republican Party and Immigration Politics*, 66.

74. Woodward and McDowell memo, "Talking Paper: Initial Survey Results and Winning Campaign Messages," July 14, 1994 (in author's possession).

75. Ibid.; Wroe, *Republican Party and Immigration Politics*, 15.

76. "Opponents Hire a Proven Winner," *Orange County Register*, November 2, 1994; "History Doesn't Favor Anti-Immigrant Initiative," *Long Beach Press Telegram*, September 16, 1994; Wroe, *Republican Party and Immigration Politics*, 75.

77. "Firm Targets Illegal-Alien Proposition," *Daily News of Los Angeles*, August 15, 1994.

78. *California Ballot Pamphlet, General Election, November 8, 1994* (Sacramento: California Secretary of State, 1994), 55.

79. "Firm Targets Illegal-Alien Proposition," *Daily News of Los Angeles*, August 15, 1994.

80. See Shultz, *Initiative Cookbook*.

81. Wroe, *Republican Party and Immigration Politics*, 76.

82. Frank Sharry, "Interested Parties" memo, December 7, 1994 (in author's possession).

83. "Taxpayers against 187 Campaign Update: Introducing the Taxpayers against 187 Staff," press release, box 319, folder 14, AB. See also Martinez, "Fighting 187."

84. On the role of nonprofits in the legalization programs of IRCA, see S. Baker, *Cautious Welcome*, chapter 5.

85. Ignatius Bau, interview with author, September 18, 2008, Oakland.

86. Jan Adams, interview with author, September 18, 2008, San Francisco.

87. Ibid.

88. Ibid.

89. "Californians United against Proposition 187: Statewide Contact List," September 6, 1994 (in author's possession).

90. "March Just a First Step, Latino Leaders Say," *LAT*, June 4, 1994.

91. Ignatius Bau, interview with author, September 18, 2008, Oakland.

92. Bau, "Immigrant Rights," 12.

93. Burt, *Search for a Civic Voice*, 319–20.

94. Mario Garcia, *Memories of Chicano History*, 314. In the early 1970s, groups such as CASA organized in undocumented communities, calling attention to abusive workplace and residential raids conducted by the INS and even calling for open borders. Pulido, *Black, Brown, Yellow, and Left*.

95. Burt, *Search for a Civic Voice*, 321.

96. Emily Goldfarb, telephone interview with author, November 6, 2008; Jan Adams, interview with author, September 18, 2008, San Francisco. For more recent organizing and advocacy work addressed toward such a framework, see the essays in Buff, *Immigrant Rights in the Shadows of Citizenship*.

97. See Simon and Alexander, *Ambivalent Welcome*.

98. "SOS Dominates California Campaign," *Migration News* 1, no. 4 (November 1994); "Feinstein's TV Attack on Immigration," *LAT*, July 10, 1994.

99. Nevins, *Operation Gatekeeper*, 1.

100. Rigoberto Rodriguez, telephone interview with author, December 2, 2008.

101. John Palacio, "Problem or Opportunity," *Orange County Register*, September 12 1994.

102. Frank Wu, telephone interview with author, November 12, 2008. For a similar position, see Park, "Race Discourse and Proposition 187," 175–204.

103. "Ardent Activism Hurting Anti-187 Effort, Some Say," *Sacramento Bee*, October 30, 1994.

104. Quoted in Wroe, *Republican Party and Immigration Politics*, 76.

105. Ibid.

106. Jan Adams, interview with author, September 18, 2008, San Francisco.

107. Wroe, *Republican Party and Immigration Politics*, 86–87.

108. "Ardent Activism Hurting Anti-187 Effort, Some Say," *Sacramento Bee*, October 30, 1994 (Munoz quote); Jan Adams, interview with author, September 18, 2008, San Francisco.

109. "Opponents Hire a Proven Winner," *Orange County Register*, November 2, 1994. The Taxpayers campaign claimed that internal polls and a Field Poll suggested the race was tightening in late October, but that the marches and walkouts sabotaged this movement. However, the largest demonstration took place on October 15, well before the polls were taken, suggesting the marches did not immediately raise support for the measure, though they certainly shaped news coverage of the campaign.

110. Quoted in Wroe, *Republican Party and Immigration Politics*, 88.

111. "White Supremacist Link Trips Prop 187," *San Francisco Chronicle*, October 13, 1994. See also "Pro-Prop 187 Group Admits It Bought Ads," *Orange County Register*, October 26, 1994. FAIR immediately sought to distance itself from Proposition 187, stating that Nelson was not working for the organization when he helped draft the measure and that FAIR had contributed no funding toward the campaign. But the Taxpayers campaign released documents showing that FAIR had arranged to purchase radio advertisements in the weeks before the election. "Both Sides Air Ads on Prop. 187," *LAT*, November 6, 1994.

112. "In Shadows of SOS," *Orange County Register*, October 21, 1994.

113. Wroe, *Republican Party and Immigration Politics*, 86.

114. "Prop. 187 Backers Counting on Message, Not Strategy," *LAT*, October 30, 1994.

115. Jacobson, *New Nativism.*

116. Bosniak, "Opposing Prop. 187," 555–619.

117. "Prop 187," aired October 16, 1994, on *Vista L.A.*, Channel 7, Los Angeles, UCLA Film and Television Archives.

118. See, for example, Newton, "Why Some Latinos Supported Proposition 187"; and Morris, "African American Voting on Proposition 187."

119. "Wilson Hasn't Decided on Controversial Prop 187," *San Francisco Chronicle*, September 10, 1994.

120. Empower America, "A Statement on Immigration," October 19, 1994, box 319, folder 14, AB.

121. "'SOS' Friends, Foes Get in Final Swings," *Orange County Register*, November 6, 1994; "In Shadows of SOS," *Orange County Register*, October 21, 1994; "Prop. 187: It's Not Racist At All, Supporters Say," *Orange County Register*, November 6, 1994; "Supporters Say 'SOS' Measure also Saving Nation," *Orange County Register*, October 29, 1994; "Prop. 187 Opponents Confront Ezell Immigration," *LAT*, October 13, 1994.

122. "For Pete Wilson, His Political Ambition Is Never Blind," *LAT*, July 23, 1995.

123. The symbolic dimensions of Proposition 187 constitute a central argument in Calavita, "New Politics of Immigration," 284.

124. Frank Wu, telephone interview with author, November 12, 2008.

125. Hayes-Bautista, *La Nueva California*, 127, 130. See also H. Johnson, *Undocumented Immigration to California.*

126. *California Ballot Pamphlet, General Election. November 8, 1994* (Sacramento: California Secretary of State, 1994), 54.

127. See Schrag, *Paradise Lost.*

128. Wroe, *Republican Party and Immigration Politics*, 96–107; "Davis Won't Appeal Prop 187 Ruling, Ending Court Battles," *LAT*, July 7, 1999.

129. Congressional Task Force on Immigration Reform, "Report to the Speaker Newt Gingrich," June 29, 1995, box 320, folder 8, AB. The committee was formed at the start of the 104th Congress.

130. For an insightful account of these developments and their impact on Asian American immigrants, see Fujiwara, *Mothers without Citizenship.*

131. Based on an analysis using the keyword search term "immigration" in the California Ballot Propositions Database, Hastings Law Library, http://holmes.uchastings.edu/library/california-research/ca-ballot-measures.html (accessed December 8, 2008).

132. The hotline group ultimately determined that 229 of these inquiries and complaints were "serious rights abuses." Cervantes, Khokha, and Murray, "Hate Unleashed," 9.

133. Pantoja, Ramirez, and Segura, "Citizens by Choice, Voters by Necessity."

134. Wong, *Democracy's Promise.*

135. Frank Sharry, "Interested Parties" memo, December 7, 1994 (in author's possession).

136. Emily Goldfarb and Ignatius Bau memo, Proposition 187 campaign, December 14, 1994 (in author's possession).

137. Adams, "Mobilizing against White Backlash," 1–6.

138. The Californians United campaign did not appear to be particularly successful at registering new voters, however. Five weekends of voter registration work in San Francisco during September only yielded four hundred new registrants, a result Adams admitted was "not gargantuan." "A Push to Get Immigrants to Vote Campaign to Defeat Prop. 187," *San Francisco Chronicle,* September 24, 1994.

139. Adams, "Mobilizing against White Backlash."

CHAPTER 7

1. "Proposition 209 Protest," aired August 28, 1997, on UPN News 13, KCOP, Los Angeles.

2. "Thousands Rally against 209" *San Francisco Chronicle,* August 29, 1997.

3. *California Ballot Pamphlet: General Election, November 5, 1996* (Sacramento: California Secretary of State, 1996), 32.

4. "Effort to Outlaw Affirmative Action Promoted in California," *Washington Post,* December 27, 1994.

5. Ibid.

6. Skrentny, *Ironies of Affirmative Action,* 216–17.

7. Ibid., 8.

8. On the Jesse Helms "Hands" ad, see Reeves, *Voting Hopes or Fears?* 17–19. See also DuBois, *Black Reconstruction in America;* and Foner, *Reconstruction.*

9. Katznelson, *When Affirmative Action Was White;* Lipsitz, *Possessive Investment in Whiteness.*

10. Hochschild, "Affirmative Action as Culture War," 285.

11. Feminist Majority Foundation poll, cited in Preston and Lai, "Symbolic Politics of Affirmative Action," 193.

12. Lydia Chavez, *Color Bind,* 24.

13. Wroe, *Republican Party and Immigration Politics,* 33.

14. "Affirmative Action Faces a Different Atmosphere," *San Jose Mercury News,* January 4, 1995.

15. "Republican Contract with America," www.house.gov/house/Contract/CONTRACT.html (accessed June 15, 2009).

16. "On Affirmative Action, Wilson's Moderate Path Veered Quickly Right," *NYT,* August 8, 1995.

17. "Conservatives Forge New Strategy to Challenge Affirmative Action," *NYT,* February 16, 1995.

18. "The New Orleans Declaration," statement endorsed at the fourth annual DLC conference, March 1, 1990, www.dlc.org/ndol_ci.cfm?contentid=878&kaid=128&subid=174 (accessed September 1, 2009); "The New American Choice Resolution," adopted at the DLC convention, Cleveland, Ohio,

May 1, 1991, www.dlc.org/documents/cleveland_proclamation.pdf (accessed September 1, 2009).

19. Lydia Chavez, *Color Bind*, 50–53.

20. Klinker, "Bill Clinton and the New Liberalism," 23–27; O'Reilly, *Nixon's Piano*.

21. "Affirmative Action Issue: Another 187?" *LAT*, February 2, 1995.

22. Lydia Chavez, *Color Bind*, 89.

23. Ibid., 100–108. See also "Summary of Results—California Affirmative Action Survey," conducted by the Feldman Group, October 1995 (in author's possession).

24. Lydia Chavez, *Color Bind*, 106. The comment was made by Connie Rice of the NAACP LDF.

25. Lydia Chavez, *Color Bind;* Feminist Majority Foundation poll, cited in Preston and Lai, "Symbolic Politics of Affirmative Action," 193.

26. Lydia Chavez, *Color Bind*.

27. "Confronting the California Anti–Affirmative Action Initiative: WE CAN WIN!!" Applied Research Center memo, n.d. (probably early 1995; in author's possession).

28. Cooper, "Fighting Waves for a Wilson Wipeout."

29. Jan Adams, interview with author, September 17, 2008, Oakland.

30. The quote was taken from "An Open Letter to My Sister, Angela Davis" and was originally published in the *New York Review of Books* on January 7, 1971, after Davis's imprisonment.

31. "Why the 'No on 209' Campaign Will Use Infuriating, Racist Messages," Californians for Justice memo, n.d. (in author's possession).

32. "Confronting the California Anti-Affirmative Action Initiative: WE CAN WIN!!" Applied Research Center memo, n.d. (probably early 1995; in author's possession).

33. Description taken from the newsletter of GSLAAP, vol. 1, no. 1 (1995) (in author's possession).

34. Quoted in Lydia Chavez, *Color Bind*, 77.

35. See Lydia Chavez, *Color Bind*, 63; Leo Chavez, *Covering Immigration*, 63. On affirmative action in the UC system, see Pusser, *Burning Down the House*, 1–2; and Post and Rogin, *Race and Representation*.

36. "UC Admission Goals Create 'Patent' Bias, Wilson Says," *Sacramento Bee*, July 7, 1995.

37. "The Curtain Pulled Back, for a Moment," *LAT*, September 11, 1996.

38. Lydia Chavez, *Color Bind*.

39. Ibid., 71–74; "Affirmative Action Ban Likely to Make State Ballot," *San Francisco Chronicle*, February 14, 1996.

40. "Regent Will Head Rights Campaign," *Oakland Tribune*, December 1, 1995.

41. "Black UC Regent Leads Fight against Affirmative Action," *Sacramento Bee*, February 28, 1995.

42. "Petitions Turned In for Affirmative Action Ban," *LAT*, February 22, 1996.

43. The state GOP contributed $250,000 toward the signature-gathering effort; Connerly and Wilson raised the balance from other Republican donors. "Rights Plan Moves Forward," *San Jose Mercury News*, February 22, 1996.

44. Lydia Chavez, *Color Bind*, 113.

45. "Affirmative Action Issue: Another 187?" *LAT*, February 2, 1995.

46. "Rights Plan Moves Forward," *San Jose Mercury News*, February 22, 1996.

47. "Foes of Affirmative Action Complete California Drive," *NYT*, February 21, 1996.

48. "Regent Fights Affirmative Action," *San Jose Mercury News*, January 19, 1995.

49. "Push Is On to Ask Voters to Kill Affirmative Action," *Sacramento Bee*, July 10, 1994.

50. "Scholars in Liberal Bastion Plot to End Legacy of 1960s," *San Diego Union Tribune*, February 19, 1995.

51. "UC Regent Pickets PG&E over Prop 209," *Sacramento Bee*, August 22, 1996.

52. Ward Connerly, "U.C. Must End Affirmative Action," *San Francisco Chronicle*, May 3, 1995.

53. "Black UC Regent Leads Fight against Affirmative Action," *Sacramento Bee*, February 28, 1995.

54. "Regent Fights Affirmative Action," *San Jose Mercury News*, January 19, 1995.

55. "Connerly: Man with a Mission," *Orange County Register*, January 23, 1996.

56. Mukherjee, *Racial Order of Things*, 219.

57. Mukherjee, *Racial Order of Things*; Goluboff, *Lost Promise of Civil Rights*.

58. "Gingrich to Dole: Back Off CCRI," *Sacramento Bee*, June 27, 1996.

59. "Anti-Affirmative Action Fever Hasn't Spread," *Contra Costa Times*, September 30, 1996; Lemann, "California Here We Come . . . ?"; Lydia Chavez, *Color Bind*, 131–32.

60. Gary Delgado, "California: Setting the Pace on Issue of Race," *National Network of Grant Makers (NNG) News* (Winter 1995).

61. Jan Adams to CFJ staff, memo, November 28, 1995 (in author's possession).

62. Ibid.

63. Description based on internal CFJ planning documents and a field-organizing campaign manual from fall 1996 (in author's possession).

64. "Voting with Their Hearts," *San Jose Mercury News*, July 22, 1996. The Freedom Summer Project involved roughly three hundred college students.

65. Quoted in Gary Delgado, "California: Setting the Pace on Issue of Race," *National Network of Grant Makers (NNG) News* (Winter 1995).

66. "Anti-CCRI Effort Seeks Low-Income Voters," *East Bay Express*, September 20, 1996.

67. Lydia Chavez, *Color Bind*, 174.

68. Bill Jones, *Financing California's Statewide Ballot Measures: 1996 Primary and General Elections* (Sacramento: California Secretary of State, 1996), www.sos.ca.gov/prd/bmc96/coverbm96.htm (accessed September 1, 2009).

69. "Winning in 1996," NOW memo (in author's possession).

70. "Deceptive 'Civil Rights' Initiative Makes Sex Discrimination Legal," Women Won't Go Back! campaign flyer, n.d. (in author's possession).

71. "Winning in 1996," NOW memo (in author's possession).

72. Quoted in "Summary of Results—California Affirmative Action Survey," conducted by the Feldman Group, October 1995 (in author's possession); Lydia Chavez, *Color Bind*, 154–56.

73. Lydia Chavez, *Color Bind*, 146.

74. *California Ballot Pamphlet: General Election, November 5, 1996* (Sacramento: California Secretary of State, 1996), 6. The elimination of "affirmative action" was mentioned in the nonpartisan legislative summaries in the ballot pamphlet.

75. For an analysis of the ad, see Mukherjee, *Racial Order of Things*, 233.

76. Lydia Chavez, *Color Bind*, 188.

77. *California Ballot Pamphlet: General Election, November 5, 1996* (Sacramento: California Secretary of State, 1996), 33.

78. "Ad Uses Klan to Attack Prop 209," *Sacramento Bee*, October 29, 1996; Eva Patterson, interview with author, September 18, 2008, San Francisco; Lydia Chavez, *Color Bind*.

79. Lydia Chavez, *Color Bind*, 137.

80. "Foes of Affirmative Action Complete California Drive," *NYT*, February 21, 1996.

81. Lydia Chavez, *Color Bind*, 124.

82. "Prop 209 Camp Debuts First TV Spots," *Sacramento Bee*, November 1, 1996; Lydia Chavez, *Color Bind*, 216–18.

83. "Prop 209 Race Gets Tighter as Election Nears," *San Diego Tribune*, October 30, 1996.

84. "Many TV Stations Reject GOP's 'I Have a Dream' Ad," *San Jose Mercury News*, October 24, 1996; Lydia Chavez, *Color Bind*, 222.

85. "The Don Quixote, Sancho Panza of Proposition 209," *Sacramento Bee*, November 10, 1996.

86. Lydia Chavez, *Color Bind*, 235.

87. *LAT* exit poll, Study no. 389, General Election, November 5, 1996, p. 3, www.latimesinteractive.com/pdfarchive/stat_sheets/la-timespoll389ss.pdf (accessed July 3, 2009).

88. Field Poll, "Prop 209 Post-Election Survey Results," Release no. 1826, November 22, 1996, p. 5, http://field.com/fieldpollonline/subscribers/Release1826.pdf (accessed October 1, 2009).

89. CFJ newsletter (Winter 1997) (in author's possession).

90. Eva Patterson, interview with author, September 18, 2008, San Francisco.

91. Jan Adams, interview with author, September 17, 2008, Oakland.

92. Eva Patterson, interview with author, September 18, 2008, San Francisco.

93. "Chipping at a Democratic Cornerstone," *LAT*, February 4, 1995.

94. "Clinton's Silence Alarms State's Bilingual Ed Backers," *San Francisco Chronicle*, March 17, 1998.

95. Bunche Center for African American Studies, "Admissions and Omissions: How 'the Numbers' Are Used to Exclude Deserving Students," vol. 3, no. 2 (June 2006), www.bunchecenter.ucla.edu/publications/Bunche%20Research%20Report-June%202006.pdf (accessed August 15, 2009).

96. "Court Bars San Jose Outreach to Minorities," *San Jose Mercury News*, December 1, 2000.

97. Gibbs and Bankhead, *Preserving Privilege.*

98. "Unz Uses Initiative for Impact" *LAT*, May 10, 1998.

99. Ron Unz, "Against Prop. 187," *LAT*, October 3, 1994.

100. Ron Unz, "Ron Unz Exposes the Failure of Bilingual Education," *Volunteer News and Events* newsletter, May 27, 1994, folder "1994 Governor," CL.

101. "The English Man," *West Magazine* (of the *San Jose Mercury News*), January 11, 1998.

102. *Lau v. Nichols*, 414 U.S. 563 (1974). See also Adamson, *Language Minority Students in American Schools*, 217–19.

103. Crawford, "Campaign against Proposition 227."

104. "Testing the Limits of Bilingual Education," *LAT*, August 8, 1997. See also K. Miller, "Reasserting Hegemony," 75.

105. "Star Latino Teacher Joins Bilingual Foes," *Sacramento Bee*, October 16, 1997.

106. Garcia Bedolla, *Fluid Borders*, chapter 1.

107. Crawford, "Campaign against Proposition 227."

108. Ibid.; "Call for Deadline to Learn English Disputed," *Sacramento Bee*, November 9, 1993.

109. Crawford, "Campaign against Proposition 227." For a discussion among bilingual educators about this debate, see *Bilingual Research* 24, nos. 1–2 (Winter–Spring 2000). See also Crawford, *Bilingual Education.*

110. "American Hispanics" (editorial), *Wall Street Journal*, June 4, 1998.

111. Crawford, "Campaign against Proposition 227." See also Schrag, *Paradise Lost.*

112. "Bilingual Foes Seek Latino Vote," *San Francisco Examiner*, October 19, 1997; *California Voter Information Guide: Primary Election, June 2, 1998* (Sacramento: California Secretary of State, 1998), 34.

113. "The English Man," *West Magazine* (of the *San Jose Mercury News*), January 11, 1998.

114. An early poll found the Unz measure favored by 84 percent of Latino voters. "Anti-Bilingual Drive's Tone is Key for Latinos," *LAT*, October 16, 1997.

115. "Bilingual Education," aired April 4, 1998, on *Vista L.A.*, KABC-TV, Los Angeles.

116. Unz, "Immigration or the Welfare State?"

117. Ibid.

118. "Conservative Trend Translates into Attack on Bilingual Education," *San Diego Union-Tribune*, March 6, 1995.

119. "Bilingual Program's Defenders Mobilizing," *Sacramento Bee*, November 23, 1997.

120. Ibid.

121. Rey is quoted from "Bilingual Education," aired April 4, 1998, on *Vista L.A.*, KABC-TV, Los Angeles. On this history, see Tichenor, *Dividing Lines*, chapter 6; Sanchez, *Becoming Mexican American*, chapter 2; and Garcia Bedolla, *Fluid Borders*.

122. "Bilingual Education," aired April 4, 1998, on *Vista L.A.*, KABC-TV, Los Angeles.

123. See here, especially, Garcia Bedolla, *Fluid Borders*, chapter 3; and D. Gutierrez, *Walls and Mirrors*.

124. "Bilingual Education," aired April 4, 1998, on *Vista L.A.*, KABC-TV, Los Angeles. For other examples of more forceful protests against the Unz measure, see "Protest Against Anti-Bilingual Ballot Measure," *San Francisco Chronicle*, January 1, 1998; and "He Speaks the Language of Activism to Community," *Orange County Register*, February 14, 1998.

125. The Republican Party ultimately endorsed the measure after a heated debate over whether such a position would continue to suggest that the party was anti-immigrant. "GOP Bid to Mend Rift with Latinos Still Strained," *LAT*, August 31, 1997. The most notable Republican to campaign for the measure was Los Angeles mayor Richard Riordan, an opponent of Propositions 187 and 209 who endorsed Proposition 227 and contributed $250,000 toward Spanish-language television ads in support of the measure. The ads featured Riordan's daughter, Mary Beth Farrell, a fluent Spanish speaker. "Anti-Prop 227 Forces Gear Up for TV Ad Blitz," *San Diego Union-Tribune*, May 21, 1998.

126. "Clinton's Silence Alarms State's Bilingual Ed Backers," *San Francisco Chronicle*, March 17, 1998.

127. "Anti-Prop 227 Forces Gear Up for TV Ad Blitz," *San Diego Union-Tribune*, May 21, 1998.

128. The rebuttal to the ballot argument in favor of Proposition 227 did assert that some bilingual programs "continue to have great success," but this theme was never emphasized in the extensive campaign advertising. *California Voter Information Guide: Primary Election, June 2, 1998* (Sacramento: California Secretary of State, 1998), 35.

129. "Big Ad Push by Prop 227 Foes: Bilingual-Ed Allies to Raise Cost Issue," *Sacramento Bee*, May 7, 1998.

130. "Ads Heat Up Fight on Bilingual Ban," *LAT*, May 8, 1998.

131. "Students Hold March in Concord," *San Francisco Chronicle*, April 23, 1998.

132. CFJ newsletter (Fall 1998) (in author's possession).

133. K. Miller, "Reasserting Hegemony," 82. Unz ultimately contributed 58 percent of the funds to the campaign.

134. *LAT* exit poll, Study no. 413, California Primary Election, June 2, 1998.

135. Jim Shultz, "Lessons of 227," *San Jose Mercury News*, June 5, 1998.

136. "Why Progressives Keep Losing California's Initiative Wars," *Media Alliance* 17, no. 4 (September–October 1998).

137. Matthew Miller, "This Man Controls California," *New Republic*, July 19, 1999.

138. For a summary of research findings on Proposition 227's impact, see Parrish et al., *Effects of the Implementation of Proposition 227*.

139. K. Miller, "Reasserting Hegemony."

CHAPTER 8

1. See Bowler and Cain, *Clicker Politics.*

2. *California Official Voter Information Guide: Statewide Election, October 7, 2003* (Sacramento: California Secretary of State, 2003), 42.

3. Ibid., 43.

4. American Civil Rights Institute brochure (in author's possession).

5. Rhodes was also a chair of the conservative Bradley Foundation, a co-chairman of the Club for Growth, and a former board member of the Heritage Foundation. He introduced Connerly to Fox News chair Rupert Murdoch during the Proposition 209 campaign, eventually helping Connerly to raise $1 million from the media magnate. See Lee Cokorinos, "The Big Money behind Ward Connerly," www.equaljusticesociety.orgresearch_bigmoney_ connerly .html (accessed April 30, 2009).

6. See Stefanic and Delgado, *No Mercy.* The awards and funders are from a list published by the American Civil Rights Institute, n.d. (probably 2001; in author's possession).

7. "ACRI Criticizes Federal Government's Rejection of a Multiracial Census Box," American Civil Rights Institute press release, July 9, 1997 (in author's possession).

8. "Racial Identity Survey," submitted to Royce Van Tassell, American Civil Rights Institute, by Zogby International, March 10, 2000 (in author's possession).

9. *California Official Voter Information Guide: Statewide Election, October 7, 2003* (Sacramento: California Secretary of State, 2003), 45.

10. "Race and Gubernatorial Recall: Can They Be Linked?" *Sacramento Bee*, July 30, 2003.

11. Ward Connerly, "No More Race-Box Classification," *Sacramento Bee*, March 7, 2001.

12. Gotanda, "Critique Of 'Our Constitution Is Color-Blind,'" 2, 18.

13. Crenshaw, "Color Blindness, History, and the Law."

324 / Notes to Pages 247–52

14. Editorial, *Orange County Register,* April 16, 2001.

15. *California Official Voter Information Guide: Statewide Election, October 7, 2003* (Sacramento: California Secretary of State, 2003), 45.

16. Ward Connerly, "Towards a Twenty-first Century Vision of Race," Interracial Voice, www.webcom.com/~intvoice/connerly3.html (accessed May 18, 2001); Lopez, *White by Law.*

17. Omi and Winant, *Racial Formation in the United States,* 55.

18. Ward Connerly, "Irrelevance of Race," *San Francisco Chronicle,* July 8, 2001.

19. For an analysis of left-oriented scholarship that takes this perspective, see Omi and Winant, *Racial Formation in the United States,* part 1.

20. Ward Connerly, "End of Race," *San Francisco Chronicle,* March 23, 2003.

21. Ward Connerly, "No More Race-Box Classification," *Sacramento Bee,* March 7, 2001.

22. "Ward Connerly and Eva Patterson Debate," aired March 14, 2003, on *Justice Talking,* National Public Radio.

23. Ward Connerly, "No More Race-Box Classification," *Sacramento Bee,* March 7, 2001 (first quote); *California Official Voter Information Guide: Statewide Election, October 7, 2003* (Sacramento: California Secretary of State, 2003), 45 (second quote).

24. Ward Connerly, "The Cancer of Race," *National Review* online, January 2, 2003, http://article.nationalreview.com/267522/the-cancer-of-race/ward -connerly (accessed January 13, 2009).

25. Memo to Equality Committee from the Office, January 31, 1961, American Civil Liberties Union, New York, box 232, folder 2, ACLU.

26. "Laws Authored and Passed by Hawkins," n.d., box 99, folder "Legislation 1935–1961 Partial List of AFH Bills Passed," AH.

27. Statement of Warren Banner, director of research, National Urban League, before Philadelphia Bar Committee on marriage and divorce, May 7, 1962, box 47, folder 5, LM.

28. "Connerly Initiative Polling Data" memo from Celinda Lake et al. to Eva Patterson, May 22, 2001 (in author's possession).

29. Mario Blanco, interview with author, September 18, 2009, Berkeley.

30. "Connerly Starts Push to End Tracking Race," *Contra Costa Times,* April 14, 2001.

31. Eva Patterson, interview with author, September 18, 2009, San Francisco.

32. "Measure Seeks to Curb Racial Data," *Sacramento Bee,* April 12, 2001.

33. The lawsuit was the *Williams v. California* case. See Elinson and Yogi, *Wherever There's a Fight.* There was considerable controversy over the impact of the RPI, since it could not ban the collection of data prescribed by federal law, including much of the data related to education. However, since the measure also banned the analysis of such data by the state, even if the federal government collected it, Connerly's opponents argued that the state would essentially be banned from utilizing it or considering it. Jean Ross,

What Would Proposition 54 Mean for the State's Ability to Collect and Use Data? California Budget Project Budget Brief, August 2003, p. 5, www.cbp.org/pdfs/2003/bb030813Prop54.pdf (accessed July 1, 2008).

34. Eva Patterson, interview with author, September 18, 2009, San Francisco.

35. Coalition for an Informed California, "Media Committee Report and Interim Proposal" memo, October 11, 2002, p. 3 (in author's possession).

36. "Summary of First Round of Focus Groups" memo from Lake, Snell, Perry and Associates to No on RPI team, May 10, 2002 (in author's possession).

37. Jean Ross, *What Would Proposition 54 Mean for the State's Ability to Collect and Use Data?* California Budget Project Budget Brief, August 2003, www.cbp.org/pdfs/2003/bb030813Prop54.pdf (accessed July 1, 2008).

38. Coalition for an Informed California, "What Is the Racial Privacy Initiative?" June 2003 (in author's possession).

39. "Budget Woes Delay Connerly Initiative," *Sacramento Bee*, May 26, 2001. Connerly initially attempted to hide the source of the donations by funneling them through the American Civil Rights Institute, but the California Fair Political Practices Commission, responding to a complaint from RPI opponents, eventually sued Connerly to disclose the names of the donors, and they prevailed. Connerly was later fined $95,000 for failing to meet state reporting requirements. Lee Cokorinos, "The Big Money behind Ward Connerly," www.equaljusticesociety.orgresearch_bigmoney_ connerly.html (accessed April 30, 2009).

40. "Racial Privacy Initiative Qualifies for 2004 Ballot," *San Francisco Chronicle*, July 15, 2002.

41. "Connerly Is Disgusted by GOP Fear of Race Issue," *Sacramento Bee*, May 10, 2001.

42. "GOP Conclave Starting on Shaky Turf," *Sacramento Bee*, February 21, 2003.

43. The recall petition was started by Sacramento antitax activist Ted Costa, who learned the intricacies of the initiative process from his mentor Paul Gann. English Only proponent Stanley Diamond was also on the board of Costa's People's Advocate Organization (see chapters 4 and 5). Norman Solomon, "California's Populist Revival," *San Francisco Chronicle*, September 28, 2003.

44. Bowler and Cain, *Clicker Politics*.

45. "Gore's Decision Will Enliven California's 2004 Primary," *Sacramento Bee*, December 17, 2002.

46. "Central Valley Groups File Challenge to Proposition 54," *Sacramento Bee*, August 26, 2003.

47. "Fund-Raising Proves Challenging for Backers of Prop. 54," *LAT*, August 28, 2003; Ward Connerly, "Not a Chance: The Electoral Journey of Proposition 54," *National Review* online, www.nationalreview.com/comment/connerly 200310150818.asp (accessed October 19, 2003). Connerly was counting not only expenditures made directly to respective Proposition 54 campaign committees but the large amounts of independent funding spent by individual candidates, the Democratic Party, and various interest groups to defeat the measure.

48. "California Recall Candidate Bustamante to Divert Funds to Prop. 54 Campaign," *San Jose Mercury News,* September 7, 2003.

49. "Summary of First Round of Focus Groups" memo from Lake, Snell, Perry and Associates to No on RPI team, May 10, 2002 (in author's possession).

50. "Strategic Summary" memo from Diane Feldman and Stefan Hankin to Larry Grisolano and Josh Pulliam, August 15, 2003 (in author's possession).

51. Eva Patterson, interview with author, September 18, 2009, San Francisco.

52. "The Recall Campaign Ad Watch: Proposition 54," *LAT,* September 28, 2003.

53. *California Official Voter Information Guide: Statewide Election,* October 7, 2003 (Sacramento: California Secretary of State, 2003), 42–43.

54. Sen, "Winning Race," 8; Wood, quoted in "Former Collaborators Clash over Race-Related Measure," *Contra Costa Times,* September 5, 2003. Wood wrote two lengthy accounts of his critique of the RPI, including "The Ideology of the Racial Privacy Initiative," March 23, 2003 (in author's possession).

55. "An Analysis of New No on Proposition 54 Radio Ad," Associated Press, September 25, 2003.

56. Ibid.

57. Mario Blanco, interview with author, September 18, 2009, Berkeley.

58. There were four ads in total: one featuring Cruz Bustamante, which ran September 16–30; one featuring C. Everett Koop, which ran September 26–October 6; one in Spanish featuring Tony Cardenas, which ran September 26–October 6; and one featuring Bustamante and Bill Clinton, which ran September 30–October 6. The CIC sponsored the Koop and Cardenas ads. HoSang, "Polling Trends during the Proposition 54 Campaign."

59. *LAT* exit poll, Study no. 490, California Special Recall Election, October 7, 2003.

60. KTLA news feed, October 7, 2003. The consensus among the CIC Steering Committee and consultants was also that the CIC campaign was primarily responsible for the dramatic swing in the Proposition 54 election. "Memo to Interested Parties" from the Feldman Group, December 2003 (in author's possession).

61. Ritu Kelotra, *Civil Rights Groups: Proposition 54 Defeat Is Victory for All,* www.civilrights.org (accessed October 10, 2003).

62. Bob Baker and Steve Carney, "Talk Radio Is Still in Attack Mode after the Election," *LAT,* October 9, 2003. In addition, before the announcement of the recall, voters who were unaware of the initiative initially supported Proposition 54 in large numbers after hearing a summary from pollsters. But by late September, those same unaware voters leaned heavily against the measure. Therefore, voters who received no information about the initiative followed the same trends in opposing Proposition 54 as those who had received information of some kind. HoSang, "Polling Trends during the Proposition 54 Campaign."

63. *LAT* exit poll, Study no. 490, California Special Recall Election, October 7, 2003.

64. Field Poll, Release nos. 2096, 2091, 2084, 2079, 2071, and 2040, www.field.com/fieldpollonline (accessed October 30, 2003).

65. Ward Connerly, "Not a Chance: The Electoral Journey of Proposition 54," *National Review* online, www.nationalreview.com/comment/connerly200310150818.asp (accessed October 19, 2003).

66. Eva Patterson, interview with author, September 18, 2009, San Francisco; Mario Blanco, interview with author, September 18, 2009, Berkeley.

67. "Prop. 54 Defeated Soundly," *San Francisco Chronicle*, October 8, 2003.

CONCLUSION

1. Bell, "Referendum," 14–15.

2. The theoretical foundations of this argument can be found in Karl Marx, "On the Jewish Question," in *The Marx-Engels Reader*, ed. Robert Tucker, 26–52 (New York: W. W. Norton, 1978).

3. Hartz, *Liberal Tradition in America*, 284, 91. On the limitations of Hartz's analysis of race in U.S. politics, see R. Smith, *Civic Ideals*, chapter 1.

4. See Field Poll, "Prop 209 Post-Election Survey Results," Release no. 1826, November 22, 1996, p. 5, http://field.com/fieldpollonline/subscribers/Release1826.pdf (accessed October 1, 2009).

5. "The Road Ahead," prepared for delivery at the Negro Leadership Conference dinner, November 25, 1961, Los Angeles, box 32, folder 6 "Loose Speeches of Loren Miller," LM.

6. L. Miller, "Farewell to Liberals." King's "Letter" was originally published as "The Negro Is Your Brother." See also Anzaldua and Moraga, *This Bridge Called My Back*.

7. Aanerud, "James Baldwin and the Critique of Racial Liberalism," 61.

8. Baldwin, "On Being White, and Other Lies," 91.

9. Ibid.

10. Baldwin, *Fire Next Time*, 334.

11. Baldwin, "On Being White, and Other Lies," 91–92.

12. Ibid., 92. See also Baldwin, "White Man's Guilt."

13. For a similar account rooted in the U.S. South, see Lowndes, *From the New Deal to the New Right*.

14. For a full elaboration of this argument, see Guinier and Torres, *Miner's Canary*, 10–13.

15. Burd-Sharps, Lewis, and Martins, *Measure of America*, 171–72. The California congressional districts in the bottom 10 percent are 18, 31, 43, 34, and 20 (ranked last). It is interesting to note that these districts span highly urbanized areas, sprawling suburbs, and rural communities, but all contain large concentrations of people of color.

16. Didion, *Where I Was From*, 71.

17. Burt, *Search for a Civic Voice*.

18. "Findings in Brief," in *California Opinion Index*, vol. 1 (San Francisco: Field Institute, 2000); Baldassare, *California in the New Millennium*; Field

Research Corporation, "The Changing California Electorate," August 2009, p. 1, http://field.com/fieldpollonline/subscribers/COI-09-August-California-Electorate.pdf (accessed October 1, 2009).

19. Lee, Ramakrishnan, and Ramirez, *Transforming Politics, Transforming America.* For case studies on the role of community organizations and immigrant political participation, see Wong, *Democracy's Promise.* On other factors fueling the growth in naturalization rates in the wake of 1996 federal reforms, see Fujiwara, *Mothers without Citizenship,* chapter 4.

20. "Wyland Backs New Prop. 187," *North County Times,* August 4, 2004; "Measure Fails to Qualify for Ballot," *LAT,* April 27, 2004.

21. Field Research Corporation, "The Changing California Electorate," August 2009, p. 1, http://field.com/fieldpollonline/subscribers/COI-09-August-California-Electorate.pdf (accessed October 1, 2009).

22. According to a 2004 analysis, "African Americans make up 6.5% of the [state] population, but they make up nearly 30% of the prison population, 36% of second strikers, and 45% of third strikers." Ehlers, Schiraldi, and Lotke, *Racial Divide,* 2.

23. Ehlers, Schiraldi, and Ziedenberg, *Still Striking Out,* 11.

24. *Official Voter Information Guide: November 2, 2004* (Sacramento: California Secretary of State, 2004), 46. On polling trends for this election, see Field Poll, "Late Breaking No Votes on Prop. 66," Release no. 2146, October 30, 2004, www.field.com/fieldpollonline/subscribers/RLS2146.pdf (accessed October 15, 2009). The measure passed 53 percent to 47 percent.

25. On Horton, see Mendelberg, *Race Card.*

26. Campaign-related materials at UCLA Campaign Literature Archive, http://digital.library.ucla.edu/campaign (accessed October 23, 2009).

27. Connolly et al., *From Classrooms to Cell Blocks.*

28. See proponents' and opponents' campaign Web sites and commercials at UCLA Campaign Literature Archive, http://digital.library.ucla.edu/campaign (accessed October 10, 2009). The campaign also demonstrated that while Wilson's influence in the California GOP might have waned, he was still a political force in the state; it was his intervention as the election approached that jumpstarted the opposition campaign. "How Prospects for Prop. 66 Fell So Far, So Fast," *LAT,* November 7, 2004.

29. Baldassare and Katz, *Role of Direct Democracy in California Governance.*

30. For a discussion of these dynamics, see Center for Governmental Studies, *Democracy by Initiative.*

31. Consider, for example, that reproductive rights opponents qualified three nearly identical initiatives for the California ballot between 2005 and 2008, limiting abortion rights for minors. Though losing narrowly on all three parental notification initiatives, they focused unprecedented new attention on the issue. See Shen, *Reproductive Justice at the Ballot Box.*

32. Williams, *Marxism and Literature,* 113.

Select Bibliography

ARCHIVAL AND MANUSCRIPT COLLECTIONS

California State Archives, Sacramento

Campaign Filing Statements (CFS)
Paul Gann Papers (PG)
Terea Pittman Papers (TP)

California State University, Urban Archives Center,
Oviatt Library, Northridge

Alan Robbins Collection (AR)
Max Mont Papers (MM)
Zero Population Growth Collection (ZPG)

Huntington Library, San Marino, California

Alexander Pope Papers (AP)
John Anson Ford Papers (JAF)
Loren Miller Papers (LM)
Marie Koenig Papers (MKP)

Loyola Marymount University, Center for the Study
of Los Angeles Research Collection, Los Angeles

Catholic Human Relations Series Records (CHRS)
Fredrick Dockweiler Papers (FDP)

Southern California Library for Social Studies and Research,
Los Angeles

California Democratic Council Records (CDC-SCL)
Charles Bratt Papers (CB)

Civil Rights Congress of Los Angeles Papers (CRC)
Dorothy Doyle Papers (DD)
Register of the California CIO Council Union Research and Information
   Services Records, 1935–56 (CIO)

Stanford University, Department of Special Collections,
Palo Alto, California

Eduardo Quevedo Papers (EQ)
Ernesto Galaraza Papers (EG)
National Council of La Raza Collection (NCLR)

Stanford University, Hoover Institution, Palo Alto, California

Samuel I. Hayakawa Papers (SH)

University of California, Berkeley

California Federation for Civic Unity Records, 1946–52 (CFCU)
Ellen Leary Legislative Papers (EL)
Institute for Governmental Studies (IGS)
National Association for the Advancement of Colored People Records, Region I,
   1942–86 (NAACP-UCB)

University of California, Los Angeles

American Civil Liberties Union of Southern California Records (ACLU)
Anthony Beilenson Papers (AB)
Augustus Hawkins Papers (AH)
California Democratic Council Records (CDC–UCLA)
Campaign Literature Archive (CL)
Chicano Desegregation Collection (Carlos Haro Papers) (CD)
Clarence Gillette Papers (CG)
Clifford Clinton Papers (CC)
Deborah Louis Collection (DLC)
Edward Roybal Papers (ER)
Film and Television Archives (FTA)
Jacob Zeitlan Papers (JZ)
Los Angeles Times Photo Archives (LAT)

University of Southern California, Los Angeles

Los Angeles County Chamber of Commerce Papers (LACCP)

OTHER SOURCES

Aanerud, Rebecca. "James Baldwin and the Critique of Racial Liberalism." In *James Baldwin Now,* edited by Dwight McBride, 56–74. New York: New York University Press, 1999.

Adams, Jan. "Mobilizing against White Backlash: Where Prop. 187 Lost—Lessons from the San Francisco Campaign." *Resist* 4, no. 4 (1995): 1–6.

Adamson, Hugh Douglas. *Language Minority Students in American Schools: An Education in English.* Mahwah, N.J.: L. Erlbaum Associates, 2005.

Akers Chacón, Justin, Mike Davis, and Julián Cardona. *No One Is Illegal: Fighting Violence and State Repression on the U.S.-Mexico Border.* Chicago, Ill.: Haymarket Books, 2006.

Allport, Gordon W. *The Nature of Prejudice.* Cambridge, Mass.: Addison-Wesley, 1954.

Allswang, John. *The Initiative and Referendum in California, 1898–1998.* Palo Alto, Calif.: Stanford University Press, 2000.

Almaguer, Tomas. *Racial Fault Lines: The Historical Origins of White Supremacy in California.* Berkeley: University of California Press, 1994.

Alvarez, R. Michael, and Tara L. Butterfield. "The Resurgence of Nativism in California? The Case of Proposition 187 and Illegal Immigration." *Social Science Quarterly* 81, no. 1 (2000): 167–79.

Alvarez, Roberto. "The Lemon Grove Incident: The Nation's First Successful Desegregation Court Case." *Journal of San Diego History* 32, no. 2 (1986): 116–35.

Anzaldua, Gloria, and Cherrie A. Moraga. *This Bridge Called My Back.* New York: Kitchen Table, Women of Color Press, 1983.

Baker, Keith Michael. *Inventing the French Revolution: Essays on French Political Culture in the Eighteenth Century.* Cambridge: Cambridge University Press, 1990.

Baker, Susan Gonzalez. *The Cautious Welcome: The Legalization Programs of the Immigration Reform and Control Act.* Santa Monica, Calif.: Rand Corp.; Washington, D.C.: Urban Institute, 1990.

Baldassare, Mark. *California in the New Millennium: The Changing Social and Political Landscape.* Berkeley: University of California Press, 2000.

———. *A California State of Mind: The Conflicted Voter in a Changing World.* Berkeley: University of California Press, 2002.

Baldassare, Mark, and Cheryl Katz. *The Role of Direct Democracy in California Governance: Public Opinion on Making Policy at the Ballot Box.* San Francisco: Public Policy Institute of California, 2007.

Baldwin, James. "The Fire Next Time: Letter to My Nephew." In *The Price of the Ticket,* 333–80. New York: St. Martin's/Marek, 1985.

———. "On Being White and Other Lies." *Essence,* April 1984, 90–92.

———. *The Price of the Ticket: Collected Nonfiction, 1948–1985.* New York: St. Martin's/Marek, 1985.

———. "White Man's Guilt." In *The Price of the Ticket,* 409–24. New York: St. Martin's/Marek, 1985.

Bass, Charlotta A. *Forty Years: Memoirs from the Pages of a Newspaper.* Los Angeles: C. A. Bass, 1960.

Bau, Ignatius. "Immigrant Rights: A Challenge to Asian Pacific American Influence." *Asian American Policy Review* 5 (1995): 12.

Bell, Derrick A. *Faces at the Bottom of the Well: The Permanence of Racism.* New York: Basic Books, 1992.

———. "The Referendum: Democracy's Barrier to Racial Equality." *Washington Law Review* 54 (1978): 1–29.

Bennett, David H. *The Party of Fear: From Nativist Movements to the New Right in American History.* New York: Vintage Books, 1990.

Bernstein, Shana Beth. "Building Bridges at Home in a Time of Global Conflict: Interracial Cooperation and the Fight for Civil Rights in Los Angeles, 1933–1954." PhD dissertation, Stanford University, 2004.

Bosniak, Linda S. "Opposing Prop. 187: Undocumented Immigrants and the National Imagination." *Connecticut Law Review* 28, no. 3 (1996): 555–620.

Bowler, Shaun, and Bruce Cain, eds. *Clicker Politics: Essays on the Recall.* New York: Prentice Hall, 2005.

Bowler, Shaun, and Todd Donovan. "Information and Opinion Change on Ballot Propositions." *Political Behavior* 16, no. 4 (1994): 411–35.

Boyarsky, Bill. *Big Daddy: Jesse Unruh and the Art of Power Politics.* Berkeley: University of California Press, 2008.

———. *The Rise of Ronald Reagan.* New York: Random House, 1968.

Brechin, Gray. *Imperial San Francisco: Urban Power, Earthly Ruin.* Berkeley: University of California Press, 1999.

Brilliant, Mark. "Color Lines: Civil Rights Struggles on America's Racial Frontier, 1945–75." PhD dissertation, Stanford University, 2003.

Brimelow, Peter. "Time to Rethink Immigration?" *National Review* 44 (1992): 30–46.

Brown, Wendy. *Regulating Aversion: Tolerance in the Age of Identity and Empire.* Princeton, N.J.: Princeton University Press, 2006.

Buff, Rachel, ed. *Immigrant Rights in the Shadows of Citizenship.* New York: New York University Press, 2008.

Burd-Sharps, Sarah, Kristen Lewis, and Eduardo Borges Martins. *The Measure of America: American Human Development Report, 2008–2009.* New York: Columbia University Press, 2008.

Burt, Kenneth C. "The Fight for Fair Employment and the Shifting Alliances among Latinos and Labor in Cold War Los Angeles." In *Labor's Cold War: Local Politics in a Global Context,* edited by Shelton Stromquist, 79–109. Urbana: University of Illinois Press, 2008.

———. *The Search for a Civic Voice: California Latino Politics.* Claremont, Calif.: Regina Books, 2007.

Cacho, Lisa Marie. "'The People of California are Suffering': The Ideology of White Injury in Discourses of Immigration." *Cultural Values* 4, no. 4 (2000): 389–418.

Calavita, Kitty. "The New Politics of Immigration: 'Balanced Budget Conservatism' and the Symbolism of Proposition 187." *Social Problems* 43, no. 3 (1996): 284–305.

California Legislative Black Caucus. *The State of Black California 2007.* Sacramento: California Legislative Black Caucus, 2007.

Cannon, Lou. *Governor Reagan: His Rise to Power.* 1st edition. New York: PublicAffairs, 2003.

Carmichael, Stokely, and Charles Hamilton. *Black Power: The Politics of Liberation in America.* New York: Random House, 1967.

Casstevens, Thomas. *Politics, Housing and Race Relations: California's Rumford Act and Proposition 14.* Berkeley: Institute of Governmental Studies, University of California, Berkeley, 1967.

Caughey, John, and LaRee Caughey. *School Segregation on Our Doorstep: The Los Angeles Story.* Los Angeles: Quail Books, 1966.

———. *To Kill a Child's Spirit: The Tragedy of School Segregation in Los Angeles.* Itsca, Ill.: F.E. Peacock, 1973.

Center for Governmental Studies. *Democracy by Initiative: Shaping California's Fourth Branch of Government.* 2nd edition. Los Angeles: Center for Governmental Studies, 2008.

Cervantes, Nancy, Sasha Khokha, and Bobbie Murray. "Hate Unleashed: Los Angeles in the Aftermath of Proposition 187." *Chicano Law Review* 17, no. 1 (1995): 1–23.

Chavez, Leo R. *Covering Immigration: Popular Images and the Politics of the Nation.* Berkeley: University of California Press, 2001.

Chavez, Lydia. *The Color Bind: California's Battle to End Affirmative Action.* Berkeley: University of California Press, 1998.

Chen, Anthony S. *The Fifth Freedom: Jobs, Politics, and Civil Rights in the United States, 1941–1972.* Princeton, N.J.: Princeton University Press, 2009.

———. "From Fair Employment to Equal Employment Opportunity and Beyond: Affirmative Action and the Poltics of Civil Rights in the New Deal Order, 1941–1972." PhD dissertation, University of California, Berkeley, 2002.

———. "'The Hitlerian Rule of Quotas' Racial Conservatism and the Politics of Fair Employment Legislation in New York State, 1941–1945." *Journal of American History* 92, no. 4 (2006): 1238–64.

Chen, Anthony S., Robert W. Mickey, and Robert P. Van Houweling. "Explaining the Contemporary Alignment of Race and Party: Evidence from California's 1946 Ballot Initiative on Fair Employment." *Studies in American Political Development* 22, no. 2 (2008): 204–28.

Chin, Gabriel J. "The Civil Rights Revolution Comes to Immigration Law: A New Look at the Immigration and Nationality Act of 1965." *North Carolina Law Review* 75 (1996): 274–345.

Citrin, Jack, Donald P. Green, Christopher Muste, and Cara Wong. "Public Opinion toward Immigration Reform: The Role of Economic Motivations." *Journal of Politics* 59 (1997): 858–81.

Citrin, Jack, Beth Reingold, Evelyn Walters, and Donald Green. "The 'Official

English' Movement and the Symbolic Politics of Language in the United States." *Western Political Quarterly* 43, no. 3 (1990): 535–59.

Collins, Patricia Hill. *Black Feminist Thought.* New York: Routledge, 1991.

Connolly, Kathleen, Dan Macallair, Lea McDermid, and Vincent Schiraldi. *From Classrooms to Cell Blocks: How Prison Building Affects Higher Education and African American Enrollment in California.* San Francisco: Center on Juvenile and Criminal Justice, 1996.

Cooper, Marc. "Fighting Waves for a Wilson Wipeout." *The Nation,* September 18, 1995, 266–68.

Cox, Oliver C. *Caste, Class, and Race: A Study in Social Dynamics.* Garden City, N.Y.: Doubleday, 1948.

Crawford, James. *Bilingual Education: History, Politics, Theory, and Practice.* Trenton, N.J.: Crane, 1989.

———. "The Campaign against Proposition 227: A Post Mortem." *Bilingual Research Journal* 21, no. 1 (1997): 1–29.

———. *Hold Your Tongue: Bilingualism and the Politics of English Only.* Reading, Mass.: Addison-Wesley, 1992.

———, ed. *Language Loyalties: A Source Book on the Official English Controversy.* Chicago: University of Chicago Press, 1992.

———. "What's Behind Official English?" In *Language Loyalties,* edited by Crawford. Chicago: University of Chicago Press, 1992.

Creighton, Sandy. "Proposition 1 and Federal Protection of State Constitutional Rights." *Northwestern University Law Review* 75 (1980–81): 685–733.

Crenshaw, Kimberle Williams. "Color Blindness, History, and the Law." In *The House That Race Built,* edited by Wahneema Lubiano, 280–88. New York: Pantheon Books, 1997.

———. "Mapping the Margins: Intersectionality, Identity Politics, and Violence against Women of Color." *Stanford Law Review.* 43, no. 6 (1991): 1241–99.

Dallek, Matthew. *The Right Moment: Ronald Reagan's First Victory and the Decisive Turning Point in American Politics.* New York: Free Press, 2000.

Davis, Angela. "The Color of Violence against Women." *ColorLines* 3, no. 3 (Fall 2000): 4–8.

Davis, Mike. *City of Quartz: Excavating the Future in Los Angeles.* New York: Vintage Books, 1990.

———. "The Social Origins of the Referendum." *NACLA Report on the Americas* 29, no. 3 (1995): 24–28.

Denton, John. *Apartheid American Style.* Berkeley: Diablo Press, 1967.

Deverell, William. *Whitewashed Adobe: The Rise of Los Angeles and the Remaking of Its Mexican Past.* Berkeley: University of California Press, 2004.

Deverell, William, and Douglas Flamming. "Race, Rhetoric, and Regional Identity: Boosting Los Angeles, 1890–1930." In *Power and Place in the American West,* edited by Richard White and John Findlay, 117–43. Seattle: University of Washington Press, 1999.

Diamond, Stanley. "English—The Official Language of California, 1983–1988." In *Perspectives on Official English: The Campaign for English as the Official Language of the USA,* edited by Karen L. Adams and Daniel T. Brink, 111–20. Berlin: Mouton de Gruyter, 1990.

Didion, Joan. *Where I Was From.* New York: Alfred Knopf, 2003.

Dochuk, Darren. *From Bible Belt to Sunbelt: Plain-Folk Religion and Grassroots Politics in California's Southland.* New York: W. W. Norton, forthcoming.

Domanick, Joe. *Cruel Justice: Three Strikes and the Politics of Crime in America's Golden State.* Berkeley: University of California Press, 2004.

Donovan, Todd, and Shaun Bowler. "Direct Democracy and Minority Rights: An Extension." *American Journal of Political Science.* 42, no. 3 (1998): 1020–24.

DuBois, W. E. B. *Black Reconstruction in America: An Essay toward a History of the Part Which Black Folk Played in an Attempt to Reconstruct Democracy in America, 1860–1880.* New York: Harcourt, Brace, 1935.

Duggan, Lisa. *The Twilight of Equality? Neoliberalism, Cultural Politics and the Attack on Democracy.* Boston: Beacon Press, 2003.

Durham, Joseph. "Sense and Nonsense about Busing." *Journal of Negro Education* 42, no. 3 (1973): 322–35.

Dyste, Connie. "Proposition 63: The California English Language Amendment." *Applied Linguistics* 10, no. 3 (1989): 314–30.

Edelman, Murray. *Constructing the Political Spectacle.* Chicago: University of Chicago Press, 1988.

Edsall, Thomas Byrne, and Mary D. Edsall. *Chain Reaction: The Impact of Race, Rights, and Taxes on American Politics:* W. W. Norton, 1992.

Edwards, Lee. *Reagan: A Political Biography.* San Diego: Viewpoint Books, 1967.

Ehlers, Scott, Vincent Schiraldi, and Eric Lotke. *Racial Divide: An Examination of the Impact of California's Three Strikes Laws on African Americans and Latinos.* Washington, D.C.: Justice Policy Institute, 2004.

Ehlers, Scott, Vincent Schiraldi, and Jason Ziedenberg. *Still Striking Out: Ten Years of California's Three Strikes.* Washington, D.C.: Justice Policy Institute, 2004.

Elinson, Elaine, and Stan Yogi. *Wherever There's a Fight.* Berkeley: Heyday Books, 2009.

Ethington, Philip J., William H. Frey, and Dowell Myers. *The Racial Resegregation of Los Angeles County, 1940–2000.* Public Research Report no. 2001–04. Los Angeles: University of Southern California; Ann Arbor: University of Michigan, 2001.

Ettinger, David. "The Quest to Desegregate Los Angeles Schools." *Los Angeles Lawyer* (March 2003): 55–67.

Fair Employment Practices Commission. *Fair Practice News,* no. 22 (November–December 1965).

Fields, Barbara J. "Slavery, Race, and Ideology in the United States of America." *New Left Review* 1, no. 181 (May–June 1990): 95–118.

Fine, Doris. *When Leadership Fails: Desegregation and Demoralization in the San Francisco Schools.* New York: Transaction Books, 1986.

Fischel, William. *The Homevoter Hypothesis: How Home Values Influence Local Government Taxation, School Finance, and Land-Use Policies.* Cambridge, Mass.: Harvard University Press, 2001.

Flamming, Douglas. *Bound for Freedom: Black Los Angeles in Jim Crow America.* Berkeley: University of California Press, 2005.

Fogelson, Robert M. *The Fragmented Metropolis: Los Angeles, 1850–1930.* Berkeley: University of California Press, 1993.

Foner, Eric. *Reconstruction: America's Unfinished Revolution.* New York: Harper & Row, 1988.

Freer, Regina. "Charlotta Bass: A Community Activist for Economic and Racial Justice." In *The Next Los Angeles: The Struggle for a Liveable City,* edited by Robert Gottlieb, Mark Vallianatos, Regina Freer, and Peter Drier, 49–62. Berkeley: University of California Press, 2006.

Freund, David. "Marketing the Free Market: State Intervention and the Politics of Prosperity in Metropolitan America." In *The New Suburban History,* edited by Thomas Sugrue and Kevin Kruse, 11–32. Chicago: University of Chicago Press, 2006.

Frye, Billy E. "Quarrels with the Courts: A Comparative Study on Three Anti-Busing Community Groups Formed in Response to Mandatory Busing." Master's thesis, University of Southern California, 1981.

Fujiwara, Lynn. *Mothers without Citizenship: Asian Immigrant Families and the Consequences of Welfare Reform.* Minneapolis: University of Minnesota Press, 2008.

Gaines, Brian, and Wendy Tam Cho. "On California's 1920 Alien Land Law: The Psychology and Economics of Racial Discrimination." *State Politics and Policy Quarterly* 4, no. 3 (2004): 271–93.

Gamble, Barbara S. "Putting Civil Rights to a Popular Vote." *American Journal of Political Science* 41, no. 1 (1997): 245–69.

Garcia, Mario. *Memories of Chicano History: The Life and Narrative of Bert Corona.* Berkeley: University of California Press, 1994.

Garcia, Matt. *A World of Its Own: Race, Labor and Citrus in the Making of Greater Los Angeles, 1900–1970.* Chapel Hill: University of North Carolina Press, 2001.

Garcia Bedolla, Lisa. *Fluid Borders: Latino Power, Identity, and Politics in Los Angeles.* Berkeley: University of California Press, 2005.

Gerber, Elisabeth, Arthur Lupia, Mathew McCubbins, and D. Roderick Kiewiet. *Stealing the Initiative: How State Government Responds to Direct Democracy.* Upper Saddle River, N.J.: Prentice Hall, 2001.

Gerstle, Gary. *American Crucible: Race and Nation in the Twentieth Century.* Princeton, N.J.: Princeton University Press, 2002.

Gerstle, Gary, and Steve Fraser, eds. *The Rise and Fall of the New Deal Order, 1930–1980.* Princeton, N.J.: Princeton University Press, 1989.

Gibbs, Jewelle Taylor, and Teiahsha Bankhead. *Preserving Privilege: Califor-*

nia Politics, Propositions, and People of Color. Westport, Conn.: Praeger, 2001.

Gilmore, Ruth Wilson. "Fatal Couplings of Power and Difference: Notes on Racism and Geography." *The Professional Geographer* 54, no. 1 (2002): 15–24.

———. *Golden Gulag: Prisons, Surplus, Crisis, and Opposition in Globalizing California.* Berkeley: University of California Press, 2007.

Gilroy, Paul. *Ain't No Black in the Union Jack.* Chicago: University of Chicago, 1987.

Gitlin, Todd. *The Twilight of Common Dreams: Why America Is Wracked by Culture Wars.* New York: Henry Holt, 1996.

Glenn, Evelyn Nakano. *Unequal Freedom.* Cambridge, Mass.: Harvard University Press, 2002.

Goluboff, Risa Lauren. *The Lost Promise of Civil Rights.* Cambridge, Mass.: Harvard University Press, 2007.

Gonzales-Day, Ken. *Lynching in the West: 1850–1935.* Durham, N.C.: Duke University Press, 2006.

Gonzalez, Gilbert. "Segregation of Mexican Children in a Southern California City: The Legacy of Expansionism and the American Southwest." *Western Historical Quarterly* 16, no. 1 (1985): 55–76.

Gonzalez, Jerry. "A Place in the Sun: Mexican American Identity, Race, and the Suburbanization of Los Angeles, 1940–1980." PhD dissertation, University of Southern California, 2008.

Gossett, Thomas F. *Race, the History of an Idea in America.* Dallas: Southern Methodist University Press, 1963.

Gotanda, Neil. "A Critique Of 'Our Constitution Is Color-Blind.'" *Stanford Law Review* 44, no. 1 (1991): 1–68.

Gramsci, Antonio. *Selections from the Prison Notebooks.* Edited by Quintan Hoare and Geoffrey Nowell-Smith. London: Lawrence and Wishart, 1971.

Green, Donald, and Joseph Cowden. "Who Protests: Self-Interest and White Opposition to Busing." *Journal of Politics* 54, no. 2 (1992): 471–96.

Guinier, Lani, and Gerald Torres. *The Miner's Canary: Enlisting Race, Resisting Power.* Cambridge, Mass.: Harvard University Press, 2002.

Gutierrez, David G. *Walls and Mirrors: Mexican Americans, Mexican Immigrants, and the Politics of Ethnicity.* Berkeley: University of California Press, 1995.

Gutiérrez, Elena R. *Fertile Matters: The Politics of Mexican-Origin Women's Reproduction.* 1st edition. Chicana Matters Series. Austin: University of Texas Press, 2008.

Haefele, Marc. "The California Shipwreck." *Boston Review* 20, no. 2 (April–May 1995).

Hajnal, Zoltan, and Hugh Louch. *Are There Winners and Losers? Race, Ethnicity, and California's Initiative Process.* San Francisco: Public Policy Institute of California, 2002.

Hall, Stuart. *The Hard Road to Renewal: Thatcherism and the Crisis of the Left.* London: Verso, 1988.

———. "The Problem of Ideology: Marxism without Guarantees." In *Stuart Hall: Critical Dialogues in Cultural Studies,* edited by David Morley and Kuan-Hsing Chen, 25–46. London: Routledge, 1996.

———. "Race Articulation and Societies Structured in Dominance." In *Sociological Theories: Race and Colonialism,* 305–45. Paris: UNESCO, 1980.

———. "Variants of Liberalism." In *Politics and Ideology,* edited by James Donald and Stuart Hall, 34–69. Philadelphia: Open University Press, 1986.

Haro, Carlos Manuel. *Mexicano/Chicano Concerns and School Desegregation in Los Angeles.* Los Angeles: Chicano Studies Center Publications, University of California, Los Angeles, 1977.

Harris, Cheryl I. "Whiteness as Property." *Harvard Law Review* 106, no. 8 (1993): 1709–95.

Hartz, Louis. *The Liberal Tradition in America.* San Diego: Harvest, 1991.

Haskell, John. *Direct Democracy or Representative Government? Dispelling the Populist Myth.* Boulder, Colo.: Westview Press, 2001.

Hayes-Bautista, David E. *La Nueva California: Latinos in the Golden State.* Berkeley: University of California Press, 2004.

Hayward, Steven F. "Ronald Reagan and the Transformation of Modern California." In *The California Republic: Institutions, Statesmanship, and Politics,* edited by Brian Janiskee and Ken Masugi, 237–56. Lanham: Rowman & Littlefield, 2004.

Hendrick, Irving. *The Education of Non-Whites in California, 1849–1970.* San Francisco: R & E Research Associates, 1977.

Hero, Rodney, and Caroline Tolbert. "Race/Ethnicity and Direct Democracy: An Analysis of California's Illegal Immigration Initiative." *Journal of Politics* 58, no. 3 (1996): 806–18.

Higham, John. *Strangers in the Land: Patterns of American Nativism, 1860–1925.* 1955; New Brunswick, N.J.: Rutgers University Press, 2002.

Hirsch, Arnold. "Massive Resistance in the Urban North: Trumball Park, Chicago, 1953–1966." *Journal of American History* 85 (1995): 522–50.

Hochschild, Jennifer. "Affirmative Action as Culture War." In *A Companion to Racial and Ethnic Studies,* edited by David Theo Goldberg and John Solomos, 282–303. Malden, Mass.: Blackwell, 2002.

Honig, Bonnie. *Democracy and the Foreigner.* Princeton, N.J.: Princeton University Press, 2001.

Hood, M. V., III, and Irwin L. Morris. "Brother, Can You Spare a Dime? Racial/Ethnic Context and the Anglo Vote on Proposition 187." *Social Science Quarterly* 81, no. 1 (2000): 13.

Horne, Gerald. *Fire This Time: The Watts Uprising and the 1960s.* New York: Da Capo Press, 1997.

Horton, Carol A. *Race and the Making of American Liberalism.* Oxford: Oxford University Press, 2005.

HoSang, Daniel. "Beyond Policy: Ideology, Race and the Reimagining of Youth." In *Beyond Resistance! Youth Activism and Community Change: New Democratic Possibilities for Practice and Policy for America's Youth,* edited by Pedro Noguera, Shawn A. Ginwright, and Julio Cammarota, 3–20. New York: Routledge, 2006.

———. "Polling Trends during the Proposition 54 Campaign: A Preliminary Analysis." Unpublished paper, 2003.

Igler, David. *Industrial Cowboys: Miller and Lux and the Transformation of the Far West, 1850–1920.* Berkeley: University of California Press, 2001.

InnerCity Struggle. *A Student and Parent Vision for Educational Justice in the Eastside.* Los Angeles: InnerCity Struggle, 2007.

Jacobson, Robin Dale. *The New Nativism: Proposition 187 and the Debate Over Immigration.* Minneapolis: University of Minnesota Press, 2008.

Johnson, Hans P. *Undocumented Immigration to California, 1980–1993.* San Francisco: Public Policy Institute of California, 1996.

Johnson, Kevin R. "An Essay on Immigration Politics, Popular Democracy, and California's Proposition 187: The Political Relevance and Legal Irrelevance of Race." *Washington Law Review* 70, no. 3 (1995): 629–73.

Johnson, Marilyn. *The Second Gold Rush: Oakland and the East Bay in World War II.* Berkeley: University of California Press, 1993.

Johnson, Marilyn, Robert Korstad, and Nelson Lichtenstein. "Opportunities Found and Lost: Labor, Radicals, and the Early Civil Rights Movement." *Journal of American History* 75 (1988): 786–811.

Johnson, Tammy, and Menachem Krajcer. *Facing Race: 2006 Legislative Report Card on Racial Equity.* Oakland: Applied Research Center, 2006.

Karst, Kenneth, and Harold Horowitz. "*Reitman v Mulkey:* A Telophase of Substantive Equal Protection." *Supreme Court Review* 39 (1967): 39–80.

Katznelson, Ira. *When Affirmative Action Was White: An Untold History of Racial Inequality in Twentieth-Century America.* New York: W. W. Norton, 2005.

Kazin, Michael. *Barons of Labor: The San Francisco Building Trades and Union Power in the Progressive Era.* Champaign: University of Illinois Press, 1987.

———. *The Populist Persuasion: An American History.* Ithaca, N.Y.: Cornell University Press, 1998.

———. "Reform, Utopia, and Racism: The Politics of California Craftsmen." In *Working People of California,* edited by Daniel Conford, 311–43. Berkeley: University of California Press, 1995.

Kennedy, David. *Freedom from Fear: The American People in Depression and War, 1929–1945.* Oxford: Oxford University Press, 2001.

Key, V. O., and Winston Winford Crouch. *The Initiative and the Referendum in California.* Berkeley: University of California Press, 1939.

King, Desmond, and Rogers Smith. "Racial Orders in American Political Development." *American Political Science Review* 99, no. 1 (2005): 75–92.

King, Martin Luther. "The Negro Is Your Brother." *Atlantic* 212, no. 2 (1963): 78–81.

King, Richard H. *Race, Culture, and the Intellectuals: 1940–1970.* Washington, D.C.: Woodrow Wilson Center Press; Baltimore, Md.: Johns Hopkins University Press, 2004.

Klinker, Phillip. "Bill Clinton and the New Liberalism." In *Without Justice for All: The New Liberalism and Our Retreat from Racial Equality*, edited by Adolph L. Reed, 11–28. Boulder, Colo.: Westview Press, 1999.

Kruse, Kevin. *White Flight: Atlanta and the Making of Modern Conservatism*. Princeton, N.J.: Princeton University Press, 2005.

Kurashige, Scott. *The Shifting Grounds of Race: Black and Japanese Americans in the Making of Multiethnic Los Angeles*. Politics and Society in Twentieth-Century America. Princeton, N.J.: Princeton University Press, 2008.

Laclau, Ernesto. "Politics and Ideology in Marxist Theory." In *Politics and Ideology*, edited by James Donald and Stuart Hall, 27–32. Philadelphia: Open University Press, 1979.

Laham, Nicholas. *Ronald Reagan and the Politics of Immigration Reform*. Westport, Conn.: Praeger, 2000.

Landis, Jeanne Thiel. "The Crawford Desegregation Suit in Los Angeles, 1977–1981." PhD dissertation, University of California, Los Angeles, 1984.

Lassiter, Matthew. "De Jure/De Facto Segregation: The Long Shadow of a National Myth." In *The Myth of Southern Exceptionalism*, edited by Matthew Lassiter and Joseph Crespino, 25–48. Oxford: Oxford University Press, 2009.

———. *The Silent Majority: Suburban Politics in the Sunbelt South*. Princeton, N.J.: Princeton University Press, 2005.

Lee, Taeku, S. Karthick Ramakrishnan, and Ricardo Ramirez. *Transforming Politics, Transforming America: The Political and Civic Incorporation of Immigrants in the United States*. Charlottesville: University of Virginia Press, 2006.

Leonard, David Jason. "'No Jews and No Coloreds Are Welcome in This Town': Constructing Coalitions in Post/War Los Angeles." PhD dissertation, University of California, Berkeley, 2002.

Leonard, Kevin Allen. *The Battle for Los Angeles: Racial Ideology and World War II*. Albuquerque: University of New Mexico Press, 2006.

Lewis, Howard. *Analysis of Proposition 14: The CREA Amendment*. Palo Alto, Calif.: Self-published, 1964.

Lipsitz, George. *The Possessive Investment in Whiteness*. Philadelphia: Temple University Press, 1998.

Lo, Clarence Y. H. *Small Property versus Big Government: Social Origins of the Property Tax Revolt*. Berkeley: University of California Press, 1990.

Loewen, James. *Sundown Towns: A Hidden Dimension of American Racism*. New York: Basic Books, 2005.

Lopez, Ian Haney. *Racism on Trial: The Chicano Fight for Justice*. Cambridge, Mass.: Belknap Press, 2003.

———. *White by Law: The Legal Construction of Race*. New York: New York University Press, 1996.

Lowndes, Joseph E. *From the New Deal to the New Right: Race and the Southern Origins of Modern Conservatism*. New Haven, Conn.: Yale University Press, 2008.

Lustig, Jeff, and Dick Walker. *No Way Out: Immigrants and the New California*. Berkeley: Campus Coalition for Human Rights and Social Justice, 1995.

Magelby, David. *Direct Legislation: Voting on Ballot Propositions in the United States*. Baltimore: Johns Hopkins University Press, 1984.

Martinez, Ruben. "Fighting 187: The Different Opposition Strategies." *NACLA Report on the Americas* 29, no. 3 (1995): 29–32.

Marx, Karl, and Fredrich Engels. "The German Ideology: Part I." In *The Marx-Engels Reader*, edited by Robert Tucker, 146–203. New York: W.W. Norton, 1978.

Mauer, Mark, and Ryan King. *Uneven Justice: State Rates of Incarceration by Race and Ethnicity*. Washington, D.C.: Sentencing Project, 2007.

McGirr, Lisa. *Suburban Warriors: The Origins of the New American Right*. Princeton, N.J.: Princeton University Press, 2001.

Mehan, Hugh. "The Discourse of the Illegal Immigration Debate: A Case Study in the Politics of Representation." *Discourse Society* 8 (1997): 249–70.

Mendelberg, Tali. *The Race Card: Campaign Strategy, Implicit Messages, and the Norm of Equality*. Princeton, N.J.: Princeton University Press, 2001.

Micklethwait, John, and Adrian Woolridge. *The Right Nation: Conservative Power in America*. New York: Penguin, 2004.

Miller, Kathryn. "Reasserting Hegemony: English for the Children and the Politics of Bilingual Education." Master's thesis, University of Colorado, 2008.

Miller, Loren. "A Farewell to Liberals: A Negro View." *The Nation*, October 20, 1962, 235–38.

Molina, Natalia. *Fit to Be Citizens? Public Health and Race in Los Angeles, 1879–1940*. Berkeley: University of California Press, 2006.

Moore, Shirley Ann Wilson. *To Place Our Deeds: The African American Community in Richmond, California, 1910–1963*. Berkeley: University of California Press, 2000.

Morris, Irwin. "African American Voting on Proposition 187: Rethinking the Prevalence of Interminority Conflict." *Political Research Quarterly* 53, no. 1 (2000): 77–98.

Morrison, Toni. *Playing in the Dark: Whiteness and the Literary Imagination*. The William E. Massey Sr. Lectures in the History of American Civilization, 1990. Cambridge, Mass.: Harvard University Press, 1992.

Mukherjee, Roopali. *The Racial Order of Things: Cultural Imaginaries of the Post-Soul Era*. Minneapolis: University of Minnesota Press, 2006.

Myrdal, Gunnar. *An American Dilemma: The Negro Problem and American Democracy*. New York: Harper & Row 1944.

Nelson, Bruce. *Divided We Stand: American Workers and the Struggle for Black Equality*. Princeton, N.J.: Princeton University Press, 2001.

Nevins, Joseph. *Operation Gatekeeper: The Rise of the "Illegal Alien" and the Making of the U.S.-Mexico Boundary*. New York: Routledge, 2002.

Newton, Lina Y. "Why Some Latinos Supported Proposition 187: Testing Economic Threat and Cultural Identity Hypotheses." *Social Science Quarterly* 81, no. 1 (2000): 180–93.

Ngai, Mae M. *Impossible Subjects: Illegal Aliens and the Making of Modern America*. Princeton, N.J.: Princeton University Press, 2003.

Nickerson, Michelle. "Women, Domesticity, and Postwar Conservatism." *OAH Magazine of History* 17, no. 2 (2003): 17–21.

Nicolaides, Becky M. *My Blue Heaven: Life and Politics in the Working-Class Suburbs of Los Angeles, 1920–1965*. Chicago: University of Chicago Press, 2002.

Norval, Aletta. *Deconstructing Apartheid Discourse*. London: Verso, 1996.

Oakes, Jeannie, John Rogers, David Silver, and Joanna Goode. *Separate and Unequal 50 Years after "Brown": California's "Racial Opportunity Gap."* Los Angeles: UCLA Institute for Democracy, Education, and Access, 2004.

Omi, Michael, and Howard Winant. *Racial Formation in the United States*. New York: Routledge, 1994.

Ono, Kent, and John Sloop. *Shifting Borders: Rhetoric, Immigration and California's Proposition 187*. Philadelphia: Temple University Press, 2002.

O'Reilly, Kenneth. *Nixon's Piano: Presidents and Racial Politics from Washington to Clinton*. New York: Free Press, 1995.

Orfield, Gary. "Lessons of the Los Angeles Desegregation Case." *Education and Urban Society* 16 (1984): 338–53.

———. "Public Opinion and School Desegregation." *Teachers College Record* 96, no. 4 (1995): 654–70.

———. *Public School Desegregation in the United States, 1968–1980*. Washington, D.C.: Joint Center for Political Studies, 1983.

Orfield, Gary, and Chungmei Lee. *"Brown" at 50: King's Dream or Plessy's Nightmare?* Cambridge, Mass.: Harvard Civil Rights Project, 2004.

Pagan, Eduardo Obregon. *Murder at the Sleepy Lagoon: Zoot Suits, Race, and Riot in Wartime L.A.* Chapel Hill: University of North Carolina Press, 2003.

Pantoja, Adrian, Ricardo Ramirez, and Gary Segura. "Citizens by Choice, Voters by Necessity: Patterns in Political Mobilization by Naturalized Latinos." *Political Research Quarterly* 54, no. 4 (2001): 729–50.

Park, John S. W. "Race Discourse and Proposition 187." *Michigan Journal of Race and Law* 2, no. 1 (1996): 175–204.

Parrish, Thomas B., María Pérez, Amy Merickel, Robert Linquanti et al. *Effects of the Implementation of Proposition 227 on the Education of English Learners, K-12: Findings from a Five-Year Evaluation*. Palo Alto, Calif.: American Institutes for Research and WestEd, 2006.

Pascoe, Peggy. *What Comes Naturally: Miscegenation Law and the Making of Race in America*. Oxford: Oxford University Press, 2009.

Post, Robert, and Michael Paul Rogin. *Race and Representation: Affirmative Action*. New York: Zone Books, 1998.

Preston, Michael, and James Lai. "The Symbolic Politics of Affirmative Action." In *Racial and Ethnic Politics in California*, vol. 2., edited by Michael Preston, Sandra Bassm and Bruce Cain, 161–98. Berkeley: Institute of Governmental Studies Press, 1998.

Pulido, Laura. *Black, Brown, Yellow, and Left: Radical Activism in Los Angeles.* American Crossroads. Berkeley: University of California Press, 2006.

———. "Rethinking Environmental Racism: White Privilege and Urban Development in Southern California." *Annals of the Association of American Geographers* 90, no. 1 (2000): 12–40.

Pusser, Brian. *Burning Down the House: Politics, Governance, and Affirmative Action at the University of California.* SUNY Series, Frontiers in Education. Albany: State University of New York Press, 2004.

Rarick, Ethan. *California Rising: The Life and Times of Pat Brown.* Berkeley: University of California Press, 2005.

Ravitch, Dianne. "The 'White Flight' Controversy." In *Busing U.S.A.*, edited by Nicolaus Mills, 238–55. New York: Teachers College Press, 1979.

Reeves, Keith. *Voting Hopes or Fears? White Voters, Black Candidates and Racial Politics in America.* New York: Oxford University Press, 1997.

Reimers, David M. *Unwelcome Strangers: American Identity and the Turn against Immigration.* New York: Columbia University Press, 1998.

Rice, Richard, William Bullough, and Richard Orsi. *The Elusive Eden: A New History of California.* 3rd edition. Boston: McGraw Hill, 2002.

Robinson, Cedric. *Black Marxism: The Making of the Black Radical Tradition.* London: Zed, 1983.

Roediger, David R. *The Wages of Whiteness: Race and the Making of the American Working Class.* London: Verso, 1999.

Rosenbaum, Walter. "Legislative Participation in California Direct Legislation, 1940–1960." PhD dissertation, Princeton University, 1964.

Rubin, Lillian. *Busing and Backlash: White against White in a California School District.* Berkeley: University of California Press, 1972.

Ruiz, Vicki. *Cannery Women, Cannery Lives: Mexican Women, Unionization, and the California Food Processing Industry, 1930–1950.* 1st edition. Albuquerque: University of New Mexico Press, 1987.

———. "South by Southwest: Mexican Americans and Segregated Schooling, 1900–1950." *OAH Magazine of History* 15, no. 2 (2001): 23–27.

Saito, Leland. *Race and Politics: Asian Americans, Latinos and Whites in a Los Angeles Suburb.* Urbana: University of Illinois Press, 1998.

Sanchez, George. *Becoming Mexican American: Ethnicity, Culture and Identity in Chicano Los Angeles, 1900–1945.* London: Oxford University Press, 1993.

———. "Reading Reginald Denny: The Politics of Whiteness in the Late Twentieth Century." *American Quarterly* 47, no. 3 (1995): 388–94.

———. "'What's Good for Boyle Heights Is Good for the Jews': Creating Multiculturalism on the Eastside During the 1950s." *American Quarterly* 56, no. 3 (2004): 633–61.

Santa Ana, Otto. *Brown Tide Rising: Metaphors of Latinos in Contemporary American Public Discourse.* Austin: University of Texas Press, 2002.

Saxton, Alexander. *The Indispensable Enemy: Labor and the Anti-Chinese Movement in California.* Berkeley: University of California Press, 1995.

———. *The Rise and Fall of the White Republic: Class Politics and Mass Culture in Nineteenth-Century America*. London: Verso, 1990.

Schattschneider, E. E. *Semisovereign People: A Realist's View of Democracy in America*. New York: Harcourt Brace, 1975.

Schiesl, Martin J. *Responsible Liberalism: Edmund G. "Pat" Brown and Reform Government in California 1958–1967*. Los Angeles: Edmund G. "Pat" Brown Institute of Public Affairs, 2003.

Schildkraut, Deborah J. *Press One for English: Language Policy, Public Opinion, and American Identity*. Princeton, N.J.: Princeton University Press, 2005.

Schlesinger, Arthur M. *The Disuniting of America*. New York: W. W. Norton, 1992.

Schmidt, Ronald. "Defending English in an English-Dominant World: The Ideology of the 'Official English' Movement in the United States." In *Discourses of Endangerment: Interest and Ideology in the Defense of Languages*, edited by Monica Heller and Alexandre Duchene, 197–215. London: Continuum International, 2007.

Schneider, Anne L., and Helen M. Ingram. *Deserving and Entitled: Social Constructions and Public Policy*. SUNY Series in Public Policy. Albany: State University of New York, 2005.

Schrag, Peter. *Paradise Lost: California's Experience, America's Future*. Berkeley: University of California Press, 2004.

Schuparra, Kurt. *Triumph of the Right: The Rise of the California Conservative Movement, 1945–1966*. New York: M. E. Sharpe, 1998.

Sears, David O. "Whites' Opposition to Busing: Self-Interest of Symbolic Politics?" *American Political Science Review* 73, no. 2 (1979): 369–84.

Sears, David O., and Harris M. Allen. "The Trajectory of Local Desegregation Controversies and Whites' Opposition to Busing." In *Groups in Contact: The Psychology of Desegregation*, edited by Norman Miller and Marilynn B. Brewer, 124–51. New York: Academic Press, 1984.

Self, Robert O. *American Babylon: Race and the Struggle for Postwar Oakland*. Princeton, N.J.: Princeton University Press, 2003.

Selig, Diana. *Americans All: The Cultural Gifts Movement*. Cambridge, Mass.: Harvard University Press, 2008.

Sen, Rinku. "Winning Race." *ColorLines* 6, no. 4 (December 2003).

Shen, Eveline. *Reproductive Justice at the Ballot Box*. Oakland: Asian Communities for Reproductive Justice, 2008.

Shultz, Jim. *The Initiative Cookbook: Recipes and Stories from California's Ballot Wars*. San Francisco: Democracy Center, 1996.

Sides, Josh. *L.A. City Limits: African American Los Angeles from the Great Depression to the Present*. Berkeley: University of California Press, 2004.

Simon, Rita J., and Susan H. Alexander. *The Ambivalent Welcome: Print Media, Public Opinion, and Immigration*. Westport, Conn.: Praeger, 1993.

Singh, Nikhil Pal. "Liberalism." In *Keywords for American Cultural Studies*, edited by Bruce Burgett and Glenn Hendler, 139–45. New York: New York University Press, 2007.

Sitton, Tom. *Los Angeles Transformed: Fletcher Bowron's Urban Reform Revival, 1938–1953.* Albuquerque: University of New Mexico Press, 2005.

Skowronek, Stephen. "The Reassociation of Ideas and Purposes: Racism, Liberalism, and the American Political Tradition." *American Political Science Review* 100, no. 3 (2006): 385–401.

Skrentny, John David. *The Ironies of Affirmative Action: Politics, Culture, and Justice in America.* Chicago: University of Chicago Press, 1996.

Smith, Daniel A. *Tax Crusaders and the Politics of Direct Democracy.* New York: Routledge, 1998.

Smith, Daniel A., and Caroline J. Tolbert. *Educated by Initiative: The Effects of Direct Democracy on Citizens and Political Organizations in the American States.* Ann Arbor: University of Michigan Press, 2004.

Smith, Rogers. *Civic Ideals: Conflicting Visions of Citizenship in U.S. History.* New Haven, Conn.: Yale University Press, 1997.

Sonenshein, Raphael. *Politics in Black and White: Race and Power in Los Angeles.* Princeton. N.J.: Princeton University Press, 1993.

Stanfield, John H. "Urban Public School Desegregation: Reproduction of Normative White Domination" *Journal of Negro Education* 51, no. 2 (1982): 90–100.

Stears, Marc. "The Liberal Tradition and the Politics of Exclusion." *Annual Review of Political Science* 10 (2007): 85–102.

Stefanic, Jean, and Richard Delgado. *No Mercy: How Conservative Think Tanks and Foundations Changed America's Social Agenda.* Philadelphia: Temple University Press, 1996.

Stern, Alexandria Minna. *Eugenic Nation: Faults and Frontiers of Better Breeding in Modern America.* Berkeley: University of California Press, 2005.

Stone, Deborah A. *Policy Paradox: The Art of Political Decision Making.* New York: W. W. Norton, 2002.

Sugrue, Thomas. *Origins of the Urban Crisis.* Princeton, N.J.: Princeton University Press, 1996.

Tatalovich, Raymond. *Nativism Reborn? The Official English Language Movement and the American States.* Lexington: University of Kentucky Press, 1995.

Theoharis, Jeanne. "'We Saved the City': Black Struggles for Educational Equality in Boston, 1960–1976." *Radical History Review* 81 (2001): 61–93.

Thernstrom, Abigail, and Stephan Thernstrom. *America in Black and White.* New York: Simon & Schuster, 1997.

Tichenor, Daniel J. *Dividing Lines: The Politics of Immigration Control in America.* Princeton Studies in American Politics. Princeton, N.J.: Princeton University Press, 2002.

Unz, Ron. "California and the End of White America." *Commentary* 108, no. 4 (November 1999): 17–28.

———. "Immigration or the Welfare State?" *Policy Review* 70 (1994): 33–39.

U.S. Commission on Civil Rights. *Hearings before the United States Commission on Civil Rights.* Washington, D.C.: U.S. Government Printing Office, 1960.

Valelly, Richard M., ed. *The Voting Rights Act: Securing the Ballot.* Washington, D.C.: CQ Press, 2006.

Vargas, Zaragosa. *Labor Rights Are Civil Rights: Mexican American Workers in Twentieth-Century America.* Politics and Society in Twentieth-Century America. Princeton, N.J.: Princeton University Press, 2005.

Williams, Raymond. *Marxism and Literature.* Oxford: Oxford University Press, 1977.

Winant, Howard. *The World Is a Ghetto: Race and Democracy since World War II.* New York: Basic Books, 2001.

Wollenberg, Charles. *All Deliberate Speed: Segregation and Exclusion in California Schools, 1855–1975.* Berkeley: University of California Press, 1976.

Wong, Janelle. *Democracy's Promise: Immigrants and American Civic Institutions.* Ann Arbor: University of Michigan Press, 2006.

Woolard, Kathryn. "Voting Rights, Liberal Voters and the Official English Movement." In *Perspectives on Official English: The Campaign for English as the Official Language of the USA,* edited by Karen L. Adams and Daniel T. Brink, 125–38. Berlin: Mouton de Gruyter, 1990.

Wroe, Andrew. *The Republican Party and Immigration Politics: From Proposition 187 to George W. Bush.* New York: Palgrave Macmillan, 2008.

Zimring, Franklin E., Gordon Hawkins, and Sam Kamin. *Punishment and Democracy: Three Strikes and You're Out in California.* Oxford: Oxford University Press, 2001.

Index

Abdul-Jabbar, Kareem, 90
abortion rights, 123, 232, 312n43, 328n31
Action for Grassroots Empowerment and Neighborhood Development Alternatives (AGENDA), 210–11, 221, 223, 227, 241
Adams, Jan: on anti-Proposition 187 campaign, 190; anti-Proposition 209 efforts of, 208–9, 217–18, 220; Californians United against 187 launched by, 183–84; long-term objectives of, 189; organizing work of, 183, 200; on Proposition 187 passage, 199; on Proposition 209 passage, 229; voter registration estimates of, 220, 317n138
affirmative action: Democratic disavowal of, 205–6, 226–27, 228–29; media coverage of, 234; paradoxes of, 202–5; Proposition 209 voting results and, 228, 228 t. 6; quotas and, 215, 224; Republican support for, 204–5; Unz ads opposing, 231. See also California Civil Rights Initiative (CCRI); Proposition 209 (1996)
African Americans: civil rights organizations, 35; fair employment laws and, 26, 37–38; formal segregation of ended, 94; as homeowners, 61;

immigrants as viewed by, 193; incarceration rates, 273, 280n16, 328n22; as judges, 19; labor movement of, 32; as legislators, 16, 28; in post-WWII California, 280n13; Proposition 1 rejected by, 124; in pro-Proposition 1 campaign, 108, 110–12; Rumford Act and, 79, 80; South Gate white rights activists and, 96; voter eligibility, 185; West Los Angeles population of, 295n126. See also Blacks
African Methodist Episcopal Church, 298n43
agribusiness: FEPC opposed by, 34–35; immigration policy geared to, 169–70; immigration promoted by, 166
Ahmanson, Howard, 217, 219 fig. 13, 239
Alameda County (Calif.), 155
Alatorre, Richard, 145
Alcindor, Lew, 90
Alien Land Law (1920), 40, 45–47, 138, 165
Alinsky, Saul, 31
"All Men Are Brothers" (speech; Murphy), 14
American Civil Liberties Union (ACLU), 109–10; anti-Proposition 1 lawsuit filed by, 126; anti-Proposition 14 efforts of, 82; anti-Proposition 21

Labor Committee against Proposition 11, 44
Labor Committee to Combat Intolerance (AFL), 38
labor unions: African-American, 32; in anti-FEPC coalition, 44; in anti-Proposition 1 coalition, 122; in anti-Proposition 54 coalition, 244, 255; in anti-Proposition 63 coalition, 150; in anti-Proposition 187 coalition, 178–79, 181–82; in anti-Proposition 209 campaign, 221; ballot measure to restrict power of, 1, 238, 279n1; civil rights organizations aligned with, 50–52, 51 *fig. 1*; decline of leftist influence in, 45, 49; Mexican-American, 32; in pro-FEPC coalition, 32–33, 37; Proposition 14 approved by, 83; Proposition 209 opposed by, 206; segregated locals, 26, 27, 52. *See also* American Federation of Labor (AFL); Congress of Industrial Organizations (CIO); *specific union*
labor unrest, 32, 33, 35
Laclau, Ernesto, 11
Lai, Irvin R., 152
Lakewood (Calif.), 58
Lancaster, Burt, 77
language discrimination, 148, 267
language minority groups, 135–36, 148, 305n13
Latin American immigrants, 1, 148, 161
Latinas, representations of, 167
Latino civil rights groups, 151
Latino Civil Rights Network, 185
Latinos: advocacy community, 166; anti-CCRI campaign targeting, 208; bilingual education and, 236–37; as English for the Children spokespersons, 233; immigrants as viewed by, 193–94; incarceration rates, 280n16; political participation of, 185–86, 240, 271–72; post-209 university enrollment figures, 230; Proposition 1 supported by, 124; Proposition 63 rejected by, 154;

Proposition 187 and, 189–90, 198, 232; Proposition 209 opposed by, 221; Proposition 227 supported by, 321n114; as Reagan Democrats, 235, 271; undocumented immigrants as viewed by, 175–76; violence against, 198; Wilson as viewed by, 189–90, 221, 235
Lau v. Nichols, 232
Lawyers against Proposition 14, 77
Lawyers Committee for Civil Rights (LCCR), 182–83, 250
Lazarus, Emma, 140
Leadership Conference on Civil Rights, 260
League of United Latin American Citizens, 110
League of United Latin American Citizens et al. v. Wilson, 197
League of Women Voters, 102, 122
Lear, Norman, 122
Lee, Rex, 126
Levy, Louis, 38–39
Lewis, Howard, 290n45
Lewis, Pamela, 226
liberalism: political subjectivity and, 266–67; racialized, 19–20; racism as viewed in, 30–31; shared political principles of, 13–14, 265–66. *See also* racial liberalism
Limited English Proficiency (LEP) students, 232–33, 234, 238, 241
Lipsitz, George, 20
Lockyer, Bill, 251
Long Beach (Calif.), 258
Los Angeles (Calif.): African American population of, 295n126; anti-CCRI campaign in, 210–11; anti-Proposition 14 campaign in, 77–78; anti-Proposition 187 campaign in, 184–85; anti-Proposition 209 campaign in, 220; CFJ membership in, 220; Chicano student "blowouts" in, 99, 109; civic unity organizations in, 13; CORE anti-residential segregation activism in, 60; immigrant population of, 139; immigrant rights

gration restrictionism and, 166–69; impact of, 162, 197–200, 220–21, 230; implementation of, 196–97; passage of, 1, 161, 196, 197 *t. 5*, 201; political whiteness and, 162, 167, 193–94, 262; Proposition 227 campaign and, 235; racial liberalism and, 191–94; Republican endorsement of, 179, 194; title of, 164–65; white support of, 208; Wilson and, 169–72, 192, 195, 258. *See also* anti-Proposition 187 campaign

Proposition 209 (1996): ballot qualification, 211–17, 212 *fig. 10*; campaign for, 225–26, 239; grassroots campaigns to defeat, 217–21, 218 *fig. 12*, 272; implementation of, 201, 230, 253–54; mainstream campaign to defeat, 221–26; partisan involvement in, 226–27, 228–29; passage of, 1, 227–28, 228 *t. 6*, 230–31; political legacy of, 241–42, 272; political whiteness and, 262. *See also* anti-Proposition 209 campaign; California Civil Rights Initiative (CCRI)

Proposition 215 (1996), 279n1

Proposition 226 (1998), 238, 279n1

Proposition 227 (1998): ballot arguments, 322n128; campaign for, 231–35, 239; campaign to defeat, 235–38, 239–40, 251, 272; civil rights language used in, 202, 242, 268; court challenges, 240; fundraising for, 239; implementation of, 241; Latino support of, 321n114; passage of, 1, 239–40, 240 *t. 7*; political legacy of, 241–42, 272; political whiteness and, 262; Proposition 187 campaign and, 235; Republican endorsement of, 322n125

Proposition O (San Francisco), 135, 136–37, 138, 143

Public Health Institute, 253

public health organizations, 244, 252–53

public schools: closings, 180; crisis in, 8;

enrollment drop in, 196; inequalities in, 267; Latinos as supporters of, 271

public services, crisis in, 8

public transportation, 271

Quebec separatist movement, 134

quotas, 215, 224, 231

race-based affirmative action programs, 204

race-based hierarchies, 8

race data collection, ban on, 253–54. *See also* Proposition 54 (2003); Racial Privacy Initiative (RPI)

race relations groups, 29–31

racial categorization, 247–50

racial conservatism, 1, 25, 86

racial formation theory, 279n3

racial innocence: antibusing campaigns and, 111–12; defined, 31; Proposition 1 and, 121–22, 126–27; Proposition 63 and, 153–54, 157; Proposition 209 and, 214; Reagan and, 88–89; rise of, and race relations groups, 29–31; school segregation and, 94, 106–7. *See also* colorblindness

racialized ballot initiatives: apartheid and, 7–8, 264; future prospects, 274; historical examination of, 1–4; political impact of, 2, 3 *t. 1*, 271–74; political whiteness sustained through, 22, 262, 265–69; racial liberalism rejected in, 264–65; as set of propositions about race, 4, 279n3; voter ideologies expressed through, 10–11. See also *specific initiative*

racial justice: anti-Proposition 54 campaign and, 244–45, 262–63; decline of, and racial liberalism, 267–69, 280n16; political whiteness and opposition to, 21–22, 241; post-WWII political culture and, 2–4; pre-WWII activism, 28

racial liberalism: anti-Proposition 11 usurping of ideas of, 25, 45; in California public discourse, 15–16, 264–65; defined, 281n7; English

AMERICAN CROSSROADS

Edited by Earl Lewis, George Lipsitz, Peggy Pascoe, George Sánchez, and Dana Takagi